THE
DIRECTOR'S VOICE

VOLUME 2

THE
DIRECTOR'S VOICE

VOLUME 2

EDITED BY JASON LOEWITH

THEATRE COMMUNICATIONS GROUP
NEW YORK
2012

The Director's Voice, Volume 2 is copyright © 2012 by Jason Loewith

Foreword is copyright © 2012 by Arthur Bartow

"The Ground Has Shifted" is copyright © 2012 by Jason Loewith

The Director's Voice, Volume 2 is published by Theatre Communications Group, Inc., 520 Eighth Avenue, 24th Floor, New York, NY 10018-4156.

The publication of *The Director's Voice, Volume 2* through TCG's Book Program is made possible by the New York State Council on the Arts with the support of Governor Andrew Cuomo and the New York State Legislature.

TCG books are exclusively distributed to the book trade by Consortium Book Sales and Distribution.

CIP data information is on file at the Library of Congress, Washington, D.C.
ISBN: 978-1-55936-352-5

Photographer credits for the directors' headshots may be found at the back of the book.

Book design and composition by Lisa Govan
Cover design by Mark Melnick

First Edition, September 2012

CONTENTS

FOREWORD

It's been more than twenty years since TCG published *The Director's Voice*. It's a pleasure to see that this new *Director's Voice, Volume 2* includes some directors who were omitted for lack of space from that first volume side-by-side with those who have risen to national and international prominence within that twenty-year interim.

While the not-for-profit theater tradition (tradition being a term we might not have used two decades ago) created the hothouses where these directors found their bearings, a majority of them have since crossed the Broadway border to prominent commercial success. They run the gamut from being in charge of prestigious not-for-profit theaters to freelancing; from being masters of the classics to creating new work; from experimental to traditional and every degree between; from the West Coast to East; from theater to opera, film and the classroom; and from being celebrated as masters of their genres to recognition as unique artists.

Only a few of these featured directors were formally trained for their discipline. Initially, most studied or apprenticed in some combination as actors, artists, dancers, dramaturgists, writers, community activists and, yes, academics. The degree to which they internally live in each of these disciplines appears to determine their point of departure in shaping their work. For instance, the directors who entered this process with a foundation in acting seem more focused on a result dictated by emotion-based techniques. It is a heady group, more deeply exposed to experimental influences and more predisposed to theory than their predecessors. But many have been inspired by and, in some cases, mentored by the directors appearing in the first *Director's Voice*. Those in both books have in common their love of reading, of art, of music, a passion for absorbing ideas from great thinkers, and research, research, research.

Since directing as a profession first came into being in the late nineteenth century, directors have used their skills to reflect the progress of America through its cultural phases, mirrored always by its political, economic, educational and religious influences. No one yet has codified a comprehensive set of principles, a framework of exercises or theories, to identify and train a director as those developed for the actor. Therefore, each directorial awakening is unique. During the past two decades, however, the use of the Viewpoints technique has proliferated among directors. Viewpoints was developed by Mary Overlie as a training method for dancers, and adapted for actors to deconstruct and rearrange the conventional elements of theater. It has been embraced by directors not only as a shared language with actors but as a method for creating and staging new work and reimagining established repertoire. This framework of thinking with its own language is especially useful when working in a company atmosphere as exemplified by Anne Bogart and Moisés Kaufman.

Viewpoints is perhaps the only indigenous American training technique yet developed, though it was conceived to deconstruct the terminology inherited from Russian theater traditions. It was inspired by the American postmodern dance movement, and it parallels the emergence of the digital age in America, an age that is in the process of gauging its cognitive effect on our society and future audiences and artists. What will be its influence on theater of this new age with its rapid fire multitasking transitions, short attention spans, cryptic interpersonal electronic relations, time-bending leaps, elevation of irony, rejection of realism and distrust of the facade of words? We can see some hints of coming to grips with this within the work of this diverse group, an assemblage whose experience bridges the gap dating from the founders of the regional theater movement through experimentation to the new age of the digitally enlightened. Perhaps the full effect of this cultural transition will be reported twenty years from now in *The Director's Voice, Volume 3*.

While the nature of our culture is always changing and societal transition, like the universe, evidently is accelerating at an ever faster pace, theater audiences for the most part appear to be remnants of those developed twenty years ago—young Americans who have not embraced theater as their central storytelling experience have created alternate ways of looking at their world. A new generation of directors is struggling to find techniques for telling the truth about our condition to this potential new audience without breaking faith with supporters from the past. In theater this transition is represented in part as a journey from a psychological- and emotional-based approach espoused one hundred years ago by Stanislavski to an intellectual, theoretical and technical approach influenced by such visionaries as Grotowski and Mary Overlie. The work forms an arc from postwar realism to the dawning age of digital nativism.

Both director books have a triple purpose: to guide, provoke, seduce and enliven the ambitions of would-be directors; to refresh and validate already established theater workers; and to enshrine the ennobling ideals of the art of directing. Neither volume is a comprehensive how-to guide, although each director shares precious and essential information. Both confirm for directors certain noble points of view and provide touchstones that encourage them to trust their own vision of the world and to act on their desire to physically acknowledge those observations theatrically—in short, to be directors rather than imitative ciphers. These directors relate the struggles and victories that have led them to lifetime commitments in craft. The significance of these directors' journeys moves beyond their own experiences and insights to embrace a larger community of theater workers and audiences. Directors become noteworthy only when they succeed in enlarging the perspectives of those around them.

The men and women interviewed in the first volume represent a theater that has now passed the torch to this new generation, even though most of those interviewed in the first volume are currently active and at the peak of their theatrical powers and success. As is true of each generation, they stood on the shoulders of previous theater workers. Their influences were drawn from role models active just before and following World War II, which were in turn based on the craft of the 1930s. In order to create themselves, they were forced to circumvent the establishment Broadway theater, which was closed to them and, in doing so, created not-for-profit institutions to support their own work. The not-for-profit theaters they created have become the establishment, and these establishment institutions, having passed from the forceful control of their director-founders into the control of their boards of trustees, are more likely to play it safe and less likely to continue the convictions and risks self-imposed by their founders. So I am struck by how many of the directors in this book have been inspired and even trained by the directors in the first *Voice* book but, just like them, have found it necessary to invent their own theaters, their own companies, their own aesthetic. These directors are beholden to the courage of the past generation but not necessarily captive to its processes.

So maybe it never gets easier. Perhaps the next generation of directors will despair of ever finding the comfort of a true profession that progressively cultivates its artists, providing ever higher levels of challenge and celebration as each milestone is met. Is this always to be the nature of our theater, requiring unending struggle? We know that in other countries artists are celebrated differently and in some of those cases subsidy can lead to a highly refined mediocrity. We see like-examples of this most frequently in our commercial theater, as George C. Wolfe defines it, " . . . a place where recycled emotions and images are cele-brated and erratic brilliance is punished . . ." That is the flaw in our cap-italistic system, where frequently everything is reduced to a commodity that must be sold and, in doing, must meet a median common denom-inator. But is that the fault of our theater or the demand of its audi-ences? Is it the common good or expediency? To feed the need for con-sensus success we have encouraged competence over depth of thought, and in those cases where we have depth of thought we often lack com-petence. Great theater requires both.

So let us lift our hats to the directors in this book who possess both qualities and are fighting the good fight, keeping theater very much alive in America by peering into the past akin to archaeologists, the present like psychoanalysts, and the future in the spirit of shamans. If those of you reading this book want to follow their example, do so at your own peril—and to your own unparalleled sense of satisfaction.

Arthur Bartow
New York
April 2012

THE GROUND HAS SHIFTED

Much has changed since 1988, when Arthur Bartow's *The Director's Voice* was published, but no transformation has been more influential in the field than the flight from risk to commercialism in the American not-for-profit theater. Eager to stand on the shoulders of their innovative predecessors, the directors interviewed in *Volume 2* have instead found the ground shifting, radically, beneath their feet.

Bartow's volume of interviews arrived at the tail end of the "Reagan Revolution," which lurched the country toward a conservatism felt most strongly in the arts two years later, when NEA Chair John Frohnmayer vetoed four peer-reviewed grants to performance artists Karen Finley, Tim Miller, Holly Hughes and John Fleck. By the time the Supreme Court ruled in 1998 that the NEA Chair was, indeed, entitled to adjudge grants based not just on artistic merit, but also on "general standards of decency and respect for the diverse beliefs and values of the American public," the Reagan Revolution's evolution in regards to art-making and risk-taking in American culture was complete. Olivier Award—winning playwright Simon Stephens recently argued that British "state-subsidized theaters [should] stage work that is not going to find an audience . . . that's what state subsidy is for." Would any American theater artist in 2012 be taken seriously if he or she made the same argument about our not-for-profit institutions?

As Bartow notes in his Foreword to this book, the directors in that first volume created (or at the very least embraced) those very institutions because they needed a safe space to experiment, and "the establishment Broadway theater . . . was closed to them." Now, the culture wars of the eighties and nineties have imperiled them by putting the free market front and center: blockbuster museum shows, star-casting of regional and Off-Broadway productions, cash-cow *Nutcrackers* and *Christmas Carols* . . . Not-for-profit arts institutions once hedged the risk of audience distaste with public and private subsidy—now they are forced to balance it, pandering to the same audience they're supposed to serve with artistic risk. The result is an ever-growing distance between an "elite" (and ever-older) audience accustomed to artistic adventure, and a much larger (and younger) public, trained to believe art should play by the same free-market rules as, say, a car dealership or the for-profit cinema.

What's a theater artist to do?

Stand on the shoulders of those who come before you, and strike a precarious balance.

Asked about their influences, the directors in this volume frequently pointed to those directors who came of professional age in the late sixties and early seventies: JoAnne Akalaitis and Lee Breuer of Mabou Mines, Robert Wilson, Ariane Mnouchkine and Richard Foreman. While one's glasses would have to be awfully rose-colored to imagine their early work was embraced by wide swaths of the population, the cultural appetite for artistic experimentation at the time gave those visionaries the freedom and impetus to create. That appetite has evaporated. Today, the distinction between not-for-profit and commercial theater has blurred so much that the two are, in many instances, indistinguishable except by union rules and zip code.

Nonetheless, the directors in this book have armed themselves with the experimental tools pioneered by their predecessors (and in some cases, created their own). They are resilient, and have succeeded by negotiating the shifting boundaries between art and commerce in a new century, and a new cultural context.

Even if artistic experimentation itself was a victim of the culture wars, the innovators of the sixties and seventies succeeded in one remarkable way: because of them our audiences have diversified to an extraordinary degree, and theaters have proliferated to tell a multiplicity of stories. More theaters than ever now bring work to more audiences, from underserved populations in our largest cities to those in the country's most remote rural areas. Theater for the youngest and theater for the oldest is being made in every state, and more professionally and artfully than ever before. No metropolitan center can be considered culturally aware without having, for example, Latino theaters, black theaters, gay and lesbian theaters, theaters serving the disability community . . .

And because of the groundbreaking work of these earlier directors, the directors in this volume are equipped with an overflowing toolbox that includes dance-based techniques like the Viewpoints and now-ubiquitous technology; they are telling stories for community-specific audiences, experimental audiences and commercial audiences as well. This collection of artists sketches a compelling portrait of directors in the new century, creating plays that speak to different audiences, often each time they work. Of the many revolutions since 1988, the fragmentation of the audience is perhaps the most significant, and the one that resonates most profoundly in this digital age, when every individual can curate his or her cultural experience on a moment-to-moment basis. As Bart Sher notes in his interview here: Americans are hungry for cultural experiences, and we are consuming more of them, and more kinds of them, than ever before.

Rather than find themselves threatened by this cultural fragmentation, the artists in this volume are doubling down on their commitment to live performance as a vital thread in our changing cultural fabric. They recognize they can no longer speak to a single audience, and they also recognize that the experience theater provides—great reckonings in little rooms—will always fulfill an essential social need. They don't fear the future; they embrace it.

> "I find that way too often, books of interviews with actors/directors/ playwrights, etc., almost never deal with a thorough (or even more general) approach to their craft and their development as artists, in artistic terms (as opposed to a resume-styled list of places). Since I seem to not exactly fit the mold of what schools are looking for . . . and have no desire to take out ridiculous amounts in loans in order to study . . . I have decided to officially pursue the path of an autodidact for now."
>
> —E-mail I received from an early-career director
> regarding this book in early 2012

I began work on this volume in 2002, just after I was appointed artistic director of a small theater company outside Chicago. The timing of these interviews roughly coincided with my tenure there as artistic director and—lacking an MFA degree—I readily confess that I stole everything these directors told me to use in my own work. The days of apprenticing oneself to a director and opportunity suddenly falling from the sky are long gone. Today, directors start theater companies, get MFAs, assistant direct for years (if they've got a good trust fund). Or in my case, get an amazing gig interviewing master directors.

Recognizing the multiplicity of paths out there, I've tried with these interviews to strike a balance between the art's mystery and the craft's technique. They're tinged by the experiences of a theater practitioner in the trenches, succeeding and failing and succeeding in rapid succession. That's why you'll find these conversations run the gamut from rudimentary and practical questions to, I hope, the ineffable.

Of course, the ineffable can't be put into words. Asking a director to talk about his or her work is like asking a painter to talk about brushstrokes: they intuitively understand what's required when applying color to a canvas, but the transformation from craft to art is lost in translation. Furthermore, directors often lack perspective on the work they create. When asked what defines it, many were at a loss. Without knowing how other directors work, without understanding *their* processes, how could they explain how their work differs? A finished production leaves only traces of the artistry required to make it. One recognizes the elements of craft that were required, but has no real sense of how the artistry came to being.

So these interviews are only traces. There are some things we can generalize about: most of these directors (though not all) speak of their tremendous respect for actors; all of them have an absolute confidence in their vision and trust their instincts, even if they can't define what those instincts are, or whence they come. In the end, I was left only with impressions and glimpses. Artistry is artistry *because* it's a mystery, and not a series of techniques.

I'm saying it up front: there are directors missing from this book. A *lot* of them. It verges on the criminal. As we were going to press I started making a list of the directors I *wished* I could have interviewed, and came up with thirty-five without taking a breath. Then I breathed and added fifteen more. To those who want to know why their favorite director isn't in this book—and to those directors who themselves feel excluded—I can offer a justification and a defense. In the first case, we did our very best when we selected the directors (which happened between 2002 and 2006) to be inclusive, representative of the community and artistically exceptional. In the second case: two directors did not agree to be interviewed— and you'll never know who they are. (For those of you who were not included but think you should have been: *that* can be your defense.)

On time: when we started this work, there was no Amazon.com, and iPads and Kindles belonged to the realm of *Star Trek* and its tricorders. Yes, it took a long time to get this book out. I will forever be grateful to the heroic editors at TCG who fact-checked these interviews (and my introductions) in excruciating detail. That work, over hundreds of pages of transcripts, could not be completed quickly. Knowing that time marches on mercilessly, we have tried to retain what was freshest in these interviews, and what stayed true to the book's mission of being a combination how-to manual, book of mysteries and guide to the American theater at the start of the new century.

The good news is that, though the bulk of these interviews were completed by 2007, I was able to reedit them five years later from a different perspective. In those early interviews, I was a first-time artistic director, thrown into a high-profile directing position without training, looking for clues . . . and believing, mistakenly, that the work of the director happened primarily between the time rehearsal began and the time it ended each day. That the director's art could somehow be discovered in scenework, in blocking, in what was said to the actors. The more interviews I conducted, the more elusive the art of the director became: their artistry evolved while they watched other productions, or in conversations with designers, or in previews, or walking through life as culturally aware individuals, or just within their minds. That realization has been of great value to me as my career has progressed.

"Within a gesture," Anne Bogart told me, "you can find the whole tenor of a play." Within an interview, can you find the art of directing theater in the early twenty-first century? Probably not. But you can catch a glimpse.

I am indebted to many individuals who helped bring these interviews to print. First, to TCG's Terry Nemeth and Kathy Sova, whose amazing editors—Nicole Estvanik, Molly Smith Metzler, Ted Thompson and many others—kept me from getting too purple in my prose. I'm also grateful to a number of folks outside TCG who transcribed unintelligible tape recordings (that's how long ago we started), looked at drafts and provided invaluable feedback: my partner Ned Cramer, my partner in crime Bonnie Grisan, Carol and Margaret Loewith and Bill O'Connor.

Among the many extraordinary professionals who have mentored me, I gratefully mention: David Esbjornson, Michael Halberstam, Beth Hogan, Celise Kalke, Peter Lackner, Todd London and Charlie Newell, each of whom instilled precious knowledge to me at a formative time, and thereby shaped my approach to the directors in this volume. Ben Cameron, Emilya Cachapero and Jim O'Quinn at TCG have also been models, providing me with many opportunities to fail, succeed and grow.

Also, a huge thanks to three of my closest artistic collaborators, who win special awards for persistence: now I never have to hear Chelsea Keenan, Mike Osinski or Joe Wycoff ask me that dreaded question again: "When's your book coming out?"

Finally, these interviews would certainly be less interesting without the mentorship of David Savran, whose book *In Their Own Words* was as much a model for me as Bartow's *Director's Voice,* and whose energizing seminars at Brown University kept me from falling into a Reagan-era intellectual abyss. Until the time I encountered David, my most influential theater experience was probably David Merrick's 1980 production of *42nd Street* on Broadway (directed by Gower Champion, who died on opening night). Thanks to David, I saw—and was appalled by—the Robert Woodruff production of Brecht's *Baal* ten years later, during Anne Bogart's brief tenure at Trinity Rep. Woodruff's orgiastic portrait of the artist as a decadent, violent and omnisexual middle-aged man left me furious; I remember yelling at David, tears in my eyes, that you just couldn't *do* that to a paying audience! You couldn't force them to sit through three hours of neon-infused, rock-and-roll, postmodern hedonism! But of course, it was brilliant, too . . . and I will forever find myself as an artist torn, somewhere, between *Baal* and *42nd Street*.

Baal closed in April 1990. Two months later, Anne Bogart was out at Trinity Rep, and the National Endowment for the Arts changed the American cultural conversation by defunding four performance artists. But Tony Kushner's angel reminds us that the storm of the past propels us into an unknown future. The directors in this volume are changing the conversation again, so that the artists in *The Director's Voice, Volume 3* can stand firmly on their shoulders.

Jason Loewith
Washington, D.C.
June 2012

THE
DIRECTOR'S VOICE

VOLUME 2

ANNE BOGART

A Global Viewpoint

FOR A WOMAN KNOWN TO HAVE A famous system rooting her process—the Viewpoints—Anne Bogart is anything but systematic in conversation. As the world's preeminent authority on this pervasive actor-training system, Bogart might be expected to speak like a rigid missionary on its behalf. Instead, Bogart talks about direction with refreshing ambiguity. Phrases like "state of grace" or "delight" or "terror" are far more likely to enter into the conversation than the specifics of Viewpoints. Approaching a production, Bogart never asks how the process will play out. Instead, she asks (in her book, *A Director Prepares*), "How can we, in a climate of racing for survival, generate gifts with presence and generosity?"

Viewpoints was originally developed by choreographer Mary Overlie in the 1970s as a way of breaking down and then codifying six essential elements of staging dance: Space, Time, Shape, Movement, Story and Emotion. Bogart encountered Viewpoints theory in 1979 while on the faculty of the Experimental Theatre Wing at New York University, and thereafter expanded on Overlie's work to create nine Viewpoints for her work in theater, split into Time (Tempo, Duration, Kinesthetic Response, Repetition) and Space (Shape, Gesture, Architecture, Spatial Relationship, Topography). Bogart's work combines an ensemble awareness of these elements with extensive "sourcework" (an improvisation-based research process) to create a foundation for most productions she directs, and this in turn has become known as her System with a capital "S."

That's opposed to Method with a capital "M." Because of its reliance on a completely different set of terms, a specificity in staging, and a physical paradigm as opposed to an emotional one, Viewpoints has frequently been called the postmodern response to Method acting, taught famously by Harold Clurman and Lee Strasberg, and learned famously (to a greater or lesser degree) by actors from Marilyn Monroe to Dustin Hoffman. The terms of that Method are things like "emotional recall" or "sense memory," and through the 1980s and 1990s it seemed as if Viewpoints and the Method were at war over the soul of actor training in this country. Bogart assailed the Method's narcissism: "If I'm feeling it," the actor is conditioned to believe, "then the audience must be feeling it, too." The split between Viewpoints and the Method became more pronounced through the 1990s, with companies springing up solely based on Viewpoints. Of these efforts, Bogart has said, "The point [of Viewpoints] is a way of learning to speak together, not an end product."

Nonetheless, with Viewpoints gaining adherents throughout the industry, Bogart's ideas found an important place at the actor-training table. Viewpoints classes are ubiquitous in undergraduate and graduate training programs alongside more traditional, naturalistic approaches. In fact, when I first learned about Viewpoints, I considered it simply as a way of codifying what I knew intuitively as a director: that diagonals are more interesting than horizontals; that interacting with a piece of furniture (Architecture) is better than ignoring it; and so on. Viewpoints worked for me as a sort of checklist—if this scene isn't working, perhaps I haven't really considered Tempo or Repetition. It was yet another tool in my director's toolbox, right alongside sense memory, and Meisner and whatever else helps us get to where we're going.

But many adherents of Viewpoints use it far more exclusively and seriously, among them director Tina Landau and actor Jefferson Mays. The work these artists create, at its best, blends unexpected and rigorous physicality with visceral, emotional force. The same and more can surely be said of Bogart's work.

Bogart was born in 1951 to a Navy family that moved around frequently. In *Anne Bogart: Viewpoints* (Smith and Kraus, 1995), she writes of her first encounter with professional theater, when she was fifteen years old and her father was stationed at Newport, Rhode Island. It was a production of *Macbeth* at the Trinity Repertory Company in Providence.

> The production terrified, disoriented and bewildered me.
> I couldn't figure out my orientation to the action. The witches
> dropped unexpectedly out of the ceiling, the action surrounded
> us on big runways, and I didn't understand the words. The

> unfamiliar spoken language . . . and the fantastic visual language . . . was my first encounter with the poetic language of the stage where size and scale were altered. The experience was frightening but compelling . . . I knew instantly that I would spend my life in pursuit of this remarkable universe.

Seven years later, in 1974, she graduated from Bard College and began her professional career. Fourteen years after that, at the end of 1988, she became the second artistic director of Trinity Rep, the Tony-winning theater of Rhode Island. Though it sounds like a marvelous bookend, the truth is far more complex. Bogart abruptly resigned after a single controversial season. As Bogart says in *A Director Prepares* (Routlege, 2001), "Reality is a construct of thought that desires continuity. Actually, the expectation of continuity is a glorious fiction."

In the years between Bard and Trinity, Bogart had established a reputation for innovative, physically based work, creating a number of original theater and dance-theater works in various downtown Manhattan and Brooklyn venues such as P.S. 122, St. Mark's Church and BACA Downtown. Her journey in those first years was similar to the journeys of many young directors: "I worked site specifically because I could not find a theater in New York willing to take a chance on a young, untested director." By the time she won a Bessie Award for her innovative production of *South Pacific* at NYU's Tisch School in 1984 (set in a clinic for emotionally disturbed veterans), Bogart had begun to marry her physical approach to found texts rather than ones she created. A fruitful artistic relationship with writer Mac Wellman followed, parallel to a deepening interest in classic writers: Americans such as Clare Boothe Luce and Kaufman and Hart, and Europeans such as Büchner, Strindberg and Brecht.

She formed the Via Theater with Brian Jucha in 1987 [which had the same name as a company she'd been a part of at Bard in 1972, but was otherwise completely separate] to give voice to some of these interests. Her production with Via of *No Plays No Poetry*, an adaptation of Brecht's theoretical writings, brought Bogart her first OBIE Award, along with the notice of Robert Brustein at American Repertory Theater in Cambridge, Massachusetts, where she worked several times in the ensuing years. By this time, Bogart knew she needed her own company to grow artistically.

Her mounting reputation brought her to the attention of the board of directors of Trinity Rep. Replacing founding artistic director Adrian Hall—who had built a two-theater complex catering to a vast subscription base—with Bogart was a risky proposition, and was greeted with skepticism in the press. She programmed an aggressive mix of radical classics, such as Robert Woodruff's production of *Baal* and her own

Summerfolk, with more standard fare; the mixture was too volatile for Trinity and its subscribers, and Bogart only lasted a year. "What I did learn," Bogart explains in *A Director Prepares,* "is that you cannot take over someone else's company. You have to start from scratch."

And so she did. After winning her second OBIE in 1992 (for Paula Vogel's *The Baltimore Waltz* at Circle Repertory Company), she cofounded the Saratoga International Theater Institute with Tadashi Suzuki, a Japanese theater director and the creator of the Suzuki Method, a physically and mentally rigorous actor-training technique. SITI Company, as it is now known, was originally to be a cross-cultural collaboration between Bogart and Suzuki every summer in Saratoga Springs, New York, convened to help revitalize the American theater via physical technique. Eventually, it became a company of artists led by Bogart with a year-round season in New York City and a summer training season in Saratoga. The actors in her company are trained in both Suzuki and Viewpoints, which Bogart says "results in strength, focus, flexibility, visibility, audibility, spontaneity and presence." More than anything else, the work Bogart has created with SITI Company affirms her central place in American theater.

Her series with SITI of shows on figures of genius (*The Medium* [1993] about Marshall McLuhan, *Bob* [1997] about Robert Wilson, *Room* [2000] about Virginia Woolf, *Score* [2002] about Leonard Bernstein and so on) are tours-de-force that leave an actor bathed in sweat by the end of the performance. The discipline, the rigor, the exactitude of the physical world Bogart creates, married with a fiercely intelligent attachment to narrative, mesmerizes the spectator. *New York Times* critic Mel Gussow called it a "'gestural vocabulary,' the body language that links people but also separates them." The gestures enfold meaning, the sheer rigor of the performance inspires awe, and the text almost becomes a hallucinatory afterthought.

Bogart's work on the classics—from *The Adding Machine* (1995) to *Hay Fever* (2001) to *A Midsummer Night's Dream* (2004)—also makes use of Suzuki and Viewpoints training. But when constrained to a classic text, her playfulness finds escape either in radical settings, or in the liminal world between actor and character. Her *Midsummer* featured eight actors performing more than twenty roles; in her production of Marivaux's *La Dispute* (2003), the young lovers were played by actors at least twice the age of their characters. It is no wonder she was tapped in 1998 to stage Brecht and Weill's *Seven Deadly Sins* for New York City Opera, in which the main character is textually split in two—a dancer *and* a singer.

Although she's best known for stage biographies and classics, Bogart has an extraordinary track record with new plays by some challenging contemporary playwrights, among them Vogel, Wellman, Charles

L. Mee and Eduardo Machado. In any genre, however, one is aware of productive tensions: between Bogart's vision and the text, between performer and text, between performer and challenging physicality, between performer and character, between movement and text. Vogel explains in *Anne Bogart: Viewpoints* that Bogart "instinctively understands that to separate the elements of her production, to layer and fragment the meaning, she must incorporate sites of resistance to her own interpretation, whether it's the design, the performance or the text."

A number of directors interviewed for this volume expressed envy for Bogart, lamenting their lack of a codified system with which to tackle a play. But that envy is surely misplaced, because Bogart's work is no more systematized than any other director's. She does, however, speak passionately about a system of training for performers, and the fact that her company shares that training and practices it every day—like a concert pianist playing scales—means that her productions are the result of a unique and rigorous collaboration. (She has said that she shares a "collective vision" with SITI Company members.) Bogart forces herself to march forward even when she doesn't have an idea, hoping by the time she reaches the stage she'll get one. Her confidence comes from knowing that her collaborators—artists who have been trained to view the stage the same way she does—are waiting at the other end.

Because of Viewpoints—and because Bogart herself is not only a prolific writer but a captivating speaker—a great deal has already been written by and about her. Our conversation covered only a small portion of her tremendously varied career. We spoke at the offices of SITI Company in New York City in the summer of 2004. At that meeting, the company was doing its exercises in preparation for a rehearsal—SITI happily opens its rehearsals to outside observers—and the atmosphere was relaxed, one of camaraderie and anticipation. Bogart was an island of intensity, of deep thought and great connections. Phones rang, company members came and went, but her focus in conversation remained acute and piercing. It's no surprise she is sought-after on the arts lecture circuit: her ideas electrify. A true phenomenologist, she speaks of theater as an event between performer and text, between performer and audience . . . and that connection, which she personifies, is what all directors are after.

The cast of Hotel Cassiopeia *by Charles L. Mee. SITI Company, Actors Theatre of Louisville, Humana Festival of New American Plays, 2006. Credit: Harlan Taylor. Used by permission of Actors Theatre of Louisville.*

JULY 2004, SITI COMPANY OFFICES/REHEARSAL ROOM, NEW YORK CITY

You're a choreographer, you're a theorist, you're a director . . . How do you introduce yourself to someone you don't know?

I always say I'm a director. Period. I hate the words "experimental" or "avant-garde" or any qualifier. I hate the words "physical theater." I think that all theater's physical. I hate those rubrics.

So I would say that I am a director. I'm not really a choreographer. I'm not an actor at all. All I've ever done in my entire life from when I was a little girl is direct. I'm one hundred percent a director.

What are the strengths you draw on when you direct?

It feels to me like it's juggling. You know those tests that people take to find out what their natural proclivities are? I'm sure if I took the test it would say I should be something like a director. I enjoy juggling an unbearable number of things simultaneously. And I think if there's any quality a director needs, that's it. To find joy in that, not terror. It means juggling psyches, and juggling ideas, and hearing them all at the same time. Some people's natural proclivity is to zoom in on one thing and go really deep—that's what a lot of the actors I work with do, and they're really good at it. I'm more interested in being able to see a global viewpoint, to feel and hear a global picture, to find ways of shepherding all the disparate elements into one worldview.

You've said in your writing that when you get lost, one of your methods is to focus on a detail. How does that help you return to the big picture?

It's almost like a formula, because you can easily get overwhelmed. Even though I like juggling, I can suddenly just have no idea what the hell I'm doing. In that case, rather than stressing about it, I focus on one small thing. God is in the details; I believe that. And inside any detail lies the entire world of the larger picture: the micro-macro. Within a gesture, you can find the whole tenor of a play. Any gesture in a play should express the entire play.

At what point in your journey did you realize that your personal theories ran counter to American acting tradition?

When I first came to New York in 1974, I was certainly galvanized by the Open Theater, the Performance Group, Richard Foreman, all of that. And when I looked at any other theater, I found it deadly boring. What I was seeing was what I was hearing. And to this day, I find that not very interesting, because in life *people don't do what they say*.

What I found more interesting was the dance world and the really huge innovations of the Judson Church era. I found those things so applicable to theater, and such an antidote to what I thought of as "couch plays," that I gravitated to them right away. I felt an affinity for the dance world, which is why you called me a choreographer. I took dance classes and I threw myself into them: I was in love with that world. I was not in love with conventional theater.

You've documented many turning points in your life as an artist: being in Berlin and realizing you were an "American artist," for example. Talk to me about those turning points.

There have probably been seven moments in my life—I documented them in *A Director Prepares*—when everything I'd understood up to that point was challenged. It was the first time I ever saw a professional play, in Rhode Island; it was the moment I saw *Sommergäste* [the film of Peter Stein's production of Gorky's *Summerfolk*, which he directed for his legendary ensemble company, the Schaubühne, in 1974] in a movie theater; it was a moment in a discussion with Ariane Mnouchkine about the necessity for a company. And in those moments, I've known I have to act. I can't go on living the way I've lived. I have to be ready to abandon every relationship that I've built up to that moment to pursue this new unknown adventure. And if I deny that, I know deep inside me my art will die. I hope to constantly tease the edge of who I am and what I need.

Through those transitions, what stayed the same?

The very first play I directed on a stage with a real audience was *The Bald Soprano* when I was fifteen. Sometimes I think that nothing has changed since that first time—that I have the same sense of rhythm, the same sense of humor, the same sense of space and spatial composition, and that I'm itching for the same things. There are certain things that drive me crazy, like if a chair is on the wrong angle. I just can't rest until it's moved, even if it's only an inch and a half. I don't know where that comes from. Is it a search for a kind of visual harmony? Those things don't seem to change. My company knows my aesthetic so well now that they put the chair in the right place, and I don't have to ask them to do it. They get my obsession that way, God bless them!

James Baldwin wrote that the purpose of art is to "lay bare the questions which have been hidden by the answers." What questions does your work lay bare?

A lot of my work is based on the question, "Who the hell is this person?" I do a lot of work about individuals: Virginia Woolf, Orson Welles, Bob Wilson, Robert Rauschenberg. You could say that's the same question, but it's about different people.

Are they all questions, then, about the nature of genius?

I'm fascinated by people of genius. I want to own them, I want to eat them, and stand on their shoulders. I want them to be inside of me. So if I spend two years with Orson Welles, it's because I want to assimilate him. There's something in him that I want not only to eat for myself, but to share with other people. There's a double necessity in that. I did a show about Bob Wilson because when I was a young director, I used to follow him down the street. (He doesn't know that—unless you publish it here and he reads it. But he won't; he doesn't read!) I followed him mainly because I couldn't understand how a person like that could exist. How could this tall Texan make these strange shows? I was completely attracted to and puzzled by his genius, even though at times I just hated it and other times I loved it.

Whenever I get an idea to do a show, I get, literally, a *frisson de corps*—a shake in my body. Based on the physical reaction to the idea, I know if it's going to sustain, and for how long. If I don't get the *frisson*, I know I'm going to lose interest. I remember sitting on a bus in Salzburg reading a book on the Group Theatre and I suddenly got this huge *frisson de corps*. This one was so big, I said, "This project will last a good three to four years."

That Group Theatre piece, *Reunion*, is still in development. What's the question that you want to answer with that project?

Again: who were they? It's the first time in my life—because I have a theater company that's now twelve years old—that I have a completely ripe opportunity to do a play about a theater company. SITI is moving into a kind of middle age, which brings up issues that the crises of the Group Theatre lay bare. I wanted for us to live through those questions, through the lens of another company. Who were they? Who was Stella Adler; what was she about? I wanted to enter into the devil's cave; I'm so denigrating of the Method and of Strasberg, and yet Strasberg is a major character in the play. What would happen if my company actually played around with affective memory [the Stanislavski acting technique that Strasberg championed]? Those questions are vital to me on a daily basis: who are we becoming, and what problems emerge in the fabric of the company?

I've also interviewed Ping Chong, with whom you've worked and who dissolved his company after sixteen years. One of the reasons he says he did that was because company members were becoming constrained by the financial realities of middle age. Your company is only a dozen years old, and you already talk about it being middle-aged. What's SITI Company's future?

A company is nothing but extreme paradoxes. Every year, the actors in my company refresh their affirmation of my ability to cast how I feel. Nothing is a given in casting. They have to reaffirm it every year. They say, "Cast the way you feel it, and if we're left out, that's our problem."

The paradox is that I care deeply about their livelihoods; they have kids, and some have mortgages and country houses, and I like that, but it can also bog things down. I actually like the problems that presents. They're big problems. How do you take care of a group of twenty people?

The thought fills me with terror . . . which is also something you have talked about: terror at the inception of the process. And of course there's the terror of, "Will I survive?" That second terror seems antithetical to the kind of terror you want to have in your process.

There are issues about survival that come up constantly, and I refuse to act on them. I don't want the company to be based on the fear of falling apart. I'd rather be afraid of falling apart because of aesthetic reasons, not for political reasons or financial reasons. Again, that's a big paradox. I'm trying to create an institution that has longevity and, at the same time, I don't want to do the things that *ensure* longevity.

Because you rely so heavily on actors as collaborators, what do you look for in actors when you cast outside the company?

It's a hard thing to describe. When I met Henry Stram, he walked in the room and was a phenomenon. When I met Laila Robins, she walked in the room and everyone else disappeared. They're both just a phenomenon. It's not like they leave a certain part outside; they bring their whole being into the room. A lot of actors think that only parts of them belong at an audition or in a rehearsal room. The fact that they bring all of their nerves and doubts is what makes them interesting.

Then the second thing I look for is that they can differentiate moment to moment. That I think, "Oh, I know who that is," and, "Wait, who's that, and where are they going?" That's the central art of acting: that one moment is different from the next. And you can't do it technically, really. You can learn how to act it, but it's tricky.

They have to be smart. And then there's another thing, it's very difficult to talk about. It's the "T" word: taste. An actor's taste. On a craft level: the piece they choose, and the way they dress, yeah, that's the most obvious. But it's the taste of how they walk into the room.

Once you've got the ideal company of actors for a project, how do you decide on your questions for "sourcework"?

I usually spend two years thinking about a project before I do it. I'm sharing the questions I've asked myself. And the questions are thought of deeply; they are not spontaneous at all. I try to get to what I think the essential questions of the play are.

The first big one I'd ask if I were doing a classic is, "What was the original energy that this play released? And how is that equivalent in our times?" In doing *South Pacific* I said, "In 1949, when it was first staged, what happened?" It opened in a country that just finished a war. It was a hit. It had a certain energy, it dealt with certain issues, it touched a nerve. If you do a visual equivalent of that, you don't actually get at the energy. What would get at a similar kind of energy? That's one of the major questions of sourcework.

Spring Awakening is about sexual awakening. Say you and I are in a room and we want to attack that: what questions would I ask you that would make you remember, in an active memory sort of way, your sexual awakening? So that the source of the *play* and the source of *you* meet somehow. Those questions allow you to access the energy of the play. The questions that the play was born with relate to our times, and ourselves, and our dreams.

In *Anne Bogart: Viewpoints*, the actor Ellen Lauren explains how, after the tablework and sourcework are done, you tend to put the actors on their feet, staging with Viewpoints and without the text. Can you explain the particulars of that process, and then why it is so valuable?

It's pretty straightforward and very traditional. I have to start at the beginning. I can't go from Act One, Scene 1 to Act Three, Scene 6. Can't do it, impossible. Because I don't know what got us there. I work chronologically, with the exception of dance numbers and songs. In terms of the dramatic through line of the play, until I find out how you enter into the first scene, I can't do the first scene. The entrance determines how the next scene happens.

In the company, we "train" for half an hour before rehearsals begin. We do Viewpoint improvisation, and then I say, okay, I know these things about how this scene starts: I know that it involves a diagonal, for example. Then I'll give a list of things I don't know, and then we start and rehearse. We stop a lot. We never improvise. Sometimes I'll stage a scene without the words, though that's not the general rule. Always, it's about how do we get from *this* to *this*? Of course we go back the next day and change things. But it's about setting things each day.

You've written that there's a cruelty in setting a moment; for an actor to keep it fresh, he or she must "resurrect the dead." That creates a tension, a happening contained in a certain physical box, against which you must continually push. Is that the idea?

That's partially it. Every time you do it, you have a different experience, different emotions. It's not about routine emotions. It's about finding a physical structure that supports a renewal every time, even though it's the same.

Every director is going to want to know how you do that.

Number one, I never tell an actor what to do completely. I will say, "I think I know that it's about a diagonal line." I will say things like, "Make a choice, and try that choice on the word *it*." Or maybe, "Your hand should be at the edge of the table." But the actor has made the choice to put his hand down. A lot of people misunderstand that about my work. They think I tell everybody what to do all the time. I don't make up the initial things. I make adjustments and I coordinate actions.

I don't say, "Now start here, and go here, and do that." But I stop a lot. If I said to you, "Go," and you stood up and turned left, I might say, "Great, could you start again and maybe turn left on this word?" And then you do that again, and maybe that doesn't work for you, and that's okay. Because you are the leader. And I'm following you. That's the most misunderstood part of my work.

Why do you think people misunderstand your work? Is it because they conceive of you as this Brecht-like "I've got a technique" person? I can't tell you the number of directors I've interviewed who've expressed envy because you've got a "technique."

I think people are looking for a method. And what I am doing is not a method. The Viewpoints work is fantastic training, and it makes speaking in rehearsal easier, because I can say, "Can you fix your Spatial Relationship?" But the idea that the Viewpoints is a technique for directing . . . that technique does not exist. Directing is painstakingly slow, like painting or practicing the piano, or any art form.

Let's talk a little bit more of the specifics of the process, and use one of your amazing actors, Tom Nelis, as an object lesson. His performance with gesture in *Score* [her one-man show about Leonard Bernstein] was extraordinary. How do you create that kind of performance? I presume a lot of it comes from him?

One hundred percent.

How do you help him find those gestures, go to those places?

What I said earlier about the diagonal—that was specifically about him in *The Medium* [her play about communications theorist Marshall McLuhan, who was played by Nelis]. The first time we got away from the table, I said, "I know two things, and I can't tell you why, but I just know that you enter on a diagonal, from upstage right, and come down stage left. And I know he's something like the Lincoln doll [the audio-animatronic mannequin in Disney World's Hall of Presidents, that moves in a stilted, robotic manner as it "speaks"]; he's suffering a stroke and can't speak, that something's wrong with him. And that's all I know. Go!" Tom listened to me: he went on the diagonal and something was wrong with him. It took us two days to get that diagonal. I just kept going over and over it again.

But then we found it. It dawned on me: "Oh, my God. The whole play is in that moment of his losing his voice [for a theorist concerned with communication, McLuhan ironically suffered a debilitating stroke before he died]. The whole thing is about speaking. [Writing in *The New York Times*, Ben Brantley lauded Bogart's ensemble for "presenting a mechanistic universe of brain-scrambled automatons, who demonstrate the ways in which we have become technology's slaves in the twenty-some years since McLuhan was on the best-seller lists."]

So it's an intuitive process. And that's a scary thing to say to an actor: "There's something wrong with you, and it's on a diagonal." We have a joke in the company. It's a quote from Nikos Psacharopoulos, who used to run the Williamstown Theatre Festival. He would say to his actors [with a thick Greek accent], "Medea must kill for love. Go!" So whenever I give a hard direction, somebody's bound to say, "*Medea must kill for love. Go!*"

I've done more than half of the interviews for this book, and there's pretty much nothing in common among you all except an absolute faith in yourselves. Young directors are the opposite: they think they need to know the answer to every question before rehearsal starts.

I come into rehearsal with stacks of books, but it's all the things I *don't* know that are interesting. I'll say, "This research triggered *this* in me,"

Tom Nelis in Score, *created by SITI Company. College of DuPage Performing Arts Center, 2005. Credit: Michael Brosilow.*

and that's also what I imbue in the students at Columbia: the idea that directing is not about knowing. It's about having the questions. And those kinds of questions, through you, are contagious. They're contagious not only for the actors and the designers, but for the audience.

With so many questions, I'd imagine your rehearsal processes can be really, really long.

No. I'm grateful that I don't live in Russia and have two years to direct. I think it's healthy to have three weeks. Time pressure's always there. The question is: how do you function inside of that pressure? Whether it's three weeks, or four weeks, or five weeks, what are you doing with that time, and how do you handle it? Do you close down and say, "Well, because I have a short amount of time, I'll only do *this*," or do you say, "Breathe, be present, trust."

And I think the word isn't "faith," it's "trust." Trust the people you're in the room with, trust in yourself. Certainly have an awareness of time. I think of the rehearsal process as an hourglass. You turn it over and, boom, there's this much time. And the sand is very light, very beautiful, and there's no sense of hurry, but you will hurry. And that's what a rehearsal is. It's an incredibly finite amount of time: the sand, the lightness in the room.

You have talked about disagreement as an essential part of the creative process. Can you give me an example of productive disagreement?

It happens in every rehearsal. If I said, "In this scene, you're angry" (I would never say that, of course), and the actor said, "Okay, I'm angry," and he was angry, there'd be no disagreement, and there'd be nothing there except someone doing something I said.

But if the actor takes that, and brings something contradictory to it—that he's actually giddy, say, or happy—then that's a disagreement. And if he doesn't give me a disagreement, then there's no point in us being in the room. Then it's a parent/child relationship; you're doing what I tell you to do. So in every moment there needs to be a disagreement. Disagreement is a terrible word—I like the word *Auseinandersetzung*, which means you set yourself apart from each other in order to create.

We do suffer in this country from the disease of agreement. If you think that a rehearsal is doing what the director wants, then there's something sick in the room. That's why Robert Wilson's work has gotten better with German and Danish actors. They disagree with him as they're doing it. That's why there's a tension. When American actors do Bob Wilson's work, there's no tension. They're saying, "Bob Wilson's asked me to count, so I'll count, okay: 'one, two, three.'" Instead of doing what the Germans do, which is going, "Fuck you, you sucker!"

The first grown-up production I ever did, with actual union actors, was with the Music Theater Group in 1985: *The Making of Americans*. At one of our first rehearsals I said to an actor, "Cathy, what are you doing?" And she turned to me and said, "Fuck you, Anne." And I was so happy. I thought, "Now we can really work." Because I was so tired of people saying, "Okay, whatever." For that kind of feisty disagreement, I think there has to be a "Fuck you, Anne" in the room. Not like, "Fuck you, Anne, I'm not going to do it," but, "Fuck you, Anne, how about this instead?"

That kind of disagreement demands that everyone be passionately involved; that they share the burden of ownership.

I am most proud of the moment when I stop doing anything and the actors completely take over. Always. Because I feel like I'm succeeding. If I'm doing all the work, then I don't feel like I'm doing very well. There are moments when suddenly I just stop because things happen, they're doing it!

The word that comes to mind when I think of those moments is "grace." You have to plant the seeds for grace; yet you can't make grace happen. And I would say if there's anything I'm looking for in my life, it's grace, for those moments of grace that are absolutely thrilling.

There's a little pet peeve I have that's related to this—and it's actually something rather glorious. On opening night, I never have anywhere to put my jacket. Everyone in the theater has somewhere to put their things—the stage manager, the people who work in the offices, the actors—but all of a sudden, there's no place for me to put my jacket.

I've worked at New York Theatre Workshop so many times and complained that I had no place to hang my coat on opening night, that now a hook in the box office says "director's hook." I'm responsible for that little director's hook, and I'm very proud of that.

But when I'm wandering around thinking, "Where could I put my bag and my coat?" that's such a great metaphor for what my job is. Essentially, a director's job is to make herself obsolete. You plant all those seeds, you work really hard, and you succeed if you suddenly have no *place* there. Every director knows that feeling in the pit of the stomach when one is not needed anymore. It's both wonderful and horrible.

In your books, you describe the process between actor and spectator (and actor and director, and director and text, etc.) as a phenomenon to be broken down and comprehended, as a series of sensory and sensual responses. ("Art is understood through experience, not explanation,"

you've said.) You privilege the *experiences* of theatergoing and theater-creating, rather than their politics, or their historical context. And yet, your work is intellectually rigorous. So what do you think is the nature of the exchange between artist and audience? Is it emotional? Physical?

I think it's both of those things, and that's why I love the theater. It is emotional, it's philosophical, it's intellectual. The only original theory that I ever came up with—everything else is stolen, but I really claim this one—is about the seven human needs the theater fulfills [as described in her book *And Then You Act*: empathy, entertainment, ritual, participation, spectacle, education and alchemy]. All of the really truly great experiences in theater do all seven.

And so, to answer your question, I think that the multiplicity and diversity of that audience-actor relationship is part of the magnetism of the theater. The more we are in front of our computers and DVDs, the more we need that magnetism. It's more rarefied to be in a room with actors. It's not quite so much a part of the fabric of the everyday; it's special.

Part of the reason that theory helps me is that I got an MFA in what's now called "Performance Studies" at NYU. I'm really grateful that I didn't go to directing school. Those teachers who were there at the time in the mid 1970s—Richard Schechner (still there), Michael Kirby, Ted Hoffman, Brooks McNamara—cultivated in me an interest in anthropology and sociology. So I don't ask, "How am I going to stage this play?" I ask, "What is this play, how does it function in the world, what is its audience?" And it instigated in me an appetite that continually gets bigger, to look at the phenomenon of the theater more than the particulars of a convention of doing theater. So I'm grateful that I had those two years of reading and studying and having my mind opened by those particular four white guys who helped me cultivate a particular attitude toward the theater. And I use the word "attitude" very consciously. I believe in attitude. You brought an attitude to this interview. I bring one back. And we create something.

You just referred to "four white guys" from whom you learned a way of looking at theater. Do you feel, as a woman working in the theater, that the playing field is level?

I had a revelation last fall. We were doing our play, *Room*, about Virginia Wolf, near Washington, D.C. The college that organized it [University of Maryland in College Park] put together a symposium. On the panel with me were Molly Smith [artistic director of Arena Stage] and Tina Packer [artistic director of Shakespeare & Company]. In the middle of the panel discussion I suddenly realized that all three of us had chosen, subconsciously or consciously, to go through the back door to get to the front. Tina Packer left England and the Royal Shakespeare Company and started a company up in the Berkshires, making it on her own in order to come back into the mainstream. Molly Smith graduated, started a theater in Juneau, Alaska, and now runs Arena. I disappeared into downtown. I couldn't get a theater, so I did it on the street corner. All three of us, in a sense, avoided the male-dominated theater hierarchy. I think we did it because we felt we'd be more free working on the side, but we were always interested in being in the middle of the theater world.

So to answer your question: no; I just do my plays, whatever. But actually the path to getting where I want to be has been particular. It hasn't been a conscious choice. The fact that I have a company means that I initiate the work. I don't wait for somebody to call; I make it happen. And I think that's partially in reaction to the fact that women get less of a chance to do work.

Do you feel free to create whatever art you want, or do you think American culture has become conservative about what it's willing to accept?

I think there is major censorship since 9/11, in every single realm. It's something we have to deal with on a daily basis. Money is used as an excuse, but the real issue is that we're a country that's paranoid as hell. So our times, if anything, are a call for action and articulation.

I wonder how much dissent is possible when you're not in control of the finances of your own company.

It's too easy to say money's the problem. I don't think there's enough resistance on the part of the artists; the size of the obstacle defines the size of the resistance. To meet a big obstacle, you have to "dilate" as human beings, and I think we're afraid of being big. That's why I like Orson Welles, who was big—not just physically—he was a big person. I'm interested in the notion of the dilation of the human being. On the stage I'm looking for a dilated human being. As a creator I want to be dilated. And I would ask that we try to be dilated in relationship to the difficulties of our times in order to offer resistance. It's a big part of our role in the world, to be resistant. To be the sand in the shell.

Think about your students in Columbia University's directing program. What kind of world are you sending them out into?

I'm sending them out to be revolutionaries. I'm sending them out to start over. None of them expects to find a prescribed life by entering into the regional world. They all know they have to make it up. You go out, you trailblaze. The only thing you can do is question the assumptions of what you're expecting to happen. And try to stay awake to the kind of culture you're in, and be connected to something outside of you, something you want to explore.

I don't think that there's such a thing as an unemployed director. It's true that you can be an unemployed actor. But twenty-five percent of what a director does is initiate projects. And if he's not working, he's not a director. I hate hearing directors say, "Oh, I'm unemployed." It's bullshit. It's not an option. If you want to be unemployed, be an actor.

What are the things that make you look at a young director and say, "Ah! There's a spark. There's something that needs to be nurtured"?

That's something I think about all the time. When I audition directors, I look for somebody who's on a quest somehow, who would do something even without the training. You know when people are so desperate they'll say, "Oh, if I could just work with you, I could figure out what I'm looking for"? I want to find people who already seem to be on journeys of their own.

Of the 115 applications we get, I bring about 20 to 25 of them in for a weekend. The first thing I do is I sit them in a big circle and ask them five or six questions. They think I'm listening to their answers, but actually I'm learning how they handle a group. Because, number one, a director is in the room with other people. How they interact, how they talk, how they're "pointing" is what I look for. I believe from the depths of my soul in Ludwig Wittgenstein's notion that if you can't say it, you should point to it. So I look for a director who can speak with intent. I look for people who are going outside of themselves, toward something that's not *them*. If it's all about them, I'm not interested.

I think that's true in any relationship: you're not attracted to somebody who's clingy, you're not attracted to somebody who's full of him or herself. You're attracted to somebody who's doing something interesting, who has something going on. Someone who has the ability to be in the room with other people, and to listen and make associative leaps. Because if you're too literal, there's no room for the poetic language of the stage.

Once you've accepted students into the program, what do they do?

In their first year each director has to do two fully produced plays a week. They're under half an hour, but they're fully produced: staged, off book, designed. After the third week, every idea they had in their career is finished. They have nothing left. In their second year, they get to spend a whole semester working on two projects.

So, it's a backwards program. It's all about making the work and putting it in front of an audience, and looking back, over and over. It's the opposite of: learn a few things, and we guide it to the end into a project. Instead it's like, put it out, put it out, put it out, and get criticized for it over and over and over again, until you just break down.

I'm so proud of my students. They don't come out of Columbia asking, "What's the corporate ladder to directing?" They go out and *rock the world*. They come out with muscles.

MARK BROKAW

Bumping into the Play

SOME OF THE DIRECTORS INTERVIEWED IN this book espouse specific methodologies in their work. Understanding how Anne Bogart uses Viewpoints to create a unique world, or how Elizabeth LeCompte or Ping Chong blend technology with the actor, can be daunting to an early-career artist. But Mark Brokaw, an actor-turned-director from the Midwest, talks about his work in a radically different way. His thoughts on developing and fine-tuning characters, and how those characters must "bump" up against a play's obstacles, seem refreshingly simple. Brokaw begins by filtering every element of the work—acting, design, direction—through one overarching idea, one "central transaction."

This simplicity has served him especially well with complex new plays. Among his best-known credits is the Pulitzer Prize–winning *How I Learned to Drive* by Paula Vogel (Vineyard Theatre, 1997), a deeply nuanced and ruthlessly intelligent story of a young woman's improper relationship with her uncle. When Brokaw first approached Vogel about staging it minimally, she was skeptical. But in the end, Vogel told the *New York Times* after the play opened, Brokaw "embraced what the actual magic of theater is, which isn't based on spectacle. [He understands] you can create a far greater spectacle from actors and words alone." His designers' work is always elegant in its spareness, and his simplicity of staging has become a hallmark. It may be the combination of that simple approach with complex texts that has been key to his success. Brokaw bumps up against a play and refuses to get caught in its nooks and crannies until he figures out the play's grand mechanism.

Brokaw grew up on a farm in Illinois, and went to college to learn short-story writing. After graduating from the University of Illinois at Urbana-Champaign in 1980, he spent three years with a small theater in Urbana, Illinois, called the Celebration Company, where he mostly acted, and ultimately tried his hand at directing. The experience so energized him that he ended up in Yale's MFA program. He worked relentlessly there, learning to love research as he put on play after play. Since Yale, Brokaw extensively researches every play he directs, often bringing piles of books into first rehearsal.

After his 1986 graduation from Yale, Brokaw was a Fall Fellow with the Drama League's Directors Project. That fellowship, in turn, led directly to a relationship with Off Broadway's Second Stage Theatre, where his career working on world premieres written by some of the country's most exciting voices was launched. Thereafter he shelved his original plans to work regionally in order to stay in New York.

A steady stream of relatively small Off-Broadway shows followed in the next ten years, culminating in one of the most extraordinary seasons to befall an emerging director. The years of 1996–1997 saw his first collaboration with Kenneth Lonergan, *This Is Our Youth*, for the New Group, followed by the Drama Dept.'s *As Bees in Honey Drown* by Douglas Carter Beane and Vogel's *How I Learned to Drive*. All three were critically acclaimed, and the third went on to garner OBIE, Drama Desk and Lucille Lortel awards for Brokaw's direction.

Why all this success with new plays? Undoubtedly, Brokaw's gentle midwestern demeanor helps when he's walking the fine, diplomatic line with a writer. "Mark has an immediate rapport with writers," Second Stage's Carole Rothman told the *New York Times* in 1999. Rothman, whom Brokaw calls his "fairy godmother," explains: "He listens and he serves the script. He is not one of those directors who calls attention to himself."

That rigor in service of the playwright has meant that Brokaw gets plenty of return invitations from playwrights, and from those not-for-profit theaters that prize new work. He's worked with particular frequency Off Broadway at the Vineyard, directing Vogel's *Long Christmas Ride Home* (2003) and a pair of Craig Lucas premieres there. He reunited with Lucas (and the actress Mary-Louise Parker, who starred in *How I Learned to Drive*) on the director's first Broadway gig, *Reckless*, in 2004. Produced by two not-for-profit theaters (Manhattan Theatre Club and Second Stage), *Reckless* was followed by two more not-for-profit Broadway productions, both with Roundabout Theatre Company: a revival of *The Constant Wife* (2005) and Patrick Marber's play *After Miss Julie* (2009).

The Constant Wife, a 1929 play by W. Somerset Maugham, was not the first time Brokaw has branched out to the classics. He directed Molière's *Tartuffe* for the Public Theater's Shakespeare in the Park (1999), and the Roundabout's revival of Tennessee Williams's *Suddenly Last Summer* (2006).

And why not try new musicals? After an out-of-town tryout at La Jolla Playhouse in 2007, Brokaw directed *Cry-Baby: The Musical* in his first commercial venture on Broadway in 2008. Based on John Waters's 1990 film *Cry-Baby*, the show did not please critics and ran a scant three months. But that hasn't dimmed the director's passion for new musicals. He serves as Artistic Director of the Yale Institute for Music Theatre, which has developed works by early-career composers, lyricists and bookwriters since 2009.

Nonetheless, Brokaw realizes his greatest strengths lie in the service of new plays. His most recent project at the time of this writing started once more at Off Broadway's Vineyard Theatre, where he tackled Nicky Silver's new play *The Lyons* in 2011. The show was such a big hit that the production transferred to Broadway the following year. Brokaw was back in his element, even if you don't see his name in the headlines. While Silver and the show's star, Linda Lavin, have been garnering accolades, Brokaw has been quietly, sensitively, bumping up against another new play.

MAY 2003, PUCK BUILDING, NEW YORK CITY

Talk to me about how you began in theater.

I grew up on a farm in Illinois on the other side of the state from Chicago, near the Mississippi on the Iowa border, and there really was no theater around. I think I actually got started doing it to entertain myself. I was the cliché—I wrote the plays in grade school, in junior high; I would rehearse them with the cousins when they came for holiday dinners and we'd put them on for the aunts and uncles. I was constantly doing puppet shows, and hauling in my family to watch them.

I'm a little baffled myself about where the interest in theater came from, but there was something about the magic of it. You know, growing up on a farm, spending so much time alone because your community is spread out . . . I spent a lot of time on my own in the fields, back in the woods, living in my own imagination. The theater became an extension of that.

From the fields to Yale?

I went to college at the University of Illinois, where I was a short-story writer. I got my degree in rhetoric, which allowed me to take any course I wanted: theater courses, film courses, literature courses . . . And the work I did as a short-story writer had a profound effect on me as a director in terms of the way I look at dramatic literature, storytelling and narrative.

My favorites were the John Cheever stories and the Raymond Carver stories and the Chekhov short stories. That's where I started to learn about structure. All those people share an ambiguity in the center of their storytelling. It's been influential to me, still, in the kind of material I'm drawn to. The other thing about short-story writers is that they tell stories with very lean characterizations.

When I was at the University of Illinois, I got involved with a semi-professional group called the Celebration Company. I worked there all through my college years, and I stayed for three years after.

What were you doing there?

I was an actor and a director and a writer. It's where I directed my first play—my first six plays. It was a converted train station—a 100-seat flexible black box—and the trains would roll by during the performances. You would have to hold, and then you'd pick up and go on.

I'll never forget: we were doing *The Hot L Baltimore,* and the girl was talking about the train going by—and during her train speech, *the train went by.* Magic, just magic!

It was a truly golden time. A great group of actors, very talented people; some of them are still there and many others have gone off across the country. Some of the finest work I've ever seen to this day was done with that group.

And also it was *poor theater.* We didn't have a lot of money, so I learned that the greatest magic was a bare stage and a chair, and that you really could create an entire universe from that. In that space, I learned how to take truly imaginative leaps.

When did you decide directing was your calling, as opposed to writing or acting?

I thought I wanted to be an actor also, and I thought I wanted to be a playwright, but the thing is that *I stunk.* I was a terrible playwright! And I was a worse actor.

But really, I always knew that I wanted to be a director, even when I didn't know what it was. When I wrote those plays or did those puppet shows on my own, there was something about being the magician at the center of it all that I found the most satisfying. To be the one at the center, to create that whole universe.

One of the first professional plays I ever saw was when the Acting Company [a touring company based in New York City] came through the University of Illinois [in the early 1980s]. I saw Garland Wright's production of *The Country Wife*. It was truly one of the formative moments in my life, because I saw what was possible, what being a director could be: how vast the task was, how much you could achieve. It really was one of the most complete productions I've ever seen.

Seeing that made me want to be a director. It also made me realize how little I knew. Back in those days, my work was about *eliciting performance*. But if I went back and looked at the performances now, I don't know if they all fit together into a world. I don't think I had a clue about how to create the *world* of a play. But I knew about how to help people give a good performance, or be able to use themselves in a way that would help them give a good performance. That's why I knew I wanted to be in a program where I could learn. I needed technique, something I could hang my hat on.

So after three years I ended up at the Drama School at Yale, which was the perfect place to land because it wasn't an academic program, and I am *far* from an intellectual. It really was about production. I had no professional experience. Before I went to Yale I had probably seen five professional productions in my lifetime outside of the Champaign-Urbana area.

My first year there, I was involved in twelve productions: as an actor, as an assistant director and as a director. I didn't do that again because I just about wore myself out. But it was exhilarating to be in a place where everybody was doing the same thing every day. It was like going to church every day, but it was *fun church*.

I was there as a tabula rasa, a blank slate. I had many wonderful teachers. Through Earle Gister I really learned what the actor's task was, and David Hammond took the next step. He had been a student of Earle's at Carnegie Mellon, and he incorporated that into what a director does with the actor. That's what I walked out with: besides the confidence of having done a lot of work, and having been able to observe the work of professionals at the Rep, I walked out with the beginnings of technique.

What is the actor's task?

I should start with the director's task and fill in from there. It's to give the piece of material an *active point of view*. And from that active point of view, one learns that every play has a central transaction. There's a central struggle embodied in every play, and in every play it's different.

And the director's job is unlocking that, identifying what that is. That's the work you take to the designers: you say, "This is a world in which *this* happens." Then you create a physical world in which, when the characters walk into that world, that action is inevitable. It *must occur* because there is no other choice but for it to occur.

So if a director's job is to give a production an active point of view, and to identify what that struggle is, then the actor's job is to have an *active investment* in that point of view.

As a director you're creating an entire world. That's what the rehearsal process is about. You're bringing the world of this play to actors. And you are identifying what the world is, and what the parameters of the world are, and what is actively going on in that world, *without naming it* for them—guiding them to it, so that they can come to it on their own, discover it on their own.

I understand the value of ownership, but why is it important that you don't name it? Why shouldn't a director at the first rehearsal say, "Here's the play, here's the central transaction . . ."

No, to me, the first day of rehearsal is merely about making people excited about coming back to the second. That is the goal. I'm wary of a lot of talk. I try to be careful about what I'm talking *about*.

That first day of rehearsal is about introducing people to the world of the play. I bring all the research—everything I used as a connecting point—whether it's pictures, paintings, pieces of music, a collage I made, newspaper articles, whatever it is—and I share all of that with everybody. And I say, "I was drawn to this for *this* reason." "This was a window into the play in *this* way." And then, everybody starts to enter the play *in an instinctive way*.

The main task of the director is to be the critical mind. And what you're trying to do is allow the actors to act on instinct. I want them to be the intuitive side of the brain, and to trust me to take care of the rest.

The talk, for me, is more about given circumstances. Forget initially what happens in the world; I'm more interested in, "Who are you? What is your relationship to everybody else? What is your relationship to this world?" And we keep filling in the world and your relationship to it.

Because if I name it, they're going to try to play *toward that*. And what's more exciting is to suggest what that is, what that central struggle is that everyone has an investment in, without truly naming it in terms that will make them intellectualize. Let me worry about that. I want them to *bump up* against the play and respond to it. I want them to *bump up* against the world of the play.

And then my job as the director is to help them solidify their path through the world. That's really what you're rehearsing. It's like being in a pinball machine. You release the ball, and it bumps off the paddles, and bounces one place to another: that's the actor's journey in a play. The characters come in wanting something, and how they go about getting that is all a result of what they bump up against from one end of the play to the other.

Or, it's like filling in the dots. At the beginning of rehearsal, we've got five big dots; that's all we've got. And each day we rehearse, we're filling in more dots, and filling in more dots, and filling in more dots, and *bump bump bump bump*. Until eventually, by the end of the rehearsal process, it's a solid line, so they can't get lost. There's *no way* to get lost. And that's how they can repeat their performance from night to night. Because I walk in with an immediate past, into the immediate present, I *bump* into the world, and I'm *on my way*. And I'm *propelled* through the play. And that way, the play is able to work on *me*, rather than *me* working on the play.

Do the dots end up in different places than where you expected them to be?

Oh, absolutely—hopefully so.

Since I work so much on new plays, I feel very strongly that our job in rehearsal is not to rewrite the play. I always say, "We've got to treat this like this is Shakespeare. It is completed, it's done, it's over." And that's how we have to approach it every day. We have to test it for the writer. The only way the writer can know what's going on, or that *we* can know, is to fully invest in what it is. It's not our job to sit around and say, "Well, I wouldn't say this," or, "Well, this wouldn't happen." You give it your best shot. And that way, the writer is able to say, "You know, they *wouldn't* say that." You always get in trouble when you violate that rule.

A maxim I apply in rehearsals, in my work with the actors, is that *I always say yes*. If they come to me with an idea, I say, "Yes." I'm very influenced by that Bill Ball book, *A Sense of Direction*. He talks about positation in that. If you say, "Yes," then in two minutes of trying an idea you find out if there's gold in it or not, rather than sitting around talking about it for twenty minutes.

He also says, "You always have to say [yes] three times." The first time, an actor is surprised, and you try [his or her idea]. The next time they ask you just to test you, if you're really going to let them try this thing. And then the third time, it seals the deal. And after a while, everyone just starts sending down *gold*. You get to the end of the process, and *every* idea is a fantastic idea. It's truly a way to unleash their intuition actively and instructively, and to help them use the part of themselves that is most valuable for the particular project you're working on.

Another rule is to always answer a question with a question, whenever possible. Whenever somebody asks a question, he or she has a sense of an answer already. It's not about absolutes. There is no *real answer,* it's only what works.

You work with so many of the same actors—is that because you can trust that saying "yes" to them is going to yield that gold you talk about?

I think [that method works with] anyone. It's that Martha Graham maxim, which I'm going to paraphrase: Education is not about putting in, but *about letting out.* That's what directing is, too. It's not about coming into a room and saying, "Okay! Here's what it is!" You walk into a room, you say, "Here are the possibilities. Here's a world where *this happens.* And now, I want to unleash in all of you the part of you that responds to that world, that is right for this role."

I love actors who are transformational. I love actors who don't use the same parts of them over and over again, who aren't "personality actors." I love those actors who are willing to go out on a limb and use different parts of themselves. And that's my job in the rehearsal hall: creating an atmosphere where people feel willing to risk in that way, willing to risk exposing a part of themselves that maybe they haven't exposed before, but is right for this particular role.

Let's take the example of David Morse in *How I Learned to Drive*. Here's an actor who has to play an incestuous pedophile. How did you unleash a willingness to go to those risky places and yet create a character that was so simple and beautiful?

Well, I was lucky because it was perfect casting! He had all the right qualities for that part. He's a big guy—he's six feet, four inches—a very gentle spirit, has a sense of mystery about him, there's something hidden in him. You don't know what the whole story is, and I don't mean that in a negative way at all.

But that character needed to be someone we could empathize with. That's Paula's great trick with that play, in how it's structured: you *do* come to care for him. She structures the play in such a way that you have a window into his soul, and can empathize with why he is troubled and damaged in the way he is, before you actually see him commit the acts that make you gasp. Your love-hate relationship with him breaks your heart.

But with David . . . It's interesting.

I am a massive preparer. However much time I have, I try to put it to its greatest use in terms of gathering all the information I can about whatever the play is that I'm working on. Because I think preparation is

Mary-Louise Parker and David Morse in How I Learned to Drive *by Paula Vogel. Vineyard Theatre, 1997. Credit: Carol Rosegg.*

freedom. The more I know, the more I'm open to other things people have to offer. If I only have three things I know, I'm going to hang on to them *really tightly*. But if I go in with as much information as possible at my fingertips, and know how it connects to what I think the active point of view of the play is, then I can be open to other things.

With David, I had done all this preparation. Because it deals with incest, I had done all of this case-study research on incest between uncles and nieces or nephews. I spent days in the library, and I felt like I had a handle on the pathology.

I brought that all into rehearsal on the first day. We did a read-through, took lunch, came back, and I showed all the [general show] research. Then I put [a different] pile of stuff on the table, and I said, "Here is the research that deals specifically with incest."

And David just looked at me and said, "I don't think I'm going to look at any of that." My jaw dropped!

Then he said, "You know, I can't look at it that way. I can't look at it as somebody who's sick. I love her. That's how I have to look at it. *I love her.* And we can look up *why* I love her, and *why* I need her, and *why* I do what I do. But we can't look at it [from the viewpoint that] there's something wrong with me." It was such a valuable lesson.

It also gave me a clear window into how he was looking at the play. That reinforced my point of view on the play, but, also, it specifically guided how we were going to work on that character. It's why we empathize with him so much. Because the heart of that play is a really twisted, tangled love story. As Paula said, that play for her is about the gifts we get from the people who harm us. I thought that was a very smart way to think about it.

He was someone who worked very methodically, who would not take the next step until he had taken the step before it. There was no short-cutting with him. He made me keep my nose to the grindstone in a very positive sense. And his performance blossomed late in the process. It blossomed just as we were moving into the theater for tech.

So with him you tried to be more hands off, to let him discover?

No, I was there with him every step of the way, but it's about: when is someone ready to take the next step? And every actor works at a different pace. It's a great mistake to say to a group of people, "This is how we're going to work." There are some things you can say to one actor on the second day of rehearsal that you can't say to another actor until the fourth week of rehearsal, that you can't say to another actor until you're three weeks into previews, and that you could never say to another actor because it would totally flummox him! It's something you're constantly learning: how to best help each person at the moment when he or she needs it the most.

What has changed most about you since you came out of Yale?

When I first got out of that training program, I had a great desire to do it *right*. That's a trap in a training program, sometimes. And I've learned over time (and it's been very liberating) that there is no such thing. There are no absolutes. The glory of the work is that it does live in the gray area. I am becoming more and more interested in the gray ambivalence at the center.

The more I work, the more I am drawn to plays that celebrate that. That's why the great plays live on. That's why Shakespeare's romances live on, why Chekhov's plays live on. Because those plays at their center deal with all the great questions that cannot be answered. At the center of all those plays is a great ambivalence, and that's why we keep investigating them. I would love to do the *The Cherry Orchard*. And I'm interested in delving into *The Tempest* and *Pericles*.

For a long while you've been connected to youth plays and youth culture. What do you think it means to your journey as an artist that you're attracted to different plays now?

There have been a number of turning points. I got out of school and had no plan to come to New York. I thought that what I would do was go back to Chicago, and hopefully I'd be able to direct at the Goodman and the Court and all those other theaters, and I'd have an associate position somewhere, and I'd be able to do Chekhov, Shakespeare and Shaw for the rest of my life.

Instead I ended up in New York on a Drama League fellowship. And through that I met Carole Rothman and Robyn Goodman at Second Stage, and they became my fairy godmothers here in New York. They gave me my first big opportunity, a revival of Lanford Wilson's *Rimers of Eldritch* [1988]. And then two seasons later, the Lynda Barry play [*The Good Times Are Killing Me*].

Because of the success of that play in 1991, I had the opportunity to do a lot of commercial work. But I very purposefully made a decision *not* to go that route, and instead to continue working on new plays in the not-for-profit sector, because I thought the work that was coming to me wasn't right for me. It wasn't work I could invest in. Had I gone the other route, and taken some of those opportunities, I think my life would have been very different. I'm thankful that I was smart enough at that time to take the less-well-paid route and stay in the not-for-profit world, because I had opportunities to work in a lot of regional theaters, and a lot of the resident theaters in New York, and to really get my feet wet.

That went on until 1996, when I was just starting to lose faith with that decision. I was starting to feel that directing was a *job,* you know? And then I had a very fortunate year: *This Is Our Youth* happened, and *How I Learned to Drive,* and *As Bees in Honey Drown*—that was all in one season. And it kind of renewed my faith in being a freelance director.

I was being considered for artistic director positions and had been thinking very heavily about not being a freelance director anymore. Because your life is so fractured. You don't have one artistic home; your life is made up of a series of artistic homes. And your artistic family is made up of your collaborators: your designers and the actors and the playwrights that you're working with over and over again. After a while, you begin to yearn for an investment larger than yourself. You start to feel your life is only as large as "me." You yearn to have a connection to a community, and something you can invest in, where you feel you're really making a difference.

I was on the verge of taking that leap, or at least investigating that leap, and then I had that very lucky, fortunate year—it just came out of the blue, not planned at all. And they were three such different plays. They were critically well received, and well received by audiences, and I believed in them so much.

I see what my friends who are artistic directors go through. The battle! . . . I guess I was selfish, you know? I thought, "Do I want to raise money, or do I want to direct?" And I chose to direct, and I had the opportunity to do it, so I grabbed it. And I do regret it sometimes; I don't regret any of the work I've done, but sometimes I wonder what it would be like to lead a company.

We haven't touched much on collaborating with writers. You said before that you try to accept the script as it's given to you, as if it were Shakespeare—

It's important that I'm telling the same story that the playwright intends to be told. If not, then I'm the wrong person to be working with him or her, because we're going to be at loggerheads the whole time. So that's where I always start. When I read a play and meet with the writer, I say, "This seems to me a story where *this* happens, where *this* occurs." And if we're in agreement about that, then it's a beginning place for us.

When I meet with a writer, I have a list of questions: "These are things that struck me, or that I have questions about, logically or structurally . . ." That begins to be my window into his or her head. And I like writers to be involved in the process; I like them to be in the room. They're a director's living encyclopedias. There are certain things you can tackle prior to rehearsal—times when you know before you go in that this doesn't need to be 185 pages long; it really would be much better served if it were 120 pages long—and there are some things that you just have to wait and see how they'll pan out. Sometimes you have questions about a scene when you read it, but once you put it on its feet, you go, "Oh, you know, that *does* work."

Have you run into intractable situations with a playwright?

No, because it always comes out in the wash. There are many times I'm *so* convinced about something—I know in my heart this is true—and then, lo and behold, in the rehearsal process, I turn to the writer one day and go, "You're absolutely right. That works. That scene that was a mystery to me is actually essential to the center of the play, and I don't know how I missed it." Or they do the same thing. And it's always about reaching consensus.

How do you discover rhythm in a play?

The rhythm is all in the punctuation. I think actors probably get tired of me. Just today, I said, "No, on page thirty-one, look at that punctuation in that speech again. Because you're putting *your* punctuation on it."

The better the writer, the more you have to honor the punctuation. Because the rhythm of the soul of that human being is *in his or her speech*. That's its manifestation. That's what the theater is: it's language presented *actively*, through an active exchange between people—living, breathing human beings. How that punctuation all adds up, character to character to character, is the rhythm of the play, it's the rhythm of the world. And it's all there waiting to be unlocked.

Sometimes an actor or a director wants to impose his own rhythm on it. Actors have their own speech patterns, their own gimmicks. The trick is helping them unlock what's on the page. There's a mystery in that treasure map of punctuation.

One of my favorite phrases used to describe your work on *How I Learned to Drive*—and it can be applied to other plays you've done, certainly—is "deceptively simple." Can you talk about how you help actors get to a "deceptively simple" place?

It's stripping it down to what's absolutely essential. It's about what is needed to allow the play to speak for itself. Once again, it goes back to the Celebration Company. I found the idea of a bare platform and a chair to be the most thrilling possibility of all. Even in design choices I make, it tends to be a spare world, because I just trust in the imagination of the audience. I trust them to fill in the blanks. That's the excitement and the exchange; it's why you go. You don't go to be told everything. I go to participate as an audience member, and to be challenged in that way. If there is a spareness to what ends up on the stage, it's because of that.

For a long time I had a great distrust in scenery that moved! I'm learning to get over that now.

Talk to me about what the design process is like for you.

It's different with every play, and affected by whether I'm working with a designer with whom I've got a shorthand, or working with somebody new. I've done probably twenty plays with Allen Moyer, and I've done a lot of plays with many other designers: Neil Patel, Riccardo Hernandez, Mark Wendland, Mark McCullough, Ken Posner, Michael Krass, Jess Goldstein.

But it's also kind of the same every time, whether I've worked with them many times or not. I always go to the shelves and start pulling out the books. My window into the play is through pictures, photography or painting. I don't even know what I'm looking for. I'm guided by that Peter Brook quote, his "formless hunch." Whether it's a color or a smell or something—it's the beginning of his conviction of what the play is about. And without it, he can't work on the play.

And at the beginning, it *is* kind of a formless hunch. You have a sense there's something in there, but it's something you can't quite get your hands around. But the more that you read the play, and allow the play to work on you just through that exploration of its given circumstances, that central transaction rises to the surface, based on where you are in your life at that point in time—which is why, if you go back and work on something at different times, you respond to it differently, because your given circumstances are different.

Very often, I just have piles of all my picture research, and I *lay it all out*. And the designers go, "This reminds me of . . ." and they bring out *their* research. And we talk about the play, but we don't tend to talk about the play intellectually. If I have a whiff of that central action, I share that with them, because that's what unites all of our work together: we want to create a world where *that will happen*.

I was working with Neil Patel on *Nocturne* [by Adam Rapp] at Berkeley Rep [2001], and I brought with me a copy of a Gerhard Richter painting. And I said, "To me, this just *is the play*." It was a painting with a portal opening in it. And that became the set! That was the backdrop, this portal into this guy's mind, his journey trying to recover from this inexorable grief.

Sometimes it's that direct. Or for instance, with the Jeremy Dobrish play [*Eight Days (Backwards)*, 2003, at the Vineyard], we looked at *so much stuff*. Eventually, it boiled down to a Diane Arbus photograph on one side—it's that famous photograph [of the castle at Disneyland with a swan, 1962] that's a little smudged, and it has a sense of mystery and magic about it. And also there's something just a little off-kilter about her. And on the other side there's this George Tice photograph. He has that famous series of photographs with something small in the foreground, like a phone booth against a very panoramic dark countryside behind. Or another famous photograph with a gas station, and, towering behind it, in silhouette, very dark, one of those big petroleum tanks. And we kind of figured out: that's what this play is. It's about slices of life in front of another world.

And I said, "This Diane Arbus photo—the magic of this is right. This George Tice is too grim. Really what we're looking for is a world that is on an empty page between the two. That guided our work.

I love to be able to meet as many times as possible, with as many of the designers together as possible. That's when the real glory happens—when you have all those people in the room at one time, and you're all batting it around, and you're saying, "What if this? What if that?"

When you're able to have a process like that, it's the sound designer who solves the dilemma of the set designer! And it's the costume designer who solves the dilemma of the sound design . . . It's that collaboration that's most truly exciting. *That's* how you're creating a universe.

What tools must you have to be a director?

All directors have different tools, but I think you have to have empathy. You have to present that ability to put yourself in other people's shoes. You have to be a chameleon. You have to have an agenda beyond yourself. I think you have to love collaboration. And you have to have boundless patience. Because unleashing what is inside all your collaborators takes time. It's not something you can force, and you have to be able to enjoy that.

And you have to want to create an *alien culture*. When you walk into a play, you are creating an alien culture, something that is brand new. Even if it's a realistic play that takes place on a street in Manhattan, still, it is an alien culture, because it is a response to what is going on right now in the world.

When I did *Nocturne* at Berkeley Rep, our first day of rehearsal was 9/11. And it was so serendipitous to be working on a play about a man coming to terms with inexorable grief, something unnameable. It was so cathartic to be able to work on that play at that time. People responded to it accordingly, because they walked into the room with that event imprinted on their souls.

I think there's a place for every kind of play. Just as much as everybody else, I love to be entertained. I love to be able to go in and just laugh. But at the same time, the plays I love to work on the most, I'm drawn to the most, are plays that have something to say beyond themselves, have an expansiveness, have an agenda beyond themselves.

Theater is not easy; it's not easy to go to, even. You have to make a decision to go; it's not like you just turn on the TV and you flip through until you find something interesting. It's not like checking out a book. You're making a bargain. Just as the actors have active exchange between them, there's an active exchange between the audience members and them.

There's that book by Bert States, *Great Reckonings in Little Rooms*. That title has always seemed to me so apt; it's what the theater is. That is what's so *moving* about the experience of going to the theater. I've made a commitment, I've made a bargain to take witness with this group of other people, at this given time.

Do you feel hopeful about theater in this country? About challenging audiences?

I think there's less work happening—even in New York—the number of productions that the resident theaters are doing, and regionally, they've dropped, just for economic reasons. And the line between the commercial theater and the not-for-profit theater has blurred as well. I've spent my entire working career in the not-for-profit theater. I've had some plays that have moved to commercial runs, but I have spent my life in that arena. I have seen a change in the kind of material that is being done. I have the greatest empathy for people at the heads of those institutions, trying to balance all the things they have to balance and still do what they think is challenging material.

I'm of the *Field of Dreams* opinion: if it's good, they will come . . . I have great faith in that. If the play is good, and it has something to say, regardless of how mainstream or non-mainstream it is, people will go and participate in it.

What about writers?

That's the other big change—the proliferation of films and cable channels. There's little financial reward in the theater. If you're doing it for that reason, you're probably in the wrong business. I understand totally the need to make a living and the need to have a home to raise your children. So there is a talent drain: it's true of actors, it's true of writers, it's true of directors.

I don't know what the solution is. If I did, I'd be sitting in a very plush office in a consulting business answering a lot of other important questions. All of my playwright friends write screenplays or work in television sometimes.

I explored that world for a while, the television world, and found it wasn't the right place for me—and I've been lucky, I've been able to make a living in the theater. I feel lucky and blessed to say that. But it is not always an easy haul.

Tell me about a moment you created of which you're particularly proud.

One that comes to mind is from *How I Learned to Drive*. It's when L'il Bit has gone to her uncle's hotel room at the end of play, and they're lying together on the bed. It would have been so easy for that to have been a very unseemly, lurid moment—distasteful. And that whole play had to be structured so that in that crux of them lying together, he is testing her and saying, "Please, if you just lie next to me for a moment . . . Tell me what you feel." And of course she is so conflicted; she feels so much, but knows that it's wrong and that it's not going to happen.

I think I was so pleased that audiences were able to go to that place at that moment in the play, and didn't pull back from it. In that moment you understood the central dilemma between those two people, and you understood the central dilemma that existed inside each of them, too. That came from careful planning from the very beginning.

That image sticks with me also. Can you talk about how you found it in rehearsal? How did you make it inevitable?

Well, that's always the goal, that it seems that the play is inevitable, it *must happen*. When those characters walk out on stage, they have to say what they're gonna say. But I think I had a hunch about that moment. After we had worked through the play once, then twice, I realized how important it was for us to be on his side at that moment.

AUGUST 2006, VIA PHONE FROM NEW YORK CITY

In our previous interview, you talked a lot about central transactions. You just helmed the New York premiere of another Paula Vogel play: *The Long Christmas Ride Home*; can you put your finger on its central transaction?

This is the way I might start to address it with the designers, but not necessarily how I might put it to the actors: it's a story about a character who's allowed one day a year to visit the Floating World, our world. Each year, he revisits a series of events that make up the action of the play. And on this day, he gets to revisit his sisters (who are still living), and he gets to breathe in a breath of life from the living to sustain himself for another year.

How would you speak differently with your actors about it?

Ultimately, I *would* talk in those terms to the actors, but not at the beginning. As I said earlier, I try to avoid naming something initially. It's better to lead people down the path to discover it on their own. And once it's discovered, you name it like gangbusters, because you want to hang on to it. Once it's been discovered and it's being played, then you're able to name it and say, "See? This is the lifeblood of the play. This is the active center of this world, and here's your piece of it."

I don't think the transaction or the center of the play ever changes for me as I'm working on it. I might discover something new about it that would mean, wow, I'd like to do another production of this play at another time and explore that. I may even discover things that could potentially work against the central transaction I've figured out, but when that happens, I save those for another production.

Catherine Kellner, Will McCormack and Enid Graham in The Long Christmas Ride Home *by Paula Vogel. Vineyard Theatre, 2003. Credit: Carol Rosegg.*

Turning to new challenges: you've got *Cry-Baby* coming up.

It's certainly the biggest musical I've worked on, and it's also the first totally original musical I've worked on, other than *Avenue X* at Playwrights Horizons [1994], which was on a much smaller scale. This has twenty-four people on stage. The music is by Adam Schlesinger of [rock band] Fountains of Wayne, and lyrics by David Javerbaum, and a book by Mark O'Donnell and Tom Meehan.

It's exciting to be a part of such a large project from the beginning, and also to work with two bookwriters who have such a firm grasp on structure. To me, working on a musical is very similar to working on a play in that the songs are just an extension of the book. The impetus for the songs starts at the beginning of the scene, and they're just a natural, inevitable outgrowth of the scene. It's also a much longer development process. So you're able to really test things out, go back to work again, and test them out again.

With a commercial Broadway production, there's got to be a whole other set of pressures.

Certainly, because there's lots of money at stake. But I'm fortunate in that I've got a great team of producers who are very supportive of me, and of the process. It's the same only moreso. The process that I go through is the same, except there's music involved. Up to this point I've not found it frustrating; if anything, I've found it freeing to have more people to bounce ideas off of. Check back in with me in a year!

And what about film?

I finished a film since we last spoke! An adaptation of [Rebecca Gilman's Play] *Spinning into Butter,* with Sarah Jessica Parker, Beau Bridges, Miranda Richardson, Mykelti Williamson and a whole bunch of great people.

Doing film feeds into a strength of mine, which is preparation. As I said before, I prepare and prepare and prepare, and for film, it's absolutely key; you *cannot* be too prepared, because things are constantly changing on you. You prepared for one thing, and all at once you can't have that location, so you have to punt really quickly. It moves so fast that once you get to the point of actually having film in the camera, you don't have the time or money to experiment. You have to have a clear sense of where you're headed.

I have to say I loved it. I enjoyed the rigor and discipline of it. And I think I loved it for all the opposite reasons that I love the theater. What I love about the theater is that it *is* new each time you come to it. Every time you go to see that same production of that play, even with the same cast in it, it still is *new* that night: there's a new audience there; those people on stage have lived a life that day . . . *Anything can happen.* With film, you're able to create something that, from your point of view, *is perfect.* And then will *always* be perfect, time after time.

And that's what I loved about it. Getting to work on it through the production phase, and the editing phase, and to just keep tinkering. It's amazing how a tiny little alteration of pace or rhythm or point of view can totally transform the meaning of the moment and how it lands emotionally. The flexibility was astounding to me.

Back in 2003 you talked about a freelance career versus artistic directing. Have your thoughts changed?

Being a freelancer gets harder and harder. So the prospect of running a company becomes more attractive. It's that constant struggle between art and commerce, to keep the work from becoming just a job, to maintain that investment, that almost religious conviction in the work that I think is necessary. And as the economics become dire, you're faced with the danger of even more conservative programming—right at the time when you need daring the most. In the last few years, I've begun to wish we lived in a world where subscriber audiences weren't a necessity. Because I think there's a danger in trying to please that audience, especially when that becomes the primary goal of the institution. Plays get chosen just to please them, which leads to a narrowing of perspective. The plays that exist outside that box have less and less of a chance of being seen.

That's why I was really proud to have worked on a production of Craig Lucas's play *Reckless,* produced by Second Stage and Manhattan Theatre Club at MTC's Broadway home, the Biltmore. To me, that was an ideal marriage of the not-for-profit and the commercial world. It was a very challenging, funny and humane play that still was full of ambiguity. It didn't tie everything up into some easily satisfying answer. I was very proud that that play got seen in a Broadway situation.

Another turning point for me recently has been my involvement as a mentor in the Open Doors program founded by Wendy Wasserstein and administered by TDF [Theatre Development Fund]. You take a group of eight inner-city high school students to see shows six times during the course of the year. It's a very competitive program; they have to apply to be a part of it. And after each outing you spend an hour and a half discussing the play.

To witness a play or a musical with a group of young people, most of whom have had very limited exposure to the theater, is so moving—to hear them discuss the work afterwards, how they find the connections to their own lives or the lives of their community or the world, and how it unleashes something new or powerful in them. It gives them another tool with which to understand the world, and have compassion for those around them.

The biggest surprise of all is how we bind together as this mini-audience that travels from show to show during the year, and how much that life raft comes to mean to all of us. In a way, [that sense of community] is the hope and the savior of the theater. It's given me such great faith that the theater can have a meaningful future, and can speak to young audiences, and engage them in a desire to participate and to share in an evening with a group of strangers, and not be so alone.

PETER BROSIUS

Speaking Up to Kids

PETER BROSIUS, THE ARTISTIC DIRECTOR OF Minneapolis's Children's Theatre Company, possesses boundless charisma. As he talks about his career, he lurches about, almost dancing, reliving the excitement of every moment. It's no surprise that this fiftysomething man—who leads what became in 2003 the first children's theater to win a Tony Award—should be so childlike. Prone to hippie phrases ("What's up, brother?"), Brosius exudes a sixties-ish call to theatrical arms, appropriate for a man at the forefront of an ongoing revolution in theater for young audiences (TYA) in this country.

Prior to the 1980s, children's theater in the United States was generally moribund, in many cases populated by second-tier artists who couldn't find work elsewhere. As Linda Hartzell, the revolutionary artistic director of Seattle Children's Theatre, told *American Theatre* magazine in 2000, "Back then, it was starter theater for people who were only doing it until they stepped up to what they thought was legitimate." Now, nearly every metropolitan area in the country has a major TYA, employing some of that community's foremost artists.

It was around the time Hartzell took over her theater in 1984 that the landscape started to change. Top professionals began devoting their careers to TYA; theaters such as Dallas Children's Theater and

Childsplay in Tempe, Arizona, were attracting national attention; and major playwrights began tackling work well beyond the standard children's repertoire. Forget *The Ugly Duckling*: come see a children's play about AIDS (David Saar's *The Yellow Boat,* 1993 at Childsplay) or the Holocaust (James Still's *And Then They Came for Me,* 1997 at the George Street Playhouse). TYA was suddenly playing a major role on the national stage.

Into this unique historical moment came Peter Brosius. Raised in California and educated on the East Coast, Brosius's first real encounters with TYA came during an influential post-college fellowship in Germany. Productions at the GRIPS Theater (an avant-garde youth theater in Berlin) really stunned him, along with work by the other adult-theater luminaries of 1970s Germany. Between those radical experiments and the theater he saw while getting his master's in directing at New York University in the late 1970s, Brosius gained a sophisticated and adventurous theatrical education. Bringing that level of sophistication to TYA has been his mission ever since.

He tried to start the City Youth Theater in New York in 1979, but the timing wasn't right. Instead, in 1982 he stumbled into a home at Los Angeles's flagship not-for-profit theater, the Mark Taper Forum, where he ran its Improvisational Theatre Project and commissioned major playwrights for youth-oriented work. He stayed with the Taper for twelve years, where he earned critical acclaim for his adventurous leadership, especially for those plays he commissioned and productions he helmed that explored social and political issues through a multicultural lens. His 1987 production of Colin Thomas's *One Thousand Cranes,* a powerful exploration of children's feelings about nuclear war, toured internationally and became a signature piece for him; that year, the Improvisational Theatre Project won the coveted Margaret Harford Award from the Los Angeles Drama Critics Circle. During his tenure, Brosius also directed plays for adult audiences for the Taper, South Coast Rep and the 1990 Los Angeles Festival, among others.

He left the Taper in 1995, frustrated by the scarcity of budgetary and space resources available to youth theater. "The prospects for growth in the short term were certainly limited," he told the *Los Angeles Times.* "It is hard for me to leave not having established a space for young people's theater . . . the young people need it, the artists need it, the life of the city needs it."

After two short (but productive) years as artistic director of the Honolulu Theatre for Youth, Brosius landed at Children's Theatre Company in 1997, where he has been able to marshal the resources he needed to establish that space.

The move to CTC cemented Brosius's position at the top of American youth theater, where he remains a much-admired fixture. In CTC's state-of-the-art facility, with more than twenty thousand subscribers and a budget that in Minnesota is second only to that of the Guthrie, Brosius combines urbane dramaturgical tastes, a startling visual imagination and his passion for youth culture to direct meaningful and inspiring work. His productions are so often magical because of his confident and committed juxtaposition of traditional children's theater tropes—the colorful costumes, the oversized gestures, the energetic performances—with complex and elaborate theatricality. Consider how the chilling expressionist butcher Mr. Zyclo in Naomi Iizuka's 2006 adaptation of *The Odyssey, Anon(ymous),* or the Hindu choreography of 2010's *Iron Ring* by Charles Way, ups the intellectual ante for traditional children's fare. It's no surprise that Twin Cities critics so often call his work "inventive," along with so many other superlatives.

And in his programming choices at CTC, whether choosing an OBIE-winning sound designer (SITI Company's Darron West) to direct *Lilly's Purple Plastic Purse* or commissioning an adaptation from Pulitzer Prize–winner Nilo Cruz, Brosius applies the rigor and curiosity he learned in Germany. As Saar, Childsplay's founding artistic director, told the *New York Times* in 2003, "The Children's Theatre feels now like it's serving the entire field better than at any time in its history. Peter is charting new territory artistically, and it's wonderful to see that with an organization that large and that complex, they are still taking artistic risks."

So for every crowd-pleasing production like *The Wizard of Oz* that Brosius programs, it seems there's a play he's commissioned from some groundbreaking voice on challenging themes: from Kia Corthron about tensions between the Somali and African-American communities in Minneapolis, from Jeffrey Hatcher about a Holocaust victim, and many more. His choices are frequently more varied and more dynamic than those found at the regional theaters that supposedly cater to an intellectually rigorous mindset. No matter how hard I tried in my conversation with him, I couldn't get Brosius to say that TYA is any different from theater made for adults. The result is that Brosius's audiences are perhaps better trained to experience unusual theatricalities and different issues than most adult audiences.

I visited Peter at CTC in 2004 in the wake of their Tony Award win. Its production of *A Year with Frog and Toad*, a musical by Robert and Willie Reale that premiered in 2002, had ended a momentous run on Broadway, and the place was stretched thin with so much activity. The organization was collaborating simultaneously with local, national and international artists (for example, the British director Greg Banks had just staged his promenade-style *Antigone*). In the center of it all Peter stood, taking in the energy from all those artists and sending it back doubled, tripled, to engage in the work with renewed vitality and passion.

SEPTEMBER 2003, CHILDREN'S THEATRE COMPANY, MINNEAPOLIS

Before we get into process, let's talk influence. You graduated from NYU in 1980. And you've spoken about being influenced by the Wooster Group, Mabou Mines . . .

I was in New York at a really amazing time. Richard Foreman's work was happening; the Wooster Group was happening; Ping Chong, Meredith Monk. I was also very fortunate in my early years in L.A. to see Ariane Mnouchkine's work at the Los Angeles Olympic Arts Festival. And I saw the early work of El Teatro Campesino, when I was an undergraduate at Hampshire College. They were touring nearby with *Carpa de los Rasquachis*. It was an amazing, celebratory, communal piece that was just so powerful, all about the power of theater and community. And other work in New York—like *Bloolips*—watching work that spoke to a specific audience was really inspiring. It articulated an aesthetic, a politic, a set of concerns. Watching the relationship between the audience and performers, seeing that something truly dynamic was happening—that was also an important influence.

I got to work in Europe in Cologne, right after I graduated from NYU; that was hugely important. Jürgen Flimm was the intendant, the artistic director, of Schauspiel Köln. And George Tabori was there, and Luc Bondy (who later took over the Schaubühne in Berlin). Also, Cologne is a very short drive to Wuppertal, where Pina Bausch's company is. The work of Pina Bausch was just jaw-dropping: the theatricality, the use of choreography, the *verity* of it. You know, the reality of it inside a *gorgeous metaphor* was always really profound.

And then Brecht, because I studied with Carl Weber . . . Thinking about Brecht, hearing stories about him as a director—about his obsession with beauty, which is something you don't think about with Brecht. Some of the stories I heard (I don't know whether they're apocryphal or not) were so delicious: someone distraught coming to Brecht about *Mother Courage* and saying, "Herr Brecht, it's all *brown,* it's *all brown!*" And he said, "Yes, but it's *four hundred shades* of brown, and it's beautiful!" Understanding first and foremost you're making a work of art, no matter what you're doing—making work that needs to stand as a thing of beauty—you don't think about Brecht doing that.

It wasn't a very long fellowship, but it was fabulous. I was in Europe three or four months.

You saw all that work in three or four months?

Yeah, I did. I also found out about the video library at the Goethe-Institut in Munich, and went down there to watch productions I'd heard about. There were videos of the work of the director Peter Zadek; they had a whole series of early films of the work of Karl Valentin, the great cabaret artist who was such an important influence on Brecht. There I am, sitting alone in this library, watching these films—I don't know if anybody's seen them! Those images are still in my head: the wildness, the chaos, the anarchy, the violence and the control of Karl Valentin's work . . . it was *incredible*!

And just watching George Tabori work. Or Jürgen Flimm: the first day in the rehearsal of *Leonce and Lena*, what Jürgen did was one of the most amazing moments I've ever had in my life as a director. The opening scene (as I remember it) had to do with the young actor playing Leonce, spitting. For *four and a half hours, this actor spat*. Working on a perhaps twenty-seven-second moment that finally made it into the show.

No one talked about Brecht, but it was that sense of totally investigating a moment. We played Vivaldi, we played rock 'n' roll; he went up on a ladder, he went downstage, he spat lying on his back, he spat in rhythm, he spat with people lifting him . . . and at the end of that day, we had totally investigated that moment to see which image lands, which speaks to that character. There was no rush, no franticness, no *angst*. Just: what are the ways that this gesture can *live*? And it was so exhaustive in its investigation that it was stunning, truly inspiring. No stone was going to be left unturned.

And that's how the work proceeded. They have a longer time than we do, but it was just the *spirit,* you know? There's a better idea down the road; there's something more interesting if you keep looking, and you keep working. If you create a world in the rehearsal room that is safe, that is a world of work, that is a world of investigation, that is a world of collaboration . . . Yes, there's a first idea, but there's probably something much more interesting. And we'll note this idea, but we'll come back to it, and we'll find something stronger and better.

There was one other moment that was very important for me, when Luc Bondy was doing the Scottish play. They were doing the banquet scene, and behind the table were Luc, his two directorial assistants, the designers and their assistants, and the dramaturg and her assistant, and everyone, one by one, just got up to start to work on the scene, throw out ideas, and rearrange. At a certain point, the designer got up and changed everything: he got eighteen more gallons of fake blood, so we'd just pour the blood, running down . . .

And the director was part of this extraordinary team of artists all working together, not necessarily hand-in-glove, but all exploring the moment with rigor and immense curiosity. He was at the center of this, but not needing to control it, accepting the genius of the collaborators. There was a multitude of good ideas, and out of all the good ideas in the room, something much more magnificent *might*—not necessarily, but *might*—emerge.

Sounds like you love rehearsal.

This may sound naive or Pollyannaish, but I think it's about the spirit of the room, that sense that we are here to investigate. The rehearsal room is a collaborative laboratory. Ideas from the actors, from the stage manager, from the accidents that happen in the room, from a question that happens, allow the work to just *keep going*. Yes, most resident theaters here have three to six weeks, but I think it's about the attitude. There's an openness to the new idea. It's about delaying closure: you set it, but you also know you're going to reopen it completely the next time you get to it.

I try to delay running a show as long as possible. I fight for every chance to go back over the scenes and back over the moments, giving ourselves as much time as possible to be in the scene, to explore it, to have the actors' input.

Why is it so important to delay running? Doesn't running a show allow for new investigation too?

It's such a different mindset than the kind of detailed work you do by making adjustments, putting a different set of circumstances on it, creating structured improvisations that explore either backstory or what the stakes actually are. It's important to allow time for that to be fully part of the room, not just the homework.

You learn massive things in running it, but for me, it's making sure you've had as much bloody time as possible to investigate the scenes, to play, to find the inner life, the choreographic life, the movement life, the image life. Some of it for me is inspired by having watched that work in Germany. It's all in the detail and the specificity of how each object is handled, how you sit up, how you stand, what's in the pockets, what secrets the actors carry. And you find those secrets by fighting for that time. It's more important that this intense work with the actors happens, because that's usually where the play lives.

And it sets the groundwork, so that when you *are* running, and you're in tech, the actors are so full, everyone's on the same page, and *they're* throwing out ideas. For example, one of the things I wanted to do in *Amber Waves* [by James Still], the show I'm directing now, was to figure out how to use these "layerings." The set is basically a very empty stage (it's really about the sky and the earth and the survival of the farm in the middle), and we had certain ideas. One was about film and isolation—the use of slip-stages [a platform or wagon that traverses the stage for rapid scene changes, usually by means of a recessed track], so things move. Things are in continual motion, which is the reality of a farm, even though one thinks of it as stasis. In point of fact, it's *always* changing, it's always surprising; you never know where things are coming from. So part of the goal was not only to create a filmic sense of transition and continual movement and surprise, but also a layering of the reality. I asked the actors to be my partners in layering that reality by having a continuous set of images upstage while the main action continued downstage.

But what we found once I started trying to layer that reality was that this approach didn't feel right. It's a piece so much about micro-focus: these events upstage ended up diminishing rather than enlarging the world. We set it up as a goal in the room; we looked at it in tech; we threw some things out; but every time we tried it, it was like, "No, stay focused. Bring the lights down. We need the focus. Wrap that focus down to a *tiny little pin*, and let that event just *soar*." It was one of those things that seemed like a fabulous idea . . . and then it wasn't, and we just had to let go of it and stop worrying about it.

That's really important for a director, to be able to let go of things that don't work.

You try them first. The proof of the pudding's in the eating. Just set it up and do it. Often I'll say, "This is an idea I guarantee won't make it in the show; it's such a bad idea! But I need to see this, and I need you to try it." And something happens, I whisper an adjustment in the actor's ear, and while it may not be right, *something* happens in there.

Let's step back. Somewhere between watching Jürgen Flimm get a guy to spit for four hours in Cologne and trying to start the City Youth Theater in New York, you had a change of direction.

In addition to seeing the work of Tabori and Bondy and other extraordinary work in Germany, I also was seeing some of the brilliant work of the European youth theater. I was in Amsterdam, seeing work at the De Krakeling, which is the space for new work for young people. I was seeing work in Berlin for young people that was beautiful theater, extraordinarily refined, engaged work, wonderful aesthetically. I was also seeing work that engaged a specific audience, that challenged that audience. It wasn't serving that audience; it was an *ally* to that audience.

Part of me wanted to make work that had a sense of being *necessary*, in partnership with a community, that was challenging and moving. And some of that you feel in the world of new-play development, making work for adults, because you're in the service of artists who are wrestling with their own ideas, and you're desperately working to understand their breath and their blood and their history. That was a huge part of my life at the Taper as well. So it wasn't out of nowhere.

Were you surprised by the work you saw, this European theater for youth?

I had no image of it whatsoever. I wasn't in the community; I hadn't studied it. I didn't come with either a negative or a positive point of view; it just wasn't part of my life.

It made a huge impression, though, because after that you ended up doing youth theater at the Taper, which catapulted your career. Connect those dots for me.

I tried to start a company in New York called the City Youth Theater to do new European theater for young people, but soon got hired at South Coast Rep to teach at its conservatory. While I was there, I called up the Taper out of the blue and said, "Can I come and meet with you?" L.A. was very welcoming. Everyone would meet with you. It was so different from New York. The doors would just open. I was nobody; I'd done very little.

So I sent some scripts to the Taper, but they never wrote back! I don't think I ever got a response. (Now, as an artistic director, I feel guilty when I look at my e-mail and I think, "My God, it's been six months!")

A year or so later I thought I'd call the Taper again. And the person on the phone said, "We were just talking about you the other day," and I was like, "Yeah, right!" But they said, "Can you come tomorrow? We're doing this workshop and we're interested in talking to you about it."

At the meeting I learned that the Taper had found some money to develop a show for high school students in a whole new way. It wasn't actually a "show" initially; it was just a workshop to explore contemporary material, which was working in a whole different way for me. Three weeks later I started work.

I made lists of all the performance tropes, and improvisational tropes, and had these fabulous actors go out and interview hundreds of people. At the end we showed the work, and it was wonderful. We pulled in all kinds of formal framing devices, and things I'd seen in various performance pieces, and created a whole body of material based on the interviews, refracting them in more formal, theatrical terms.

What kind of material?

It was pretty broad—these were high school students. What are the things you fear? What are the things obsessing you? We went to Catholic boys' schools, we went to Asian drug clinics, Jewish community centers, schools, backyards . . .

We went all over, and then we came back and did all these improvs, and the Taper asked if I would write it into a play. And not having a job, and not having a nickel, I said, "Sure!"

And let me tell you, that play ranks up there with *Moose Murders* as one of the worst plays ever written! Watching the folks at the Taper as we did this reading! . . . It was just one bad idea after another. And I remember looking around at the faces and thinking the play had crashed. So I said, "It's no problem, I'll rewrite it, I'll fix this."

And I went back and rewrote it entirely, and went into rehearsal with an entire company of remarkable people. Chloe Webb was in it, and Diane Rodriguez. And it became a success. It dealt with contemporary issues in a way the theater hadn't done before. They invited me to come back and do it again for a younger audience, and I did. And then they asked me to join the staff.

So the overarching sense of that journey is: you went away from your community, learned all these amazing things you wanted to share . . . and as you brought them back, you started to find your own aesthetic.

It's always been my agenda to make new work. Take *Mississippi Panorama* here at CTC [2001, by Kevin Kling], which came out of spending time with political historians, and people talking about the power of the Mississippi River and how it was a force here in transforming the Upper Midwest, bringing black culture and white culture together, and connecting the North and the South. And then we discovered the story of John Banvard [a 19th century panorama painter] creating an allegedly three-mile canvas panorama, and suddenly we're in a room putting the Mississippi River on stage, and it's a process like nothing we've ever done. And does it have politics in it? Yes, but it also has a wonderful, wacky Kevin Kling sense of the Midwest, and an epic nature. It has nothing whatsoever to do with what I saw in Europe, but it's those roots that fed me.

[Brosius displays a picture from the production]

That's a very striking shot. Gobos, stars, a proscenium within the proscenium . . . Can you tell me how you arrived at this image?

This was a codirection with a very gifted theater artist, Michael Sommers. John Banvard, a young artist in our imagining, had a vision to

The cast of Mississippi Panorama *by Kevin Kling. Children's Theatre Company, 2001. Credit: Mitchel Anderson. Used by permission of Children's Theatre Company.*

travel the length of the Mississippi and paint it as one canvas. What attracted us to that idea was the madness of that, and that it was epic. In that moment, you've got an artist creating a new art form: the art of the panorama.

The image shows this character, the spirit of the river, Professor Leaky, who did actually leak on stage. And then these other characters are the river sprites, modeled on the fairies in *A Midsummer Night's Dream*. And the idea here is that like in old-time popular theater, the show would take place inside this little proscenium, with supertitles.

And then we had an actress *a vista* [in view of the audience] in the pit, holding this mirror ball. It was important that we *revealed the magic,* yet this is still a spectacular image. The lights come from a place you've never seen—from below, going up. We tried it initially with her down in the pit so you couldn't see her. But it's so much more interesting that she's *there,* and some people could see the mirror ball and some couldn't. It's like, "Look what an actor can do with a mirror!"

This is perhaps one of the most collaborative processes I've had the great good fortune to do. The team was remarkable; Michael is an extraordinary artist. And Kevin is a wonderful writer, actor and performer. Kevin also, in his way, became part of the directorial team: he'd get up and whisper something into an actor's ear that neither Michael nor I nor the stage manager had heard, which often involved a line change and an adjustment!

Beverly [Emmons, the lighting designer] also has very strong opinions. And Darron [West, the sound designer], having worked for years with Annie Bogart, would also, in the middle of a moment, stop us and ask the actor to try something else, to restage it another way or pause in a different spot. So there were two official directors, and then Darron came into the process, and it was quite interesting, because the actors were thrown for a loop. Michael and I had a pretty good groove going; we'd talk to each other at the table, and I think there was only one time that he said "red" and I said "blue." It worked very well, but then having Darron *also* come up and give adjustments . . .

At a certain point, we faced this situation. Shall we stifle what Kevin's doing or what Darron's doing? And we said, "No." We made sure the company knew that *we knew* what was going on, and that we felt it was the best way to move forward. And we were getting everyone's best efforts because they were so invested.

We found John Banvard in the first of two workshops. Not a word had been written. I said, "I want the Mississippi River on stage, and there *may* be something about this John Banvard." So we spent the first couple of weeks exploring the idea of the Mississippi River. It was a hot summer; we were pouring water all over each other; we were gargling and singing, "M-I-S-S-I-S-S-I-P-P-I." We created one tableau after another about the river. Each actor brought in music that inspired him or her about the idea of the river and made mini performance pieces.

Then I read this rather cheesy biography of John Banvard—it's a young adult book, it's not particularly well written—and I began to read chapters out loud. And suddenly, in terms of focus, we went from the Mississippi to John Banvard. The rest of the workshop was all about him: what he saw along the river, from slaves escaping, to the whole world he would have seen during that time.

This specific image had a lot to do with that young man seeing the moonlight on the river, and getting inspired by it, and perhaps finding the courage and the inspiration in a very poetic way to take this mad journey. So it had to happen in very poetic terms; the river comes alive, the spirit speaks to him, the moon's alive, and the world opens up in a variety of ways with music, sound and movement.

This production was one of those rare moments when, for me as a director, it all came together. You can count such moments on your hand; I think I can count four or five shows when it all came together.

I don't think I ever saw another performance of it that *landed* the way that opening night did. There was something alchemical and magical. It was just one of those nights when what had really been a collection of ideas on Tuesday preview became by opening a piece that wove and spoke and soared in its metaphysics—and also was filled with silliness—and was unbelievably beautiful, and unlike anything anyone had ever seen here. It's a funny thing about directing: I always say, "If I can just see it *once* . . ." Because it's rare that you go back and watch it and it's there again! You just want to see it *once*.

Does that kind of aesthetic, that highly designed world, define a Peter Brosius show?

I have no idea. What do I try to do? I'm certainly someone who grew up in a world saturated by music. I'm interested in the way music can play under, around and through; the way music can be both underscoring and juxtaposition. And I love the work with designers. And so the work with design in creating a world is very important to me, the visual sense is really keen.

Why do we love theater? Because every person who comes to it can take away something entirely different from the person sitting next to him or her. The audience members sitting in the chairs are the editors, because they're assembling their own performance. Of course, you can direct their attention with light, with movement and staging, but we make it differently than film, because really it's *their assemblage*. I pay a lot of attention to design, a lot of attention to light. Because I know that you can create an image that can last for decades in someone's head.

What are the first questions you ask in early design meetings to create that specific, physical world?

The first thing I do is spend a lot of time examining what each of those locations is in the piece. I think of them in a way as *worlds*. What are all the things about that *world*? Whether it's the Olson kitchen, or Johnny Diamond's farm, or the school, as in *Amber Waves* [2003]. I do a lot of free-associating—every image that comes to my mind about that world, from the play, from my research—words, adjectives, descriptions.

What are the things those worlds do? How are those worlds active? What are the things that happen inside them? How do they act on people? You know, architecture is an *actor*, architecture determines behavior, architecture affects thought. Locations are also machines: a school is a machine, and a farm is a machine, and a bedroom. All these things have ways of *working* on people. So you just spew, spew, spew, trying to figure all this out.

And then, what is the dominant metaphor? In *Amber Waves* it was about the hugeness of the sky and the vastness of the earth and the solitariness of a person. Farmers are really up against immense forces of land and sky. The family farm means being alone in a very profound way. I knew I wanted to break some of the rules that made things successful in my theater here. When you're doing a small play—and this is an immensely small play, it's a tiny chamber play—I usually try to ratchet down the proscenium, bring it way forward, you know, *break* that theater, because it's a big hall.

And here, it was the opposite. We're going to have a conversation around the kitchen table, but this is going to be *against the sky*. It's going to be in the bigness of that theater, against an immense sky and in an immense field of earth. And it filled me with terror. Because I've watched things, particularly big crowd things, on our immense stage, where if it's not choreographed within an inch of its life, it can feel pathetically small. So I'm going to have one person standing alone on that stage, and there's nothing on it except the sky and the earth, and *can this sell*? Because of the nature of the way our stage works, it's going to have to be slightly upstage of the proscenium, so I've got this huge separation from the audience.

Now, back to the design process. We went through every possible way of making this world transform: it's one of those plays with multiple scenes. So we said, "Okay, it's ten inches of dirt, nothing moves, and then there's the sky—that's the first thing." Then we went to painters— Anselm Kiefer's *Falling Angels* was a huge image for us—and then we walked through the play, scene by scene, again and again. And then we built a turntable in a model form; then a turntable with a wall. I like to work with designers who are willing to rip the model apart, put it back together, try it a lot of different ways.

We went through seven or eight more ways of making this whole story work. The first image was filled with photographs; photographs were iconic objects throughout. Then we eliminated all the photographs, because we wanted to keep moving forward. I didn't want to stop and analyze, I wanted us to be caught in the change of seasons, in the challenge of this family falling apart.

And then, I said the word "slip-stage." I'd never worked on a slip-stage. My designer and I built the slip-stage; staying up all night, working through it, and suddenly: "This is it! This is going to work!"

And we had a wonderful meeting with the costume and lighting designers, and out of that came the idea of: "How do you zoom into close-up?" So the next time the family came on stage, instead of the entire working kitchen, you only needed a table and a chair. Every time they came out, the scene was refracted, focused. A continual transformation.

Out of that conversation came a simple metaphor: the ever-present cornfield. In every single scene, the cornfield is there, because you can never forget that the crop is dying; you can never forget the challenge of the drought and the single crop that needs to sustain this family.

So we had trashed corn, we had winter corn, we had spring corn, we had corn outside the fairgrounds, we had corn that was [indicating chest height] this tall, we had corn way in the distance that was [indicating knee height] this tall. An actor was in a tiny pinspot way down left doing a monologue, but then we'd sidelit this tiny stalk of corn, so that wherever you were, you could never forget that the rain hadn't come. You didn't escape it. Farmers don't; they can't take two-week holidays. And we got these wonderful moments, like this little kid in the audience going, "That's winter corn, isn't it? It's different from the other corn." Noticing the metaphor, tracking through the piece!

That metaphor came out of always believing there's a better idea. It's just like the rehearsal room. We sit down around the table and re-design the show, many, many times.

Young audiences can be so forgiving and refreshing in receiving metaphor, unlike adults—

But no. Look at how Mary Zimmerman or Robert Wilson do their work. A theater of images. If you sculpt a world that has its poetry, I don't see the difference at all.

When I was in graduate school at NYU, it was brutal; there had been no compliments, all criticism, three long years. And at the end of my senior year project production, I was surrounded by people congrat-ulating me, and the head of the department came over and said, "Peter, don't always believe the audience." And he walked away. I almost wept. I was so hurt, so angry. After three hard, expensive years of graduate school, to have this one night of triumph shot down in a comment was almost too much to take. Now, some number of decades later, I'm so grateful. Because you have to be relentlessly self-critical. If the audi-ence loves it, it doesn't mean you've done the work. If the audience hates it, it doesn't mean it's bad work. When I did *Imperceptible Mutabilities in the Third Kingdom* [by Suzan-Lori Parks, Odyssey Theatre Ensemble in L.A., 1993], half of that audience was fighting to get out of that theater, hating that piece. And the other half of the audi-ence sat in that theater for twenty minutes after the show had ended. They just stayed quietly, some talking, some just sitting. For some rea-son, people needed to soak it up because it was so unique or moving. Or *Eh Joe*, when I did it at the Taper in 1990: I had the crazy idea to adapt a Beckett television play for the stage. I had the idea to use hidden video cameras so that we could zoom in on the actor, live, and then have him projected on the scrim box in which he was sitting so that he appeared inside his own head, and then inside his own eye . . . Again, for some of the audience members it was a little hard. And for others, it was a revelatory Beckett experience, because it was so emotionally true.

You've said: "We're about conversation. We're about community dialogue. We're about bringing people together. And we're also about doing extraordinary theater." Given the reactionary climate, how can you be sure you're *leading* the conversation, rather than responding?

Speaking as a director or as an artistic director, there are different answers. As a director, you choose work that speaks to you; you choose work that you feel must be done; you choose work that you feel has a currency either because of a theatrical possibility, content, style, work with actors or design. You choose to do a piece because it *terrifies you*. It's brilliantly poetic and powerful, and urgent to be told. And it's coming in a theatrical language that is exploding in ways that you've never imagined. And you don't get it, but you know that something major's going on. And then you wrestle, wrestle to find the theatrical language to communicate that genius.

What is an artist? An artist is a curious person; an artist is a person bedeviled by questions more than answers. An artist is thrilled by the unknown, delights in being in the unknown, delights in creating a world in which there's no guarantees. No matter what you do there's risk. If you're doing *A Midsummer Night's Dream* with a group of people who've done it fifty times, there's no guarantee the production'll have any *life*.

And yes, sometimes there's a thing in the world you want to respond to, and you hope to find the artist to be your partner in that when you're not a writer and you're not a composer. We're developing a project [*The Lost Boys of Sudan*, 2007] with Lonnie Carter, and I've just been reading new scenes this morning. Why Lonnie Carter? Here's a man who writes epic poetic theater pieces, who finds incredible theatricality in the ordinary, who has an affinity for communities different from his own (whether it's Filipino or African-American). As a director, I'm thrilled to be on that ride together with him, watching that work get created, knowing that we're going to tell a story that hasn't been told, knowing that we're going to say something that will matter, I hope, in a way that's so *vividly theatrical*. I mean, this is all in *rhyme*! It's wild! These epic poetic structures—who does that? *Nobody* does that!

These kids [the lost boys] come from civil war and have been orphaned, and now they come to Fargo to this world of escalators and electric can openers and microwaves and *lots and lots of white people*. Can we create a vivid moment of theater out of that? Yeah! Was there a call to do that by the community? No.

So that's very clearly leading a conversation. These are the questions that bedevil you, and you're looking for people to be deviled by them, too.

If you're an artistic director, you respond to ideas that you think can spark artists. You respond to questions in the community that seem to you to be complicated. I'm not directing the piece *Snapshot Silhouette* that we're doing with Kia Corthron [2004], but I realize that the world of immigrants here, the Somali community here, is opaque to a lot of the population. It's the community that I drive through every time I come to work. So I bring Kia in here, and she digs in and explores the tensions inside both the African-American and the Somali communities. And you hope that the artist can not only speak to these communities, but also to those that are neither African-American nor Somali.

Let's talk about rehearsals. Can you give me an example of how you recently worked through a roadblock?

There was one monologue at the end of *Amber Waves* that was very difficult. The father has just learned about the suicide of one of his neighbors. We were working through it, and [the actor] Terry Hempleman and I were sharing the frustration that we weren't getting it. It was right at the end of the day, and we hadn't nailed it. It had been in the same vocabulary as the rest of the piece—kind of measured, kind of "understood." I just went up to him and said, "How are you doing?"

He said, "All right."

"Can we just do it one more time?" And I said something like: "Your son is leaving. Your son's never, *ever* coming back, if you don't stop him now. And the only way you can do that is that he has to see a side of you he's never seen." I think it was pretty general, like that.

And he got up and said, "Okay, let's try it." And suddenly, it was this man who was so *unbearably* vulnerable, unable to hold himself together: he saw himself in the same space as this farmer who'd killed himself, how they were exactly the same person. It was one of those moments when, at the end of it, the whole room knew something had happened.

And I said, "Terry, you opened a door!" That became the template on which we built the next work: the fact that suddenly, instead of the line-reading [gruffly and loud], "Don't go!"—which is what he said to his son constantly—it was [gently and slowly], "Don't . . . go." It was the silence, it was the quietude, it was the release; it was the pain, it was the impossibility of standing up and being the demanding father anymore. At the end of the day, we knew the play was going to be different, and the world had shifted. We had opened the door to the other side of this character, which was going to be key to the scene.

The cast of The Lost Boys of Sudan *by Lonnie Carter. Children's Theatre Company, 2007. Credit: Rob Levine. Used by permission of Children's Theatre Company.*

One of the other things I've learned over the years—which you *don't* do as a young director but you do as you get more shows under your belt—is say, "I don't know." And you say it to the whole company. And I've had actors say to me, "You're supposed to know. You're the director! What are we supposed to do if you don't know?"

I try to relieve myself of the pressure to know it all. I will have created a movement score, an image score, I'll write the fable of the piece, I'll write all the questions I have, I'll write everything I know, I'll write everything I don't know, I'll do all my process; I'll go through the whole piece scene by scene with costume designer, set designer, know what each clothing piece *can* do, *can't* do . . . But then it's a whole different thing when you've got the actors. Ultimately, I'm in it to be surprised. If all we're doing is putting my ideas up there, I'm not particularly interested.

What do you do in common on each show?

Once we've read the work—even though I'll have worked through the storyboarding quite specifically with the designer—I'm always much more interested in what the actors are going to do initially on the set, and in working off of their first impulses, rather than what my first impulses were. I've got those; they're not going to go away. But if actors have good ideas, I'm more interested in their impulses.

So the first time you put a scene on its feet, do you define the rough contours?

No.

You say, "Get up and do it."

Yes. Almost always. I let them know where the doors are; we walk it through. We spend a lot of time looking at the model. I talk about it, I make sure they know what they're wearing. But I'm almost always more interested in what they'll bring to it. And if those ideas sing, we'll develop those, and I may scrap *entirely* every notion I had. Or find a way to merge mine with theirs.

I pay a lot of attention to gesture and what the body is doing. And maybe that's because my first work was as a dancer making performance pieces, spending a little bit of time as an undergraduate looking at movement therapy and how the body tells stories and how the body *doesn't lie.* The body is a conveyor of *tremendous* information. I spend a lot of time on what the walk's supposed to be, and gestures—not necessarily setting them, but supplying frameworks for the actor to play in.

Do you say different things to young actors?

No, because they're so smart. With young actors I may do more physical improvisations, so that the understanding of the physical world of the play is more real and in their bodies. In one show I did, a young actress played a character who had done this heroic thing of running to the grocery store to get food for a really poor neighbor whose mother was schizophrenic. And all of it was being hidden so her family wouldn't know. So she had to enter the scene completely calm.

I said to the stage manager, "Get me a sack, and fill it full of books." We were rehearsing up on the fourth floor. I said to the actress, "Take this sack, and run down to the first floor, and then run back up. And do it again." And she was dying. "Do the scene. Now do it again," until she got it. She began to get the hard, taxing work that this character had to do every day.

Or, in *Amber Waves*—the young girl playing Deb [Celeste J. Busa] was fantastic—but there was one scene that wasn't landing: what it means when you overhear your parents fighting. I could remember my mom and stepdad arguing when I was a child, lying in bed, hearing that. And I talked to the actress, and talked to her, and talked to her, and I wasn't getting anywhere. So I said, "Okay, just lie in the bed." I turned off all the lights, and I said to the adults, "Just play the scene, and develop it, in the dark, till I tell you to stop." And then I sat there on the bed and talked her through it.

"The line in the piece is that you feel they're fighting because of you. That means you have to *believe* this; it's not a question. You're asking the question *because* you believe it." And I made her list a litany of all the things that were wrong with her family because of her. And it kept going and going and going. Insisting that she *own* all of that, so that she could play this scene that has this terrible question: "Are you getting divorced?"

Most of the time with adults, I don't find it quite as necessary to use those kinds of exercises to get the stakes, to get the backstory, to get the given circumstances. Sometimes with young actors, that's a difference. They have to feel it, truly experience it, understand it in their bones.

There was a physical piece of comedy at the end of the play, where her brother puts ice down her back, and she only quietly says, "Oh." I told the stage manager, "Get some ice." I kept it a secret. And I told the actor playing the brother to really put ice down her back. He did, and she screamed! She chased him around, a whole lot of physical comedy came out of it. This is what happens when you get ice down your back! It can be that simple.

There's also a physical thing I do: "You've got two minutes with this blanket—show me thirty-seven things you guys can do with it, torture each other, like brothers and sisters really fighting." Sending actors off to work on a problem like that, they'll often come back with a whole series of ideas. I do this sometimes with adult professionals as well, often with a piece of physical comedy, letting their imaginations drive it, and later I can edit it.

You tackle some challenging themes. What are the ground rules?

I don't think about it in terms of ground rules at all. Every country is different, every state is different, in terms of what subjects people feel are inappropriate. This'll sound odd, but what I say as an artistic director about that, or as a director sometimes, is, "What are the bigger targets?"

I know that, for example, certain uses of language can stop the audience from receiving the piece. Now, is it more important to say this word or that word in a particular context? Or is it more important to have people sit in the seat to see a piece that is about the savage differentiation of class? We're after a bigger fish. Either I'm taking them on an aesthetic journey that will make them excited or challenged, or I'm delving into content. But I want to take away those things that are easy excuses not to listen.

For example—and this is minor—in the script of *Amber Waves* there were two uses of the word "damn." Now, it's a minor word, and it may seem a trifle, but nonetheless to some parents it's offensive. Elissa Adams, our director of new-play development, came to me after the first preview and said, "We should cut those two words."

And I said, "I agree." Because we felt a change in the audience. It distanced itself from the play in those moments, and in effect turned against it. It was unfortunate, and the momentary disengagement was painful. Does it hurt the actor's intention to say "darn" or "dang" instead? Does it diminish the stakes? It's perhaps less shocking. But do I want the audience to get so offended that it can't stay and go after the big target, which is that this family is coming apart? I'm not going to give any easy outs so that you can reject this piece.

That's one answer. One has to be attentive, also, to issues of sexuality, which is culturally different around the world. How it plays in Holland is totally different than how it plays in Honolulu. For me, you just note that and attend to it, because, again, it's about a bigger fish. Often it just requires a translation of that language or that image.

Still, I don't feel I shy away from things [in programming for CTC] because of content. We did *Starry Messenger* [by Kari Margolis, 2000] about the persecution of Galileo at the hands of the Church; we did Nilo Cruz's *A Very Old Man with Enormous Wings* [2002], which looks at neo-colonialism through Gabriel García Márquez; we've done many pieces, which, because they posit an alternate cosmology—whether that's an Inuit cosmology, in *Whale* [by David Holman, 1999], or Chinese cosmology in *Dragonwings* [by Laurence Yep, 2001]—offend some people.

But that's an easy one: the world's a big place. There are *many* cosmologies. And we cannot be alive today without accepting the breadth of human experience and spiritual experience. And no, we aren't going to posit a single answer: that would be retrograde of us and irresponsible and offensive.

You know, after 9/11, having Carlyle Brown's *The Beggars' Strike* on our stage, which all took place inside the Islamic community, and opened with a call to prayer, was amazing. We opened it in January 2002, when Islamic people were being hounded; the world was quite a complicated place. I called Tazewell Thompson, the director, to talk about the play, and he said, "You're calling to cancel?"

I said, "No, why would I do that?"

He said, "I just assumed."

Our first preview of *The Beggars' Strike* was one of those amazing moments. The play opened with this beautifully choreographed, elegant call to prayer. A company of twenty-five bowing, and the voice of the imam filling the theater. They folded up their blankets and stood up, under a beautiful sky drop, and the audience burst into applause.

I was like, "Is this applause for acceptance and tolerance? Is this applause for, 'We should embrace this'? Is this applause because it was beautiful?" It wasn't spectacular; it was quiet, very still and precise, but it built and kept building. (That moment never happened again.)

Was it appropriate to bring the world of Islam to a world that maybe was wrestling with Islam for the first time? Yeah!

What about young audiences and the classics? How do you make them connect?

Last year we did *Antigone*. We were launching our teen programming. I brought Greg Banks in from England, having seen his work. When we met, he said, "I'm thinking about doing *Antigone* for the National; would you be interested?" The National passed, and we took it.

We talked about doing it promenade-style, where you tear out all the seats. So we didn't do it in our theater. We did it at a nearby venue. The environment felt like a Berlin nightclub: graffiti walls, slightly punky/gothy costume world. And it was muscular, visceral, participatory— when Creon wins, he strides through the crowd, pulling girls up to his side, checking them out; he's got a beer bottle in his hand, celebrating; the crowd is screaming and yelling, musicians moving around.

And this teen audience had never seen anything like it. Political, brutal, funny, pathetic, moving, physical, surrounding you, surprising you, tender.

Do you make different aesthetic choices when directing for a younger audience?

I don't know if there's a profound aesthetic difference. Some of the difference, I hope, is a generosity of spirit . . . What works for us is when there's that wild dance between the obsessive pursuit of an artistic vision and the incredible generosity of inclusion and respect and love, even, which may sound a little odd. You're giving this incredible gift of this story. Take the deconstruction we did of the Brothers Grimm [*Once Upon a Forest*, 2003, by Moniek Merkx and Elissa Adams]; it was extraordinarily formal and European, very dark, but at its core it was an invitation, and a welcome. I don't know how that manifests itself, but you know when the work is only self-referential, as opposed to being a wonderful dialectic between the impulse of the artist and the hunger to push the audience, and bring them, and connect.

How do you know what a twelve- to fifteen-year-old audience wants?

Well, there are a couple of things you can do. One is to make the work you most want to make and invite them in and talk about it. Second is to do what my colleagues in Europe do: be in continual conversation. What are the issues in your life? What excites you? Bring them in for improvisational sessions; bring them in as your dramaturgs: what are the moments that are alive, vivid? When did you check out? You know, really ask them, rather than ask for their endorsement.

And never, in any way, shape or form, underestimate the stakes of their emotional lives. The emotional journey of a young person's day is extraordinary: the peaks are higher, the valleys are lower. Adults live in a more flatlined EKG world. You may be annoyed at work, or stuck in that traffic jam, or pissed off. But you aren't *crushed*, or *exhilarated*. You aren't suddenly part of the in-crowd, or suddenly banished from the gates of Heaven, or humiliated in class and feeling that it's a scar across your forehead—the way you are as a young person. Those stakes are vivid; the losses of those friendships, those exhilarations, the degrees of that boredom, are massive. So do not underestimate. Do not dismiss or patronize.

Start with a massive respect for your audience! Assume they're smarter than you, because they are! That they're braver than you, because they are! Do not lie to them, in the same way you should not lie to any audience. Be *so endlessly vigilant* about not lying, which is the great danger in any art. You can manipulate them—pop culture manipulates them brilliantly. Marketing geniuses spend many hours a day thinking about how to manipulate them into purchasing this, that or the other. It *is* possible. I remember seeing a show in Russia at the Central Children's Theater: it had the strobe light, had the fog, had the magic tricks, had the audience participation . . . relentless manipulation, and it *all worked*! It wasn't good, or satisfying, but did it work? Yes. So be mindful of it.

Do you agree with Linda Hartzell, who said in *American Theatre* magazine in 2000 that what's most important about TYA is that you leave them with hope rather than cynicism?

Young people are not cynical. At least not till early adolescence. They're not ironical. That comes later. Do we think about hope? Yes. I'm thinking of the end of *Korczak's Children* [2003], which Jeffrey Hatcher wrote for us: on the one hand, Dr. Korczak and all the children walk off to Treblinka, the concentration camp. That's the reality, that's what happened. On the other hand, as he's walking out with them, he's telling them a tale. A tale of possibility. A tale of transcendence, about the power of imagination. He's suggesting there are people out there who are their allies, who are creative, who believe in the power of children. The victory is: we're doing a play about him in 2003. He's gone, but he still has an immense power. So what happens at the end is a kind of deeply spiritual hope.

At the end of *Amber Waves*, too, the tiniest hope: we're renting out some of the land. It ain't over till it's over. Did they make it through this period? Yes. Are these challenges going to come up again next year? Yes. Are they better equipped as a family to stop being in denial? Maybe; I think so. Because they opened up and spoke to each other, there's the potential for that kind of hope. But again, it's the difference between a false hope, a lie, and a kind of profound engagement in the possibility of renewal.

Why are we theater artists? We believe people can change. We wouldn't do this if we didn't think people can change, that they can come into this space and learn something, be moved, be excited, be intellectually challenged, have questions, and become someone slightly different. We believe in the possibility of transformation.

PING CHONG

Outsider

THE WORK OF PING CHONG DEFIES categorization. A veteran of New York's downtown avant-garde, Chong creates theater that can be alternatively classified as multimedia performance, documentary, dance or performance art. In a career spanning four decades, this Chinese-American artist has revolutionized the use of technology in theater; at the same time, he's returned performance to its most elemental and ritualistic.

Chong's pieces range from nearly wordless music-movement fantasias to documentary theater pieces written and performed by refugee children. They are created in places as diverse as the Netherlands, Vietnam and his hometown of New York. For his nontraditional experiments, he has been repeatedly honored, both by the establishment (six National Endowment for the Arts fellowships, a Kennedy Center commission) and its alternative (OBIE and Bessie Awards for sustained achievement). The acclaim has brought big-budget shows at the Brooklyn Academy of Music, Lincoln Center and dozens of other major presenting houses across the globe as well as community centers across the country.

It's ironic that Ping Chong hasn't devoted his time to traditional filmmaking, given his great admiration for the form and its influence on him. (Chong studied filmmaking at the School of Visual Arts and the

Pratt Institute in the 1970s, but his experience is limited to his use of film, video and projections within his performance works.) A Ping Chong production may have a budget in the hundreds of thousands of dollars, or it may be radically smaller, but the work always teases the viewer's perspective with the same control a filmmaker's does. Chong pioneered the use of filmic elements on stage like highly integrated sound design, projections and digital animation. Though some of these advances now seem commonplace, Chong's employment of them was radical and revolutionary when he began.

In his theatrical experiments, moving scenery, the illusion of a split screen, the manipulation of focus from long shot to zoom and stylized choreography seduce the eye into a realm of visual spectacle more commonly associated with the cinema. For example, his enormously successful puppet shows *Kwaidan* (1998) and *Obon* (2002), based on Japanese ghost stories, almost defy visual logic by altering scale, tempo and expectation. Even his low-budget projects, such as the ongoing *Undesirable Elements* series, defamiliarize the spectator by turning witnesses into performers: a narrative trick of perspective.

In addition to this interdisciplinary and filmic style, the other trait common to all of Chong's work is its interest in exploring how "the other" is conceived, created and treated in society. Chong frequently talks about being an outsider himself—a Chinese-American boy in a primarily white high school, an American interviewing people abroad to write a script, a nontraditional artist in a traditional theater world. And despite being a longtime New Yorker, he is kept out of New York much of the year by his punishing touring schedule. Ping Chong is thus both a citizen of the world and a stateless refugee. Long before multiculturalism became an American obsession, Chong was a living example of the advantages and challenges that multiculturalism presents to American society. The culture shock of his youth (and being frequently perceived as "the other") fueled his artistry and still defines it.

Born in 1946 and growing up in New York's Chinatown, Chong says film was his earliest and strongest influence. Though his parents were Chinese opera veterans, Chong turned to the burgeoning international cinema of the 1960s for inspiration. The freedom of New York's tumultuous art scene at the time led him to the Pratt Institute and the School of Visual Arts (where he studied filmmaking and graphic design), and soon after he graduated in 1969, he joined Meredith Monk's House Company, where until 1978 he was a performer and frequent collaborator in the legendary dancer's work. He learned from Monk that he needn't adhere to any preconceived notions of artistic expression.

With this background of heterogeneous influences, he formed the Fiji Company (now Ping Chong & Company) in 1975, and began blending all these disciplines together. Chong was part of a movement that eschewed traditional narrative, working assiduously to redefine how the stage could be used as a storytelling medium.

For fifteen years, he trained his anthropologist's eye on his beloved New York, investigating the greedy American culture of the 1980s in *Nosferatu: A Symphony of Darkness* (1985), or American attitudes toward the immigrant with *Kind Ness* (1986), among other topics. It was a prolific time for Chong, and his experimental approach became a favorite with the Brooklyn Academy of Music's influential Next Wave Festival.

It wasn't until 1990 and the start of his *East-West Quartet* that Chong finally looked to Asia to address the issue of otherness. In this series, many critics feel he found his strongest and most visceral expression. The four works of the *Quartet* (*Deshima,* 1990; *Chinoiserie,* 1995; *After Sorrow,* 1997; and *Pojagi,* 1999) travel through time to analyze the West's perception of Japan, China, Vietnam and Korea, respectively, through both a historical and personal lens. These poetic documentaries feature a familiar blend of Chong's multimedia expression—dance, theater, projection, sound and so on—to examine the effects of Western imperialism and colonialism on these countries, and in the process they reveal just how "other" Eastern culture remains in Western eyes.

Chong begins with a desire to educate his audiences about the East, but the eloquence of his stage imagery overwhelms the history lesson. These works often become powerful by forcing the spectator to forge links through time: *Chinoiserie,* for example (which Chong has called a "docu-theater-concert-dance-piece" and in which he himself performed as an on-stage narrator), juxtaposes the story of an eighteenth-century meeting between a Chinese emperor and the emissary of a British king alongside that of the racially motivated murder of a Chinese man in 1980s Detroit. Chong even uses the technique in his puppet shows: *Cathay* (2005) uncovered China with stories from the Tang Dynasty, World War II and today.

But the mainstay of his work of late—and the clearest assertion of Chong's personal mission to explore the outsider in American culture—is the *Undesirable Elements* series, which has run parallel to Chong's other endeavors since 1992 and which he has mounted in dozens of communities worldwide. The most important qualification in casting these works, Chong says, is that the actors must have traveled from one culture to another, and they must have stories they're willing to share on stage. The process is not dissimilar to that pioneered in Los Angeles by Bill Rauch and Cornerstone Theater Company, but rather than use those community members to adapt an extant text or create a new fiction, Chong uses their own words to create a powerful Theater of Testimony that speaks directly to the community where it's performed about the intercultural issues they face. Within the *Undesirable Elements* framework, Chong has created pieces with groups of legal and illegal immigrants, adult refugees as well as children (in the twentieth install-ment *Children of War*, 2002), people with disabilities and other margin-alized communities. As Chong said in 1999, "As an artist, I'm an out-sider in American society. As an experimental artist, I'm an outsider in the art world. As a person of color, I'm an outsider; as an immigrant, I'm an outsider; as a gay man, I'm an outsider. It's the position that fate has allotted me, but it's a valuable position to be in, because I think every society should have a mirror held to it by the outsider."

MARCH 2003, OFFICES OF PING CHONG & COMPANY, NEW YORK CITY

I know that your parents' background in Chinese opera was very impor-tant. Was becoming an artist a foregone conclusion for you?

Obviously, I'm not a theater artist in the traditional sense, because I'm a synthesis of a lot of different interests. There was an amalgam of influences on me.

I got into the arts because one of my father's closest friends was a scenic prop painter. He gave me a lot of art books to look at, both Western and Eastern, and that's how I started getting into drawing. Growing up in America, it wasn't until high school that I saw Western theater. Up to that point it was all Chinese opera, if I saw theater at all.

I never wanted to go into the theater. That was never, never in my plan at all. Actually, my great love was film, and still is; it's the form that has disappointed me the least.

I was originally going to start as a painter when I was in high school. But that was complicated because the painting I studied in art school was Western art. I was going from one culture to another, and it was very conflicting for me to deal with Western art. Film was more international.

What kind of films did you like as a kid?

Everything. Mostly Hollywood films and Chinese films. Not the inter-national cinema, because that didn't really start until the late 1950s, or the beginning of the 1960s. I remember the first foreign films I saw were *The Magician* and Alain Resnais's *Last Year at Marienbad*. Quite a heady stew. It was certainly above my head at that point.

You said film is the form that has disappointed you the least. Could you expand on that?

I think from the very beginning of my career, my contribution to the field of theater has been the use of sound, because of my film background. From the very beginning there was never any question that sound for me is a part of what theater *is*. At this moment, you know, sound design is a major player on Broadway. And I'm very proud of that aspect of my work.

But why has film disappointed me the least? Because the problem with theater, especially in this country, is that there is very little courage. The regional theaters do not generally demonstrate that much courage.

To be fair, it's a difficult field economically. Not that international film isn't. I'd say most of the films that are interesting are not Hollywood films. In a way, you could say I'm talking about the fringe cinema, but I'm not: I'm talking about international cinema. Though in a way it *is* fringe, because lots of things that I like are often fringe in their own countries as well.

But theaters have to appeal to their immediate populaces. We're talking about local theater, local populations. And that defines the work a lot, because if your audience is not interested, there is not very much you can do about it.

I remember when I was at Milwaukee Repertory Theater at the invitation of John Dillon. John was a wonderful artistic director in the sense that he saw the world in a less provincial way than many artistic directors at regional theaters do. He saw an international world; he didn't just see American theaters. He knew that, in order to not be provincial, you need to include the world. It seems obvious to me; and certainly it was to him. He was presenting a series of Chilean plays while I was working there. And some of the patrons were going, "One Chilean play, okay. But why so many?" It's a very provincial mindset; and that's not just Milwaukee.

I guess I still see a lot more courage in filmmaking. A lot more vision in terms of exploring, taking chances. Coming out of that 1960s visual theater world, I have seen very few things in the last twenty years of a similar nature. There are very few people coming up to continue that tradition. We're still talking about the Wooster Group, Anne Bogart, Richard Foreman, Mabou Mines and . . . you know, we're the old guys!

The Builders Association [of New York City] is one of the few groups I find interesting. Cloud Gate Dance Theatre [of Taiwan] is kind of interesting . . . and Annie-B Parson and [her company] Big Dance Theater are on the cusp between theater and dance. So I know there *are* some [companies doing experimental work]. But there are fewer than there ever were before. Granted, I came out in the sixties, which was one of the most exciting times in terms of exploration and process. But I know that for the last twenty years, it's just been diminishing.

Do you think it's mostly a financial issue?

I think it is *partly* a financial issue. It is much more difficult to live in New York now, as opposed to when I started out, and arts funding is reduced. The climate is much more conservative for all of those reasons.

You have received a lot of strength from the funding community—yet you call yourself an outsider. Do you have to be an outsider to be a creative artist?

No. I don't. Because I see myself as an artist in the theater, as opposed to a theater artist.

In 1997, I was at a conference at UCLA that the Ford Foundation put together. It was a collaboration between Asian and American artists. There was a Taiwanese theater director from a very well-known international company. They do Chinese opera in a very avant-garde form, meaning that they're taking the form of Chinese opera into this century.

When I saw him talk about his work, I realized that I'm not a theater person in the traditional sense. His whole *life* was in Chinese opera; his life was completely in the theater. I came from an ancestry of three generations of the theater—when I was a kid I was making little Chinese operas at home in the basement—but I transferred to film very early, I was making cartoons that I called films.

Recently, Susie Farr (who is executive director of the Clarice Smith Performing Arts Center at the University of Maryland) was interviewed about me in an article about a project I did called *Children of War*. And she said, "I don't know what to call him!"

I said, "Susie, if you think of me as an *artist*, then it makes complete sense, because an artist will work on *anything* that is of interest to him, whether it is a fashion show or an installation or whatever." But this attitude is not common in the theater.

But you've found a home for your art within the theatrical medium.

And I'm comfortable in it now. People have asked me, "Would you make a film?" And I say, "Only if someone has signed the contract and faxed it!" But otherwise I'm happy to be a passive lover of film, and let everybody else have the headache, because I know what it takes to make a film. I'm not getting any younger, and that's a brutal, punishing medium. I don't even like tech week in the theater.

George Drance (behind) and Federico Restrepo in Angels of Swedenborg *by Ping Chong. Ping Chong & Company, Williams College, 2011. Credit: Damia Cavallari.*

That's interesting because your work is so . . .

Technical! I know! But that's why I don't like tech week! Although it's getting better, because it's about working with the right people. In the last ten years, I've finally found people I can completely trust. And I know that they'll whip themselves more than I will ever have to whip them if they fuck up in any way. Their sense of responsibility and self-respect is just as high as mine, and I won't have to worry about it.

That's mostly true of my major designers. I'll deal with a designer's idiosyncrasies if the product is worth it. I'm very family-oriented. I've been working with the same stage manager as much as possible over the last twelve years. The same lighting and set designer, the same costume designer—but I've worked with a variety of sound people, because I think I wear them out.

So how did you come to find your comfort level in theater? What was the journey?

Well, if you talk about the first decade of my work, it really shows my visual arts roots, because those pieces were not *activated* in the way theater is activated, and I never thought of them as theater. Those early works were very still, very silent; there is sound, but not text. They were not literary in any way, very visual, and very enigmatic, more like poetry than prose.

There was not much in the way of dance, because at that time I was working with Meredith Monk, and I felt like dance was her territory. The work she and I were making together was totally choreographic; it was music-theater, really. It wasn't unrelated to what I was doing, but my early work and the work I did with her was very different. The common elements that I use—projections, recorded sound—were there in my early work. Dance showed up more toward the end of the first decade of my career. What I learned from Meredith is the use of gesture. I also learned it from Chinese opera, which is all gesture. You might say that meeting Meredith returned me to my own culture.

The next decade was a decade of inspiration . . . all kinds of inspiration, like elaborate media projections in relationship to my music. Also, funding arrived! I only had one or two fellowships in the first decade. It wasn't until around 1980 that I started to get into federal and state funding.

And that gave you an opportunity for other, more expensive media?

Well, not really, because I was very low-budget even then. I was still making work for a couple thousand dollars.

The eighties was a period when I was unconsciously finding my vocabulary. As an artist I was there already with the visual, the sound, the sense of time, the filmic aspects. And design, which I never thought of as "scenery," but as the sculpture of space. But now I was finding a more elaborate use of those elements.

And also, I was developing a vocabulary with my performers—the performers from Meredith's group, and the performers who were new to my work. This group made up my company, the only time I had an acting company, for about eleven years. It's amazing that I had eleven years to work with the same people.

There was no common denominator: one performer came from dance with Meredith. One was a physical theater person, from a kind of street theater, but also with some traditional theater training. The third was a mime. And then there was an extended family of another two or three people. It was a very motley mix, and very small to start.

Over time I realized that they were all conceptual. They were not passive performers as you have in traditional theater. Traditional performers tend to be passive in relationship to the director—unless they're divas! I realized I was drawn to conceptual performers who were themselves interested in the making of the work. At the very beginning, I didn't write anything. Mainly, the words were created in an improvisational process with the company. And I functioned in a way as an art director. I decided what stayed and what didn't stay.

As one of my performers said, "More often Ping knows what he doesn't want than what he wants, and by the process of elimination he gets what he wants."

By the end of the eighties, my approach became all about process. With some shows I was vaguer than others: I would come in without any idea of what I was doing. I'd say, "Let's put two chairs on the stage, play a piece of music, the set's going to be all white, and then just improvise." And then something emerges out of this. Like a painter with a piece of canvas: you have to put the first mark on the canvas, but you don't always know, especially at the top of a series of paintings, how it will turn out. It is about exploring some problems you want to solve, and the hardest part is the very first one. Because after that, you're chasing that solution to solve the problem.

Nosferatu [1985] was my signature piece in the 1980s. The theater community took notice of me with that piece, partly because it was related to theater in a recognizable way, and also because it was kind of a weird comedy of manners. It was like a Buñuel film on American society. A satiric work about the yuppies, and the plague (the AIDS epidemic, which, though never mentioned in the show, was very present in the consciousness of the country at that time) and about consumerist society. The eighties was the time when greed became acceptable behavior. This was a work addressing *that,* addressing Western society.

Could you talk a little about the process?

Nosferatu was inspired by a novel called *How German Is It* by Walter Abish, about modern-day Germany, and its suppression and denial of its recent dark past, and how in this spic-and-span materialistic new Germany, the rot comes through the walls. In fact, *How German Is It* would make a very interesting play or film in its own right. But at that time, I was really more moved by what was happening to my city. I'm a New Yorker, so what's happening *here* is personal.

So I asked everybody to read that book. And then I was thinking about Calvin Klein underwear, which was a big deal at that time: the fashion statement, advertising, logos. I did a lot of interviews with yuppies. And then I said all the characters were going to be named after the original characters from the Bram Stoker novel *Dracula,* and all of this was going to take place in a loft in a big city. I shot single frames from the original *Nosferatu* film on slides—the subtitles, everything, all the way from the beginning to the end of the show—and that was the only linear narrative.

So you came into rehearsal with all of that in your head?

Yeah, that piece was more thought through than some other work at the time. I would put on a piece of music, and the two characters would be at home in their underwear, looking like models, going through their mail. As they went along, I might say, "Do this, say this," and that's how we'd go. In my work in the eighties, the script always came after the show was made!

That decade we also did *Angels of Swedenborg* [1985], which was largely textless, totally choreographic, totally movement-oriented: mime, mask, dance. And then after *Angels* I said, "Too much tech, let's strip down." So we did *Kind Ness* [1986], which had six actors and nothing on stage. I would alternate between these very elaborate technical dances and, "Let's do something simple."

Thematically, I was always exploring the outsider. The outsider theme started out as a very personal theme of cultural adjustment, but over time, it became clear that it was incredibly rich and universal. Within that, theme varied greatly. *Kind Ness* was a seminal work in the age of multiculturalism; it was before people really got hot on it. Obviously, for me, it was always a hot issue.

In 1991 I did my last show with that core company. Working with an acting ensemble was a kind of utopian dream, and reality reared its ugly head, as it always does. The performers were getting older and they wanted to start families and stop touring all the time. And I was changing artistic directions, too. I said, "It's time for you to go and do your own thing." [Chong's company is now an informal core group of artists with whom he collaborates on a project-by-project basis.]

Our last show together was called *Elephant Memories*. It was kind of like William Gibson cyberpunk, in terms of language. At the same time, it was nonstop movement, and the performers never left the stage. It was a physically challenging piece, but they did it, and they were good . . . but it was clear that those days were going to become more and more difficult. I'd worked with them for a decade. I was accommodating *their* needs as well as my own. I wasn't able to explore other areas because of the limitations: we'd outgrown each other to some extent.

You didn't think about a new company?

No, because it was hardly the time to form a new company. By the nineties, the world had changed irrevocably. In the first decade, nobody asked for salary—because people could afford not to, and I didn't have the money. Idealism was the first decade. And then by the end of the eighties, you couldn't get *anybody* to do *anything* for nothing anymore. Of course, actors should be paid for their work. The way we pay actors in theater is shameful.

So economic circumstances had a big effect on how your work evolved.

The economics had less to do with *me* and more to do with *them*, because Ping Chong & Company was pretty stable as an organization after Bruce [Allardice, the managing director] started in 1988.

In the early 1990s, without your acting ensemble, you started *The East-West Quartet*.

This is how *Deshima* [part one of the *Quartet*, 1990] started: from 1979 till 1990, I went to Holland every two years to make work (and anybody can tell you that in the seventies and early-eighties, Europe kept the avant-garde alive). The Mickery Workshop Theater there asked me if I was interested in doing a show about Vincent van Gogh. In researching van Gogh, I learned he was born when Commodore Perry was in Japan and said, "Open your doors to trade." At the same time, the Impressionists were totally influenced by Japanese woodcut prints. Between the eighteenth and nineteenth centuries, Chinoiserie and Japonnais were all the rage, and influenced the Impressionists: the flattening of the pictures, the painted surface. It was the beginning of Modernism in painting, in a way.

At the time, the press was unfairly attacking Japan—Mitsubishi had bought [a controlling interest in] Rockefeller Center, and there was all this crap about, "We're losing our patrimony." (Meanwhile, Britain, Holland and Canada were buying much more property than Japan was, and no one complained about that, so this was clearly racist.) So I decided to do a work about the history of Japan and the West.

I was in a transition phase. By the end of the eighties, I felt I was spinning my wheels artistically. I'd started doing installation art. It was just a fluke: I was feeling really stale, and it was time for a change. I was asked to do a visual arts installation in 1992 [at Artist Space in New York City] called "A Channeling and Containment of Undesirable Elements." It was designed as a three-dimensional quarantine space for "undesirable elements." But what "undesirable elements" *were* was not defined. The audience that came to see it was quarantined on bridges; and then there were these pools of yellow and black liquids that were not defined, so you could read them any way you wanted.

The director of the space said, "We want this to be a multidisciplinary art space, so would you consider doing a performance in your installation?" At that time I was interested in doing a performance in multiple languages, so I thought, "Here's a chance to do something modest, in many languages; something I don't want reviewed, a work-in-progress." That's how *Undesirable Elements* started, as a forty-minute piece.

Soon after that I was invited to Cleveland to do another version of it, and that's when it dawned on me, what the project was. With the first one, I just barely had an idea of it. I was learning the skill of interviewing, which was something totally new. And *Undesirable Elements* was absolutely unlike anything I'd ever done before, which took me by surprise as well. Even in the early stages, people told me the show would have legs. Also, the project has allowed me to address needs I had as an artist and as a human being.

Chinoiserie [1995] did that, too. I didn't know it would be the second part of my *East-West Quartet*. I got invited to work with a string quartet in Minneapolis at the Walker Art Center, and that's when I hooked up with Guy Klucevsek, the composer. At the time, Hong Kong was about to be returned to China, and I realized that no one knew what that history was about and that I had to do a piece on China, too . . . and that the series had to be a trilogy. I didn't know what the third one was going to be, but I knew it had to go on.

So I said, "Let's do *Chinoiserie*. I know we can do it at BAM; I want a big explosion with this." The content was very personal, too; except for *Fear and Loathing in Gotham* [1973], the third piece in my career, *Chinoiserie* was the only [other] time [up to that point] I had addressed the personal cultural-schism thing.

I'd had a cowriter on *Deshima*, Michael Matthews, with whom I had worked on another Dutch production. He was an American ex-pat, and we hit it off. So I asked him to cowrite *Chinoiserie* with me.

I hadn't written anything completely by myself until *Undesirable Elements*. I was starting to write much more extensively than I had done in the first two decades of my career. I'd forgotten that I like to write. I'd written a lot of poetry in my college years, which is funny because I'm thought of as a visual director. And now, if anything, there's a hell of a lot of words in my work!

Chinoiserie was a music-theater work with singers—so you see what I was saying about [the limitations of an acting] company? None of my performers had been singers, really, except one. I was always moving toward a total performer.

Chinoiserie was drawn from historical sources, though the development of some of the scenes was collaborative. We used trained martial artists and Chinese opera and Restoration gestures. And I had the good fortune of having Chen Shi-Zheng, who was at the time working with Meredith Monk, and who later directed *The Peony Pavilion*. He was Chinese-opera trained, so [he spared] me having to go through the tedious process of that gestural stuff secondhand.

Chinoiserie would never have happened if *Undesirable Elements* hadn't already existed. All that work was coming out of *Undesirable Elements* and *Deshima*.

But then, the cutbacks in 1995–1996 [the NEA's Congressional appropriation dropped from $162 million in 1995 to $99 million in 1996]: a real crisis moment for us; the bottom dropped out. We had to cancel two tour dates for *Chinoiserie*, which I'd never had to do before or since. And at the same time we had to decide what to do with the Vietnam piece [*After Sorrow*, the third work in *The East-West Quartet*, 1997], because there was no money.

I went to Vietnam to do research, but because we were in a period of cutbacks, I didn't have enough money to go to France. I really wanted to deal with the French, even more than the Americans: the French colonial history is not well known. But we couldn't.

I couldn't figure out what the show was about until I got to this book about a Quaker woman who had gone to Vietnam during the war, and then went back during the embargo to see: who are these women, these people that we fought? I was going from epic—*Deshima*, which had fifty costume changes—to *Chinoiserie*, which was a little narrower. It was like a pyramid: it got narrower and narrower until it got to this personal history, this encounter between the Quaker woman and a Vietnamese woman, and then the tragedy of the war for both of them emerged. Reduced to two human beings. *After Sorrow* was constructed like a meditative ritual about war. You never see the Vietnamese woman, you only hear her voice.

When a Korean director friend of mine said, "You have to do a piece about Korea" [which became *Pojagi*, 1999], I said at first, "I don't want to do this anymore!" The research on these things is tedious and time-consuming; not uninteresting, but tedious! Each of these things would take a year of research. I wish I could avoid research; it drives me crazy.

Undesirable Elements influenced not only *The East-West Quartet*, but a shift towards more overtly political work and Theater of Testimony.

The *power* of that show is that you're witnessing the person these things happened to, or this person's family. If a performer did it, it wouldn't have the same power. We've experimented over the years with casts that are all performers. And it doesn't really work. The genuineness of these human beings on stage is what makes it effective.

What's astonishing about *Undesirable Elements* is that it's seven people with a script in front of them, sitting in chairs for an hour and a half . . . and they can hold an audience of 700 to 800 people. It just is so powerful to hear. Each of the participants is a vessel of history. Many of them can't act, really. You discover that in the audition process. But in the end, it's a very simple act of storytelling, with very little acting.

What happens in the interview process?

Well, they have to have stories. And I don't want generalities . . . Generalities are useless to me. They have to want to tell their stories. There are times when people are too angry, in which case they can't tell their stories in a dispassionate way, and I don't want to work with them. They're subjective about what's happened.

You've done this many times now. How long does it take you to do one of these?

Usually there are two weeks of prescreening, finding the people I want, and I have six weeks before opening.

In a recent online Q&A for washingtonpost.com [during the February 2002 run of _Undesirable Elements_ at the University of Maryland in College Park], you said: "Right now I am very interested in stories of homeless kids,

Kristin de Groot, Arnaud Kokosky Deforchaux, Michael Matthews and Nita Liem in Deshima, _conceived and directed by Ping Chong in collaboration with Michael Matthews. Ping Chong & Company, Mickery Workshop Theater, Utrecht, Holland, 1990. Credit: Bob van Dantzig._

gay kids and the millions of kids who are living in America below the poverty line and have no public voice at all." Why are children's stories of such interest to you now?

Well, there are lots of things that I don't get to do until I find the right partner for it, the right time to do it. With gay kids, I've wanted to do that for some time, but it's never panned out. And I'm not willing to give up my other work to do only this. Because these projects are very intense. This year, for example, I'm going to Berlin [to create an *Undesirable Elements* production]. I've been wanting to do a German piece for a very long time.

Why is that?

Because in Europe there's always criticism of our American problems— our war problems, our race problems. Yet meanwhile, they're totally dissembling and hypocritical. They're old-world liars. The old world is much more sophisticated about how to colonize people and everything else. When all the shit started hitting the fan in Germany and France about guest workers and repatriation and all that stuff, I wanted to get at it.

I wanted to do one on Israel, too. They were like, "Who's this Chinese man coming here to talk about our problems?" And that's exactly the point—because I don't have a vested interest there. That's why I'm the better person to talk about it. But I knew that was completely quixotic.

The best thing I got out of that was that I got to go to Israel. It was wonderful to have that experience, but it was very, very sad. I was there that night: the bombing in Tel Aviv [the Purim holiday bombing in March 1997, which killed three Israelis]. The next day I was in the Old City of Jerusalem, and it was tragic for both sides. Can anything be that implacable . . . you know what I mean?

I guess it's nothing new. Not to mention that there are Jews in Israel who can't even talk to other Jews, never mind Palestinians. I'd never get a Hasidic Jew on stage to agree with another Jew: forget it! It's fanaticism we're talking about here, but I thought I'd give it a shot. But the producers were too nervous about the idea. They didn't have the courage to do it. Because if it had happened, all the people on stage would have had to be open-minded; that would take courage on their parts.

So is theater a really dangerous place anymore?

It would be a dangerous place if they let you do it!

In Harvard's *Arts Spectrum* newsletter [September/October 1999], you said: "There's no such thing as safety for an artist in America. We're not safe in this country. We're totally vulnerable, not accepted; we're really scapegoats because we're threatening the establishment. We have no security. We are exploited all of the time by all kinds of things, organizations, all kinds of producers. We are really workers, and we don't make much money. There is no safety net, so I don't understand that term, 'risk-taking.' By definition, being an artist means taking risks."

What's the difference between muzzling an artist by dictatorship, and muzzling an artist by not giving him the money to do it? What's the difference? It's no different. If you have a voice that no one can hear, what's the difference? You're marginalized to the boundaries.

That's the reason *Undesirable Elements* exists. Even though it's only at a grassroots level. You either light a candle or curse the darkness and sit in the dark, you know? People say, "You're preaching to the converted," but you know what? I don't buy that line anymore. Because the converted need to be preached to.

And I don't always reach the converted. To do one of these shows in front of black students at [an urban public high school], and to watch them go beyond laughing at the fact people on stage are speaking different languages and come to respect their experiences is, to me, valuable.

Do you feel it's risky, putting these "undesirable" voices on stage?

I don't see myself taking risks with this project. This project subverts criticism, because you're trying to build bridges here, so who can disagree with that? Politicians want to look like they're doing good deeds anyway. The show is certainly political, and I certainly put my two cents in. I see this as fulfilling a need in me as a human being, to do my civic duty.

At the beginning of my career I was more a European-influenced artist, seeking the approval of the "colonial master," you might say. From the nineties on, I rejected that. Now, I don't give a flying fuck about European approval. For the last ten years I've been going to Asia a lot more—I've been identifying myself more as an Asian with American roots.

I guess the bottom line is that the West has become more and more heartless, and more and more inhumane. That's not to say that Asia is the answer. We didn't have the Enlightenment in Asia, and that's made things a lot worse there. Spiritually, I'm not a certified Buddhist, but still, I'm closer to that.

But for me, risk is really about *personally* doing something. For me, to direct a two-and-a-half-hour Mozart opera as I am about to do [*La Clemenza Di Tito*, Clarice Smith Center for the Performing Arts at the

University of Maryland, College Park, April 2003] . . . I've only directed one opera before, and that was a one-act opera [Benjamin Britten's *Curlew River*, Spoleto Festival USA, May 1997]. So that's a risk.

Can you tell me about a moment you've created of which you're very proud?

In the opening of my puppet show *Kwaidan*, there's a tiny puppet of a monk in a huge landscape, a cinemascope landscape of Japanese pine trees. This little puppet who's lost sees a hut in the distance, and descends down an invisible path. Then, nothing's changed, only the lighting changes and a large puppet comes in to the third window, the center window, and he descends down the center window, and the lights change. Then a much larger-scale puppet comes in, and goes back up toward the hut.

It's totally magical, and it's completely simple. From my point of view, that's what's missing in most theater. A film would never do it that way. Could not do it that way. It's pure theater. And that's coming from someone who says he never wanted to be a theater artist—but now it comes full circle. Because in the Chinese opera, for example, a character will do this kind of circle, semi-dance, semi-walk; and by the time he completely stops, he's *arrived* at the place he's going to. That's theater. And there is very little of that in American theater. You hope for the audience to use its imagination, which is in short supply now in this country.

How did you plan that moment?

I storyboarded it that way, and then communicated it to my designers. The whole puppet show had to be storyboarded beforehand, to figure out how all design elements should be constructed in order to make this magical moment happen on stage.

The difference between live actors and puppets is that you can have the same character in three different sizes. I was playing with that point of view thing. In fact, originally, there was even going to be a moment when he's looking for a place to stay for the night, and you see a close-up of his face, looking in the window. So it was all there in my storyboard. But I don't think I had any idea how effective that would be.

The irony is that *Kwaidan* is a puppet show, yet it's pure theater. I don't think I've ever had as much satisfaction as I had watching *Kwaidan* from the audience and hearing a *gasp* at certain things that happened in that show. It was totally low-tech. No wires or people flying around or any of that.

What would a Ping Chong show be like on Broadway?

Oh, I have no idea. But recently, I was at the Getty Museum [in Los Angeles], which is famous for the battle in the late nineties between Richard Meier, the architect, and the artist Robert Irwin. And they both had a tremendous amount of money, and that doesn't bring out the good side of artists, in my opinion!

That's my answer to you about Broadway. It's a hard call, because we have to be so parsimonious most of the time when we are making work, that it's hard to resist (when the money's available) doing all kinds of stupid things. Limitations are your best friend in making art. And I welcome limitations, because that's when I can be the most creative.

Undesirable Elements is as limited as it gets. It's a very simple show, but it's actually very sophisticated in terms of construction. Doing twenty of them, I learned to use a more refined plan in terms of set, how to get the effects. But it's a very narrow band of creativity, like a haiku.

Do you use the same format with each group that you talk to?

The format is identical, except that even now I'm finding things I've never done before. Very small, but that's what's interesting about it. Within this *extremely narrow band*, can you find new ways into it? I still do.

My last questions have to do with the profession and young professionals. You're currently mentoring Michael Rohd. What are you hoping to achieve there?

I don't think about that, really. Mentoring came to me; I didn't come to mentoring. People started to see me as a senior citizen, you know what I mean? I understand my responsibilities to them. I'm not a person who wants people to do what *I* do. I've talked to Michael about his work; he doesn't have a lot of ego problems. He's a great man that way. So I can be very frank with him about what I see, the limitations that I'm seeing. We talk very openly about that. As someone who's worked for thirty years I'm happy to do it. But in the end everyone should realize their own vision, not my vision.

What else can be done to encourage young artists to achieve their own vision?

I've always said this to old and young people: you shouldn't narrow your interests in terms of the world, in terms of other art. You should be open to looking at all the arts, past and present. Because it can only make you richer.

There are no absolute rules in making art. There are lots of people who are *not* interested in the rest of the world, who have very narrow areas of interest, but they create their own world. So, I tend to tell people to be more open to the world, because all our problems come from the fact that we're not open to the world. And having had the privilege of traveling around the world, I know that I've got a view of the world that most people don't have.

SEPTEMBER 2006, VIA PHONE FROM NORTH FOURTH ART CENTER, ALBUQUERQUE

Let's talk about the evolution of the *Undesirable Elements* project, which you're now working on in New Mexico. You've expanded again, this time to the disabilities community.

It's largely with actors with disabilities, but it's also talking about border issues, because this is, after all, New Mexico. So we're also talking about illegal immigrants and the Mexican border.

They're both border issues, in a way. Why did you put them together?

Most of these shows have a thematic thrust, but within that there are secondary themes. And they all relate in the end: it's always about the issue of undesirability or otherness or outsiderness . . . or *empowerment.* Really, the *Undesirable Elements* project is about empowering voices.

Last time we spoke, you said that you were still finding great artistic challenges despite the project's small budget.

This project wasn't designed to have a big budget, and budgets don't mean anything in relationship to it. But this *production* is certainly a challenge, because I've never worked with a disabled community before. We have a cast member with cerebral palsy, who can only articulate with her head. The technology of her wheelchair allows her to speak electronically. And then there's a cast member who's deaf, and a cast member who's blind . . . so that's a challenge in rehearsal. I'm going to have to improvise a little bit, because there are a lot of unknowns.

But it's been incredibly enlightening, because the disability community is something I know very little about, and it's interesting to learn about that history now, the fact that during the sixties and seventies, they, too, had their revolution.

Did you make an earlier trip to start casting?

This project now has an in-house collaborator, Sara Zatz. She has done two of these productions without me, and she's the administrator for all of them. For the production in Albuquerque, she did the initial interviews, and I'm doing the second interviews. We're sharing the writing as well.

That's allowing you to concentrate on your other work, the multimedia work such as *Cathay: Three Tales of China* [2005].

That's right. Last year, the Kennedy Center mounted the largest per-forming arts festival from China in the history of this country. And we were the only commission as far as performance goes. The Kennedy Center had already presented *Kwaidan,* my first puppet show, and they had seen a puppet troupe in China, and wanted me to collaborate with them. So I went to China and met with the company and agreed to do it.

How did the collaboration go?

Fantastic. I actually said no, twice! I said, "This is too dicey, I've heard some horror stories about what can happen in China." And the only way I would agree to do it was if the production was largely to be made here in the United States, so I could have some control over it, though I would say seventy-five percent of the puppets were made in China.

This group [Shaanxi Folk Art Theater] is from Xian, which is the most historic city in China. It was for a thousand years the capital, the most global city in its day—as much as Rome was, if not more so. It was also the largest city in the world at the time of Rome. So the artists from Xian had something to prove, because Beijing was coming to the festi-val, Shanghai, Hong Kong . . . But I was leery, because they're a tradi-tional puppet company. And I said to them openly: "We should not do this unless you're open to doing something very, very different from what you're used to doing." And they were totally open. It was a real challenge for them, but they were great sports, can-do people. It was an incredibly harmonious cross-cultural project.

How did you pick the three stories you dramatized?

Since this was a festival of China that was happening at the Kennedy Center, and since Americans are relatively ignorant about what China *is,* or *was,* I thought I should do a show that gave them some sense of Chinese history. And where China is today.

And since I was in Xian, the most historic city in China, the first story took place in Xian during the Tang Dynasty, which was one of the highest economic and cultural points in Chinese history. That choice was natural. The second story, about the Second World War, was very close to me personally because my sisters lived through the war in China. And the third story, as I've been going to China since 1993, had to be about the incredible transformation of that nation on every single level—politically, socially, economically.

Time traveling through significant periods to link narratives is a common thread in your work.

Absolutely. I love to travel! I'd travel through time if it were possible, but it's not. It is and it isn't, if you know what I mean. That's an ongoing thing with me, because I'm interested in showing the constants of human behavior over time, and the artifice of human culture over time. It's this anthropological viewpoint that I carry around with me, and which is very much a part of my signature, my vision.

After the Kennedy Center in 2005, *Cathay* went later that year to the New Victory in New York and Seattle Repertory Theatre in 2006. Was there a difference in audience response, given that the New Victory is geared towards young adults, and Seattle Rep is a more traditional venue?

For Seattle Rep, *Cathay* was kind of landmark because it's not the kind of thing they do. But we sold out even before we opened. A lot of theaters don't have the courage to do something new and meanwhile their audiences are aging and the young people aren't coming . . . that's a big problem. The younger folks are doing experimental stuff on a *nickel* and are struggling for obvious reasons. It's difficult for them to reach an audience.

Young audiences are the future, and New Victory is one of the best theaters in the city because they do creative and innovative work. It's not really looked up to because they do "young peoples' work," but I think they're really cutting-edge.

You've always been on the forefront of new technology in theater. Are you branching out in terms of technological innovation?

Cathay did exactly that. We used digital animation in collaboration with shadow puppets. That's a first. It was just amazing. We had built shadow scenery for the show, and then I said, "Can we cut the latticework windows to make the place look a little more shabby?"

And my projections designer said, "Well, I can just photograph that and *digitally* give you the same thing." So he gave me *virtual scenery*. I actually removed all of the scenery (except one piece to which a puppet was tied). It was all virtual, which was *great*. Because as it is, *Cathay* travels in a forty-foot truck!

Usually technology on stage takes a great deal of preproduction work, but it sounds like you did that just in rehearsal?

There's always some improvising in every element in theater anyway. Since I've been working with technology from the very beginning, I know how to plan it, but also remain open to the possibilities that could occur at any moment. I'm working on a show right now [*Cocktail*, about AIDS and the drug industry, Swine Palace at Louisiana State University, April 2007]; even though I'm writing out an entire list for my projection designer of what I want in each of the scenes, there will be a lot of adjustment after she's done some work and while we're there in the theater.

What elements are hardest to adjust once you're in rehearsal?

Set items are the hardest to change, and in terms of the puppetry, you can't change very much with puppets because it's so time-consuming. It's a very peculiar form. First of all, the entire script has to be written ahead of time, because I've already had to determine what size the puppets are, and if I've made a mistake, I'm in trouble. So far, I've been fortunate.

There was one scene I had built into *Cathay* that I took out because of how much stuff there was backstage, and how much time it took to go from one scene to another. You have to be open to cuts while you're working on your feet. I always say you can separate the boys from the men and the girls from the women by seeing who's willing to be ruthless about editing. No matter how good something is, if it's in the way, you've got to get rid of it.

DAVID ESBJORNSON

Along the Continuum

ALTHOUGH DAVID ESBJORNSON FINDS IT hard to speak about directing ("One becomes a director as a way of expressing what one *can't* talk about," he told me), something he *can* talk about (and will, without hesitation) is the importance of theater to American culture. His is an intellectual, cultural-materialist point of view; theater is always negotiating a place along a continuum between education and entertainment.

He knows that continuum well because he's worked comfortably on so many parts of it, from obscure experimental texts to the classics to the entertainment-dominated world of Broadway. Only a few other directors in this book, such as Frank Galati, Michael Mayer and George C. Wolfe, have traversed such disparate territory with comparable ease and success.

Esbjornson's back-and-forth journey between not-for-profit institutional leadership and Broadway work is rare in the field. Both as an artistic director and a freelancer, Esbjornson has built a career that straddles the seemingly impenetrable boundary between challenging work not intended for a mainstream audience, and its opposite. He's maintained that delicate balance, even as many large not-for-profit theaters have reached their tipping points.

Esbjornson was born in Minnesota, where his father was a high school drama teacher, and he went with his family to see his first professional theater production (*The Miser* with Zoe Caldwell and Hume Cronyn) at Minneapolis's legendary Guthrie Theater, the birthplace of the American not-for-profit regional theater movement. Beyond planting the seed for the form and the classics, the experience introduced him to the idea of regional theater as community resource. He graduated in 1975 from a small liberal arts college in Minnesota and headed to San Francisco, where he was a house painter and a window designer. He didn't consider himself a theater artist until he moved to New York and enrolled in the MFA program at New York University, from which he graduated in 1984. Among his classmates were Mayer and Tony Kushner. Kushner was to play a major role in Esbjornson's career; Esbjornson himself was to give a significant boost to Mayer's.

Seven years directing Off Broadway and regionally followed, with some very challenging texts, including Franz Xaver Kroetz's *Farmyard* (New York Theatre Workshop, 1986) and Romulus Linney's *April Snow* (Manhattan Theatre Club, 1988), culminating with the world premiere of Kushner's *Angels in America, Part One: Millennium Approaches* at the Eureka Theatre Company in San Francisco (1991). (*Angels in America, Part Two: Perestroika* was still in development at the time; Esbjornson mounted a workshop production of the piece to go with part one.) Esbjornson's production was hailed at the Eureka, garnering seven Bay Area Critics Circle Awards.

The acclaim boosted his career. Although he didn't direct any of the future incarnations of *Angels,* he has stayed close to Kushner, and installed him on the board of directors of the first major institution he helmed: Off Broadway's Classic Stage Company, a small and dynamic not-for-profit. Esbjornson was hired in 1992 after the departure of artistic director Carey Perloff (who left to lead San Francisco's American Conservatory Theater), and his seven-year tenure there helped generate renewed interest in revisionist and intellectually engaging text-based work with the classics. He did this in part by championing adaptations from writers outside the mainstream: the world premieres of Kushner's adaptation of Pierre Corneille's *The Illusion* (1994), James Magruder's adaptation of Marivaux's *The Triumph of Love* (giving Mayer's directorial career a helping hand in 1994), Ellen McLaughlin's *Iphigenia and Other Daughters* (1995) and Migdalia Cruz's adaptation of Federico García Lorca's *The House of Bernarda Alba*, called *Another Part of the House* (1997). But Esbjornson's tenure at CSC is probably best known for his own spare and provocative takes on Beckett: *Krapp's Last Tape* (1993) and *Endgame* (1995, featuring Kathleen Chalfant as Clov, a casting move that nearly stopped the production due to pressure from Beckett's estate) were among the productions that led to CSC's Lucille Lortel Award for its body of work, awarded just months after his 1998 departure.

But the not-for-profit ground had shifted dramatically during his time with the company. Though artistically invigorating, Esbjornson's work at CSC was not financially successful, and by the time he left the post, he was disillusioned by the changes institutional theaters were being forced to make in the wake of the Reagan years. The virtual disappearance of government funding as a major component of not-for-profit budgets necessitated painful cuts and a new emphasis on audience-friendly programming. Esbjornson felt pressure to paper over his passion for high-minded experimentation with slick marketing, and he had neither the interest nor the aptitude for the tasks that would be required.

So it's ironic that the commercial world rescued him from his malaise and dominated the next part of his career. Although he spent plenty of time in the not-for-profit theater during the seven years between leaving CSC and taking the reins at Seattle Rep—directing the world premiere of *In the Blood* by Suzan-Lori Parks at New York City's Public Theater in 1999, as well as a number of productions at the Guthrie that culminated in a premiere adaptation by Simon Levy of *The Great Gatsby* to open its new theater space in 2006—it was his Broadway career that catapulted him to such well-regarded artistic accomplishment.

Shortly after leaving CSC, Esbjornson helmed the world premieres of plays by legends Arthur Miller *(The Ride Down Mount Morgan* at the Public, 1998) and Edward Albee *(The Play About the Baby* Off Broadway at Century Center for the Performing Arts, 2001). As luck would have it, these playwrights were each about to find themselves on Broadway once again, and Esbjornson was in the right place at the right time to accompany them. Esbjornson helmed the Broadway transfer of *The Ride Down Mount Morgan* in 2000, and his close relationship to Albee after *Baby* led to *The Goat, or Who is Sylvia?* on Broadway in 2002.

Broadway success led him to more commercial, even populist fare: world premieres of Jeffrey Hatcher's adaptation of Mitch Albom's *Tuesdays with Morrie* (at New York Stage and Film, then Off Broadway's Minetta Lane Theatre, 2002) and Neil Simon's *Rose and Walsh* (at the Geffen Playhouse in Los Angeles, 2003); and productions with stars, such as Farrah Fawcett in the ill-fated *Bobbi Boland* (2003, a Broadway production that closed in previews); Sam Waterston in a starry *Much Ado About Nothing* for the Public in Central Park (2004); and Rob Lowe in *A Few Good Men* in London's West End (2005). It's hard to believe that this is the same artist who was best known in the 1990s for his interpretations of Beckett and Kroetz.

Though one might suspect Esbjornson was making a conscious U-turn away from his experimental roots, a closer inspection of this phase of his career suggests otherwise. For the most part, the world premieres he helmed were plays in which now conventional writers were staking out new territory for themselves: consider the time-traveling hallucinations of *The Ride Down Mount Morgan,* or the prospect of an older artist like Neil Simon confronting the imminent end of his career *within* his work. "I'm interested when anybody steps out of his or her mold," he told me, referring specifically to the Simon play. In the cases of both Miller and Albee, Esbjornson's productions reinvigorated their literary reputations.

I first spoke to David for this volume in 2003, in the midst of his successful freelance stretch. Despite his accomplishments, he missed being part of the artistic community he'd found in the not-for-profit world. And so, when Sharon Ott resigned as artistic director of Seattle Repertory Theatre, Esbjornson applied for the job. He was appointed to the post and began work there in 2005, at which point I sat down with him again.

But his time at the Rep was short-lived. Patrons and supporters had trouble rallying around his challenging and occasionally controversial programming, critical response was less than enthusiastic, and Esbjornson's relationship with Seattle's culture and arts scene was fraught. In April 2008, he informed the board he wouldn't be renewing his contract in 2009. Four months later, the board told him he didn't need to stay for the rest of it. The Rep's longtime managing director, Benjamin Moore, told *The Seattle Times,* "David has done a wonderful job here, but it's been quite difficult for him. He tends to be attracted to doing new work, edgier stuff with a darker equation. We've had some wonderful successes, but financial pressures have been great." Seattle's alternative paper, *Seattle Weekly,* was less diplomatic: "Apparently this was one of those breakups where the guy comes home to find all his possessions stacked outside the door."

Seattle's loss has been New York's gain. Though Esbjornson reportedly turned down offers to work back east during his tenure at the Rep, he's not been shy about answering those phone calls now. In fact, it's as if he's never left: a new play Off Broadway (Moira Buffini's *Gabriel* at the Atlantic, 2010); a well-received return engagement with Shakespeare in the Park (*Measure for Measure,* 2011); a crowd-pleasing Broadway show (the acclaimed 2010 revival of Alfred Uhry's *Driving Miss Daisy,* starring James Earl Jones and Vanessa Redgrave); and another Albee triumph, Signature Theatre's revival of *The Lady from Dubuque* in 2012. Esbjornson and the Rep couldn't find themselves in the same place along the continuum between artistic challenge and mainstream approval, but he's mastered that balancing act back in the freelance world. And he's doing so with his customary rigor, curiosity and artistry.

MAY 2003, DAVID ESBJORNSON'S APARTMENT, NEW YORK CITY

You left Classic Stage Company five years ago. What are you looking for now?

I'm looking for new challenges for myself. That includes trying to explore theater for this time, this age. I don't have any answers at this point, just questions. It just seems to me that the values that I grew up with in the theater have changed since I became a professional. I can't identify exactly what has replaced them. I know we've become more entertainment-based, more oriented to the audiences, but I don't know if we know what we're doing with the form. The sense of purpose I remember is gone . . . Maybe it's a false memory, but the theater used to be about *making change*, educating people, stimulating their thinking. Always, of course, entertainment was a component of that. Now, the theater that is the most interesting to me is the theater that seems to challenge present-day thinking, or turns the perspective slightly to the left of center, approaching the world with intellectual curiosity, or bringing up social or political questions. It's harder to get those plays on.

Do you think audiences want something else?

Sometimes. But, I also I think they'll go where we take them. Obviously, audiences are made up of individuals . . . I don't think the audiences that go to see plays on Broadway or in other commercial venues are less informed or less interesting than audiences who see not-for-profit theater. A Broadway audience will give you the first fifteen minutes free. There's something very exciting about that audience.

Is a preview audience on Broadway any more or less helpful than a sub-scriber audience in shaping the work?

You have to continue the process no matter where you are; you have to. But it is very difficult to keep all the voices out in a Broadway situation. It's a bad environment for exploration. People are weighing in a lot sooner; they're judging the results without seeing it over the long haul. The preview period is actually a bit treacherous in a Broadway situation. There are a lot of people other than the audience coming to judge the show. The preview period isn't truly an opportunity to work freely and clearly on the play. That's less true in a not-for-profit or regional the-ater: there, an audience has been groomed to understand the process, and might even come again to see a show later in the run.

Who's doing all that judging in a Broadway situation? Producers, invest-ors and such?

It can come from a lot of sources. It can come from friends who are there to "support" the actors; it can be from internet critics who want to get there before everyone else to determine if it's worthy or not. And I've always felt I needed the preview period to deliver a play. We already don't have enough time to do our work.

And what about the loudest voice of all—the playwright? I'm trying to imagine what it's like, opening a new play by Edward Albee or Arthur Miller on Broadway, all that money at stake, everyone has an opinion, you're just trying to keep it together . . . and in walks the playwright.

Yes, but working with living playwrights is such an amazing experience. They can contextualize their play better than anybody. The actors learn so much by understanding who a writer is. If everybody just opens up their eyes and ears, there's so much to be gained by the playwright being present in the room.

I know a lot of directors say they don't want a playwright to be any-where near the rehearsal room. And of course, there's a point at which it's important for the actors and the director to be alone, to talk freely about the play; it's not always good for a playwright to see that. But most playwrights don't mind giving you that space; they understand enough about the process to know the value of stepping away.

Having worked with major playwrights now, how has your process changed?

I was perhaps more formal in terms of preparation and dramaturgy in approaching a play when I was younger, and the difference now is I just *trust my process.* I go into the rehearsal room without knowing precisely what I'm looking for. Sometimes, I discover what I'm looking for from the actors. Sometimes I'll find out what I'm *not* looking for from some-thing an actor does. But somehow, we all manage to get our needs met. I don't feel compromised by being open in the process; my needs will ultimately take precedence, anyway.

On the other hand, *actors* understand the character from the inside out, or they're trying to. So it's very important to support that process for them, and to listen to what they're learning. I always talk about the actor-director relationship like this: I'm looking at it from the outside, you're looking at it from the inside, and our job is to find what we both feel excited about and comfortable with. I'm not talking about everyone being *happy* necessarily. Because, you know, I've seen *happy* companies where the work is a disaster.

But you want to get to the point where the actors feel confident executing the scenes; they know why they're doing it, and they understand what the impact is supposed to be. *And* they understand how they're playing into the design elements on stage, as opposed to being plopped down in the middle of a design to which they have no connection.

Tech is a part of this process. I think actors should know *why* something is being done, and what it looks like behind them, how their character choices relate to that. It's the job of the director to put those things together.

Can you talk about that process with *The Play About the Baby*, working with the actors on that imagistic and symbolic set? [The actors had two giant alphabet blocks with them on stage, and a mammoth rocking horse and baby carriage suspended above them.]

With that show, the set designer John Arnone (and all of us) took a huge leap of faith in terms of design. When it works, abstract stuff is great fun for the audience, but it's not necessarily all that much fun to rehearse. It's *hard work*; it's detailed, like Beckett. And Edward Albee— when he's writing like that—is the closest we have to Beckett.

With *The Play About the Baby,* you're laying in a subtext that has been invented by you and the company. Obviously there are clues taken from the text, and if Edward hated the interpretation, he would let me know. But it would be different with different actors and different directors. I knew Brian Murray [who played Man]; I'd worked with Brian on *Entertaining Mr. Sloane* and *The Entertainer* [both at CSC in 1996]. And I knew Marian Seldes [who played Woman], not from first-hand experience, but from seeing her work. It was a different kind of work for Brian; Marian had already done Albee's *Three Tall Women*. She had a sense of his world. Both were willing to go down new paths.

So are abstract plays harder than realistic plays?

I don't know that it was harder to do. In some ways there's an expectation for things to come together with a conventional script that maybe there isn't in an abstract play. On the other hand, the logic in an abstract play has to be crystal clear. The movement from moment to moment has to be credible.

For actor and audience?

For the actor, so the audience doesn't feel disengaged. That doesn't mean you add it up for them. The audience has to add it up any way they want—that's what's fun about it. I love how in *The Play About the Baby*, the plot doesn't begin until after intermission. Actually it doesn't begin until after the Man spends another ten or fifteen minutes talking about how intermission "went."

So really, the play—the plot, if you want to call it that—is only a small portion, maybe a quarter of the text. The audience just went with that. And they went with that because what was going on up there was engaging enough and specific enough to hold their interest.

That's got to be hard work for those actors.

Yes, it is hard on the actors. Most of the writers I've worked with create such dense, rich text that there's much for all of us to do. It's difficult for the actors to do all that homework, have it in their heads; it's natural that you reach a point where that subtext can be overwhelming. Obviously in the first performances there's going to be *air*, because there's too much thinking going on. Eventually, you have to get rid of the homework. You continue to trust the homework, and know that the choices that were carefully made will be there for you. That's always the scary point for the actors; but for me, and for the audience, that's when it gets exciting.

How do you push actors out of their comfort zones, so instead of having that happy cast, the actors are working hard?

It is a very specific one-on-one situation with each actor. Some actors are prepared to go to very dark places, but maybe they need to find other choices that balance that, to keep their performances from being too one-note.

So it's more than just "creating an environment of trust."

Yes, it is, but I think you get the best work out of people when there's a sense of respect and trust operating at all times. Whenever people get crazy, it's because they don't feel respected or understood. That has to be the basic component of your environment, of your rehearsal room.

If that's in place, the challenges can happen, naturally. Sometimes it means that you talk to an actor separately—but generally speaking, I don't do that. If I'm speaking, and I'm giving a direction (even if it's of a more conceptual nature, like, "How do we want the audience to view this play?"), having other actors hear what I'm saying is not a bad thing, because they also get to see how that direction is affecting that specific performer. And if I'm right, I'm being proved out in the rehearsal room.

So it's a sort of competition: if one actor has taken a leap, that enables another actor to take a leap—

Right, exactly, but he or she may find that leap uncomfortable. Sometimes you have to let actors be uncomfortable, give it up for a while and come back to it later. Usually, I find that actors will be truthful about their needs. If they disagree . . . well, we *can* disagree, because the room has been set up that way. It's okay for them not to be good soldiers and do everything the way they're told to do. I've heard stories about tyrannical directors with staging concepts that weren't negotiable. I think that if you're connecting personally to actors, and you can make them understand your point of view about a text, and they buy into it and they *trust* you, then they'll try anything in rehearsal. And, if they succeed, then they'll love doing it every night.

How about *The Ride Down Mount Morgan*? How did you help Patrick Stewart become comfortable playing such an unlikable character?

Patrick has a charisma, a kind of warmth to him and familiarity that counterbalanced Lyman's negative qualities. Obviously, if you're playing a flawed character, you want a sense of humanity in him—you don't want a cartoon portrayal. But it's sometimes difficult to get that balance. The biggest struggle will come with a particularly difficult role like Hedda Gabler or Lady Macbeth, when the actress is going to have to accept the fact that there will be portions of the audience that will *dislike her,* rather intensely. And she's going to *feel that!*

That happened with *The Goat, or Who is Sylvia?* There were certain audience members who *could not go there.* Especially in the early days, when we were still trying to calibrate things, there were groups of people who were sending harsh, negative energy toward those actors on stage, not making the distinction that they were characters, not real people—just throwing their vibes at the performance, which the actors, of course, feel.

And then the actors start pulling back?

They sometimes do. That's what separates good actors from great actors. "Great" actors somehow have the courage to do whatever's required. But having said that, I think it's up to the director and the playwright to allow for as much humanity to exist as possible, so those actors have a fighting chance.

Now, there's a form of theater that intends to alienate. But I think we have shifted away from that. I don't know too many people who believe anymore that alienation is the way to handle an audience—nor to talk down to them, preach to them or scold them. But there are times when actors really must have the courage to be seen as grotesque and selfish.

So do you have long conversations with actors before you cast them?

I do.

For example, "You have to understand, Laila: you're playing Hedda Gabler, and that means you've got a certain responsibility"?

Not in that instance [casting Laila Robins as Hedda Gabler at the Guthrie in 2000]. As we were moving to the later stages of that production, in previews, we did have that discussion: about the negativity of the character and the way that she was perceived. We also exploited the tremendous amount of humor inherent in Ibsen, which balanced the more strident and harsh aspects of the character.

In almost all the difficult work I've done, humor has been a major component. It's extremely seductive, and it's full of humanity, and it helps an audience go to difficult places.

I'm thinking of Beckett's *Endgame* at CSC in 1995, and Irma St. Paule coming out of the trash can: "Time for love?"

There's just no substitute for bringing that out in plays. And I'm not talking about cheap humor. I'm talking about humor that comes from pain, humor that has irony, humor that eases the absurdity of the human condition.

The tricky thing about *The Goat* was holding the audience back. There were so many funny lines in the beginning, and you had to hold the humor down, keep the pain inside the situation. When that didn't happen, the performances weren't as effective as when they felt like they came out of something real, difficult and wholly unexpected.

I watched the opening, and that audience went straight to the humor: people were primed for irony, ready to laugh. But I'm sure the audiences before and after were different.

They were all different. Sometimes they were more susceptible, sometimes more sophisticated. Sometimes they'd laugh in all the right places, stop at the right time; at other times, a "rogue" audience would simply not want to go to the darker places. But *The Goat* is such a particular type of play in that regard. It's trying to do many things simultaneously.

So many people think of Beckett as not being funny. They have seen many dry, droll, academic versions of Beckett, and feel that's the way it is. And even some productions of his work that he directed weren't stellar in that regard. But I can't read his plays without seeing a tremendous amount of humor and irony and pathos! It strikes me as odd to put those works on stage without it.

Kathleen Chalfant (top) and Irma St. Paule in Endgame *by Samuel Beckett. Classic Stage Company, 1995. Credit: Gerry Goodstein.*

Looking over your body of work, what else do you see as identifying characteristics? For example, you have a background in visual design, and your productions have a great integrity of design.

I do think it's true: I need to understand the physical world of the play, its environment. That is one thing you *can* prepare for prior to rehearsal. Of course, you can prepare for working with the actors, but there's something about that which is so organic, and needs to have a certain freedom in the moment.

But the impression that I have about a play scenically is usually very strong. It has a lot to do with the feeling of it: is it edgy? Is it rough? Does it need to be fluid? Does it need to have poetry? *How does it need to function?* Will we be moving quickly from one reality to the other? What makes that happen? Do you want to see scenic elements as part of the choreography of transition, or do you want to get the sense that nothing is changing and you're coming up in a new place? Transitions are often the exciting part. That's why it's so much fun to do plays where there are scene shifts, and things are on wheels, and you can constantly be moving, transforming.

The hardest thing for me is doing plays around furniture. It is so much more challenging to try to find creative imagery in that. You become so accustomed to the chairs and the couches, it's almost a cliché.

Now, I did *Who's Afraid of Virginia Woolf?* at the Guthrie [2001], and that's a furniture play . . . but because it was done on that wonderful thrust stage, it pushed the play into a different dimension. You don't necessarily make naturalistic moves on a thrust. You need to create movement that is right for the space, so you end up making a lot of secondary choices that open the play up, shift it out. You might stage it more on the diagonal. All of that helps to create wonderful kinetic energy. The thrust has always been a big influence on me: as you know, CSC was a modified thrust, and I've always tried to use those tools of staging on a thrust in my other work where possible.

What I can't bear is when I go to see plays in which it feels the movement is entirely arbitrary, that a story isn't being told through movement. Again, this isn't something you have to shove in the actors' faces. But if, at the end of the day, the story isn't being told by the staging, then you haven't really done your job as a director.

Have you ever had a design process go absolutely contrary to where you expected it to go?

I honestly don't think so. There are times when I've had to do work too quickly, or when I've worked on a second production of the play and got to change aspects of the design I wasn't happy with. But no. I know there are directors who always design as they work, like Richard Foreman: all the aspects of the design are critical, and he must have it just the way he sees it. If changes are needed, he's going to make them. I agree that it's my prerogative to make changes if necessary. But seldom has it gotten to the point where I had to override the designer.

I'm always amazed when a director says, "The design wasn't that good; that was one of my problems." Well, if the design wasn't good, why did you accept it? It's your job to design as a director, just as it's your job to understand what an actor is thinking from moment to moment in a scene. It's all your responsibility.

But if you're working with wonderful, talented people, you must listen to their input; you must fold their creativity and their vision into the production. You evolve the production together, *in the time you have*.

That's why American directors are constantly envying their European counterparts. They're jealous of the fact that Europeans get an enormous amount of time in discovery, allowing them make all sorts of changes after they have been tested in front of an audience. Naturally, those productions can be pretty stellar, because they've worked out all the bumps along the way. American directors have to make choices hard and fast, and that's why many directors work with the same set of designers, and even actors, as often as they can.

With a lighting designer, I'm painting pictures in the theater. That's a live and active thing that happens during tech. And, for me, sound always comes in rehearsal after I've gotten a sense of what the play's about, what the tone is. With sound, you want to have the ability to shift and change, have a number of choices, set your soundscape as part of the preview period. The same with lighting, though visually you've always got to understand how lighting is going to affect the scenic elements; the flow of it, the cueing of it, is better done once the production has found its own rhythm. Good lighting designers will support that rhythm. For me, lighting is the final touch.

So you have a lot of design conferences with set and costumes early on?

Yes, and I always involve the lighting designer in a conceptual discussion of the scenic design, so that he or she can give input about what we're planning.

How many meetings do you have with a set designer before a show?

It depends on the show, but at least half a dozen.

The costume designer is also a major influence, not only with design, but in terms of creating characters. I always try to find costume designers who have tremendous empathy for actors and their process. The costume designer is an important dramaturg, and a link to the actor; actors will express things to him or her about their physical appearance, insecurities that are important for a director to understand. You always want actors to feel terrific in whatever they're wearing—and sometimes when you get into very low-budget situations, it's challenging. Nobody understands that modern dress is the most difficult thing to do! Everyone thinks, "All you have to do is go out and buy it at the store!" Well, nothing's more difficult than buying something that's precisely right, in the right time of year, that an actor feels absolutely comfortable in. Keeping in mind that *everybody* has an opinion about a modern costume, and how it looks on a particular actor and whether it's right for the play. I guess because we all shop! It's also twice as difficult to control the palette in modern dress because you're limited to what you can *find*. You can draw it, but unless it's being made, you can't have that sort of full, perfectly rendered world that you have when everything is created in a costume shop.

Talk to me more about building character with actors.

Again, I feel it's important to do that mostly on your feet. You can talk conceptually for days and never even get close to the truth of a character, or the truth of a play. Some people are really good at talking about plays; they don't always make the best directors. I think there's something absolutely essential about getting in there, rolling up your sleeves and figuring it out. And until you do that, until you're actually going through it, I don't think it makes a lot of sense to talk about a character.

Sometimes actors want to have a conversation before rehearsal starts, so they'll call you at home and you'll have a conversation. Or maybe you're trying to get an actor to *do* a play, and he needs to feel like he understands enough about what you're going to do, how you're going to approach it, to be comfortable signing on. But most of the time, we get in the room, we read the play, we talk to the playwright—or, if it's not a living playwright, we present the dramaturgy, the designs, the research we've assembled. It's about touching all the things that you know before you begin the process.

You cast that actor because they've brought a certain something to the role that has captured your imagination. So you want to support *that*. That's how you put together your company: this person in contrast to that person. What you don't want is for them to *meld* and become less interesting or less clear; yet at the same time, you want them all to be in the same play, the same world. That's one of the most challenging things for the director, how to find a way to take actors from completely different backgrounds and training, and get them into the same place stylistically. It's very exciting when that happens, because you realize we all bring a little something different to the work. It's celebrating the fact that we arrive at a common goal through a variety of paths. What a wonderful metaphor for how I wish the world worked.

Can you give me an example of a moment you created in rehearsal of which you're particularly proud?

There are moments in *Hedda Gabler* when Ibsen almost tips into a surreal place; or at least I interpreted Ibsen as being able to support a kind of surrealism. So I created a world that was kind of ghostly. There were moments that were operatic, like when she burned the manuscript: this very high, powerful music played, and Hedda, with her face in the fire, arched her back in ecstasy. It was a beautiful ending to the first act.

I structured the play differently, changed the act breaks. It was a dramaturgical choice, making the "Lovborg section" the center of the event. And at the end, after Hedda shoots herself, for the last little coda, just three or four lines: I moved those into a completely abstract place. I put all the characters in pools of light, and they said their lines in separate parts of the stage. The door blew open, and a ton of yellow leaves blew onto the stage around their feet.

That play would break me on certain days. And then other days I'd think, "Yeah, I got it!" It was one of the hardest rehearsal processes I've been through. People criticize melodrama; but what is melodrama other than extreme activities concentrated in a short period of time? And that happens all the time! Look at the World Trade Center tragedy . . . To me, melodrama is *not false*. It happens in life constantly.

I have favorite moments from *Mount Morgan,* too. There's a moment—when everything just floats and falls away, and we come back to the hospital for the final time—that just felt beautiful. In *Summer and Smoke* [Guthrie, 1999], some of the transitions were magical; I used all the actors in every transition, blending the two households. There was some choreography in that production that I was very proud of. A lot of the work I feel strongest about was for productions at CSC— *Iphigenia and Other Daughters, Entertaining Mr. Sloane*, the Beckett work—and also at the Guthrie. I think to some extent it's because they are places that I call home.

Going back to Hedda burning the manuscript: when did you know the moment would happen that way?

I was trying to decide what burning that manuscript was like for Hedda. And I thought it must contain *ecstasy*. Because, in her psychology, she has come to a point where that kind of destruction turns her on; she feels dead to herself and this act gives her a feeling of life. It's such a twisted psychological moment, but it felt absolutely right after we tried it.

It was planned design-wise only in this sense: we knew we wanted to grow the light. Ken Posner was doing the lights, and we didn't know how far it would go—whether it would even be perceptible. When we put the music in, we really wondered if we were going too far. And then we decided to go the distance. So we grew the light until she was completely immersed in firelight. The rest of the light on stage went down; the music swelled; and when Hedda came to a high point, we pulled everything out. It had that sort of chill up the back of the neck effect.

And did you just say, "Laila, arch your back"?

No, Laila understood instinctively what the moment was. She's an actress who, if you explain what you're going for, will try to help you get there. She's not afraid of that.

You have to possess a fearlessness, and tremendous instinct, to be a good actor. What must you have to be a good director?

I think you need to be intelligent. And you have to have a fairly clear political viewpoint.

Why?

Because we don't do theater in a vacuum. We have to be aware of what's going on around us. You can say a lot with a play.

I often think that young people feel the political concept for a play is its overarching idea. It can be. But it can also be a series of smaller choices that happen all the way through the play, that at the end form a political or social viewpoint. It may be the way a female character is handled that is less conventional, or a sexist or racist attitude that is slowly brought to light by smaller actions . . . or a production can put the play in a historical context that helps to illuminate its politics.

Directors *always* put themselves on the stage. You can never separate the production from the director. The more abstract the production, the more you see the director. You can't hide behind your actors, and you can't hide behind the text, because you've been completely involved in every aspect of those choices. There's a personality, there's a feeling that the production has; the kinetic energy, the passion . . . the personality of the director is always there. And to any other director, it's quite perceptible.

You know I'm going to ask: what's your personality on stage?

No, let's get back to the other question! You need to have a brain, you need to have a heart. And you can't be timid about using either. I do think that without providing context, making choices that relate to the world, you're being somewhat irresponsible to the craft.

Speaking of politics: you've gone from introducing the world to perhaps the most radical political voice of our generation—Tony Kushner—to introducing the world to the latest play by Neil Simon, a man generally regarded as the least radical political voice of our time. Is there a point at which you just want to take the work that pays? Or is there something redemptive about working on that Simon play? You've said to me before, "You don't find the work, it finds you." So tell me why Mitch Albom, Neil Simon and *Bobbi Boland* are the works that are finding you now.

Why am I doing this kind of stuff, you mean?

Let's talk about *Tuesdays with Morrie* as an example. I think what we managed to achieve with that play was an evening that allowed people to explore, without being maudlin or cloying, death and dying. And I did that play because I think people need to be able to engage with that subject. And they need to do it in a life-affirming way.

Does it have resonances of commercial exploitation? Yes, there's no doubt about it. And we fought that the entire time we were working on it. We were very aware that the book was a best seller, and that this play might make money for people, maybe even for us. That was the least interesting part of it for me.

What we were interested in was creating an event in which people felt like they were truly meeting Morrie. We needed a highly skilled actor of exactly the right age, who had many of the qualities that Morrie Schwartz had, and we found him in Alvin Epstein. We also tried to find ways in which the play moved with a kind of "edge" and difficulty between the two men as their relationship grows. The story isn't all a walk in the park. It is full of conflict—characters disagreeing about things and learning something from each other. Morrie is not a saint in this production; he was somebody who occasionally said things that were insensitive.

It was hard-won to get to the point where the play wasn't senti-mental; the audience could both laugh and cry at the end, and feel that contradiction. So many people were touched by the production, and *needed* that catharsis, so it felt completely relevant for me.

It's not dissimilar to the Neil Simon play, *Rose and Walsh*. Neil was trying to write a play that's different from other plays he's written. He was writing a play about a creative person, a writer coming to the end of

Mercedes Ruehl, Bill Pullman and Jeffrey Carlson in The Goat, or Who Is Sylvia? *by Edward Albee. Broadway, 2002. Credit: Carol Rosegg.*

her life. The central character is trying to face the fact that her skills are diminishing, and she's trying to prepare for the inevitable.

I thought, "Well, if he wants to make this departure from his comedy writing, and he wants me to do it, I'm there. I'm going to have that experience." Because Neil has an ability, a craft, that is amazing. Some of the best comedies have been written by this guy—extraordinary plays, tight plays that work beautifully.

I'm interested when anybody steps out of his or her mold. It's something I've always wanted to be able to do as a director. I don't want to be labeled. I want to be able to go from classical material to new plays—to new forms. I think almost every director has that wish, just like actors don't want to be typecast. To support that desire for a writer is an interesting adventure. Whether it works, whether it's as profound as Arthur Miller's plays, is not a question I'm trying to answer now. I'm just trying to go through the process of helping each play live. There's time for judgment later.

I've taken jobs in situations where I've said, "Oh, I'll have to leave town, I don't want to do that," and then I've had an incredible experience that taught me something. Two people in the profession probably saw the show, but I got something out of it that was so important that I've just given up trying to make judgment calls. I try to find out if there's some integrity in what is being attempted—emotionally, politically. And it's not like any of the stuff I've done in commercial venues has been typical; it's been Albee and Miller.

I don't think anyone would accuse you of selling out—

That's not what I'm paranoid about. I don't know if I've ever had that experience, the *true commercial play*. Directing Neil Simon doesn't mean I'm in that camp. I think I'm actually trying to negotiate a more difficult and more specific kind of work.

A lot of people would feel working with Neil Simon on a new play is the ne plus ultra of what being a director is.

That may be, and there are other people who are going to feel that way about Arthur Miller, and other people are going to feel that about Suzan-Lori Parks. As long as I can continue to work with people like Tony Kushner and Suzan-Lori, as long as that's part of the mix, I'm going to be happy. I want to move back and forth among not only genres and venues, but also among younger and older voices.

Now, working with some of these more established writers is a thrill in and of itself, so you have to make sure to say, "Is it the thrill I'm excited about, or is it something about the work?" And I've been lucky in that I haven't had to make that distinction. I haven't had to say, "Okay, I'll do this because it'll be good for my career." I think I can safely say that there's always been something of great interest to me—in the way the play is designed, or how it moves, or what it's trying to say.

You're lucky, because so much of the not-for-profit world has become cautious in producing risky work.

Why is there such caution? I think it just costs so much to put on plays. It's pretty simple. It costs too much to go to them, to recoup—all those dumb, obvious factors having to do with economics. There's a dwindling audience. That's what producers are dealing with, whether they're not-for-profit or commercial. It's more acute for commercial producers because they don't have a loyal subscriber base.

But the caution comes from the fact that producers need a lot of people to like and accept the work. That means a well-known play with stars—and what constitutes a star is limited. Even that is beginning to fall apart. You talk about very well-known actors, and the conversations now are, "Yeah, but I don't know if they're box office. Are they *enough* to bring an audience in?" I don't know how people determine that, but they do all the time.

So the caution is understandable, but if something has risk and integrity in it, there is a portion of the audience that will respond to it. Sometimes the least likely things turn out to be the biggest hits—like *Urinetown* and *Metamorphoses* and *The Goat*.

As long as there are those kinds of projects happening, as long as not-for-profits are taking ideas and putting them into the commercial mix, as long as we get this cross-fertilization going . . . I think that's probably the most exciting trend we can cultivate now. As long as we can keep doing that, I think there's some hope for the theater to survive.

It seems that not-for-profit culture, by trying to reduce risk, is making the situation worse. It's conditioning the audience to avoid risk.

I think you're stating the crisis that American theater is in, to some extent. You just have to take a deep breath and risk it if you want to be vital. In smaller theaters, it's a little bit easier to do that. You're living a little precariously anyway; certainly that was true at CSC. We did some things that other places might not do—it was part of the mission of the theater, and helped us stand apart.

But CSC to some extent was as much for the theater community as it was for the audience at large. The theater community knew the plays that we were adapting; it was interested in the literature being drama-tized. Or it liked the fact that certain plays were getting a newer and slightly off-center interpretation. That may be entirely valid for a the-ater to be that for a community—a place where "artistic juices" can start to flow. A place like CSC may help artists inform their work, or be a place of departure that generates a good discussion.

Do you think the not-for-profit world takes itself too seriously?

I don't know. I come out of that world, so it's very hard to be objective. Regional theaters were attempting to do something that was very important. They were trying to say that there are other values, other things to celebrate than box office. There are works that should be seen and experienced by people, but for that to happen, it requires subsidy.

I watched not-for-profit funding get cut while I was at the helm at CSC. The culture shifted so quickly, and it was such a philosophical shift that it was hard to know how to respond except to stick with the values I understood. I still want those values to be part of my work, and I expect other artists to do the same thing. But there's a pragmatic side of me that recognizes I can't expect everyone to think exactly like me.

Some situations will be closer to your liking; others will not. It's important to infuse your projects with whatever you value. That has to do with the way you work with people, the way you treat them; it deals with process and making sure that you are at the center of it.

Do I skirt the issue too much?

I think you're giving an honest answer.

I just don't know where we are in the world right now.

As an artistic community, we've become incredibly middle class. We want the *jobs*, we want the paychecks, we want all of those things. Probably the most radical and effective artists live outside the system. If you're really going to be politically effective, you can't be co-opted. And yet there isn't anybody in this country who doesn't seem to get co-opted.

You can't keep going, year after year, without some kind of support. I remember going in front of the committee when I applied for my grant [the NEA/TCG Career Development Program for Theatre Directors in 1989], and they said, "You've done six plays; that's a tremendous amount of work for a single year. How much did you make? You must have done very well." I added it all up, and it came to $8,500. And that was for six productions, during which I was really only able to do my day job sporadically. So when I got the support of that grant, I felt like I had been liberated. It wasn't really that much money. But combined with one good regional theater gig, it put my salary over $20,000 that year. I thought I'd died and gone to heaven! I was a working theater director for the first time in my life.

We're also not spending a great deal of time doing the kind of theater that questions the establishment. Open questioning doesn't seem part of our world anymore. Perhaps because the politics are so complex and difficult to understand.

That's part of why Tony Kushner is so successful: he has the natural ability, the political sensibility, to pull things apart and make sense of them! I think most of us are just reeling with all the complexities and uncertainty of the world. There aren't that many writers who can help create clarity anymore.

I guess what I'm trying to say is that *overtly political* work wouldn't necessarily be supported now. Maybe it will be left to the independently wealthy to bring about a new generation of political directors. How's that for irony?

Time to answer: what is your personality on stage?

I don't know. I'm always uncomfortable, as a midwesterner, talking about myself in that way. I think that one becomes a director as a way of expressing what one *can't* talk about, or discovering something about what one doesn't know. What is so wonderful about the craft is that it's always a bit of an enigma. When you're channeling something beyond you, that's when it's *great*, that's when you feel it's almost not you doing the job. There's something else in the room helping you do it and understand it.

But, *forced* to speak about it, I would say that I hope my work contains a kind of intelligence in terms of the choices; that it is passionate or cool, depending on the world. I like to think that the personality of the text has been responded to fully, and that there's a quiet political expressiveness beneath it. And I want it to be as visually interesting as possible, and always theatrical.

JUNE 2005, SEATTLE REPERTORY THEATRE, SEATTLE

First, the big and obvious question: when you left Classic Stage Company in 1998, you were in despair about the not-for-profit world because values had changed so much. You had found a home on Broadway. Now you're back in not-for-profit world, at the helm of Seattle Rep. What gives?

Uh-oh! What did I say last time? [laughs] I guess I'm longing for a different kind of community and a different kind of dialogue.

What Seattle Rep offers me is an opportunity to blend the two things together. This theater is interested in maintaining a national profile, and in order to do that, you have to move some things around: you have to originate some work, and you have to participate in a national and international landscape. And it struck me as maybe the best combination of the commercial world and the not-for-profit world.

The first time I interviewed you, for *American Theatre* [July/August 2000] you were already talking about the not-for-profit world changing, and you feared you didn't have the tools for that new landscape. It looks like you've gotten the tools.

One tool you picked up seems to be a network of connections in many different places. In your first season at the Rep, you've got one project heading to Broadway [Neil Simon's *Rewrites*, which was later postponed], one to the New Victory [*Cathay: Three Tales of Darkness* by Ping Chong], and two world premieres [*Purgatorio* by Ariel Dorfman and *Restoration Comedy* by Amy Freed], which you hope to send along the regional theater circuit.

I guess my philosophy has broadened since earlier days. I believe in eclecticism, rather than having an overriding aesthetic that shapes everything at the theater. I feel like it's the best way to make sure that everyone has a place at the table. That doesn't mean there can't be a certain signal sent to the audience that this theater is being run by a particular person. You can find common denominators in people's work and in the things they choose to produce. I would like to think that work I produce would always have very high acting values, and other essential elements that eventually become a signature.

But in terms of the choice of plays and the artists, the question is this: how do you support the community that you live in, and at the same time move into the national or international arena? That's the tricky part, and you don't try to do everything all the time. If you feel that supporting the immediate community is the thing that's going to feed you at that particular moment, that's what you do. Maybe next year, the thing that will feed you will be something from Thailand, or a brilliant British play that somehow puts everything into focus. Then you *must* produce it because it becomes too important not to.

Talk to me more about the difference between CSC, which functions as a niche institution, and Seattle Rep. Now you're saying, "We have no niche; we're sharing the best of what we know."

What I hope, starting out, is that maybe this theater will become defined by a set of values or choices that, over time, will become clear. That it will have as specific a profile as a place like CSC, but in another way. That may be exactly what's needed here. When I say I want diversity, that doesn't mean without a philosophical center. You're not just the marketplace. You have to stand for something.

Because being a flagship institution carries different responsibilities?

The term flagship makes me nervous; I worry sometimes about large organizations usurping other theaters. Because if you really do well, then the need for those smaller theaters is a little bit less! If you can bring in programming that's adventuresome, that had been marginalized, how does that affect the small theater down the road that exists simply for that? All over the country you can see that there's a lot of concern from smaller theaters about the big theaters in town, and what that does to their identities. Having run a small theater, I want to be sensitive to that.

But let's face it: the far more common situation at large institutions is that their bulk requires that they placate the audience as much as possible, because they can't afford to offend anyone.

This is all before me, so I don't know to what extent that will be required. If people don't buy the programming, then either I have to change their minds, or I have to give them more of what I think they want, or I have to leave.

I frustrate people because I won't tell them what I'm planning. A couple of journalists have asked, "Who are you going to bring in?" And I tell them, "I don't know; we'll have to wait and see." And it drives them crazy, but I don't understand how you can know what you're going to do next year. Theater has to be as close to an immediate response as it can be.

Even to put together a *season* is more formal than I'm comfortable with! Do I know that [Heather Raffo's] *Nine Parts of Desire* next March is going to be the most vital thing in Seattle when it has already had a New York run? Maybe, maybe not. It may have lost some of its cachet. On the other hand, does it feel important to do this play in this community? Yes. It's freaky to think that it's almost a year away. But there's no avoiding that; it goes with the territory. When you're freelancing, someone calls you, and you say, "Hey, that's great, let's go!" And you're in rehearsal in a couple of months. You can make that decision for yourself. The infrastructure of these places can get in the way of that immediacy.

What have you learned about directing in the past five years that you'll bring to directing here, at this institution?

If you're presenting a particularly difficult piece, or if there is something complex about the approach, it may obligate you to contextualize more. You rarely want your audience to feel lost. I'm not saying any of this is easy to calibrate, but we do have an obligation to hook into these emotions, the heart of our audience—not only the intellect. That doesn't mean resorting to sentimentality, nor does it mean condescending to them. People need a way into challenging material and a connection to what they're seeing on stage.

There are systematic political efforts at work to "dumb down" our culture. These efforts have gone a long way to damaging intellectual curiosity and making our job more difficult. And we may have unwittingly helped their cause a bit. I think we're still in recovery from what is generally viewed as a kind of theater snobbery: "You should participate in what we're doing here because it's good for you, and if you don't understand or relate to it there must be something wrong with you."

It's a fine line we walk in the theater. Our job is essentially to challenge. So we seduce our audience and push them around a little, piss them off and at the same time we actually need their approval to stay in business.

Is the key to finding that approval by creating work that's emotionally accessible?

I wouldn't say that, but I think there has to be a way for the audience to come into a piece, whatever it is. Sometimes it's about an emotional connection or pathos in the acting; sometimes it's a beautiful and evocative image that touches somebody deeply. You take a scene like the sleigh ride in *Peer Gynt*: what's more powerful, what's said, or the image? You can't really separate them. The best theater gives you both.

I don't dismiss purely visual art—you can be moved by dance without a word. There is something about gesture, how it's articulated, that is extremely powerful if it's done well. But that's the beauty of theater: you get the movement, the scenery, the text; you get to use all the disciplines wrapped into one. All the good stuff comes down to a connection to the audience: that they don't feel outside it, but brought into it. And we have to look at that as technicians, very harshly. Not, "Is this satisfying me?" but, "Is this satisfying *them*, or *have I gotten to them*?"

You've had great relationships with writers, and some not as good. What have you learned as a director from the difficult relationships?

I guess what I've learned is that it's really important to be clear that *you want the same thing.* It's only when you step into a relationship not knowing somebody . . . but . . . I have to contradict that by saying I have gained so much by jumping into things with new writers I didn't know or situations that I didn't completely understand. Sometimes, just as in life, you run up against someone you shouldn't go out on a date with. But you never know what will come out of a relationship.

OSKAR EUSTIS

Dramaturg at the Center of It All

BETWEEN MY FIRST AND SECOND interviews with him in 2003 and 2005, Oskar Eustis was appointed to perhaps the most powerful theater post in the country, the artistic directorship of New York City's Public Theater. As the fourth leader of this singular American institution, Eustis brings a distinct set of strengths to the high-profile position. Joseph Papp, the Public's founder, may have been this country's greatest producer, but as a director, he rated far below his successors—JoAnne Akalaitis and George C. Wolfe. Eustis's primary strength is neither producing nor directing (though he is prodigiously good at both), but dramaturgy—the art and science of new-play development.

Eustis has been a producer for nearly two decades, and has directed dozens of productions at major theaters all across the country; but as a new-play dramaturg, he has shepherded from page to stage hundreds of works by some of the country's (and the world's) greatest writers. Any given week, even as he runs one of the country's thorniest institutions, you can catch him traveling across the country, stopping in Chicago, L.A. or San Francisco to give his two cents on a reading or workshop to a writer whose trust he's earned on the theatrical battlefield. For every world premiere he's directed, there are twenty more that he's midwifed into existence, quietly, away from the spotlight.

The history of stand-alone dramaturgy is even briefer than that of play directing, which most scholars trace back to 1874, when the Duke of Saxe-Meiningen created an intensive rehearsal period to work with his touring troupe of actors. While actors, directors and producers have long provided their input to playwrights in the composition and fine-tuning of a playscript, dramaturgy as a separate function only began to emerge nationally in the last thirty or forty years. As regional theaters in the 1970s became more interested in new-play development, staff positions were added to address the need. Today, Literary Managers and Dramaturgs of the Americas boasts a membership of around five hundred.

Eustis's dramaturgical career began in 1980 at San Francisco's Eureka Theatre, a highly political company that for much of its life was run as a collective. He muscled his way into a volunteer position that put him at the center of the artistic action, working under artistic directors Richard E. T. White and Tony Taccone. Starting off as an assistant director, he quickly found himself drawn to visiting playwrights such as Caryl Churchill and David Edgar. One visitor, playwright and director Emily Mann, shifted his path just enough to turn him into a dramaturg. Mann came to the Eureka in 1981 with her play *Still Life*, and the two fed off each other's passion for theater as an instrument of social change. (On their own, each of them is a megawatt personality; together, my advice to a bystander would be simple: duck and cover.) Eustis commissioned Mann to write a play about the murder of San Francisco Mayor George Moscone and Supervisor Harvey Milk. The two worked tirelessly as writer and dramaturg, lugging suitcases of trial transcripts across the country for three years, until finally the play became Mann's celebrated *Execution of Justice*. Eustis directed the play's 1984 world premiere at the Humana Festival at Actors Theatre of Louisville in Kentucky.

During his nine-year tenure at the Eureka, which included three years as artistic director, he built his reputation for new-play development—and talent-spotting. Eustis perhaps remains best-known for commissioning Tony Kushner's *Angels in America*, and working with the playwright as a dramaturg to develop it. As he told *American Theatre* magazine in December 2003:

> When it came time for me to leave the Eureka, Gordon David-son asked me to come to the Mark Taper Forum in Los Angeles. I gave him the most recent draft of the first two acts of *Millennium Approaches* [*Angels in America, Part One*] and said, "My company has fallen apart, my father has died, socialism has failed disastrously, I don't know what I believe in, but I believe in this play. If you love it, I'll come to your theater." Gordon loved it, and I moved to Los Angeles.

Eustis stayed at the Taper as resident director, director of new-play development and then associate artistic director until 1994; while there, he directed the first workshop of *Millennium* and, with Taccone, codirected the world premiere of the full two-part *Angels*. (Who really directed the "premiere" is a somewhat contested crown: David Esbjornson gave Part One its premiere and Part Two its first staged reading—while the Broadway premiere and national tour were directed, respectively, by George C. Wolfe and Michael Mayer.) Kushner's work went through so many workshops and versions that, as Taccone told Ellen McLaughlin in *American Theatre* (September 2006), "When a phenomenon like *Angels* happens, everyone feels that they own a piece of it, or it owns a piece of you.") In 1994, Eustis was tapped to lead one of the country's foremost ensemble-based regional theaters, Trinity Repertory Company in Providence, Rhode Island.

In a successful decade at Trinity Rep, Eustis left his mark on educational theater as well. He spearheaded the creation of a major partnership between the theater and Brown University, then home to fellow new-play midwife Paula Vogel (whose MFA program generated dozens of significant new American playwrights such as Nilo Cruz and Sarah Ruhl). Complementing Vogel's program, the Brown University/Trinity Rep Consortium offered MFA degrees in acting and directing, along with a doctorate in theater and performance studies. Since its formation in 2001, the Consortium has become one of the most competitive MFA programs in the nation.

Notwithstanding two decades as a producer, director and educator, Eustis is still best regarded for his new-play wizardry. In addition to *Execution of Justice* and *Angels* he's developed and directed world premieres by heavyweights including David Henry Hwang, Suzan-Lori Parks, Philip Kan Gotanda, Ellen McLaughlin and Eduardo Machado. Even today, Mann and Kushner continue to rely on Eustis's dramaturgy skills in both formal and informal ways. As Kushner told Rebecca Mead for a 2010 *New Yorker* article, "I can't imagine writing anything and not immediately thinking, 'I have to show this to Oskar, and see if it is any good or not.'"

So why would the Public Theater, which began life as the Shakespeare Workshop, and which is now most popularly identified with Shakespeare in the Park and blockbuster directing, hire a new-play dramaturg to run the place?

When the Public moved into the former Astor Library on Lafayette Street in 1967, Papp suddenly had five theaters to fill—and one can only do so much Shakespeare. The legendary producer began presenting new plays to fill his spaces, and the theater found itself at the forefront of a new movement in American not-for-profit theater. Papp produced some of the most important new plays of the 1960s, 1970s and 1980s—among them *Hair* (which Eustis revived for a concert version at the Delacorte in 2008; it moved to Broadway the following year), *A Chorus Line, Streamers, That Championship Season* and *Sticks and Bones*. Wolfe added significantly to Papp's track record, bringing to Broadway the Public Theater productions of *Topdog/Underdog, Bring in 'Da Noise, Bring in 'Da Funk* and *The Ride Down Mount Morgan*.

But when Wolfe announced he was leaving the Public in 2004, the theater's once-mighty endowment of almost $40 million had been reduced to less than half its size. And Eustis—who had managed to double Trinity Rep's operating budget and increase its subscription base during his tenure there—looked like an excellent candidate. He was selected after an extensive nine-month search to lead the Public in the new century.

At the Public, Eustis has been smart enough to play to his strengths, embracing its core mission as a home for American artists as well as all New York audiences. He has directed rarely since coming to that theater, choosing instead to devote his energies to leading the institution, fostering an educational tie-in with New York University, and nurturing exciting new plays. He's also built a number of new programs: the Emerging Writers Group; the incorporation of Mark Russell's influential Under the Radar Festival; and the Musical Theater Initiative.

Ironically, Eustis began his theatrical career as a lefty, anti-establishment iconoclast. As a child of the 1970s growing up in Minnesota, he'd encountered a traveling group of experimental theaters. When he moved to New York in 1975, he reconnected with many from that group through NYU's new Experimental Theatre Wing. Eustis embraced the countercultural life, sleeping in the Performing Garage, and talking philosophy into the wee hours with his classmates. Right out of NYU he cofounded a company with a friend called Red Wing, the mission of which seemed to be to produce any kind of theater that would provoke, anger or mystify a traditional theater audience—not that any of them came.

Red Wing spent two years abroad impressing the Swiss avant-garde with its American-bred version and gained a certain bad-boy notoriety. Eustis wasn't yet twenty, but he was adept at producing work fashioned from what even he calls a "breathtaking" self-referential narcissism.

How did this supercilious avant-gardist turn into the keeper of the institutional flame? Eustis sees his move to the Taper as the moment that changed how he viewed the impact he could have as an artist and theater professional. "The Eureka was one of those hot little places devoted to the idea that you could somehow institutionalize the counterculture, and my leaving to go to the Mark Taper was really a rejection of that thesis," he told *Brown Alumni Magazine* in 2003. "It became clear to me that the most exciting battleground was going to be in trying to infiltrate major institutions to have an impact."

As Eustis has transitioned into the establishment he once rejected, he has taken the skills he learned as a dramaturg along the way, as well as his political and intellectual commitment. Eustis directs with precision, surgically examining the text for clues, and leading his actors toward what he's found in the operation. On stage the work is exceedingly clear, direct and often quite powerful. While he readily admits he's not the kind of director who creates visual metaphors with ease, he is the kind of director who can take a complicated new play—whether it's *Angels in America* or Paula Vogel's *The Long Christmas Ride Home*—and give it a production that captures an audience's imagination. When a new play fails, even if it's the fault of the director, the playwright gets the negative reviews. It is to Eustis's credit that the new plays he works on get his writers good ones.

JUNE 2003, THEATRE COMMUNICATIONS GROUP NATIONAL CONFERENCE, MILWAUKEE

Talk to me about what got you interested in theater.

I started getting serious about the theater through my involvement in the Children's Theatre Company in Minneapolis—an extraordinary company under John Clark Donahue, who founded the place and turned it into a major force. I acted there as a preteen-ager.

Another important influence was CETA: the Comprehensive Employment and Training Act (which was gutted by Reagan in the 1980s). I was one of the last people to get a CETA job; I think I was fourteen at the time. It was a job at the Pillsbury-Waite settlement house in Minneapolis, designed to create children's theater and tour it to public schools, and then teach workshops. We called it the Story Lorry, and the title was odd even then!

But the real reason I ended up in the theater was the fact that theater was the first and the only place I felt entirely at home. I was an extremely emotional, somewhat traumatized-by-my-childhood-in-Minnesota kid . . . and everything you've heard about Minnesota is true. I was too loud, I cried way too easily, I *laughed* too loudly and too easily, and I always felt somewhat out of step. I was very bright, but I didn't feel like I fit in anywhere. I wanted to be a ball player so badly, but I couldn't hit a curveball to save my life.

What I found in the theater was a place where everything I was interested in—not just intellectually, but also emotionally, socially—

everything I cared about had a place. To this day that remains true: I know of no other profession that by its very nature is so all-embracing. As Chekhov proves, nothing human is alien to it. And if you can't find a natural fit for it in the theater ... that's your challenge, to figure out how anything you're interested in can be made into theater. Because the theater *wants* that, the theater wants to be used in that way.

On a cruder social level, I found lots of people like me in the theater, lots of other people who were extremely precocious and emotional. (Some of them were bright, some of them weren't very bright ... but they were all *terribly present*.) And that feeling of it being all right to be "other" ... I loved comic books as a kid. And that's the ur-story in every comic book: "Once there was a kid who was *different,* and that difference made him hated and despised by his peers, but really, it's because that difference was a *special power* ..." That's what we long for as kids: to believe somehow that our difference, the same thing that other people don't like about us, is actually a source of strength. And the theater is the one place where other people really believe that. By the time I was thirteen or fourteen, I felt *home* in the theater, and I never looked back.

The other thing that happened is that I got my mind blown by a Bunch of Experimental Theaters of New York, Inc. It was an organization that included Mabou Mines, Richard Foreman's Ontological-Hysteric Theater, the Performance Group, the Manhattan Project: they had banded together, and I encountered these folks when they toured to Minneapolis at the Walker Art Center along with the Iowa Theater Lab, a neo-Grotowskian theater.

When I was sixteen, I got out of high school and ran away from home, and ended up at a new theater festival in Ann Arbor, Michigan. I was just sleeping in the woods, and—

You really ran away from home?

I mean, my parents were okay with it! I graduated high school, I wasn't going to college, so I "ran away" from home. They skipped grades for kids in my community; they didn't know then what they know now about the psychological damage!

So I was sleeping in the woods, and going to these experimental theater performances, and the one that most people were talking about was the Living Theatre. Its members had come back to the States; they were living in Pittsburgh, and they were performing something from a cycle called *The Legacy of Cain,* which was the first site-specific work I saw, a traveling work performed at different sites in Ann Arbor.

And their marriage of political and formal experimental techniques radicalized me. I was already politically radicalized; my stepfather and

Fred Sullivan, Jr. and Delroy Lindo in Julius Caesar *by William Shakespeare. Trinity Repertory Company, 1990. Credit: Del Bogart.*

mother were members of the Communist Party; my father was a very liberal Democrat; the anti-war movement, the civil rights movement . . .

But what I found in this Living Theatre performance was this ideal of the marriage of the political and the artistic, a marriage of the emotional and the intellectual. They stood outside of a bank in Ann Arbor and burned Monopoly money as a symbol of their resistance to the military-industrial complex. And I pulled out all the real money I had left in my wallet, and burned it, waving it above my head, tears streaming down my face! That was the time: "'Twas bliss to be alive in that dawn." And of course it was completely fucked-up and narcissistic and confusing, because we made no distinctions between being politically radical and aesthetically radical—and you know, what was the difference? The counterculture was the counterculture; it didn't matter whether you were spinning in circles for eight hours in the Byrd Hoffman loft, or taking your clothes off with the Performance Group, or marrying performance art and narrative with Mabou Mines, or doing political agit-prop with the San Francisco Mime Troupe . . . We were all the counter-culture! We were a bunch of experimental theaters!

Out of all of this I found out that NYU had a program; I was one of the first seven students in the Experimental Theatre Wing. At that point it was only a transfer program for third- and fourth-year students, but I talked them in to letting me go as a freshman. Although I have since occasionally made rhetorical hay out of the fact that I dropped out of college and don't have a college degree, the truth is that I completed the two-year program. At that time, there were no faculty; the teaching was outsourced to Mabou Mines, the Performance Group, Charlie Ludlam, these people I came to love.

So I moved to New York in the fall of 1975, and lived at the Performing Garage. I was still an actor at this point. But I was rapidly discovering a couple of things. First: *I wasn't that good.*

How did you figure that out?

You figure it out because the world starts telling you that you're not that good. But part of it was much more visceral. I noticed that my colleagues in that program enjoyed acting a lot more than I did. Being on stage performing gave them a pleasure that it actually never gave me. Certainly it became obvious to anyone who knew me that I was much better suited to being a director.

The relationship between performance and reality was always with me as a performer: I never lost my self-consciousness. I didn't have that ability to lose my critical distance and immerse myself in performance. And it's that instinct for critical distance that is so useful for a director. I felt more like *myself* when I was directing.

My last audition was for Joe Papp. Lee Breuer [of Mabou Mines] had just been given this gig at the Delacorte [home of New York's Shakespeare in the Park] as a choreographer for *Henry V* [1976]—that was Joe trying to help Lee out, give him a gig. So Lee got me an audition for Papp, and I went in and Papp asked me to do some Shakespeare, and I said, "I don't know any." I was such an asshole!

"Well, what *do* you know?"

"Well," I said, "I'm working on a performance piece called *Sleeping with Women.*"

"Well, do some of that."

He then let me perform a twenty-five-minute piece for him! And at the end of it, he said, "I suggest you keep doing that." And I thought, "I am never auditioning again." And I never have. I could not deal with putting that much of my life into someone else's hands.

You don't feel the same pressure as a director, once you give a performance to an audience or critics or colleagues?

Of course. But to me there is a rational distinction between saying, "I cannot control how people view my work, or value my work as a director," and as an actor, saying "I cannot control whether I'll be able to work at all, or who I'll be able to work with, or the circumstances."

When I do a show, every opening night, I'm the first person out of the theater, and I *walk*. At least around the theater, often several more blocks, by myself. It's my way of marking that I've opened a show. It's the same thing every time: I go out and I say, "This is the last moment when my assessment of this is *just mine*." And I just talk to myself until I feel like I come to peace with what I think I did. And I come back to the party, and from then on, I have to listen to what everyone says. As an actor, you don't have that moment.

As a way of transitioning from acting to directing—and as a way of controlling whether and how you worked—you formed a company called Red Wing.

Red Wing came right out of that ETW class. A young Swiss director named Stefan Müller had taken refuge at the Performing Garage. I had seen him in several workshops around SoHo, which was a tiny little village at the time. And so we started talking, and he rapidly became a very close friend, one of the best friends I ever had. We started Red Wing with the two of us as directors, although he also was the first dramaturg I'd ever met.

Did the company have a mission?

I'm sure we said things! But what we were really doing was trying to take all of the influences from the SoHo of the time, experimental theater, and combine it with the European sort of high-modernist influences that Stefan was bringing: he read Adorno, we'd spend nights listening to Karlheinz Stockhausen. It was not any more articulated than that, and indeed there were some deeply flawed aesthetic assumptions beneath the whole enterprise!

And as the 1970s went on, without ever consciously realizing it, I was drifting further and further right, more and more away from any kind of real political or cultural basis to my work. My own politics were becoming an aesthetic backdrop, a set of twisted terms I was using rather than anything that had to do with the real world. And my work was becoming more and more formalist, in a very specific sense. The form was becoming more important to me, and communication with an audience was becoming less and less important. Although I would not admit it at the time, my actual goal was to awe, mystify and impress my audience, rather than to actually communicate with it. And all this seemed to me the height of artistic purity. In the SoHo of that time, you had a couple thousand people who all agreed with what you thought was important, who would go see one another's work, applaud it, hate it, argue about it until two in the morning.

And by doing that, we set up a kind of static screen between us and the dominant culture. And that's really the goal of bohemias everywhere: to create an alternative value system. So we couldn't have given a shit about what the the *New York Times* thought; the *Times* had never seen any of our shows. We could give a shit about how many tickets we sold; we were giving tickets away half the time. I lived in New York for two years and never saw a Broadway show; it just wasn't part of my world. I never went above Fourteenth Street.

The good part about that is you can set up a value system that is resistant to the commodification of the dominant culture. The bad part of it is that in so doing, you set up an utterly self-referential and narcissistic system that fails to understand its relationship to the larger culture. And fails with a kind of a stupidity that can be *breathtaking*.

There's a seminal essay on this called "Whose Theater? Whose Avant-Garde?" by Roland Barthes. In it he argued (and it was certainly new to me) that rather than actually being resistant to the bourgeois culture, the avant-garde was a completely necessary component to bourgeois culture, and *in its resistance* served to reinforce what the dominant culture was doing.

In any case, we were doing this work, and we went out to San Francisco to tour. I was still nineteen years old at this point. I walked into the Eureka Theatre and started talking to Woody [Robert Woodruff, then artistic director], and before that conversation was finished he had invited Red Wing to be in residence at the Eureka the following fall. We went out there in 1977, spent three or four months in the Bay Area, and performed two pieces. One was a production of Peter Handke's *Self-Accusation,* and then a piece we self-created called *Kalkwerk* (that's German—talk about not being interested in communication!—for "chalk works," and it's sort of a reference to the blackboard, and a rip-off of a Thomas Bernhard novel called *The Lime Works*).

We had great success in San Francisco, and got invited to the Baltimore Theater Festival in the spring of 1978. Stefan had brought over some of his colleagues from Switzerland, and they hired Stefan and me to move to Zürich and found an experimental second stage at the Schauspielhaus Zürich, called Das Labor (the Laboratory). I also began teaching avant-garde workshops in Berlin and Munich.

How was your work received?

What I was doing was roughly equivalent to an exhibit that I saw at the Basel Zoo. It was an African steppes landscape, and in the middle of it was a grass hut. And I was told that until the 1950s there were Africans *living in that grass hut* at the Basel Zoo.

I didn't know who my audiences were in Zürich and Germany. I was absolutely, deeply intent on mystifying them, and impressing them, and coming up with exotic American avant-garde spectacles that would make audiences gasp. And we were relatively successful at that. We were received well, we caused some controversy, but the Swiss had essentially imported another exotic that they could, from the safety of their Swiss citadel, be titillated by.

Then I went home for Christmas in 1979. I was in my old bedroom with John Lennon posters on the wall, and I read an article by Joan Holden [playwright for the San Francisco Mime Troupe] in *Theater* magazine. And the opening line was something like: We are a theater that does not have contempt for its audience. I didn't sleep that night. Because I realized that wasn't the form I had been operating under.

So you ended up back at the Eureka in San Francisco, where your career transitioned into dramaturgical territory. How did that happen?

That was really two or three different impulses at once. First, during my time in Germany, I watched a lot of great dramaturgs at work—Dieter Sturm with Peter Stein, and so on—dramaturgs who were really central to the lives of their theaters. And I began to understand that there was an intellectual function, a mediating function between a work of literature and theater that was compelling to me.

I also brought back a conviction that I could not keep doing what I'd been doing. I needed to break down the distinction between my art and my politics that I had now recognized had hardened into an inappropriate one-way conversation. And also a recognition that the only way that would work was to return to plays, which I really hadn't done for years. At this point I'd been working on self-developed texts, collage texts, *anything except plays* . . . I was a creature of my time. In the late 1960s and 1970s, almost the only thing that all of those groups agreed on was that the playwright was passé. The actors and the directors and the designers were the center of the act of theatrical creation; the playwright was like some kind of antiquated literary appendage, to be ignored, rejected, torn apart.

And look what happened to you.

Yeah! I realized I was dead wrong. There had been no narrative; that was connected to the whole problem of accessibility. I was reembracing the idea of being understood by a non-elite or nonspecialized audience.

All of these different things led me back to a more mainstream idea of theater, and I began to realize that there was a ton of stuff I didn't know. Case in point: I'd been doing theater my whole life, and I'd never worked with a stage manager.

I made one attempt to revive Red Wing in San Francisco in 1980, but it petered out. And I had a real collapse, and spent a month in bed watching *The Rockford Files*, drinking Budweiser and eating Fritos. And then I walked into the Eureka (Woodruff was gone and the place was being run by Richard E. T. White [who would be succeeded in 1981 by Tony Taccone]) and said, "Nobody here remembers me, but I want to work here." I had enough money left over from my Swiss days that I didn't need to have a job, so I volunteered first to just assist. Then I realized I could remake myself as a dramaturg, and did so.

The great advantage to making myself a dramaturg, aside from reading a lot, was that it allowed me to be in the rehearsal room with directors. It gave me an excuse to be there and learn. And at this point I had never studied anything like conventional directing. I wouldn't have known what blocking was. It was a way for me to do on-the-job training.

I presume at that time you were more a research dramaturg than a writer's dramaturg. Yet so much of the dramaturgy you're known for now is with new works and playwrights.

It's amazing how quickly that started. The first thing I had assistant directed was *Mary Barnes* [1980], and [playwright] David Edgar came over [from the U.K.] and we spent two weeks together, getting to know each other; and Caryl Churchill came over when we did *Cloud Nine* [1983]. The dialogue with them was incredibly interesting. These were British writers coming out of the Royal Court, Joint Stock experience of political theater. They were developing plays in collaboration with actors and directors on political subjects, but still *they were plays*.

That tradition started to influence me and intrigue me, and, indeed, my first big commissioning project came out of a chance remark by [another British playwright] Barrie Keeffe. We were doing a production of his [in 1981] called *A Mad World, My Masters*. Barrie came to San Francisco; it was a few years after Mayor Moscone and Harvey Milk were shot, and he said, "If this were England, there'd be five plays written about this by now."

And a year after I got there, in 1981, we did a production of Emily Mann's *Still Life*. Emily came to San Francisco and immediately we sort of fell for each other. I absolutely love her!

The Milk-Moscone thing came up with Emily, and immediately we knew we had to do something with it. That began the three-year journey of developing *Execution of Justice*. And that was really the process that defined my career. I've never looked back.

Working as dramaturg with Emily was inspiring, exhausting, just absolutely fantastic. Nothing about what I do has fundamentally altered in the twenty-two years since then. I stayed at the Eureka until 1989, when the size of what I was doing—*Angels in America*, at that point— outgrew what that organization could contain.

Why Emily and that story?

We knew we wanted to do something together. Because Emily does work off documentary material, it pointed us to history. Barrie Keeffe's remark came back to me, and it seemed so obvious. Randy Shilts's book *The Mayor of Castro Street* had just come out. We started the process of trying to get the trial transcripts (which was much harder than we thought it would be). It took us three months and several hundred dollars just to get them copied. Emily lugged those transcripts around in this huge duffel bag. We worked on it in nine different cities for the next couple of years until we had a rough draft.

We knew it had to be something to do with San Francisco, because that's where we were. *Angels* was exactly the same way. The only given we had with *Angels* was that it had to be about San Francisco, it needed to deal with the AIDS crisis, and it needed to be for the actors at the Eureka Theatre Company. And though both of those plays began with a dedication to respond to the specific local life, they ended up having audiences far beyond that. That local address was the key to them being universal, not an obstacle.

What makes a great relationship between a dramaturg and a director?

It's a very tricky question, because being a good new-play dramaturg (as opposed to a research dramaturg) is akin to what Janet Malcolm called "the impossible profession," psychoanalysis. In order to be a good psychoanalyst, in a certain way you need to disappear as a human being. As a dramaturg, fundamentally, you have to listen to what somebody else's vision of the world is—a playwright or a director—and see it through their eyes. Because you're trying to help *them*, you're not trying to make something yourself. And yet, if you *really* make yourself a blank, if you really disappear, you have nothing to offer. So how the hell are you going to have enough vision of your own to be worthwhile to talk to and yet be able to submerge that? So the object of your attention isn't the realization of your own vision, but instead is the way that your insights can help realize somebody else's?

This is a humanly impossible task, as a result of which every dramaturg I know falls into one of three categories. They're either bad and useless, or they're useful and insane—with personality disorders that come from boundary issues, related to being unable to differentiate what is properly theirs and what is somebody else's—or third, what I'd like to think I've done: they are grounded by having another profession. There is something they do besides dramaturgy that allows them to have a healthy ego expression, so that when they enter into the dramaturgical relationship, they're able without too much psychic distortion to put aside their own bullshit and really listen to somebody else.

It's why I have migrated into being a director, certainly, but more importantly into being an artistic administrator and teacher. There will be moments working on something as a dramaturg when I can *feel* my own ego needs, my own desire for expression, rising to the surface, and I need to let it go if I'm going to get to a solution.

So there's a conflict between fear and ego for you.

There's more fear when you're talking about directing new plays, but something wonderful happens when you have helped frame the problem in such a way that solutions start to pour out, regardless of where they come from.

I had a wonderful experience working with Paula Vogel on *The Long Christmas Ride Home* [a Trinity Rep/Long Wharf Theatre coproduction in 2003]. We assembled a fantastic team: actors from Trinity Repertory Company; Basil Twist, the puppeteer; [light designer] Pat Collins; [set designer] Loy Arcenas; [sound designer] Darron West. And what we managed to get to in the last couple of weeks of rehearsal was *pure bliss* for me. Because day after day we'd come into rehearsal, and we had the problem defined, and I knew that my job was just to *frame the issue sharply enough to be solved.*

So is the director's task what you earlier called "managing the interplay of ideas"?

The director's task in its simplest form is to direct, meaning that it is your job to keep everything moving in the right direction. You're the one person who never gets to have an excuse about anything. You can never say that any part of a production is not of interest to you, or not your problem. It's *all* your problem. You're trying to get the best possible work out of a lot of other artists from different disciplines who are approaching this from different directions. That means you take the responsibility for saying what are the most important guiding principles of this event as a whole.

The hardest thing about directing is knowing what you need to hold absolutely firm to, and what you need to be completely flexible about. The choice comes down to the core value or principle of the piece you're presenting, and the means for executing it and expressing it. Every time I've fucked up a show, it's because I got that balance wrong. I held firm to things I shouldn't have held firm to—they were notions, they were decoration, they weren't the fundamental principle, they didn't illuminate the real event, and they turned out to be peripheral. Or I was being flexible about things that I didn't recognize I needed to be rigorous about.

Can you give me an example of that?

I did a production of *As You Like It* that was kind of a disaster. I had a very clear vision of it: the first half, in the court, felt to me like early 1960s Washington. The second act felt like 1967–1968, and the Forest of Arden was the hippie countercultural revolution.

I had that idea, but then I backed away from it because I got scared it was too literal, that it wasn't hip enough, that it was too much like what I had done with *Julius Caesar* [a modern-dress version he mounted at Trinity in 1990 and the Taper in 1991]. I was afraid of repeating myself, so I tried to do it indirectly. I tried to come up with clever ways of telling the story, and at a sudden point I realized I had created an ungodly mess. It wasn't just because there wasn't a strong historical timeline. The reason I backed away from it was fear, and that fear started to be the quality that was driving all the decisions. It felt timid and pretentious at the same time. You could feel the choices weren't coming from a purity of conviction. I was cowardly, and it showed. Because the thing about directing is that—[whispers] hey! It always shows!

The good news is that you don't have to work at putting yourself into a show; you're in the fucking show, whether you like it or not! You get a portrait of yourself. And I sat back and I really didn't like the portrait of myself that I saw. It was obviously more than just a mistake in the show, it was a moment in my life where things were not what I wanted them to be.

Let's go back to the idea that the director must frame the problem. Is that true of all plays?

Absolutely. You make the question clear at any given moment, and the stakes clear: what are we trying to do in this particular rehearsal, in this scene, in this show? And why is it important, why should we care? Those are the two things you always have to be defining. In terms of a narrative theater, that usually has to start with the definition of what the action of the play is, and what the event of a given scene is. Because I believe that's the essential unit of the construction of drama: what makes a drama *drama* is action. Not language, not spectacle, not song, not any of Aristotle's other categories. You must really understand what the action is, which means you have to understand what the reversal is, how one thing changes into another in the course of a scene, in the course of a unit of action, in the course of a play. Defining that is for me the starting point of any interpretation of a play. Discovering that is the key to cracking open a scene or a play.

Until I've done that, everything else is just fiddling around the edges. I know myself well enough now to know that I am in trouble if I start giving notes that are too detailed about line-readings or exact placement. It's a warning to me that I haven't cracked the scene yet. Because if I've cracked the scene, everything else falls into place. Of course I give detailed notes, but it's the difference between, "Adjust your hand like *this*," and, "Wait: typing is the wrong thing! This isn't about typing! It's about self-destruction! And how are we going to get to self-destruction?!" And then, I suddenly don't care what your hands are doing, because I've got the action, and I let you do what your hands are doing.

Can you give me an example of "cracking a scene"?

A character dies on stage in *The Long Christmas Ride Home*, and the stage direction is "Stephen becomes the Ghost of Stephen." We'd worked out a faux-Japanese setting, and a beautiful and quite elaborate process of him being stripped by fellow actors, lifted up, his clothes taken off slowly and solemnly. By the end he was in a loincloth and a white dressing gown. We were all in love with it. Then we got into tech, and I said, "You know, this isn't actually beautiful, it's just the *idea* of beautiful. It's kind of clumsy, and it's too much work."

And after the second preview, I just said to Stephen [Thorne, the actor playing Stephen], "I don't believe this is working." Stephen said, "What if I just take my clothes off?" And I said, "Well, that won't work, because we won't have that beautiful, dreamy quality."

But then I said, "Wait a minute. Go ahead, take your clothes off." The first thing he did was take off his boots and throw them. There was this big CLUNK. And I said, "Wait, that's what it *should* be."

It turned into him taking his clothes off, and throwing them on the floor. And it was fantastic: suddenly, a scene that was about the pretty idea of turning into a ghost became about the anger of dropping the body, turning his body into *trash*. It wasn't pretty but it was *dead right*. It was so fantastic to discover, and felt like such a group process. And in that case it was simply my job to say, "The Emperor has no clothes. We've all been telling each other this moment is beautiful, and it really isn't beautiful." That unleashed a chain reaction that led to the discovery of a different emotional motivation that really *was* beautiful, because it was real.

Let me give you one more from the third time I did my modern-dress *Julius Caesar,* at the Taper [in 1991]. There was one scene that always killed me: Act One, Scene 3, between Cassius and Casca. Cassius meets Casca on the street, and Casca has seen all of these unnatural portents—a slave with his hand on fire, lions running around the streets—that Cassius interprets to mean the fall of Caesar. I just couldn't figure out how to make sense of this. This is pure superstition . . . what does this have to do with 1962 in Washington?

And I suddenly went, "Sonofabitch! Put him in a phone booth!" This came from watching [the 1975 film] *Three Days of the Condor,* in which Robert Redford was in a phone booth. If you're in a phone booth on a deserted street, with Casca talking to Cassius, you suddenly think the phone is being bugged. The fact that technology can turn against you is exactly the kind of paranoid, *Manchurian Candidate,* early 1960s equivalent we were looking for. It worked beautifully, and I'm so proud of that. It's one of the few moments when I've had a conceptual thought, a translation that I just thought nailed it.

But that was a production when I didn't know what to be firm on and what to be flexible on. I fucked it up both ways. I hired someone whom I shouldn't have to play Brutus because I was intimidated. And then I fired him because I was intimidated. Once I hired him, I never should have fired him. It's one of the few casts I ever just *lost.* It was a terrifying experience.

Conquering fear is a theme that unifies directors I've interviewed.

I know I'm in trouble if I'm not *courting* my fear, because it means I've erected walls to keep myself safe. But once in the situation where I am afraid, I must not be driven by the fear; I have to avoid acting because of the fear. I have to let the fear go, and see through it.

JULY 2005, EUSTIS'S OFFICE AT THE PUBLIC THEATER, NEW YORK CITY

Before I get to some questions about the Public, I'd like to go back to your personal artistic journey and talk about how you went from being a dramaturg to finding your way back into directing.

I don't feel like I've actually found my way back to directing. Then again, there's a sense that I've never left dramaturgy since discovering it. For me, uncovering my vocation as a dramaturg was also an approach to directing. Since then, all my directing has been a form of applied dramaturgy. What I've been trying to do is understand and unleash the storytelling power of a particular narrative. Trying to understand what that particular story is, why it has to be told in that particular way, and how best to get that in dialogue with an audience.

A play like Rinne Groff's *Ruby Sunrise,* which I'm doing for the third time here at the Public [in 2005; he directed it the previous year at the Humana Festival of New American Plays and at Trinity Rep], is a perfect example of that: directing a show becomes the most effective way for me to be a great dramaturg on the show. It gives me a certain authority and overview of the entire play. While I've done good dramaturgy on shows I'm not directing, I don't think I've been able to do such complete dramaturgy on them.

So do you work with dramaturgs when you direct now?

Very rarely. And I feel sorry for them when I do: it's just so much my meat-and-potatoes, so much my wheelhouse, that I just *do not want help.* What's more common these days is that I have an assistant director who works in a dramaturgical capacity—research work, support work, the library side of it that I don't touch. But when I say "dramaturgy," what I'm really talking about is the new-play development aspect of it . . . and that's what I do, so I don't really need any help.

Patch Darragh and Marin Ireland in The Ruby Sunrise *by Rinne Groff. The Public Theater, 2005. Credit: Michal Daniel.*

They say that Toscanini always conducted like a cellist. And I'm a director who always directs like a dramaturg. That also defines a lot of my limitations. There's a lot of work that I don't think I'm the best director for. There are many directors who have a much stronger visual sense than I do. I've almost got no costume imagination whatsoever. Set and lights are a little different, because I do have a little more familiarity with the spatial. But it is incredibly rare—to the point of nonexistent—that there's an image in one of my shows that doesn't spring directly from the text. I'm not that kind of director.

You started the Brown/Trinity consortium. Now you're on faculty at NYU. Can directing be taught?

Yes and no. The constituent elements of directing can be taught, and that's everything from how to work with actors to text analysis to staging, how to fuse all of those. Of course those elements can be taught. How well somebody learns them is always a question. You can't make someone who doesn't have talent learn how to do something. But that's true in any profession. There's nothing mystical or inborn about directing.

What I think can't be directly taught is that every director is a leader, and every director must develop a specific style of leadership in order to draw work out of other people. That can be taught by example, but then every director has to piece together his or her own way of doing it through trial and error. I don't know anybody who has succeeded by flatly imitating the leadership style of another person. If it's leadership, it's not because you're following somebody else. And one of the toughest demands about directing is that you have to get a lot of people to *want* to do what you want them to do. There's a million ways of *failing* to motivate people; there's actually only a few successful ways to motivate them, and they're very subtle and can't really be faked.

In America we rely on our directors to be the entrepreneurs of our theater system. Certainly most civilized countries have theater systems that are more precisely evolved than ours, that are analogous to universities. Even though you have to be an original scholar and nominally a good teacher in order to succeed as a professor, nonetheless there's a system you can go into. You can move up the ranks. [In U.S. theater], every director who succeeds does so to some extent because he or she entrepreneurially invents his or her own career path. I do think that makes American directors wilier and tougher and sometimes cruder than our European counterparts, because those survival characteristics are necessary. For example, there are European directors I know who are thin-skinned in a way that would disqualify them for the profession in the United States.

Is that why you worked to create the Brown consortium, and why you're looking forward to this partnership with NYU? Does it have to do with mentorship and establishing a path?

It also has very specifically to do with wanting to put a stake in the ground for a certain kind of aesthetic. Over the course of the last twenty-five years, an aesthetic has developed within America's professional theater training that I would almost refer to as Mandarin: a highly refined, highly sophisticated, hot-house, art-school atmosphere of directing. I think there are a lot of reasons for this, not the least of which is that universities tend to want to create relatively arcane vocabularies and sophisticated, expert languages, so that one can distinguish between those who have advanced degrees and those who don't.

There is nothing wrong with this, except that I've witnessed what I'm afraid is a narrowing of the aesthetic range of professional American directors over the last twenty years. To put it very specifically, it's hard to find somebody who has gone through American professional theater training who's not heavily influenced by Viewpoints, or heavily influenced by Suzuki, or heavily influenced by one of several Bogart-esque, Suzuki-esque, methods of training. Those methods are not bad in themselves, but they are by no means a complete picture of what American theater practice can or should be.

I hope that at Brown and NYU we can establish safe havens for highly sophisticated training in a practice that is more populist, more based on storytelling, less based on design and abstraction and the style of directing that I see currently dominating American professional training.

For example, I sat down and said, "Okay, I want Central Park to be set aside for young, vigorous, American directors." And I started thinking, "I must know a bunch . . . but I'm not sure I've got any I could safely put in the park." That's a terrifying thought! Because the ones who have the technical skill to do it are mostly working in this aesthetic that doesn't interest me; it is not what free Shakespeare in the park should be about.

Last time I talked to you, you told me about your audition for Joseph Papp. Now you're sitting at his desk. It's really going to be different from Trinity Rep: you have a lot more freedom, don't you?

I have more freedom, but with freedom comes responsibility. This is the great thing with the Public, and the difficult thing about the Public: so many people feel it's their theater, and so many people feel the mandate of the theater includes them. Joe's vision was so generous and so big, but it has more missions than it can possibly fulfill successfully. That's okay, though; I'd rather cope with that than with apathy and indifference. And from what I've been able to tell, people are not apathetic about the Public Theater!

We are also in such a different time. The landscape has changed, not only since Joe founded the place, but after they'd been in the building twenty years. Manhattan Theatre Club, Roundabout, Lincoln Center, BAM, even Theatre for a New Audience are all significant players. Nothing analogous to them existed at first. There's a real competition for the Shakespeare franchise that didn't previously exist.

And of course there's serious competition for the new-play franchise. The model of not-for-profits moving shows commercially (which the Public kind of forged) is now the lingua franca of the realm: everybody not only does it, but everybody (rather revoltingly) orients their seasons around it! To try to figure out in this environment what is the ecological niche that the Public needs to fill, and what is the mandate that we need to prioritize, is a very complicated question.

You're taking the title "artistic director." That's interesting, given all you've said. Joe Papp was famously a better producer than director; George C. Wolfe, who preceded you, had the title "producer." Are you going to direct a lot here?

We'll find out. The real problem is not so much the Public as it is New York. New York is, as far as I know, the only city in the world where it is becoming more common for artistic directors *not* to direct than it is for them to direct. Tim Sanford [Playwrights Horizons], Jim Nicola [New York Theatre Workshop], André Bishop [Lincoln Center Theater]—the list of non-directing artistic directors is now bigger than the list of directing ones. And I think that's because, honestly, this place is so harsh, and the response to failure so intense, that it is extremely difficult to move from a rehearsal room—where you need to have the openness and vulnerability of an artist—to the artistic director's office, where you need to have the skin of a producer.

Will I be able to do that successfully? I don't know. I will be distressed if I have to give up directing, but I won't be devastated. Because if I have to give it up, it'll only be because I think there's something that I have to do that is more important. And, ultimately, I was not hired to direct. I am here to fulfill the mission of the Public Theater.

Why are you choosing *The Ruby Sunrise*—a remount—to start your directing career here?

I had a commitment to Rinne to do the show in New York before I got this job. And I can't take time off to go direct this play somewhere else;

I have to do it here. But the real reason is that the star of *The Ruby Sunrise* is Rinne Groff. She's a playwright I believe in, who is relatively unknown, and my sincere hope is that this production will launch her to the kind of prominence that I think she deserves as a playwright, and that it will help move her practice as a playwright to a still deeper level.

Also, the fact that I've already done it makes it less frightening to go into the rehearsal room here. It's important for me that I reduce my fear level as much as I possibly can the first time I go into a directing situation, because learning to cope with that fear on a heightened level is going to be a significant part of the task.

Does *The Ruby Sunrise* signal a new direction for the Public?

Sure. There are three major aesthetic planks that signal what I think we should be doing here. First, this should be a playwright's theater. We should be a home for every playwright in New York—those who have a talent we believe in, and those who believe in the mission of the Public.

Second, we need to create a home for independent artists whose work we can present—and that includes companies and individual artists; it embraces people who are experimental and pushing the bounds of the art form.

And finally, we've got to take a good hard look at revitalizing our Shakespeare tradition. We've got to put a lot more emphasis not just on Shakespeare in terms of those thirty-seven plays, but the classics, and what it means for us to be the resident company at the Delacorte Theater. What it means for us to be the classic theater in New York that gives away its tickets, and the implications of that not only for how we produce, but for the aesthetics and practice of how to make theater.

To me, those are the three big planks of the theater. There's an educational component that I'm still developing—but even that educational component will be there to support these three producing planks that I think will become the heart of the theater.

FRANK GALATI

Ambushed

I MET FRANK GALATI IN FEBRUARY 2004 at his beautiful Victorian home in Evanston, Illinois, a half-hour drive from the center of Chicago. It's an even shorter distance from a wealthy suburb called Highland Park, where in 1974 Terry Kinney, Jeff Perry and Gary Sinese founded a little theater called Steppenwolf. While it would be hard to pin down the moment of ascendancy for Chicago theater on the national scene, Frank Galati's induction into the Steppenwolf ensemble in 1986 played a significant role. Two years later, his adaptation of John Steinbeck's novel *The Grapes of Wrath* grabbed the attention of the international theater world. The production moved on to both the National Theatre in London and to Broadway, where it won Galati Tony Awards for Best Play and Direction.

Chicago theater's reputation grew in part from two very different roots, and Galati nourished both of them. The young actors of Steppenwolf—who, in 1985, became the scrappiest bunch ever to win a regional Tony Award—stamped Chicago as an actor's town, where the visceral connection between performer and audience is prized above all else. New York loves to put its directors on a pedestal, but one need only think of Steppenwolf ensemble member John Malkovich's searing performances in plays by Lanford Wilson or Sam Shepard to understand why the actor is king in the "City of Big Shoulders."

The other strain that propelled Chicago theater to the forefront of American drama has been its embrace of narrative adaptation (what critics sometimes call "story theater"). Examples of the form are productions created by director Mary Zimmerman, with the Lookingglass Theatre Company or the Piven Theatre Workshop, that blend narration with grounded performance and visual imagery to "tell plays" in intimate, theatrical ways. Unlike the in-your-face style of performance that made Steppenwolf (and Chicago) famous in its early days, narrative adaptation rarely shines the spotlight on the actor. Instead, the story itself—its historical sweep, its metaphorical heft, its layers of image and language—takes center stage. Zimmerman, who has done more for the form's popularity than anyone, credits Galati with Chicago's appreciation for the style.

It would be an oversimplification to say that Steppenwolf and Goodman Theatre (where Zimmerman is a Resident Director) have historically represented these disparate sides of the Chicago theater coin. But it's somehow significant that Galati, who himself became an Associate Director at the Goodman in 1987, is the only artist of stature to hold major positions with both companies. How has he managed to marry the fierce, gritty style of acting that set Chicago apart with its gentler, story-focused counterpart? The answer lies in the story of his career, and the story of his career is in large part the story of Chicago theater's rise.

Galati's ascendancy is a classic study in long, hard work. He was born in 1943 in Highland Park, and wrote his first play in high school in 1959. As an undergraduate at Northwestern University, he was mentored by the influential acting teacher Alvina Krause, and a company of her recent graduates pooled their resources to form a professional company (of which Galati was a part) in Chicago in 1965.

But external events would soon dictate a critical detour in Galati's career. With the Vietnam War brewing, Galati took a position in the speech department at the University of South Florida to avoid the draft. For two years, before returning to Chicago, he worked tirelessly, directing everything he could put his hands on, and writing a number of adaptations. After getting a Ph.D. in Interpretation from Northwestern's School of Speech (now known as the Department of Performance Studies), Galati fell in with another Chicago legend, William Pullinsi of the Candlelight Playhouse, and he started to direct professionally there and elsewhere (his adaptation of Nathaniel West's novel *Miss Lonelyhearts* for the Actors' Cooperative in 1973 earned particularly good notices and validated his narrative-theater approach). Nonetheless, Galati was still best known as an actor in Chicago until 1986.

That year saw not only Galati's induction into the Steppenwolf ensemble, but also his appointment to an associate directorship at the

Goodman, where he immediately directed his own adaptation of Gertrude Stein's works, which he called *She Always Said, Pablo*. It was part of Robert Falls's first season as the Goodman's artistic director. Falls wrote about that production twenty years later:

> *She Always Said, Pablo* was a celebration of one of the twentieth century's most iconic friendships, between Stein and the egotistical genius Pablo Picasso, arguably the greatest painter of the century. But Frank's production was much, much more than that: a sumptuous fantasia of theater, opera and dance, fusing Stein's eloquently elliptical writings with the distinctive, endlessly fascinating images of Picasso's creation. *She Always Said, Pablo* was difficult to describe but amazing to experience; it remains, in my mind at least, one of the most inventive theater pieces I have ever been a part of; a testament to its sources and to the theatrical creativity of its adaptor and director.

The work was a turning point for Galati, and he has acted only twice since then (Steppenwolf's *The Drawer Boy* in 2001, and *The Tempest* in 2009). A longtime directing relationship (begun in the late 1970s) with Chicago Opera Theater led in 1990 to the start of another with Chicago's Lyric Opera. There have been more Stein adaptations (including a musical, *Loving Repeating* for Chicago's About Face Theater in 2006), two adaptations of Haruki Murakami's fiction for Steppenwolf (*After the Quake* in 2005, and *Kafka on the Shore* in 2008) and a play he wrote about Freud and Sophocles, *Oedipus Complex*, for Oregon Shakespeare Festival in 2004, then directed it again at Goodman in 2007. In between the new scripts and the operas, Galati has made frequent pit stops to direct more "traditional" scripts, from Kaufman and Hart's *You Can't Take It with You* (Steppenwolf, 1985) to Brecht's *The Good Person of Setzuan* (Goodman, 1992). And he has staged Tony Kushner's play *Homebody/Kabul* several times: first in 2003, its Chicago premiere at Steppenwolf, starring Amy Morton; then the following year with Linda Emond (who had originated the role of the Homebody at New York Theatre Workshop) in productions at Los Angeles's Center Theatre Group and at Brooklyn Academy of Music in New York City.

Meanwhile, *Ragtime*—the musical by Lynn Ahrens, Stephen Flaherty and Terrence McNally that Galati directed on Broadway in 1998—earned its cast and creative team a total of twelve Tony nominations, and ushered in his high-profile commercial theater career. Though he has not replicated the Broadway success of that project—his productions of *Seussical* (2000) and *The Pirate Queen* (2007) were plagued by off-stage drama and poor reviews—he remains a potent force in nearly every facet of American theater.

In conversation, Galati's luxurious, voluptuous vocabulary rocks you like a ship—sometimes fiercely, sometimes gently, but always in *italics*. He seems never to have forgotten a name, and so much history competes for his attention when he speaks that it's tough to pin him down to one subject. That's in part because Galati himself is frequently overcome by emotion. He is astonished, thrilled, overjoyed, over-wrought . . . each adjective is a distinct reference to a certain expression or movement, and often he is all of them at once. A memory from thirty years ago has as much power to move him as the opening last night of his latest work.

Galati is treated with reverence by established Chicago artists, whatever their aesthetic proclivities. Though he now splits his time between Chicago and Miami (he bought a house there in 2006 with his partner, director Peter Amster), Galati is still a familiar figure on the scene, directing plays all over Chicagoland at theaters large and small. Nearly every artist and theater-lover in that town speaks with venera-tion about some production or other that he has created there. The out-pouring of love and affection for Frank is returned by him with such vivid generosity that he is apt to cry at any moment. He is, to borrow a favorite word of his, *ambushed*.

FEBRUARY 2004, GALATI'S HOME, EVANSTON

How did you become a triple threat: writer, director, actor?

I was a student at Glenbrook High School [in Illinois], where Ralph Lane was the drama teacher. ([Later] he actually sort of discovered Malkovich, and Laurie Metcalf . . . the early Steppenwolf company was formed out of his group of students [at Illinois State University]). While I was at Glenbrook, I got involved in speech contests. I won the first prize in the state of Illinois with a monologue, which was the first thing I ever wrote. So Mr. Lane (as we called him) encouraged me to write a play, and he let me direct it. The principal made an announce-ment inviting everyone to come see it because it was very unusual in 1959 for some high school kid to be writing a play.

But I never really seriously thought I was going to work in theater. I went to Western Illinois University for a year, and I did do a lot of plays when I was a freshman. I had a wonderful philosophy professor who said to me, "Why are you here at Western Illinois? Why don't you go where there's really a theater program?" I had a couple of other friends who advised the same thing: "You know, Frank, you should go to Northwestern," because in 1960 I had been in the "Cherub" program [a summer theater program at Northwestern's High School Institute].

I applied, was accepted, and became a theater major in the last couple years of Alvina Krause's tenure. She had been the star faculty member for thirty years. She was the mentor for people like Patricia Neal, Penny Fuller, Dick Benjamin, Paula Prentiss, Charlton Heston—they credited her with teaching them the art of acting.

I never took any of her classes, but I was in something she saw and critiqued, and she asked me to come to Eagles Mere, Pennsylvania, where she had a summer theater for twenty years. I was there for the last two summers before she retired. We would do nine shows in ten weeks; we had to be off book when we arrived. We would improv one show in the morning, rehearse another show in the afternoon, do a third show in the evening on stage. Although she never did Chekhov—she thought the schedule was too tight—we always did Shakespeare and a musical. I was in *Rhinoceros, Life with Father, She Loves Me, Brigadoon* . . . I played Falstaff in *The Merry Wives of Windsor*. It was an amazing crucible of intense labor. And she was a genius, really and truly a genius . . . but she was brutal.

She was a passionate person, and she often physically attacked her students. She did things that you couldn't possibly get away with now. Slapping people, beating them up about the head and shoulders. Pinching, tweaking, kicking, pulling hair . . . Of course there were many benign experiences with her; she was very kind and compassionate, and she had political fervor. She had this compelling interest in working people up—she felt that we were complacent. According to her, we didn't understand that if you were going to be authentic you had to be truthful, you had to hurt, you had to activate what was ferocious in yourself in order to gain access to serious regions of expressiveness and psychological reality.

In 1965, some of her former students (recent graduates from Northwestern) got together and formed a company here in Chicago called Eagles Mere Associates—the purpose was to produce a season of shows that Miss Krause would direct. We did [Pirandello's] *Six Characters in Search of an Author,* [Friedrich Dürrenmatt's] *The Physicists* and Shaw's *Too True to Be Good*. I designed all three sets; I acted in all three shows. We were creamed by the press, and rightly so: "They were pretentious; they were underdeveloped; the production values were nil." There was a great deal of chutzpah and arrogance for us to be doing plays of this scale and range when we were just out of college!

Some would say that's not so different from Chicago today. Nonetheless, it sounds like you were doing everything except writing and directing.

That's correct! That season was so depressing—it was during the Vietnam War. One way of getting out of the draft legally was to get a teaching job at a state school. So I got a job at the University of South Florida in the speech school, where I taught literature through performance for two years.

I was responsible for public performances on campus, and the head of the department, Jim Popovich, was very interested in promoting the program and getting more visibility, so I did three productions a year for two years. That's when I really started directing. I directed everything I had read, practically! I did *Orestes, Lysistrata, Endgame* . . . I started doing adaptations of fiction, including Vladimir Nabokov's *Pnin*. I put together an antiwar piece called *M Company* based on an article in *Esquire* magazine about following a battalion of guys from the time that they were inducted into the service through a calamitous attack in Vietnam.

[I returned to Northwestern as a graduate student, and] I finished my Ph.D. in 1973. Bill Pullinsi had opened up Candlelight Playhouse in Summit, Illinois. He was doing musicals, dinner-theater packages, blockbusters running for years. The show would run, the money would come in, and he was bored. So he built a theater next door called the Forum Theatre. And he opened with a play that was kind of hot at the time called *Child's Play* [by Robert Marasco]. I auditioned, and I didn't get cast. But Bill asked me to come to his office. He said, "I'm doing this play called *The National Health* [by Peter Nichols], and there's a part in it that I think would be perfect for you."

That's where I met Mike Nussbaum, and tons of Chicago actors. It was a huge hit that ran for nine months. Suddenly I was being interviewed, and the whole theater community came. It was really a high experience for me.

Finally, after I acted in a couple of shows, Bill said, "Why don't you direct something?" It was a casual interest because I had so much fun doing it at the college level. Of course I had anxieties about doing it, but I thought, "It's basically the same, I'll just have better people!"

How did you end up with high-profile directing positions at Steppenwolf and the Goodman, practically simultaneously?

In 1985, while I was teaching at Northwestern, [artistic director] Greg Mosher left the Goodman. In the interim year, I directed *The Inspector General* there, and I even interviewed for the job of artistic director [that went to Bob Falls]. Bob and I were friends; I had worked at Wisdom

Bridge Theater under his direction. The very first thing Bob did as artistic director was ask me if I'd like to be associate director. Then he and I invited [Michael] Maggio, and the three of us were a kind of happy fraternity at the Goodman.

At the same time, I'd been friends with [the ensemble members] at Steppenwolf for all these years. I was always on the sidelines, and they'd ask me for advice, and ask if I would direct something. I always wanted to but it never worked out. Then Gary Sinise, who was artistic director, called me one day and asked, "How would you like to direct *You Can't Take It with You* with [John] Mahoney and Rondi [Reed] and Amy Morton and Rick Snyder and Molly Regan and Bradley Mott and Del Close?" And I did, and it was a blast. About halfway into the rehearsal process, Gary called me up to his office and said, "We would like you to become a member of the ensemble." I was bowled over. It never dawned on me that I'd ever be invited to be a part of that group. I mean, you know, I was older. But I had so much fun with them; we liked each other so much. Of course I said yes.

That began my most intense period of work as a director, mainly moving back and forth between Steppenwolf and the Goodman, but also working in opera.

Up until 1985 you were best known in Chicago as an actor, not a director. But since then you've only been on stage once, in Steppenwolf's *The Drawer Boy* in 2001. Why did you stop acting?

Because I got to be directing all the time, and I really loved it. I mean, the life, the eight shows a week—I had done enough of that to not be interested in doing it anymore. The crucible of the process is intense and painful and exhilarating. But then once it's alive and going, [as a director] you can bolt, which I always do!

I hope this doesn't seem phony, but I'm rather in awe of the actor. I know I've been an actor myself. It's not because I know what it's like to be up there that I have such respect. Having spent as many years as I have on this side of the table, watching, paying attention, trying to lean into, really hear and listen to actors carving out their vision of a character, their relationships with one another, their understanding of the given text . . . it never ceases to amaze me what courage, what fortitude, what stamina they have in the practice of their art. And I do think it is an art.

To be the colleague, the witness for someone like Lois Smith or Amy Morton; to share in the evolution of the storytelling of the company I had the privilege to work with on the *The Grapes of Wrath* . . . In 1991, after we'd been working on it for nearly four years, we taped it for PBS's "Great Performances." I'll never forget the last scene, when Lois

Smith and Gary Sinise were saying good-bye as Ma Joad and Tom Joad. I was sitting in the studio, in a trailer outside the Cort Theatre in New York. I'll never forget watching them, on the camera, play that scene for the very last time. I don't know why—I got up and I walked into the theater and down the aisle, and I went on stage and the three of us put our arms around each other and wept. [he begins to cry] You have to be humble before that. [his voice breaks, wavers] Because those two human beings, as mother and son for four years, every night, went from Oklahoma to California; they watched their family fall apart. They gave their lives . . .

I think one of the reasons why *The Grapes of Wrath* was such a powerful experience in all of its incarnations is that, yes, of course, the story is gut-wrenching and satisfying because of the dignity of these people, what they survived. But you've also watched a company of actors who have gone through two and a half hours of stage time. And when they walk out together [for the curtain call] soaking wet from the flood, in their rags and tatters, part of what's so overwhelming is that *you know what they have gone through.* They've gone through it right there in front of you, and you've gone through it with them.

The cast of The Grapes of Wrath, *adapted by Frank Galati from the novel by John Steinbeck. Broadway, 1990.*

So I feel like my job is a very complicated one. One is to be in charge: you have to be an administrator and have some kind of a vision. But I feel like as a director my principal obligation is *to be there for the actors, to be the witness to their discoveries* and to be able to honestly tell them what I'm experiencing. I am their first audience. They have to be able to trust that if I laugh, I'm not faking. If I'm moved, it's because something genuine is happening. Or if something doesn't work, I will tell them, and not put them in harm's way by doing so, but rather will make the environment comfortable enough so that *they* can fail, and *I* can fail.

So the courage to be an actor, to practice that art, has to do with the potential for failure. Can you put your finger on that?

It's courage in battle, the way a warrior has to have courage, because there are enemies to be defeated. And those enemies are fear and self-doubt and not quite believing yourself, because you know that you're manufacturing something that has to be repeatable. There are millions of situations for actors when the doubt is engulfing. "I don't believe in him, I don't believe in the scene, I don't believe in the director, this design is hideous, it's overproduced, it's this, it's that! . . ." The courage also involves giving in . . . to be brave enough to take what is being given, and to run with it.

What do you do when you work away from the ensemble, with artists you don't know? How do you establish trust so quickly and enable those risks?

I have to put myself out there first. I have to articulate my own deep experience of the play as far as I've been able to get into it before the first day of rehearsal. I feel like I have an obligation to say what I think the play is about. I'm sometimes pedantic and scholarly: I write speeches for the first day of rehearsal! But I have to introduce them in as gentle a way as possible to the world that's going to be created physically around them, and with them.

I find this a very delicate aspect of the launch experience, because you show the cast a model and costume renderings and it's almost like they're looking down a very long corridor at a tiny thing that is way off in the distance, that they're going to approach, like they're supposed to *go* to it. And I feel that's wrong. That's like thinking of a character as being *out there*, like Hamlet is *out there* and I have to go out there and get him and put him on like an overcoat.

Acting is so internal and it has so much to do with the source being inside that one has to be very careful [as a director] about projecting,

"Now this is what you're going to look like, and what you're going to wear, and you're going to have red hair and a big nose and funny shoes." I've gone through that as an actor, and that can be discombobulating and scary: "Oh my God, *that's* supposed to be my character?"

Talk to me about a moment working with an actor when you were discombobulated or stumped, and how you worked through that.

The character of the Homebody [in *Homebody/Kabul*] created by Tony Kushner has a kind of intellectual, electric charge, plus she's deeply neurotic, she's on antidepressants, she's willing herself into a situation that is definitely fatal. But along with this kind of death wish, there is erudition, there is sexuality, there is sexual anxiety and fear. There's the heartbreak of a mother whose relationship with her daughter has been a complete failure. There's *bitterness,* a kind of *acerbic rage* that spits out of her occasionally. And *unbelievable* compassion. An eloquent way of expressing the mystery and beauty of a world that she does not understand, that she feels she cannot understand. She's agoraphobic, and she's an adventurer. So . . . *my God!* The opposites that are working in this personality are dizzying.

Amy Morton played it in Chicago. We worked every week for six months before rehearsal started. Once a week, we would get a little bit further into the script.

There's a crucial zone near the end of the monologue when she brings herself to say something like, "Down, down into the sunken gardens of the soul where a little voice sounding rather like mine is chattering away, chattering, chattering away . . ." All of this is deep, soul-embedded territory. At the end of the play, Khwaja, the guide, says, "Deep within, someone waits for us in the garden . . . Perhaps she is Allah . . . or she is our death. But always she is waiting in the garden." And that's what that *is*, that's *there*: in that dark garden of the heart lies our death. We carry our death with us, every day. That's a terrifying thing. It's like spiraling down into your own interiority. And Amy was timid, and very candid about it: "I don't know if I can go there, I don't know if I can do this," she said.

And as we got further on into rehearsals and then even into previews, the rigor and the difficulty of the task of sustaining this imaginative flow and emotional truth for so long would unlock Amy's emotions. And there were certain sections she would get to where she would go completely to pieces, sob uncontrollably, because what was being activated in her was overmastering her disciplined embodiment of the text.

Tony was so kind, and understood why she would go through these emotional currents. He saw the first runthrough in the rehearsal room.

Then he and I got together and we went over all his notes and he said, "You know I said you don't have to observe any of the stage directions, but there's one you *have* to observe in the monologue."

It's at the place when she's having this fantasy of the man with the ruined hand (the hatseller), and he leads her on a tour of the city, and they wind up in the palace of a prince. And she describes the prince's garment. When it comes to a close, the script says, "*She cries.*"

Every time we would get there, Amy would pass right over it. She would say, "I can't cry there. This prince was a murderer—he might have had a beautiful costume, but I don't know how to get myself emotionally stirred up by this image." And I would say, "I don't know what to tell you, except that she is so overwhelmed by the beauty of this world and its sensual appeal, *it makes her cry*. But if you can't do it, you can't do it, and I'm not going to force you to do it."

So Tony said to me, "She has to cry."

I filed that away, and he left; he wasn't coming back until the opening. So we got into previews, and one day I said to Amy, just the two of us, "Amy, you have to cry where the stage direction says you have to cry."

She says, "He wants me to cry there."

And I said, "Yes. And you know what? If you have to fake it, just stop. Be unable to go on. You don't have to sob, you don't have to weep, just be *ambushed*."

Well, it was the word "ambushed" that got her. Something was going to come over her from behind that was unexpected, that maybe didn't have anything at all to do with the silver and gold of his costume. Often our most emotional experiences are triggered by something *completely unexpected*. You don't cry when your mother dies, but you cry when you see your cousin, and you're ambushed by your feelings.

Amy absolutely got it, and it was heartbreaking. It also ambushed the audience, and they were suddenly *changed* because they saw that she was so *accidentally* real. The *weather* in the room, the whole condition in the room changed. It was a preparation, just as there would be in a musical score when a bell is struck or a chord is played or a key change occurs! It was an absolutely essential preparation for an enormous amount of what was to come, not only in the monologue, but the entire show.

I came to think that the monologue is an overture: it states the themes, it's a solo aria—but all of the musical material, all of the characters, all of the issues, everything is established, and then the Homebody *passes the baton* on to the story which then commences with her remarkable physical move into the world of Afghanistan. This was something that Linda [Emond] had never experienced, because, in the New York Theatre Workshop production where she performed it previously, the intermission was at the end of the monologue, so she got this huge ovation, and then the action of her play was over.

My ambition in working on the play structurally was to execute the transition in front of the audience, to let the Homebody be the *agent* of the shift—the lights don't go out on her and come up on the hotel, she has to, *literally, physically* walk into the world of the future, after her own death.

When Linda did it, she was completely overwhelmed. And she did something that I thought was absolutely magnificent in rehearsal—she would inhabit scenes that she wasn't in. She would sit on the bed next to her daughter; when there was combat between father and daughter, she would sit right between them, she would read her guidebook, she would be listening, she'd be in the other world. From her point of view as an actor, she felt it was very important to *feel* what her husband and daughter were like, to *feel* the tension in that household, the tension of those relationships. And it allowed her to be really specific. So when she was talking in the monologue about "my husband and his cold indifferent way," it was Reed Birney [the actor who played her husband] she was talking about.

And what it gave father and daughter was this omnipresent weight of the mother's psychosis that they couldn't shake, no matter how dead and dismembered she was.

How does your previous acting work affect your directing—do you think it makes your directing unique?

No, I don't think it makes it unique. Certainly I know what it's like to be up there, and that knowledge makes me more sensitive to the primacy of the actor in the whole process than I would be if I hadn't been an actor.

It *has* to be their choice, fundamentally, whatever it is. So: "Go here, try this, see if this impulse works, what if?" are invitations to explore, not directions to be obeyed. If someone is doing something because I told them to do it, I know it's wrong, it's false. One of the most difficult things is to keep your mouth shut. It's not what you say, it's what you *refrain* from saying that often makes the difference.

I have the sense that with the increase in narrative theater (if that's a way of putting the proliferation of adaptations of fiction and nondramatic texts like *The Laramie Project*), there's an increased awareness among us that every actor—no matter how realistic the play—is a *storyteller*, and has some obligation to share in subordinating or bringing to the foreground certain elements that are crucial for the audience's comprehension of how the story unfolds.

Miss Krause used to say, "When you're acting in a farce, you have to know—in a way that your character does not—where the prop is that's being hidden from view. You have to *know* who's behind the screen in order to play in ignorance of such." Because you have to *italicize*. Mrs. Malaprop *lands, emphatically* on the wrong word. And if she doesn't land emphatically on the wrong word, the comedy is drained of its sizzle. That's a crucial zone of negotiation between actor and director, because the director can help the actor understand in what ways she has to function to clarify the story.

Chicago is of course known as an actors' town. You played a big role (especially with Steppenwolf) in bringing that about. Is that why there are fewer auteur directors working in Chicago?

When you experience the electrifying presence of a directorial *genius* (a Robert Wilson, Pina Bausch, Peter Sellars, Ariane Mnouchkine, Peter Brook) you are aware of a controlling intelligence that does and does not dominate the actor's field. I would say that Mary Zimmerman, a Chicago director, is an auteur, with her narrative experiments, her dreamscapes, the sort of layering of images that tend to hold sway over text, which is often links of episodes, narratives within narratives. The actors are the *agencies* of these images, as well as agents of the text. But they don't come to the foreground as the embodiment of characters in psychological conflict and in relationships the way they do in other kinds of plays.

Bob Falls, also of Chicago, is someone who has a very strong, controlling intelligence, but he likes to work with the *big* plays, the naturalistic plays of the American canon. His work on Eugene O'Neill, his work with Arthur Miller, which is *towering* in its achievement, is a testament to a balance between a strong directorial vision and actors. Performers like Brian Dennehy and David Cromer and Vanessa Redgrave can match, with the ferocity of their acting, the scale of Bob's vision.

I recently saw Dexter Bullard's production of Tracy Letts's play *Bug* in New York [the production started in Chicago before transferring to New York's Barrow Street Theater in 2004]. It's knocking people out: the reviews in New York have been sensational. And there was tremendous excitement here, because the Chicago school was on display.

There's an example of a small, fierce, contained comic melodrama: gothic, grotesque, very funny and very pathologized, all contained within this hotel room in two acts. Ferocious, tremendous velocity, a kind of mystical, mysterious darkness underneath, and *deep* need, and *terrible* addiction, and a kind of perverse self-destructive strain, paranoia, and so on. And the actors are delivering *extraordinary* performances. Audiences are not as conscious as we are of what a director is doing in a production that's combustible and realistic like this one.

Of course, Dexter manages to traverse both worlds. His company, Plasti-cene, is purely physical and far from realistic. So are we talking about two different arts? What unites both approaches to create a great director?

I think it takes the capacity to read deeply. To get inside, underneath, and go to the core of a text. It doesn't matter what the text is in terms of the *style*. But if the text has a root source that is deep, then the exploration of its internal workings is what leads a good director into the style of the Gertrude Stein musical or the style of the Ferber/Kaufman play or the style of a musical like *Ragtime*.

When I was first given Terrence McNally's treatment for *Ragtime*, having of course already experienced the novel [by E. L. Doctorow] and admired it tremendously, I realized immediately that Terrence was not going to take the novel somewhere other than where it wanted to go. What he was going to try to do in his musical adaptation was to find out what the novel is like when it *speaks* and *lives in time* on stage.

That was the key for me. I could relax, I could really trust the material, because I knew it came from a really deep place, and its ardor and its passion and its complexity could fuel me and teach me how to shape it, how to help it sing, how to help it move in space.

The same thing can even be true of the most complex text. Way back before I did *The Mother of Us All* [the Gertrude Stein/Virgil Thomson opera, produced at Chicago Opera Theater in 1976], I did a fifty-minute vaudeville program of Stein material that really mystified and scared me. We did it for the Speech Communication Association, and the late Lilla Heston and the late Sandra Singer performed it. We worked on it and worked on it. They were *furious* with me, because they had to memorize this text, and they didn't understand it, and I couldn't explain it to them. But the more we worked on it, the more convinced I was that there was something very deep underneath it. Marianne Moore says in her poem "Poetry" that you know you're in the presence of poetry when you can feel something genuine. She calls that "imaginary gardens with real toads in them." You can tell! A bell rings!

How are you a different director than when you first started out?

What do you know at sixty that you didn't know at thirty? Well, *a hell of a lot*! The ways in which the life experience, the failures, the pain, the confusion, the fear, the *enormous* fear—the ways in which all of those dimensions of the life of the theater work on you, and age you and weary you, and also open you up and set you free!

I think I can say that now I feel a level of relaxation, a kind of bliss in being able to say exactly what I think without fear. Not because I'm going to be harsh or judgmental, because I don't come from that place.

I think I have learned and I keep trying to remind myself, above all, to listen. And I can see something in my head that I *have not seen*, in the same way I can see something in my head that I *have seen*. I remember space, I remember dimension, I remember color, I can remember whole paintings. And I can remember what I'm concocting in terms of space.

Let's pretend you've been asked to mount a theater production in a remote country where the people don't know you don't know you: "You were recommended to us by Steppenwolf artistic director Martha Lavey. We want to know: what makes a Frank Galati show?"

Well, I am a fairly emotional person, and I believe that aspect of my character is consistently reflected in the work I do. Although I have intellectual interests, and I am capable of a great deal of control, creating works that are glossy and finished and refined, I hope that one of the characteristics of my work is a depth of feeling, an *ardor*, *heart*, if you will.

Emotion, I once learned from my professor Wallace Bacon [chair of Northwestern's Department of Interpretation during Galati's tenure there], is "going out from yourself." When you are truly moved, you are moved away from your own local concerns. I think that's what theater aims to do: to invite an individual spectator in a congregation of spectators to share identification with, and to resonate with, the central characters in a given dramatic text. You *are* Hamlet while *Hamlet* is being played. Hamlet dies but *we survive*. And in the afterlife of the play perhaps we've come to some level of nourishment that carries us on spiritually.

Can you tell me a little bit about what a rehearsal day is like with Frank Galati?

I wouldn't say it's a fixed pattern, but I go through similar phases with each show. First of all, I feel obligated to answer the question, "Why are we doing this?" before anything else. I feel I have to explain why I'm drawn to this text and why I think it's valid to do it now, why particular interpretive choices have been made in advance of the cast coming together on the first day of rehearsal (design choices, etc.).

It varies, but I have spent as much as a week at the table, having readthroughs and then saying, "How did it feel? What do you think?" And then having a free-associating, free-flowing discussion. Then we read through it again to see if we feel differently. Then we read it again—anyone can stop and say, "Can we talk about this," "What does this mean," "What is she thinking," etc. Of course this is the period that most intimately involves the dramaturg (if there is one), with research and historical context.

Then, after I feel like we've wrestled with the details of text and textual analysis and so on, we usually get up. We start at the beginning and go one scene at a time. And I tend to be very private. I have always resisted having assistants. The assistant for *Ragtime* was absolutely fantastic, and I almost always had him with me. But there were times when I would say, "Stafford [Arima], I need to be alone with Marin [Mazzie]," or "Brian Stokes [Mitchell] and Marin and I are going to talk about this," or, "I just need the family . . ."

What does that achieve?

Well, the level of trust that has been built up between me and the individual actors is often reinforced by private time. Since *Ragtime* was a big moment in my life in terms of expressiveness as a director, I made sure we had a lot of it. The cast needed a week with the musical director to learn the score, which was choral and extremely complicated. So I said, "Could I have a little office, and could I have a meeting with every principal in the cast before we get started?" We were beginning to develop a kind of collegial intimacy, which began when we started to work on scenes with a level of trust.

If there are a bunch of spectators, if the whole chorus is there when we're working on a scene, if actors who are not involved are in the room, *all of that* leaches energy from the necessary focus on dimensions of this art that are very *fragile* and that are sometimes very *scary*. People are very vulnerable. When I worked with Audra McDonald—I mean, that song! We ultimately did "Your Daddy's Son" on this *huge* stage, absolutely empty, there wasn't a single thing on the stage except her kneeling with a little baby—and she was *extraordinary*!

Can you tell me how you got to that moment of putting her alone on stage?

The first time Audra McDonald opened her mouth and spoke, I thought someone had come into the room and was asking a question that wasn't in the script. It was so *real*—her *vitality*, her *candor* was so evident that she didn't *sound* like anybody else. Lynn and Stephen [Ahrens and Flaherty, the librettist and composer] and I were looking at each other, all thinking the same thing: her part is too small! She *dies* at the end of the first act! How can we kill her off and not use an artist of this brilliance and expressiveness?

A couple of days later I said, "The audience has got to like someone, in fact *deeply* empathize with someone, who tried to kill her own baby. Now let's talk about this." We talked about Medea, and we talked about

Audra McDonald and Brian Stokes Mitchell in Ragtime, *music by Stephen Flaherty, lyrics by Lynn Ahrens, book by Terrence McNally. Broadway, 1998. Credit: Catherine Ashmore.*

Susan Smith, the woman who drowned her children, which was a fairly recent horror at that time. Lynn Ahrens—who is a genius!—said, "You know what, the audience *has* to go there. We can't *skip* the event. She has to *take* us there and explain why she would do something so horrible." And so the idea was born that it would be a lullaby, and that she would tell the baby what she did and why she did it.

So Lynn and Stephen decided they were going to work that night, and they always work by themselves. The next morning, we went to the rehearsal hall and Lynn said to me, "Come here, I want to show you something." I think this is one of the most unforgettable and moving experiences in my whole life in the theater. She opened her computer and I stood behind her and there were the lyrics. And there was the *whole story*. "You have your daddy's hands . . . you are your daddy's son . . ."

In the second act of the song (Lynn always believes that a song is a three-act play), she reveals to the baby that his father was a ladies' man, and that he left her. By the time she gets to the last act of the song, she's completely back in that moment of hysteria when her water broke, and she runs screaming in pain to the garden and digs a hole and puts the baby in the hole.

I read it, it was there, and it was poetry; but it was real, and it was brutal. Stephen had composed the music. We brought Audra in that afternoon, and she sang it *cold*. She was completely transformed by the song. All of a sudden she had a vision for herself of the magnitude of this role. I knew from that moment that it must be absolutely unadorned in the staging: it had to be Audra alone on stage with the baby and the audience. No matter how grand the scale of the space, and no matter how big the emptiness around her, it had to be a *searing* focus on that "Madonna and Child."

This sounds wonderfully organic. Are you at other times a planning director, one who is prepared at every moment?

I'm not a very planning director, but I go through these periods of high anxiety that ultimately break open and reveal a plan. I do a tremendous amount of pacing!

Let's take *The Royal Family* [Steppenwolf, 2002]. Here's a very realistic comedy with a tremendous amount of *traffic*. The doors are really important (there are four bedrooms, a library, a terrace, a kitchen, two closets, the front door). I'd studied the ground plan of the original Broadway production, in which there was a single curved staircase. The front door to the apartment was hidden underneath it, so that anyone who was entering the apartment, after a "ding dong," came around the staircase into the room.

I thought, "The audience should *see that door*." In a way, it's a little proscenium, and [the characters are] all in show biz! We've got to find a way to do that: what if it were a double staircase? [Set designer] James Schuette was instantly able to see that we could come up with a ground plan in which we could be more responsive to the play.

It took me years to learn that the entrances and exits, the way the character is delivered to the stage and the way the character must leave the stage, are fundamental, primary choices. The ground plan is everything.

I've also come to realize that the stage house is the *head*, the human head. The stage space is the mind. As if a volume of energy is focused fiercely with its empty eye on the audience. I think I learned that from Beckett's *Endgame*: the design, which he suggests is deliberately a human skull, which contains the rattling contents of a soul at the end of its tether.

What about mistakes you've made?

I had a huge disaster with *Seussical*. The initial experience was ecstatic. We had a workshop in Toronto [on a bare stage, with actors in street clothes, in August 1999], and right after the opening number started, [the widow of Dr. Seuss, Mrs. Theodore Geisel] said, "They've got it!"

Afterwards we had a postmortem and it seemed to be so far along . . . we seemed not to have any serious problems.

But as we went into the design process, things got cranked out of shape. The chemical interaction of the individual theater artists was *toxic*. It produced strange behaviors and mistrust; it generated doubt and anxiety and suspicion . . . all of which was exacerbated by the producing cohort. And I found myself *disabled*. I lost my own strength.

By the end of the rehearsal period, the weather changed in the room. Dramaturgical problems began to emerge. There were casting issues. When we made the transition to tech rehearsals there were contractual delays that almost made it impossible for me to be involved in the costume fittings. And when I saw the clothes in Boston [for the pre-Broadway tryout in September 2000], there were problems with quick changes; the actors didn't have enough time. There were problems with the set mechanisms, some people had problems with the lighting . . . everyone had an opinion.

So there you are, sitting out of town in the kind of hell you've heard about, the kind of hell that people wish on *Adolf Hitler* . . . and it just *devolved*.

I said this at the beginning and I went out saying this at the end: *Seussical* was more like *The Fantasticks* than anything resembling a big Broadway show . . . it had the humblest of ambitions. But everything that drove it was the *mega empire* of Dr. Seuss, and the fantasy arose that, between marketing and merchandising, this was going to be a cash cow.

So what lesson should an emerging professional draw from your *Seussical* experience?

You have to be very careful of the group that's assembled, the group that is fundamentally generating the energy for the show. And in the commercial theater, the relationship between the director and the producer is just as important as the relationship between the director and the cast, or the director and the playwright. The dollar drives everything. Unfortunately, the ambition out there is to work on Broadway, to be on the world's stage. But the real creative opportunities are elsewhere. They're in Chicago, they're in Minneapolis, in Louisville and Houston and Off Broadway and everywhere *but* the Great White Way.

MICHAEL KAHN

Elder Statesman of the Classics

WHEN I FIRST MET MICHAEL KAHN IN FEBRU-ary 2003, he was in Chicago auditioning twelve hundred actors for the Juilliard School's MFA program, where he was the Richard Rodgers Director of the Drama Division. He was also audition-ing students for his own classical train-ing program at Washington, D.C.'s Shakespeare Theatre (now the Shake-speare Theatre Company)—arguably the largest and most important Shakespeare theater in the country—where he is artistic director. Running two major institutions at once was nothing new for the peripatetic director; for most of his long career, the energetic Kahn has been at the helm of more than one company while playing a leading role in the education and training of generations of American actors.

Kahn won't reveal his age, and though his *enfant terrible* days are well behind him, he still carries his six-foot-two-inch frame with an energy more common in those much younger. With gray-white hair ringing his pate, and a deep, scratchy voice, he looks and sounds like an éminence grise at the Vatican. Indeed, the many empires he's built have earned him a certain veneration from the rest of the theater field. When colleagues or those he's mentored speak of him, their voices often sound awestruck, reverential. Jane Alexander, former head of the National Endowment for the Arts, has called him "the best interpreter of Shakespeare in the country."

Though best known now for his work with the classics, Kahn spent his early career on the cutting edge. He made his Off-Off-Broadway debut in 1963 with the premiere of Jean-Claude van Itallie's *War* at the Albee-Barr-Wilder Playwrights Unit. In fact, Edward Albee became a major force in Kahn's first professional years: he produced Kahn's staging of Adrienne Kennedy's *Funnyhouse of a Negro* in 1964, which won the playwright an OBIE Award. Joseph Papp saw that production and hired Kahn to direct *Measure for Measure* for the New York Shakespeare Festival in Central Park in 1966, which won him a *Saturday Review* Award for the best direction of a revival.

That production led to three contemporary plays on Broadway in 1967 and 1968 (including Albee's *The Death of Bessie Smith/The American Dream* in 1968), which ran for a combined total of thirteen post-opening performances. Undeterred by the lack of success, Kahn returned to Shakespeare, and in 1969 assumed his first artistic directorship at the now defunct American Shakespeare Theatre in Stratford, Connecticut. And although he found great success subsequently on Broadway (including a Tony nomination for his 1983 production of *Show Boat*), and major opera and regional theater companies have come calling with frequency since then, the classics and classics-based institutions have dominated his career for the last forty years.

Part of that is the influence of his four decades at Juilliard, where he first began to teach in 1968 at the behest of the legendary John Houseman (he was the first teacher Houseman asked to join him). Running that flagship program from 1992 to 2006, Kahn's influence on classical theater training in this country is hard to calculate. His former students include such luminaries as William Hurt, Laura Linney, Kevin Kline, Patti LuPone and Robin Williams.

While still in Stratford, Kahn was called on to save the foundering McCarter Theatre Center in Princeton, New Jersey, in 1974, and he ran the two institutions simultaneously for five seasons, bringing the latter company national prominence with his productions of O'Neill's *Beyond the Horizon, 'Tis Pity She's a Whore* and Williams's *A Streetcar Named Desire* starring a young Glenn Close as Stella.

His long love affair with the work of Tennessee Williams gained serious steam after he was appointed artistic director of the Manhattan-based touring Acting Company in 1978, for which he directed ten Williams one acts Off Broadway, *Ten By Tennessee*. Soon after his appointment there, an invitation came from the Chautauqua Institution in southwestern New York to create an actor-training program; he ran that program concurrently from 1983 to 1988.

In 1986, shortly after the Shakespeare Theatre separated financially from the Folger Library in Washington, D.C., Kahn was appointed artistic director there, and he has successfully guided that institution into becoming a major, independent and vital national institution. (If you're keeping score, this means in 1986 Kahn was running the Shakespeare Theatre in D.C., the Acting Company in New York and the actor-training program at the Chautauqua Institution, while teaching at Circle in the Square Theatre School and Juilliard in New York. When I met him, Kahn had homes in D.C. and Connecticut, as well as an apartment near Lincoln Center; it wasn't unusual for him to teach in New York in the morning and rehearse a play in D.C. in the evening.)

Kahn has worked many transformations in his long career, but possibly none so thorough as that which he has wrought upon the Shakespeare Theatre: not only did he change its name, but he created an attached MFA training program in 2000, opened two major new facilities and instituted a free Shakespeare summer park series that has been seen by more than half a million people. His mentorship of now major-career directors there (and at the Acting Company) has become legendary: Charles Newell, Ethan McSweeny, Daniel Fish, Jesse Berger . . . the list goes on and on. And in 2012 his impact was recognized, when Shakespeare Theatre Company was given the Special Tony Award for Outstanding Regional Theatre.

All this, while Kahn has been directing plays. And not just one every season or two. Well over a hundred since that first Off-Off-Broadway show in 1963. Trying to pull out one or two highlights seems pointless. He's worked with hundreds of big names and thousands of small names; he's directed world premieres and more classics than most theater professionals have heard of; he's helmed operas, musicals, straight plays, gender-bending classic fantasias, straightlaced work . . . Pinning him down as a director is no easier than pinning down his travel schedule.

But that schedule finally changed in 2006, when Kahn ended his tenure as head of Juilliard. He opened the Harman Center for the Arts at Shakespeare Theatre Company the following year, which includes an additional 775-seat venue he has to program. "All my life I've divided my energy: two jobs, three jobs. And as I'm getting older, I realize I want to put my creative energy into this organization. I want to focus here."

**FEBRUARY 2003, PALMER HOUSE HILTON, CHICAGO
SEPTEMBER, 2006, VIA PHONE FROM WASHINGTON, D.C.***

How early in life did you know you'd make a career out of directing?

Well, I've never wanted to be anything other than a director. I actually directed my first play in first grade. I was a very bossy kid, an only child,

---

*Michael and I spoke twice for this interview (in 2003 and 2006); I've combined our talks into this one piece.

and smart—I guess I was smart. By the time I went to high school, I didn't have any friends, I just had *casts*. I never thought I'd go to a school [New York City's High School of the Performing Arts] where everyone was like me. My mother had read all of Shakespeare to me probably by the time I was in the first or second grade.

Why did she do that, do you think?

She had read *A Tree Grows in Brooklyn*, and in that, an Irish immigrant mother reads the Bible and Shakespeare to her daughter—so my mother read me the Bible and Shakespeare. And she cut out what she knew were the dirty parts of the Bible—I know we didn't read the Song of Solomon—but she didn't think there were dirty parts in Shakespeare, so she read me all of that.

But I didn't know I wanted to be so involved in Shakespeare until I was in college. I went to Columbia, and I did a production of *Pericles*. And then I did a production of *Peer Gynt,* and then I knew I just wanted to do really *big* plays. But that wasn't how I started out as a director: I actually started out as a very avant-garde director, at Café La MaMa, Caffe Cino.

One wouldn't suspect it, knowing you now.

Oh yeah, I did the first *America Hurrah* [by Jean-Claude van Itallie], Sam Shepard's plays, Adrienne Kennedy's plays . . . that's the kind of director I was, that's how I started.

And then Joe Papp hired me to do *Measure for Measure* in 1966. I did an enormous amount of research and studying and reading, so I came in all prepared; I had very strong feelings about what *Measure for Measure* was about. And after that, people thought of me as a classical director.

Twenty years later, you did *Romeo and Juliet* in your first season at the Shakespeare Theatre, which was considered groundbreaking. So somewhere between 1966 and 1986, you figured out who you are as a director.

I feel that I've actually discovered who I am as a director three or four times in my life. I'm happy to know I'm a very different director than I was ten years ago. And I've changed as a director—thank heavens—a bunch of times. I'm amazed at what I didn't know when I started; I think my imagination and my intelligence carried me quite a long ways and must have allowed people to put up with me, because I was also extremely temperamental. The fact that I'm still working must mean something! But I believe that I only really understood what I was doing with classical plays, *really* understood, maybe in the last ten or twelve years.

I also changed the kind of director I was by the kinds of theaters I was associated with. When I was in Stratford, Connecticut, such a large theater demanded a presentational kind of style; at the same time I was running the McCarter, another large theater. So I began to see things in rather large, epic, presentational ways.

And I got stuck in that, even got accused of it by a critic in the *New York Times*. I was very upset by that, but I sat down one day and said, "He's actually right: I've fallen into a rut." And so I didn't do any more classics for a while.

And then I was offered the [Shakespeare Theatre at the] Folger, and I thought, "This is the only kind of space I would like to work in doing these kinds of plays again, where the relationship between the actor and the audience is really intimate." [The Folger is a 240-seat theater designed as an Elizabethan inn yard, complete with three tiers of wooden balcony seating.]

And because of the Folger, and because of my teaching, my approach to classics has changed in a really healthy way. I am not in this class, but I have always admired Picasso, who continually transformed himself. I don't think I've ever quite had the courage to do that, continually transform, but that's what I admire the most.

How has your directing changed with age and experience?

I find a certain freedom now getting into rehearsal, and having an idea take me in a new way. And I also think I'm more collaborative than I used to be. An actor will come up with something, and I'll take it further, and they'll take it further, and I find that really fun.

Now I never go into rehearsal of a play knowing what it's going to be like. The fun of directing for me, now, is like the fun of reading a mystery. When I first started, I had it all written down, I had it all organized, and some of it was great. But now I find, by the time I do a play, I've read it so many times that I should know it by heart.

Now that you get such joy working moment to moment, does that make planning a season more difficult?

Yes and no. I'd love to be able to say in the middle of the season, "I don't want to do this play anymore, because I think we'd better do *this* play." And I've done that. But that's harder as you get more established. I've been very lucky that I've always surrounded myself with extraordinary people doing a lot of the work. It's been a long time since it's been all on my shoulders. So I have creative time.

But what I hate now is having to decide on the set three months in advance, and the costumes three months in advance, all that stuff that *settles* things and makes it the way you're going to do it. I wish we didn't have to do that. I wish there were a way you could say, "This is the basic idea of how we're going to do it," but, unfortunately, you have to make those decisions.

A hallmark of your work with the classics throughout your career has been its clarity in storytelling.

Somebody wrote a letter to me saying they'd tried to read *The Silent Woman,* by Ben Jonson, and they had to put it down. They really weren't looking forward to coming to see my production [in 2003]. And they couldn't believe how, when they saw it, they could follow it and like it and laugh.

It's my second Jonson, and it's a wonderful challenge and struggle to do that. I don't change the words, but I'll make edits. And I know how much work I do on lines and beats to make it clear. But I hope I change from play to play. Certainly what I want to do is to find the best way to illuminate that play. I don't even think I work the same way play by play with Shakespeare, though I have certain basic principles.

For instance, I opened [the 2002–2003] season with *The Winter's Tale,* and I did *The Winter's Tale* in my first season at the Folger. And they were very different productions. They were not different just in look; they were different in terms of what I thought about the people, what I thought of the language, what I thought about how to tell that story.

Are you a Folio technique person, spending hours analyzing the First Folio version of a Shakespeare play for clues about breaths and emphasis and so on?

No, no, no, no. I'm not a Folio person. I'm not interested in that. I'm not a historicist. I know less now about all that stuff than I did when I was starting. I used to care about that a lot. Now I think I just trust my spirit, my feelings, trying to get to the deepest part of what the playwright's trying to talk about. What my passions are, what I would like to say along with the writer.

How does your relationship to your audience, which is so longstanding, affect your work?

I hate to say something like this, but I have never thought about the audience. I've always trusted that I'm the most difficult audience this play will ever get. And so, if I can figure it out for me in some way— though I've been wrong; I've had enough flops—I really don't think about the audience. I see myself as the filter for understanding. But you know, the audience in D.C. has changed; it's gotten much younger, more diverse. And I don't want audiences who come to see classics as though this is the one safe place they can be away from the rest of the world: nothing bad's going to happen, nothing dangerous is going to happen, it's all going to be fine, and we'll be the same people when we leave as when we walked in. That's not an audience I particularly want to play to.

Certainly the interesting thing about doing Shakespeare in Washington, D.C.—the most powerful city in the world—is that there's no better playwright to deal with what's going on in the world. You often feel you're doing the play-within-the-play from *Hamlet,* and out in the audience is Claudius. Plays in Washington are often received by a significant portion of the audience as a relevant part of their thinking about what's going on. And I'm never unaware of that.

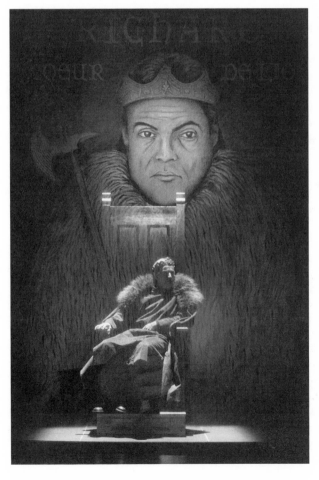

Philip Goodwin in King John *by William Shakespeare. The Shakespeare Theatre, 1999. Credit: Carol Rosegg. Used by permission of Shakespeare Theatre Company.*

I've done a lot of plays at particular times because I thought those plays needed to be done. Very rarely have I done a play just because it's *next*. That's one of the things that's sustained me my whole life. I never really did a play just for money.

Shakespeare productions are changing throughout the country. It used to be that people would simply pick a period and do their Shakespeare play within it.

That was what someone's idea of a "concept" would be, you know: "I'm going to do it like Goya."

That time seems past.

I hope so! [laughs] I can understand why people did it, because it did get imaginations working. But basically that was a gimmicky way of thinking about how you do a play. I've done Shakespeare in every period, no period, mixed periods . . . I don't think it's about the period. It's about how you illuminate *this* point about *this* play. So if I've ever chosen to change a period, it was to do that. Right now I like to do plays that aren't set in any period; I'm not very interested in period. When I started, I'd have people coming in showing us bows and curtsies and dances, and I'm not interested in that anymore. I'm interested now in letting my imagination go where it wants. I learned that from Ingmar Bergman. I went to see some Bergman productions and I thought, "You know, he doesn't give a damn, and I don't either." I don't give a damn whether this goes with that or whether this is a period play and there's a telephone there or . . . Well, it's very freeing. And there are things about myself I trust now.

There was a clear sense of freedom in the *Love's Labor's Lost* you did as part of the Royal Shakespeare Company's international festival of Shakespeare's complete works [2006]. You actually did set it in a period, at a late sixties ashram, with vivid colors and dancing cosmonauts, complete with space suits designed by Catherine Zuber . . .

When [RSC artistic director] Michael Boyd invited us, he said to me, "I'd like you to do a comedy, and I think it would be great if it had an American feel to it," because after all, he was doing an international festival. And in the sixties, I had done a production of *Love's Labor's Lost* [at American Shakespeare Theatre] that I decided would make some sense if I set it at an ashram. That was what was happening at the time: all these fashionable people, all these rock bands, were going to India on spiritual retreats.

I thought that made some sense of this play, which is an Elizabethan conceit about academe. The production back then was okay—as I say, I think I know what I'm doing a little better now—but there were things I simply couldn't fit in, or didn't make sense. So when Michael asked me to bring a play to the RSC, I thought, "I've never done *Love's Labor's* here, so why don't I take a look at it again, and maybe forty years later, one could look at the sixties in a different way?"

I think this production was sharper and wittier. The setting [scenic design by Ralph Funicello] was more authentic than it had been before. And it was interesting to see people look back at what was a big event in their lives—the sixties. It gave the play a different kind of resonance, with people remembering fondly, laughing at themselves, yet taking it seriously.

Where did the idea for the cosmonauts come up?

They have to disguise themselves as Russians to woo the girls. When I did it the last time, I had them all look like Moiseyev dancers, who were the first Russian group to come to America during the Cold War. This time, we thought: "Oh my gosh, cosmonauts!" They walked in doing this sort of moonwalk, and they'd bump into each other because they really couldn't see in those things. I wanted it to be something silly. There are a lot of lines in the play about visors—and they had visors!

Is it that kind of freedom with directorial interpretation that separates American and British directors of Shakespeare?

Directors nowadays come from so many different places. In England, some directors come from philosophy, some of them come from history, some of them come from the visual arts. They don't all come directly from theater, or from acting.

We have English directors here at Shakespeare Theatre Company, and some of them work with the actors in a language that the actors find immensely congenial, and sometimes they don't. I'm not sure that the difference is so huge between American and British directors of Shakespeare.

How about actors?

When I was growing up, the difference was enormous. English actors certainly were considered highly technical; their voices, their ability to speak verse was outstanding, but in a way they acted from the neck up. Whereas Americans were physical and emotional, but not terribly good at text. They broke up the words, or mumbled them—but they were

Aubrey Deeker, Erik Steele, Amir Arison and Hank Stratton in Love's Labor's Lost *by William Shakespeare. Shakespeare Theatre Company, 2006. Credit: Carol Rosegg. Used by permission of Shakespeare Theatre Company.*

very alive, and the British were very clear and not so alive. In an odd way, that's one of the reasons that Juilliard was formed, to synthesize the two approaches.

Now, I think there's not as big a difference. English actors want to get underneath the situations and the characters more, and Americans are getting better (because of training) with elevated text. But for the most part, I still think that Americans can physicalize in a way that is simply part of our being. And because we don't have a tradition, we can afford to be freer with the plays, as long as we have the skills to do them.

[Even so,] most American actors won't get within twenty minutes of this kind of material. But if someone wants to do it, then it's necessary to have those skills that make it comfortable, and not to try to turn it into something else.

It's very easy for American actors to try to sound natural in Shakespeare by pausing before every adjective or noun, instead of *finding* it. And it sounds okay for a little bit of time, but eventually: why bother to have verse? It's easy for an untrained actor to add emphasis by being loud or soft; or to be clear by going very slow, so that by the end of the sentence you haven't really followed it, but it *seems . . .* clear . . . because . . . you're . . . explaining . . . it. That's what you do when you don't have enough technique, to bring the same life and imagination—internal life, I mean. Reality is something you can do in modern language. You need to have the same ability to do that with verse, and that takes training.

Let's talk about being an artistic director. Shakespeare Theatre Company in D.C., the American Shakespeare Theatre in Stratford, the Mc-Carter in New Jersey—what became uniquely Michael Kahn about them?

They were about to close when I came there—that's what's the same about all of them!

I had three years with McCarter and Stratford both saying at the same time that they were going to close. But they didn't. The McCarter is still there. And there were ten more years of Stratford after I left. It just got to the point where finally I said, "I don't want to see another budget, I don't want to see another board," and I just decided I didn't want to do it anymore. And so I freelanced for a while. And again I realized that part of the joy I had in my work was that I was *in charge* of my work. It's the same reason I was a director when I was seven. I needed to be in control in some way of what I was doing. It wasn't that I minded working for other people. As a matter of fact, sometimes I was so glad somebody else was the boss. Even now if I go out to dinner and somebody says, "What should we have?" I say, "*You choose.* I've been making decisions all day long—*you* tell me what we're having for dinner!"

But I realized that not just the ability to shape my own work but the context in which I *did* my work is very important for me. There's an entrepreneurial part of me. I enjoy picking seasons. Running an institution is fun for me. I didn't want a life where you go from Cincinnati to Detroit to L.A. to Atlanta to do a play.

I felt bad a couple of years ago when people didn't want to be artistic directors. But I see that people want to do it again. The days of "I'm the artist and you have to take care of me because I'm the artist" are *long gone.* If I'm going to be responsible for my work, I have other responsibilities to the institution. The kind of ivory tower of the artist was never really part of my makeup.

So would you say, in this economy, this culture, that it's essential for an emerging director to affiliate with an institution?

Well, institutions are in trouble now. Though for me, linking with institutions is healthy. And I think a young director can have an influence on an institution. You get something back, and you also bring new energy and new ideas into an institution. I don't know how anyone makes it as a freelancer anymore. But I do understand that there are people who don't want the added responsibility of an institution, and certainly the danger of institutions is that in difficult times, they retreat, get safe. That's not good for the institution or the artist. I had that happen to me at the McCarter. It was really difficult. And I started making decisions, you know, artistic decisions that I thought were "saving the institution" decisions. It's what made me leave the McCarter.

When I got to Washington, I was not unaware of the difficulties the Shakespeare Theatre was in, both artistically and financially (in fact, I was on the NEA panel that had defunded it for artistic reasons). So I said to the board when I took the job, "I don't believe in saving institutions. I don't believe institutions *need* to be there. There doesn't need to be a third-rate or a second-rate classical theater in America. So I'm going to do the best work I know how, but if either my own work or the resources available do not lead us into being a significant theater, then I don't think we should be there." I learned that at the McCarter, when I was working so hard to save it, bringing in productions that I shouldn't have, trying to appeal to a larger audience. Because all of a sudden, I had huge audiences for plays, but they weren't necessarily going to come back for anything else I wanted to do.

So I learned that lesson: don't reduce or change what you believe in, what you think your vision is, in order to save an institution. I would urge anybody to avoid that, because the things you would do to save your institution will ultimately destroy it. So you decide to do popular programming for two years . . . well, is that the audience you want to play to forever? I know the problems, but how do you maneuver without sacrificing what you believe in?

The best thing that's happened to me in Washington is that we've developed an audience based on the work we've done. Absolutely. And the *support* I have is based on the work we've done. And how do you get an audience to trust you? By literally committing yourself to how you're going to work, and *stick to it*. And the people who don't like it go away, and the people who begin to like it see you grow with it.

I read an interview recently in which you spoke about stars in productions. In your first production in Washington, for example, you cast Pat Carroll.

Well, I'd seen her in *Gertrude Stein* [*Gertrude Stein Gertrude Stein*, 1979–1980 at Circle Repertory Company] and I knew this was a *major actor*, so that's why I cast her. I'm not going to penalize someone for becoming a star. The people I work with on this material are people who can do the material. They've all been trained to do this work. I knew Kelly McGillis from Juilliard. And I knew Stacy Keach from Central Park.

But do you worry that the audience might come to expect star-driven programming?

We've got many plays with our own actors in addition to those with well-known actors. The nice thing about Washington is that people will come if the play means something to them. Of course it helps to have a star. But Pat Carroll wasn't a star when she did that; she became a star in Washington *because* of that. And Pat was wonderful. She was wonderful as Falstaff. She was wonderful as Mother Courage. And I gave her a chance to do that when she'd been doing game shows for a long time.

Help me finish this sentence: You can't be a director if . . .

I don't think you can be a director if you don't have imagination. I don't think you can be a director if you don't have an understanding of plays. I don't think you can be a director if you . . . well, I'm going to say this though I'm not sure it's absolutely true: I don't think you should be a director if you don't have an understanding of the most important instrument you're going to work with, which is the actor. That's not necessarily the way some people think. But I would never want to be an auto mechanic and get asked to fix a car if I didn't know something about it.

I think it helps to have drive and patience. I think it helps to have a lot of energy. And I don't think it hurts to be smart.

You can't teach a lot of that.

No, but you can encourage imagination. You can see when someone stops him or herself, and you say, "No, wait: open that door." That's what you do with actors. I think what you can probably teach in directing is how to look at a play, what are the possibilities of styles, what are the possibilities of blocking. But probably, directing is in some way as inborn as acting. I've never tried to teach directing; I've tried to mentor people. I'm very shy about all that. I mean, Anne Bogart has a *system*, so she can go teach people how to do that. I don't have a system. I envy Anne that she has a system! It's fantastic! People say to me, "You ought to write a book." And I ask, "About what?"

But you did say that there are certain basic things you know how to do when you start directing a play.

Right. I know that when I read Shakespeare, I read it first for the story. And then I'll read it again once I know what the story is, and I'll read it very closely. I'll read it line by line. And then I'll read it word by word.

THE DIRECTOR'S VOICE, VOLUME 2

And then I begin to understand where all the changes are because of what I see in the text. I understand where all the transitions are. Like in a big speech, I'll see, "Oh, it starts there, but actually the thought changes *there,* and the thought changes *there,* and the thought changes *there.*" And then I think, "So why does it change?"

And if I start doing that really close work—why is that word there instead of another one? and so on—I feel the playwright's mind. I start to be in the playwright's mind as to what kind of choices he or she is making as it goes along. And that takes a lot of time.

But I've also learned how to listen to a scene and notice when the actor's skipping. We can be doing a scene, and I'll say, "Wait, wait, wait a minute. How did you *get there?* You just got there because you said it, but you didn't really *get there.*" I can hear that in an actor. And I can hear it in five actors; I can actually be living five different characters' lives moment to moment in a scene, which probably comes from teaching acting. That's why my plays are clear: because I don't skip anything.

That kind of work is tremendously exciting because all of a sudden, the play opens up. It's not just a text but a play about behavior, feeling, all of these things that are influencing the text, driving the text, in very specific terms. I think that's what made the Jonson work.

The clues aren't as clear in Jonson.

No, you have to read it, and read it, and read it, and read it. I drive actors crazy by stopping them and saying, "No, wait a minute, wait a minute, what did you say? No. That's what you *think* you said. What did you *say?*"

It's not easy, because there's not a lot of subtext in Shakespeare or Jonson. But I strongly believe it's the director's job to get the actor to the place where *they actually can't say anything else.* That there's no *choice* to say anything else. And that takes a lot of doing. Sounds easy, but most people say it next because it's *there,* which is the most uninteresting reason to say it.

So how do you get yourself situationally, emotionally, physically, imaginatively to the point that you really can't say anything other than, "To be or not to be," and mean, "To be or not to be," and not mean anything else? That's what I've come to understand, finally, in a profound way for myself.

What happens when you can't get an actor to recognize that imperative? Is it the actor's fault? Yours?

It's all of our faults. But I don't get that too much anymore! One of the other things I really have now is a sense of humor. Sure, I'm impossible, but I keep rehearsals funny. It reduces my tension.

I had Keith Baxter in rehearsal for the *The Merchant of Venice*, and I was saying, "No, no, wait a minute, wait a minute: stop!" And he just stopped, and I asked, "What's the matter? Can't you act when I'm talking?"

Have you ever gone down the wrong road with a production team? Or a cast? Or an audience?

Lord knows I've had enough failures. I did *Hedda Gabler* [in 2001] in Washington with Judith Light, and I had a really wonderful time doing it. But when I did it [in 1981] in New York at the Roundabout, it got the worst set of reviews that I've ever gotten in my life. I realize now that I was more interested in *how I wanted to do the play* than in the play itself.

I know that I'm more open-minded about things now, more interested in ambiguity. When I first did *Measure for Measure,* it was a big success, but I thought Angelo was a villain. And when I did it more recently, I realized what was going on, and that there was more complexity to the character.

My first *Henry V*, in Stratford, became a rather well-known production during the Vietnam War. It was the antiwar version of *Henry V*. It was completely influenced by Brecht and by kabuki. And I just laughed when I saw a picture in *American Theatre* magazine of an avant-garde production of *Henry V,* and it was mine from thirty years ago and I didn't recognize it! But when I came back to do *Henry V* [in 1995], I realized that the character of Henry was not just awful; I now see the complexity of people. I enjoy the complexity of people. And so therefore the productions I do are not so skewed.

Can you tell me about moments you've created of which you're particularly proud?

I'm thinking of [actor] Wally Acton in *Henry VI* [Shakespeare Theatre Company, 1996] at the end, when Gloucester has his speech: "I have no brother, I am like no brother." The play has to move toward Richard, toward *Richard III.* And we were in tech, and I thought, "This is not *fierce* enough." Yet it wasn't about being loud, or about being more scary. The speech needed to change the temperature of the auditorium completely. It had to chill the place.

So I said to Wally, "I'm going to take the lights out." I asked one of the interns for a flashlight, and I said, "Just shine it on him." You know, now it's a commonplace, with shadows on the wall, but we hadn't seen that yet.

And then I said, "Why don't you start undressing as you do this? As you work yourself up, so we actually see you without the padding, without all the stuff you do to hide your hump." And he took off his doublet, and he was in this little thin undershirt with his hump. And then I said, "Would you just throw the clothes down, and walk off the stage, and walk through the auditorium and slam the door shut?" And it was *really scary.* It went from the drama of the play and murders and all that to something that seemed to be pure evil, pure deformity. That was a really important moment. Sometimes the best things come out of rehearsal, by accident.

Just like when I was doing *'Tis Pity She's a Whore* at American Repertory Theater [1988]. We were at a dress rehearsal, and Giovanni is supposed to come in with the heart of his sister on a dagger. And during the scene before, I rushed to the costume designer and said, "Make him put on her wedding dress before he comes in." So she ran back, put the wedding dress on Derek Smith—he didn't know what the hell was going on. But he came on with her heart, wearing her wedding dress, and I thought, "*That's it.*" That's an identification with her so completely that he *is* her. That's the kind of thing that comes to you, and you think, "That's exactly what the play is about."

The most fun I had with audiences was when I did *Timon of Athens* [in 2000]. I set it in the eighties, because I was looking for a play about greed. I hadn't wanted to do *Timon*; I thought it was not a very good play, but then I thought that by setting it in the eighties, by setting it in a recognizable period, the play would open itself up. And I got a letter from someone with two subscriptions torn up, saying that I was trying to influence the elections.

And I thought, "How wonderful that somebody believes that a four-hundred-year-old play in a little theater in Washington could actually influence the elections!" She thought I'd done it about Reaganomics. I'd done it about the eighties; I had just done it about *greed*. And I did it because I thought this play was a healthy reminder that a bust could come. We were in the internet boom, and my audience was Northern Virginia; it was all internet start-ups. I thought it would be a healthy exercise, but I didn't know it was going to be *true*. My audience is now made up of internet close-downs.

I worked with Charlie Newell for a couple of years, and I hear echoes of him in you. You've mentored so many people. Who are the people that mentored you?

I had a great acting teacher in high school. And also Joe Papp believed in me when I was a kid; I think he was a major influence in my life. And then there were people I wanted to *be* like. I learned from watching Martha Graham, and Giorgio Strehler, Peter Brook. But you know, I was such a stubborn, egotistical guy: I wasn't mentoree material! I wanted to be in charge!

So you were unmentorable?

I had the courage of my convictions, and a pretty big temper. I'm amazed I'm still working. John Houseman believed in me. He hired me to teach at Juilliard without knowing a damn thing about whether I could teach or not.

I remember, when I was in college, walking up Broadway and thinking I should be a Broadway director. I was a kid in New York: I was going to Broadway! I must have been seventeen. But later I realized that my life was not the life I thought I was going to have. It wasn't going to be this Broadway-director life. And I didn't know what else there was.

I was just lucky that, you know, I found Jean-Claude van Itallie, and [La MaMa founder] Ellen Stewart . . . But I wouldn't join the Open Theater. Everybody else I knew joined the Open Theater to work with Joe [Chaikin], but I couldn't, because I wasn't mentoring material! It's true!

You've done a lot of Shakespeare and a lot of Tennessee Williams, and I wanted to ask you why.

First of all, I love the language of Tennessee Williams, and I like all the things that happen in Tennessee Williams. And he was the great playwright when I was growing up. But I didn't do any Tennessee until *Cat on a Hot Tin Roof* [a 1974 Broadway transfer from American Shakespeare Theatre].

And because I did *Cat* in the context of a classical theater, the play took on what I believe to be the definition of "classic theater": theater that takes on the big issues through the meaning of language and character. It transcends the particular time of its writing.

I've done quite a bit of Ibsen lately; I've done O'Neill. I think the thing that I love about all of those plays is that the ambition of the playwright is larger. I've always liked these huge challenges—whether I could meet them or not is less important to me! [laughs] I like it if what I'm doing is hard for me. That's why I like doing Ben Jonson: it's hard.

You know who's missing from your list? Chekhov. Miller. Albee.

My first year as artistic director in Stratford, I got together an extraordinary group of actors to do *Three Sisters*. Kate Reid, Morris Carnovsky, Brian Bedford, Maria Tucci, Marian Seldes. And I had the most awful time, the *most awful time*!

The other thing is—and this is serious—I have to see two Chekhov plays a year done by the second-year students at Juilliard. And while it's a wonderful experience for them, and an important experience for them, they're not really ready to do Chekhov in the second year, as I've seen for twenty-eight years!

Now, Albee . . . Edward gave me my first start in the theater. I owe him and Joe Papp my career. All of my first jobs were for Edward Albee. And it was that which led to Joe asking me to do *Measure*. I would love to do Albee. But I've never been in a place where I've wanted to do a play that had just been done on Broadway.

I was at the opening night of *Virginia Woolf* [1962], and I wrote Edward my first fan letter. I didn't know him yet, and I said, "This is the most beautiful, terrifying play I've ever seen." And he wrote back a letter saying, "Dear Michael Kahn, if this is the most beautiful, terrifying play you've ever seen, you haven't gone to the theater enough."

Here's a quote of yours: "People ask me, 'Aren't you sorry you aren't in New York?' and I say, 'Can you tell me where I could have done *Timon of Athens* or *Pericles* or *Camino Real*?'" My question leading out of that is—

Would I have liked to have done them in New York? Yes!

Why are the lesser-known classics so interesting to you? Are you trying to reshape the canon, or just avoiding the comparisons you'd be subject to with more popular plays?

Doing a play that I've never seen, that interests me, that I don't know how it's going to turn out, that I don't have any roadmap for . . . that is exciting for me. I want to do all of *Faust* now. I like throwing myself up against a wall and seeing if I can stand up. I really do!

I had never seen *Don Carlos*, and I'd wanted to do it for years. And then the RSC did it, and I thought, "Oh damn, they're going to bring it to BAM [Brooklyn Academy of Music], and I won't be able to do it," so I just scheduled it. And when I did it, I thought, "Why doesn't every theater do this play? This is the most interesting, emotional, political play I've done in years."

Your production sparked a mini-revolution of Schiller in regional theater.

Yes, and I think that's part of my responsibility as the artistic director of a classical theater that has some sort of national reputation: to help expand the definition of what the canon of classics is. I love the Jacobean plays. They're extraordinary plays waiting to be done.

Do you think it's easier or harder for a young director to have a career now than it was twenty years ago?

Look, I was very lucky. I worked for free for a very long time, which was very important to be able to do. My mother died when I was young, which left me a little bit of money, which allowed me to be able to take a lot of free jobs. And I had a scholarship to college, so I didn't have student loans. So I could work at Cino; I could do all those plays for Edward Albee's playwriting project, all of that stuff. I had a freedom that let people get to know me as a director, that introduced me to actors and designers. Lord knows, New York was a more thriving theater scene *then* than it is *now*; although I didn't want to do much in New York, and I got out of there pretty fast.

Sometimes when I go talk to the Lincoln Center Directors Lab and I see ninety people in the room, all wanting to be directors, I think, "There aren't ninety plays to *do* right now." So you'd better make a lot of noise to get out of the pack.

So when directors ask me what to do, I say: (1) try to assist people you will learn from, and who will put you in situations where people will actually start to think of you as a director; and (2) start your own theater company. And then just get one person down to see it.

One of the nice things in my life is that I have Juilliard. And I have the best non-program program for young directors at Shakespeare Theatre Company. Someone comes to work there for three years, and ends up getting the title of junior artistic director. And when they leave, they've done all the understudy rehearsals, they've done a lot of casting, and they're ready to do it. Would I take a chance to hire one of those young directors to direct one of my productions at Shakespeare Theatre Company? Probably not. But I *can* at Juilliard.

I feel a real responsibility. Because I was allowed to direct in major places in my twenties. People gave me a chance to run a theater when I was twenty-eight years old. A big theater.

When you choose directors at Shakespeare Theatre Company, do identity politics ever figure into it? Gay directors, directors of color, female directors . . .

I don't think about woman directors, or directors of color, other than I think it's important for inclusion. Since women and artists of color have been excluded for a very long time—though it's not so much the case anymore—it's important to do what you can do to make room. I actually support affirmative action in many ways, until the playing field is leveled.

I've never thought of a play as, "This is a play a woman should direct, or a gay person should direct." For instance, Gale Edwards doing *Richard III*—this is probably not a play you would think is necessarily a woman's sensibility. And yet her relationship to that actor, and to the text, is so strong I asked her to do it. As for me, I've been out my whole life; I'm just lucky to be in a profession where I've never been discriminated against.

You said that you're a director who continually changes. Do you feel another change coming on?

It better come on!

Why?

I think I know what I'm doing now, and I need to find something I *don't* know. When I really think I know what I'm doing, then it's time to say, "Move on." I spend a lot of time thinking, "Maybe I should be Peter Sellars, maybe I should be Andrei Serban." But then I realize: *I* am who *I* am, and maybe it's time for me just to be Michael Kahn, and find out what else I have to do.

Have you ever thought of retiring?

Well, I don't think I'm the same workaholic I've been my whole life. I want a little more time for myself to read. But do I want to retire? I don't think I know what retirement means yet.

MOISÉS KAUFMAN

A Question of Form

WHEN MOISÉS KAUFMAN AND I FIRST met in 1996, he needed a coproducer for a work he'd been writing based on the trials of Oscar Wilde. Despite some good press attention for his production of Franz Xaver Kroetz's *The Nest* (named one of the top productions of the 1994–1995 season by the *Village Voice*), his company, Tectonic Theater Project, was still struggling for legitimacy. When Tectonic couldn't find anyone to coproduce the Wilde project, the company somehow found the resources to put it up by itself. Kaufman called the play *Gross Indecency: The Three Trials of Oscar Wilde*. It became the third-most-performed play in America in 1998, according to TCG's annual survey of the subject, and generated raves from the country's mainstream press: *USA Today*, *Time* magazine, the *Wall Street Journal* . . . even *Entertainment Weekly*. Moisés Kaufman is now one of the best known and most important voices directing and writing in America's institutional theaters. And that's ironic, because Kaufman's work actively questions the assumptions on which mainstream theater is based.

Kaufman's longstanding suspicion of what constitutes "the mainstream" has its roots in Venezuela, where he was schooled as a boy at a yeshiva. In that rarefied world, Kaufman studied the Talmud, a Jewish religious text devoted to questioning and interpretation. Decades later, that kind of rigorous questioning still guides Kaufman's theatrical exploration.

Long after yeshiva, but before coming to the United States, Kaufman worked with Thespis Theater Ensemble, one of Venezuela's preeminent experimental theater companies at the time. There, he applied a Talmudic rigor to traditional theater forms. Kaufman worked as an actor in nonrealistic plays (Ionesco, Molière, Valle-Inclán), and engaged in extremely rigorous training influenced by Vsevolod Meyerhold and Jerzy Grotowski.

After moving to New York in 1987, Kaufman continued his studies at New York University's Experimental Theatre Wing, where he learned from the giants of the experimental movement. There, Kaufman embraced his mentors' questioning of theatrical form—a form that, until the 1960s, placed text at the center of the theater experience. But companies like the Wooster Group and Mabou Mines, as well as individuals like Richard Schechner, Mary Overlie and Stephen Wangh all challenged traditional notions, and translated their experiments into stage practice.

In 1991, Kaufman founded Tectonic Theater Project to mount a production of four short plays Samuel Beckett wrote for actresses, *Women in Beckett*. As with many new companies, Tectonic was small and project-driven. Kaufman's cofounder, Jeffrey LaHoste, was (and still is) his life partner; it was LaHoste's steady job that secured the bank loan they needed to produce that first production. LaHoste was the company's first managing director, and served as one of the screenwriters on the HBO film of *The Laramie Project*.

Despite now finding himself in demand elsewhere, he continued primarily to create theater with his company. (Unlike many of his contemporaries, Kaufman has not been seduced to large institutional leadership.) "Tectonic means the art and science of structure," Kaufman told me, and his company studies it as it relates to theater with reverence— he says that "form and content copulate" in his work. Whether staging plays by twentieth-century revolutionaries such as Beckett and Kroetz, or creating work from the ground up, his company pursues its founding mission to ask not only what forms or structures are possible in the theater, but how those are created. These questions about theatrical vocabularies and theatrical languages invariably generate very innovative work. The plays for which Kaufman is best known—*Gross Indecency* (as writer/director, 1997), *The Laramie Project* (again, as writer/ director, 2000), and Doug Wright's *I Am My Own Wife* (as director, 2003)—all have at their center these queries.

And because all three tackle historical figures and events, they ask these tectonic questions by turning the documentary form upside down. If a documentary is meant to present authoratative truth, Kaufman's approach subverts that assumption. He does this by investigating the artist's role as editor, just as much as he investigates the history itself.

Thus, in *Gross Indecency*, each of the three historical trials of Oscar Wilde is presented with a different theatrical vocabulary, highlighting the impossibility of knowing the truth—of the charges against Wilde, of the era itself and of the place of homosexuality in history. All the actors except the one playing Wilde are narrators at one point or another; Kaufman's staging gets less traditional as the trials progress, and the characters hold books and reference texts as if to put the word *history* in quotes. The play put Kaufman on the map, winning a slew of awards; he directed productions of it across the country and internationally.

In *The Laramie Project*, the company's investigation of the brutal murder of Matthew Shepard in 1998 is purposefully bifurcated. Created from extensive interviews conducted in Laramie, Wyoming, over the course of a year and a half, the play's first act unfolds as traditional docudrama (significantly, Shepard is the only principal figure without a voice). The second act then directly challenges the docudrama format by focusing not on the crime itself, but on the role the media played in influencing the residents of the town (and America more generally). *Laramie* thus investigates the murder, its effect on a community and the way it became history—all in one magnificent stroke. The play ultimately became one of the most-produced plays in America in the 2001–2002 season by TCG's measure; critics have compared it to *Angels in America* in terms of its scope and influence, and Kaufman's HBO film adaptation of the play was nominated for four Emmy Awards. An epilogue, *The Laramie Project: Ten Years Later*, premiered on October 12, 2009 simultaneously in one hundred cities across the country: a kind of crowd-sourced, community-based theater event.

I Am My Own Wife attacks the question of authorship and truth even more directly. What began as a traditional biodrama about the little-known life of Charlotte von Mahlsdorf, a transvestite who lived in Berlin during the Nazi and Communist eras, took a new turn when Kaufman suggested playwright Wright insert himself into the narrative as another character (a device used successfully in *Laramie*). Wright's character and the way he was interwoven in Charlotte's story was the subject of the play's extensive workshop (Sundance, 2000; La Jolla Playhouse, 2001; Chicago's About Face Theatre, 2003), and when it officially premiered at Playwright's Horizons in 2003, *I Am My Own Wife* was a smart and sympathetic investigation not only of Charlotte, but of the role of the biographer, the practice of idol-worship and the many-sided face of historical truth. Investigating Charlotte, Wright was shattered to learn that she was not the saint he imagined her to be; his crisis became a part of the drama. Charlotte can neither be condemned nor exonerated in *I Am My Own Wife*, and that's in part due to the complicated insertion of the author into the narrative: what "truth" does Wright (the character) want to portray in Charlotte's story, and what "truth" does Wright (the author) owe his audience? Kaufman's work on the play garnered Tony and Drama Desk nominations, and an OBIE Award; the play itself was awarded the Tony, the Pulitzer and a number of other high-profile laurels.

Although Kaufman's company was not directly a part of the genesis of *I Am My Own Wife*, all three of these plays were created using Tectonic's methodology. A long period of research is conducted under Kaufman's leadership (whether conducted through in-person interviews or by reading as much material as the artists can get their hands on). The results are brought into workshops, where the material is played with, filtered, edited and shaped. A Kaufman project might undergo as many as half a dozen weeklong workshops, some separated by months in order to get the right artists in the room together. Kaufman usually takes on the role of lead writer in addition to directorial duties. The workshops are presented to public audiences (press is not invited until Kaufman is ready), and extensive post-show discussions help shape the work.

Though it is particular to Kaufman's aesthetic interests, Tectonic's methodology is not without precedent. In the 1970s and 1980s, the Joint Stock Theatre Company in London used its actors to do research that eventually turned into Caryl Churchill's *Cloud Nine*. In this country, both Emily Mann and Anna Deavere Smith construct "Theater of Testimony" based on interviews they've done. But the obsession with theatrical vocabularies and how narratives are constructed is Kaufman's own stamp, and his success in putting it on stage as a subject of his work is unparalleled. The recent explosion of devised-work companies in this country (like Sojourn Theatre or Rude Mechanicals) is due in no small part to Kaufman's influence.

Another important strain in his past work is the construction of sexuality and sexual identity. *Gross Indecency, Laramie* and *Wife* all investigate homosexuality in drastically different historical contexts (Victorian Britain, contemporary America and post–World War II Europe, respectively). Kaufman's assignments regionally (within and without Tectonic) explore similar questions: his 2006 *Macbeth* for the Public Theater in Central Park emphasized the play's contrasts between masculinity and femininity. Tennessee Williams's screenplay *One Arm*, which Kaufman adapted and directed with Tectonic in a workshop production at Chicago's Steppenwolf Theatre Company in 2004 (and in 2011 at the Acorn Theatre in New York), tackles questions of sexuality and masculinity (and authorship) in its own rebellious way.

This is not to say Kaufman is constrained by subject matter: his company's latest project focused on Beethoven's writing of the Diabelli

Variations (33 *Variations*, 2007), and as of this writing, they have works in development about autism, the nineteenth-century actress Charlotte Cushman and William Golding's *Lord of the Flies*. In addition, Tectonic has established a theater-training program specializing in "moment work," a technique for writing "performance" (as opposed to writing text). Through its university and professional workshops, Kaufman and his company have passed their methodology onto thousands of students across the country.

The methodology long championed by Kaufman is now, thanks to the success of his work and his company, ubiquitous throughout the country. *The Laramie Project* receives hundreds of productions each year at high schools, colleges and other amateur theater groups, along with professional productions. As the *New York Times* said in 2002, "*The Laramie Project* has entered the mainstream of American culture in a way few plays do." That fact is important to Kaufman, whose work fosters in audience members not only a greater awareness of challenges facing others—in *Laramie*'s case, our cultural fault lines—but also the not-so-mainstream understanding that the theater as an art form must be questioned in order to remain a vital cultural force.

MARCH 2003, MUSEUM OF CONTEMPORARY ART, CHICAGO
AUGUST 2006, VIA PHONE FROM NEW YORK CITY*

Tell me about the beginning of your career.

I started doing theater out of panic. I had enrolled in the business school at a university in my native Venezuela. I was unclear about what I wanted to do with my future, and business administration seemed to me to be vague enough to allow me to delay the decision for as long as possible.

But on the first day of school, the first class was accounting, at seven in the morning. And I can't tell whether it was the subject matter that I found abominable or the hour, but I started having a panic attack. The minute it was over, I ran to the extracurricular activities center and asked if they had a theater group. They did. I immediately joined.

Since then, I have often found that decisions made in a moment of panic tend to be surprisingly wise.

---

*Moisés and I spoke twice for this interview (in 2003 and 2006); I've combined our talks into this one piece.

The cast of The Laramie Project *by Moisés Kaufman and members of Tectonic Theater Project. Berkeley Repertory Theatre, 2001. Credit: Ken Friedman.*

That theater company (Thespis) was led by a very brilliant director by the name of Fernando Ivosky. This was 1987, and Venezuela at that time had one of the most important international theater festivals in the hemisphere [Festival Internacional de Teatro de Caracas]. This director had attended workshops with Jerzy Grotowski, and had been very influenced by Peter Brook and Tadeusz Kantor. So I was fortunate enough to start my theater career in a company that was influenced by some of the most theatrically interesting minds of the century.

How did Thespis work?

The company was very rigorous. We spent months in rehearsals for each play. We would do intensive body work and voice work and dozens of theater games. The productions were very physical, and concerned with creating a theatrical vocabulary that best suited the world of the play. The repertory included things like *The Bald Soprano* by Ionesco, *The Pelican* by Strindberg, and *The Imaginary Invalid* by Molière. All of these works demanded a keen attention to theatrical languages and theatrical vocabularies. So as you see, my early influences were writers who were not dealing with realism or naturalism but with other forms, and with how theater speaks as a medium, as opposed to how one particular play builds a narrative.

I was in that company for five years as an actor. And somewhere in those five years I realized I was more interested in constructing stage events than I was in constructing a single character. But that early experience planted the seeds of my own theoretical questioning, and my own pragmatic development. Many of the techniques I use in rehearsals today, the way I work with actors, the way I talk to designers, reference my time in that company.

In addition to this, I had an uncle who lived in New Jersey. And every summer we would visit him and go to the theater both on and Off Broadway. I remember seeing *Hair*, and the thrill I felt when everyone on stage got naked . . . I remember seeing a show Tommy Tune did Off Broadway—I think it was called *The Club*—with male impersonators.

So I had a very eclectic theatrical upbringing, from Grotowski to *Hair*, from eastern European avant-garde to American musicals.

You've spoken before about how Judaism has influenced your artistic path as well.

Well, I went to a yeshiva all my life. You can picture the quintessential image of a yeshiva: people sitting around tables reading books, studying, praying. In that environment there is a great deal of attention paid to erudition, and books and learning. One rabbi says this and the other rabbi says that. It's a very dialectical analysis of both reality and text.

In fact, one of the things that made me want to come to New York was that, although I had been working as an actor for five years, I felt that I lacked the *theoretical* knowledge that I needed to generate the work. I knew all of Grotowski's exercises, and Peter Brook's, and understood some of their ideas, but I didn't know how they fit into the continuum of theater history in the twentieth century. What were the things they were revolting against? I had of course read *Towards a Poor Theatre*, I'd read *The Empty Space*; I knew *some* of the theory behind it all, but I didn't understand the context in which these ideas were being formulated. I felt that if I wanted to be a director I needed to study much more. Know more. Read more.

At that time, the Experimental Theatre Wing at NYU was influenced not only by Brook and Kantor and Grotowski, but also by the way Americans had interpreted and processed their work. They were influenced by Richard Schechner and the Wooster Group and Mabou Mines and Mary Overlie and the people who had themselves translated those directors into an American lingo. So there was a continuity to my education.

And indeed the main thing that I learned at NYU was the theoretical background to go with the practical knowledge, which helped me fully understand what I was doing. It gave me a framework on which to construct my own practices, my own theories and my own beliefs.

What theories are those?

Well, over the course of the twentieth century, one of the big questions we faced in the arts was: does form follow function, or does function follow form? And I think one of the big breakthroughs in that dialogue came when Beckett said that *form is content, and content is form*. A dam broke for me when I read that.

The way I like to think about it in Tectonic Theater Project is that form and content *copulate*. And the offspring of that copulation is the work that we do. I know that sounds somewhat pompous, but it's inspired us to think about that relationship in a different way. (And it allows us to have the word "copulate" in our mission statement.)

Whenever I go into a rehearsal, I always try to spend the same amount of time discussing the subject matter as I do talking about theatrical vocabulary and form. And it comes from this questioning of the medium. What is it that this medium can do that others can't? The age-old question!

I'm very intrigued as to why realism and naturalism are still so prevalent on our stages. These are, after all, nineteenth-century theatrical vocabularies. If you went to a contemporary art gallery today and saw a contemporary painting that looked like a Renoir, you'd say it looked like a bad imitation of a Renoir. You wouldn't accept it as a valid contemporary visual vocabulary! And yet, when we go to the theater, that's exactly what happens. We're seeing forms that are more than a hundred years old; forms that, at this point, film and television do better.

So what are the vocabularies, the forms, that will allow the theater to speak in all of its glory and beauty and grandeur? You know how they say we've only learned to use ten percent of our brain's ability? I think we've only learned to use ten percent of our theatrical ability. We've only unlocked a minuscule segment of its possibilities. And that's not to say we should avoid ever producing another realistic or naturalistic play. But should they continue to dominate our theatrical landscape?

These are the kinds of questions to pose as we enter the rehearsal room.

When we first met in 1996, you and Tectonic were just beginning to move from using the classics to investigate those questions, often in stunningly visual ways, to creating the text yourselves, or using new texts like *I Am My Own Wife*. Why the shift?

In the first five years of Tectonic Theater Project, we were staging exist-ing texts, which themselves were posing questions of form. The first production we did was called *Women in Beckett*, which was all of Samuel Beckett's short plays for women.

And look at Beckett's trajectory as a writer: he begins with very well-formed, full-length plays, *Godot* and *Endgame*. But as he continues his own theoretical pursuit, and his own formal pursuit, the plays become smaller; they become very precise theatrical machines, where you see only a mouth on stage, or a woman in a rocking chair. So he's really fracturing what, up to that moment, was a dramaturgy based almost entirely on text. And he begins to do what I think of as *writing performance. Not I* cannot exist without the image of the mouth. He's writing for the the-ater in theatrical ways: the dramatic event cannot be divorced from the full stage picture he's created. And that's one of the reasons why he was so adamant about his lines, his staging not being changed, because he *perceived* it as one thing. He started with this stage event, and then wrote texts for that stage event, which was a radical revolution.

We started doing those pieces because they spoke to us. We also staged Franz Xaver Kroetz and Sophie Treadwell—a great American expressionist. We did Naomi Iizuka and other contemporary writers. Then we staged things like the late pieces of Tennessee Williams, where he was influenced by people like Beckett and Ionesco. So I guess in essence we were looking to learn from these playwrights who were themselves interested in questions of form and theatrical languages. Tectonics is the art and science of structure—"tectonic plates," "archi-tectonic"—and so from our inception, we were trying to pose questions about form and structure.

But after four years of doing this, it became clear to me that if I was really committed to asking questions about form, I had to explore the issue of text. It wasn't sufficient anymore to keep exploring other artists' texts. It was necessary to create our own.

Can you point to that moment of clarity—what it was?

I think the problem of recounting history is that one tends to make it tidy. We have a desire and a tendency to tie up loose ends, to construct epiphanies in hindsight. You know, there's a beautiful book by Gabriel García Márquez I read just recently. It's called *Vivir para contarla (Living to Tell the Tale)*, and it's a very moving autobiography. On the first page he writes: "Life is not what one lives, life is what one remembers and how one remembers it to tell it." That's a great definition, because it talks about identity as an act of memory and reconstruction.

So when you ask me, "When was the exact moment when you knew?"—there wasn't one, because it was an organic process.

So you're even questioning the form of this interview!

Yes! [laughs] But I can tell you when I first had the idea of working on a piece about Oscar Wilde. I remember very vividly when somebody gave me a book called *The Wit and Wisdom of Oscar Wilde*. And thinking this might be the project with which to tackle the issue of text.

***Gross Indecency**, **Laramie**, even **I Am My Own Wife**—these are all plays that consider identity via the question of who owns the story.*

I think we, as a culture, have become very, very savvy about how we hear stories and how we tell stories. We're a visual culture and we're savvy about narrative. So I want to think that perhaps this kind of work is addressing questions that we're dealing with as a culture.

I was born into an orthodox Jewish community in a Catholic country. When I was nine I realized I was gay. So I was gay inside an orthodox Jewish community inside a Catholic and *machista* country. Then I left Venezuela and came to New York and became a Latino. So now I am a Jewish, Gay, Latino man living in New York (probably the only place in the world where that's not such an anomaly). For me, that makes issues of identity and representation terribly important. I'm very interested in exploring not only what identity is, but also how identity is constructed and interpreted.

One of the things that really struck me about most biographies of Oscar Wilde written before 1970 is that Wilde's homosexuality was always referred to as an "illness" or "malady" or "mental defect." I found this interesting, because if you look at Oscar's own writings, he never describes himself that way. His attraction to men is for him a thing of great beauty: something to be cherished, not condemned or reduced to clinical terms. And yet every time his story was told for the next eighty years, he was described as a person with an illness. It wasn't until the 1980s that we began to get biographies that talk about his sexuality as something other than an illness.

That was such a pivotal moment in my development as a writer, I think, because I realized that if Oscar were to tell his story, that's not the story he would tell. So who gets to tell whose stories? And how do narratives change according to who constructs them? These are incredibly helpful questions with which to enter a rehearsal room—questions to pose to the actors, designers, composers . . . all your collaborators.

Another thing that had a great impact on me was that when I originally read Oscar's narratives of the trials, I took them to be "the truth," or "the facts." But the more research I did, the more I kept finding contradictions: Lord Alfred Douglas had a different version of what transpired. Wilde's lawyer had a different version of events; so did Wilde's wife, and so on.

In my naiveté I'd been thinking, "When I finish the research, I will know who's telling the truth." Well, of course, when I was done with the research, all I was left with was a number of contradictory versions of the event.

So the question for me became: how do you write a play about the impossibility of reconstructing history? How do you create a story about the impossibility of creating *one* cohesive story? And that question led to much of the form of that play: a group of actors quoting from different (often contradictory) sources in an attempt to figure out the past. In this context, the audience becomes the constructor of the narrative. And hopefully becomes aware of the ambiguous and ungraspable nature of history.

Form and content copulating—and out comes a three-act structure.

That was dictated by the fact that there were three trials. And it was very clear that each trial affected Oscar in a very different way. Early on, I had the idea that the journey of the play was the journey between Oscar Wilde's public persona and Oscar Wilde's innermost private persona: an undressing of sorts. A lot of people have called Oscar Wilde the first performance artist, because he created this persona which he then paraded around the world: *The* Oscar Wilde. In the first trial, Oscar is at the top of his game. And it is this *Wilde* persona that attends the trial: the wit, the court jester. So I created a very public space—a very public, straightforward narrative, very presentational—a courtroom where Oscar Wilde could and does shine. But at the end, he loses the trial and is imprisoned.

In the second trial, his patina begins to crack and we begin to look into Oscar's inner self. His reality is splintering, and so is the vocabulary used in the play: it's much less realistic and linear. Because we're dealing with his sexual relationship with the boys he frequented, and with the distortion of his ideas and philosophies in the trial, our theatrical language becomes much more lyrical and sensual.

The men who testify that Oscar had sex with them enter the stage in their underwear. The world that Victorians heard about but never saw is fleshed out on the stage. So the second act becomes a journey to his sensual world, and into his more private intellectual world. I think that, for Oscar, intellect was a thing of great sensuality; he caressed, devoured, made love to ideas.

By the third act, the man is ruined. Oscar has been in jail for weeks, and has lost everything: his property, his name, his family. So the vocabulary we used in this act was deconstructed, very expressionistic.

We were now very close to his core. The same questions were being asked of him a third time and he was almost delirious. We tried to explore a vocabulary that would allow us to go more deeply into his state of mind.

Each one of those vocabularies attempts to go deeper into the mind and heart of Oscar. In the course of the workshops, I kept asking: what is the form that best reflects Oscar's state of being at any given moment?

Your workshop process is well known for its intensity, its length, its rigor.

I think if you want to be rigorous about questioning theatrical form and what happens on stage, you also have to be rigorous about how the work is made. The forms that you use in the development of the work will inevitably determine the form that the work takes.

The prevalent way in which theater is made at this time in America is that a writer goes into a room (cobwebs, vodka bottles on the floor, van Gogh–like chairs), and spends twenty years in that room. And then she comes out of the room with a play, her hair thinning and white, and she runs and gives it to the director. The director then runs with the play into another room, and after three weeks of rehearsals and a week of tech, the play is done. (Oh yes—in this second room, the playwright is sometimes not allowed.) To me, that form is very problematic.

So one of the questions we're trying to pose is, what are the other ways of creating material? Other processes?

The Laramie Project took well over a year to write because we needed to follow that town for a year. We couldn't have done that play in less time because we needed the story to conclude, and this only happened after the last trial of Matthew Shepard's murderers. Once we knew that outcome, we would have a story.

Was that longer or shorter than the process for *Gross Indecency*?

Gross Indecency was a shorter development process. I try to listen very organically to what the work requires. Not only in the writing or performance, but also in the way the rehearsals are handled. In *Gross Indecency*, it was a bunch of books on a table, and really paying attention to what was occurring around that table. And the form was arrived at from that. *Gross Indecency* tried to pose the question, "How can theater reconstruct history?" And *The Laramie Project* posed the question, "How can theater relate to American values, politics and current events?" Is there a role that theater can play in the national dialogue about current events? That dialogue usually happens in the realm of television, radio, newspapers and film. Is there something we can contribute to it as theater artists?

Jefferson Mays in
I Am My Own Wife
by Doug Wright.
Broadway, 2003.
Credit: Joan Marcus.

So what do you think *The Laramie Project* contributed to that dialogue?

When Matthew Shepard was murdered, I think that my initial response was similar to that of a great deal of people in America: horror and sadness, dismay and shock. "Oh my God, how could they do such a brutal thing?" But the thing that interested me even more in the days and weeks that followed was that you couldn't open a newspaper without seeing Matthew's picture; you couldn't turn on the television, or turn on the radio, without hearing something about the case. It became very clear that it was one of those watershed cultural moments—a historical marker—that forces a certain society in a certain time to look at itself in ways that it hasn't before.

So my hypothesis was that if we went to Laramie at this time, and we simply talked to the people of the town, we might be able to gather a document that told us about not only where Laramie was at the end of the millennium, but perhaps where America was as well. Not only in terms of sexuality, but in terms of class and economics and education and violence and gender and all of the kinds of fault lines that are splitting us up as a culture.

At the same time, I was rereading this really interesting essay by Brecht called "The Street Scene." It's a piece that proposes a form, a model for a theater. A car accident takes place on a street corner, and there's one witness. When other people approach the site of the accident, the witness says, "This is what I saw," and recounts the event. To me, it seemed like a really fascinating model. Think of a theater company going to a community, listening to the people of a town, and coming back to say, "This is what we were told. This is what we saw and heard."

The idea of one community trying to tell the stories of another community seemed rife with possibilities. It was one community, with all of its complexity and differences—

And many stories.

And many stories—trying to understand another community with many stories. As a way of working, that excited me a great deal.

When we went to Laramie the first time, we didn't know whether it would be a play, but it felt like a very valid experiment: is this a way to make a play? And now that we have a body of work under our belts, we feel more daring in making experiments, exploring and researching.

The play is a group of actors who come on stage and say, "This is what we heard, this is what we saw." That's why I never call the work we do "documentary"; the word "documentary" is based on this notion that reality can be captured and retold. When you see a documentary, it operates under the premise, or the contract with the audience, that these are the facts. But I think we as a culture are now keenly aware that as soon as you splice two frames together in a film, you have become the storyteller, you have become the creator of the narrative. The story you're telling is as much your story as it is the story you're narrating.

The way we dealt with these questions in *The Laramie Project* was for the company to become a character in the play. As if to say, "These are not the facts: this is what *we* heard, this is what *we* saw." You get to meet a little of who we are as a company, with our prejudices, identities, biographies and stories.

How does that change when the original cast is no longer performing?

When we were writing it, we were keenly aware that would be the case. We were writing an object, an artifact that we knew would have to work without us performing it. So they're two different events. When the company performs it, there's one degree of separation between the audience and the people of Laramie. It's very personal. When other people perform the work, there are two degrees of separation. The actors create a first fiction: "We are the members of Tectonic." Once the audience allows for that fiction, the rest of the event is rather similar to the way we told it. Because ultimately the focus is on the town.

So your work differs greatly from, say, a television documentary about Matthew Shepard, because it doesn't presume factual knowledge, and encourages the audience to construct its own narrative.

There's a way in which the instrument—the actor's body—becomes the recording device and the playing device. The body of the actor, his mind, his being, are the keepers and the narrators of the story. That's very powerful, and unique. And it positions the actor as an artist who has a very specific take on things—that is somewhat different from that of a journalist or an anthropologist or a camera.

It creates a space in which the artist gets to articulate current stories. Our sensibility, our subjectivity, our artistic perspective of the world is infused into every word that we speak on stage. And that infuses a certain kind of humanism into the story, into the telling of the story, and into the contract that we are entering into with an audience.

As an artist, you want the audience to be aware of the story's "constructedness": your subjectivity, the subjectivity of your collaborators and even the way each audience member receives the story. Yet you're uncomfortable with this interview "constructing" a certain Moisés Kaufman. Can't we trust the reader to recognize this interview is just one window into who you are as an artist?

I am very rigorous when I'm making my own narratives on stage. But I'm careful to avoid making every moment of my life part of a well-organized, well-mapped-out narrative. There's great danger in that. Especially when one looks at the past—with all its messiness—and tries to streamline it. Memory has a tendency to clear up the mess of the past. That's how myths are born.

For me [in theater] the departure point is the premise that there is a mystery. And the way you deal with mystery (this is a very Judeo-Christian thought) is that mysteries are there to be explored. And every day you explore it, you get closer . . . not to the resolution, but to the core of the mystery, to the mystery itself. For every question that gets answered, three more questions get posed. And that's the thing that keeps people in the theater: there's a never-ending question that keeps being posed. What I'm trying to do is keep finding ways to articulate the questions.

That's very Peer Gyntian of you.

I often feel like I'm in a nine-hour play!

What does it mean to you to be a "director"?

The great joy in directing is to keep asking how the stage "speaks" and to keep having that dialogue with the writer, the actors, the designers and all the collaborators. It's not enough to create a world in which the words can be believed. That's a theater in which the text becomes the dictator and arbiter of all things on stage. But there is a much more sophisticated relationship to the idea of text now. When theater practitioners revolted against the text in the 1960s, we tried to ignore or reject it. It was a necessary "excess" of that revolution. Now I think we have acknowledged the power of the text, and our task is to continue exploring the narrative powers of the other elements of the stage; in other words, how to continue to think and construct narratives theatrically. And that allows for all the other theatrical elements to have a dialogue with the text.

Can you give me a specific example of bringing text and form together in your recent work?

Well, for example, the third act of *The Laramie Project*. The set design has been co-opted from the third act of *Our Town*: all the chairs on one side of the stage to denote the cemetery. Our third act begins with Matthew Shepard's funeral. And the town of Laramie is forced to deal with his death and the subsequent trials. By visually referencing *Our Town*, we are posing questions about the relationship between Laramie and Grover's Corners. How does our iconic image of a small American town match our current reality? Also, in *I Am My Own Wife* there are several moments like that. In the beginning there's a moment when Charlotte crosses behind a lace wall. And it's lit in a way that you can see her but her image is diffused by the lace. She's luminous and vague. And it is such a good beginning for a play about identity, a play that asks, "Who is this person?" At the end of the first act, we have all the gramophones, which were so important to her, come to life as she sinks into a musical stupor that shields her from the harshness of the questions that are coming up about her collaboration with the Stasi. These moments use things other than text to profoundly articulate ideas and narratives that are uniquely theatrical.

Since *I Am My Own Wife* wasn't written by you and your company—the text was "privileged," in a way—it must have been a different process.

Well, Doug has written extensively about our collaboration on it. But for me it was an exciting proposition because I'd never worked with a fiction writer like him before and he'd never done the kind of work that I was known for at the time. It was a great opportunity to test some of Tectonic's ideas and methods with an outside writer.

What was the process like?

What's great about Doug is how brilliant he is and how much he loves words. We'd been friends for many years before we worked together. We were asked to come to the Sundance Lab to work on the piece for three weeks. I started by bringing in several Tectonic techniques to allow Doug to begin to find a theatrical vocabulary for his piece: I asked him and Jefferson [Mays, who originated the role] to bring in a theatrical moment (using a prop, a costume, a piece of music) that expressed what they loved about Charlotte. I did so as well. Doug brought in a gay guide to Berlin and read out loud the names of all the gay bars that are there now; we used that moment the first time Charlotte goes to West Berlin after the wall falls and discovers the gay lifestyle there. Jefferson spent the night cutting furniture out of cardboard and brought the pieces in a shoebox. He opened the shoebox and gave us a tour of the museum, pointing to the pieces he'd made. I brought in a black dress and put it on. That's how we started looking at the theatrical potential of the piece. It was really thrilling. By the end of the three weeks we had a draft of Act One.

Jefferson Mays is well known as a Viewpoints actor. Did that make it easier or harder to direct him?

I have some training in Viewpoints, so it gave us a common vocabulary. We had a funny thing happen. I would give him a note, and he would do it. And then I'd find out through Doug that he wasn't happy about it. This happened several times. I finally said, "I'm Jewish and I'm Latino and I'm gay—three very vocal cultures. If you don't like something or if something is not working for you, you have to tell me!"

So later on, I would ask him, "Did that work for you?" And he would say, "Yes." And I would say, "Is that a Latino yes or a WASPy yes?" We found a way to communicate with each other.

I love working with actors. I am always in awe of what they do. There were many runs of *Wife* where the only people in the room were Doug, the stage manager and I. We'd get this astonishing performance by Jefferson all to ourselves. And I felt like such a lucky man.

Do you find yourself using the same techniques in development today as you used years ago?

We use some of the techniques we've been developing for the last ten years, and we find new ways of working. Each new piece brings about its own challenges and its own pleasures. I'm working now on a play about a composition Beethoven wrote toward the end of his life [33 *Variations*]. We have a pianist in the rehearsal room and we continue to build theatrical moments about the music—how to articulate some of the ideas we've been discussing with this music. So each process is different.

Are you asking the same questions now as a director?

I'm very interested in exploring fictional narratives these days. In my Beethoven play I've created several fictional characters, and working from that place is thrilling. We've also begun to teach our techniques and that's been fascinating—a whole new way of approaching what we do is teaching it. There are so many people who are hungry for new ways of creating work.

Why do you think so many people are hungry for new ways of creating work?

I think actors, writers and designers rejoice in the possibility of creating work together—of writing performance together. And our work allows them to explore those kinds of collaborations.

I also think many people in the field find the current model problematic. Taking a text into a rehearsal room for three weeks to make a "show" is not the best way to develop new work. In "moment work" we're allowing actors, writers and designers to contribute to the creation of the narrative together, and people get very excited by that. We find that it really inspires writers who are working on a new idea, or actors who bring in projects they're developing, or designers—each of them exploring their own ways of constructing narratives on stage. And as I've been traveling the country, lecturing and teaching about these ideas, I see people getting excited . . . I see opportunities opening up for people that weren't there before.

JAMES LAPINE

Moving Pictures

IN 1976, A GRAPHIC DESIGN TEACHER AT YALE University was urged by his students to try his hand at directing a play. They even suggested the material: Gertrude Stein's three-page, "five-act" stage poem "Photograph." Drawing heavily on his visual arts and photography background, the first-time director used projection and ensemble movement to create images that shed light on Stein's abstract text. A surprising success, it moved to SoHo's Open Space in September 1977, where it won an OBIE Award for its fledgling director. Richard Eder in the *New York Times* called it:

> . . . a theater of the subconscious . . . The actions do not so much follow its lines as accompany and intersect them in the way that a river appears and reappears beside a railroad track . . . throughout there is a lovely humaneness, a delicacy toward the images and toward the audience, whose possible bewilderment in the face of an elliptic and abstract work is allayed with the old theatrical resources of humor, variety and a pace that respects the human capacity to sit still.

Seven years later, that same graphic design teacher used projections, ensemble movement and a "delicacy toward images" once again to create a work of lovely humaneness, in which the audience's bewilderment towards a less-than-conventional narrative was allayed by humor, variety and directorial ingenuity. That piece was *Sunday in the Park with George,* which that graphic designer—James Lapine—wrote with legendary music-theater composer Steven Sondheim. It earned Lapine his first Tony nomination for directing, and won him both the Tony and Pulitzer for his book.

Sunday in the Park sprang from Lapine's fascination with the show's signature image: Georges Seurat's painting, *A Sunday on La Grande Jatte.* (Interestingly, Lapine used the painting in *Photograph,* too.) Lapine told Ira Weitzman in a 2002 interview:

> [Sondheim and I] got together a few times and chatted . . . I'd bring over images and we'd spread them all out and look at them. I'm sure he must have thought I was crazy. But one of the images I brought over one day was the *La Grande Jatte* . . . Steve seemed vaguely intrigued so I just started writing it. In fact, I wrote an entire act and he didn't write anything . . . I had a commission from Playwrights Horizons so we gave a reading of my first act. Steve wrote the opening five chords of the show and that was it. We hauled in this big piano, Steve played the opening five chords, then sat down and we read through the play . . . I thought after a while, "Well, if he doesn't write any songs, at least I'll have a play."

Sondheim, of course, did write some songs, and the collaboration was vital for Lapine's artistic evolution: as a writer/director, he'd struck a balance between abstract visual inspiration and narrative engagement. In a way, *Sunday in the Park* is a lyrical tone poem (like *Photograph*), a "concept musical" written in response to one of the greatest visual works of the impressionist era. On another level, the piece is a simple and traditional love story traversing a century. And on its most complex level, it is a meditation on the push and pull of commerce in the service of art. The melding of these three seemingly contrary strains is what earns its place as one of the great advances of the musical-theater form.

It also marked an important point for Sondheim's trajectory. In addition to *Sunday in the Park with George,* the two created *Into the Woods* (1987) and *Passion* (1994)—widely recognized as the three greatest works of the latter part of Sondheim's career. (*Into the Woods* and *Passion* also earned Lapine Tony Awards for Best Book of a Musical.) In these innovative works, thematic complexity matches depth of characterization, and many critics see Lapine's influence as bringing about Sondheim's most intensely personal statements. Sondheim says as much in his 2011 book, *Look, I Made a Hat:*

> When I look back as objectively as I can at the shows I wrote
> before James and contrast them with *Sunday in the Park with
> George* and the others I wrote with him, it seems clear to me
> that a quality of detachment suffuses the first set, whereas a
> current of vulnerability, of longing, informs the second.

The mysterious alchemy of collaboration: Lapine's visual imagination, literary wit and "humaneness," combined with Sondheim's gifts, yielded something greater than the sum of its parts. Sondheim's music and lyrics are unforgettable, but so is the moment when the figures of Seurat's painting shift, shake and leap to life on stage. When the picture moves, it is a moment of directorial brilliance, as at home on Broadway as it might have been at the Open Space with Gertrude Stein in 1977.

Lapine and Sondheim were introduced to each other via Stephen Graham, who in 1980 produced Lapine's play *Table Settings* at Playwrights Horizons. (Lapine is also an accomplished playwright.) That production (which began his long-standing relationship with that theater) also introduced Lapine to his other great longtime collaborator, composer William Finn. While many claim credit for introducing the two, the truth (as Lapine told Ira Weitzman) was that "Bill Finn was just a maniac who pursued me to the point where I just finally agreed. I don't know why he came after me to direct a musical."

Lapine's work with Finn was also extremely influential for late twentieth-century musicals, particularly in its frank treatment of gay themes and the AIDS crisis. Lapine credits his work with graphic design ("it's all about 'signatures' and structure") with his ability to shape Finn's unwieldy genius into the composer's two great early works, both at Playwrights: *March of the Falsettos* (1981) and its sequel, *Falsettoland* (1990). When those two plays were combined into a Broadway production called *Falsettos* in 1992, Lapine cowrote the Tony-winning book with Finn. Lapine also directed Finn's work *A New Brain* in 1998 at Lincoln Center Theater in New York City; *The 25th Annual Putnam County Spelling Bee* in 2005, also in New York, at Second Stage Theatre and then on Broadway; and *Little Miss Sunshine* (for which he also wrote the book, based on the 2006 film) in 2011, at La Jolla Playhouse in California.

Between his work with Sondheim and Finn, Lapine has racked up seven Tony nominations, altering the course of American musical theater along the way. And it is a mark of Lapine's range and talents that he could be partner with two such oppositional figures in contemporary musical theater. Finn's characters are intensely personal to the composer, while Sondheim's operate more outside himself. Whereas Sondheim's music is somewhat iconoclastic (or at least challenges the notion of what a musical has traditionally been), Finn's work falls comfortably into normative musical form. Where Sondheim's personality cannot easily be discerned in his musicals, Finn's is often their subject. And with both composers, Lapine's directorial worlds are visually striking, appropriate to the spaces in which they're set, and reflective of the words and music that live within them.

It is also a mark of Lapine's directorial talents that, notwithstanding his success in musical theater, he has accomplished much along the way with straight plays. He has directed Shakespeare three times for the Public Theater: *A Midsummer Night's Dream* (1982, at the Delacorte Theater in Central Park); *The Winter's Tale* (1989); and most recently, *King Lear* with Kevin Kline in 2007 (featuring incidental music by Sondheim). He also directed a well-received Broadway revival of *The Diary of Anne Frank* (1997) starring a young Natalie Portman, and co-conceived and directed Claudia Shear's Mae West revue, *Dirty Blonde,* at New York Theatre Workshop in 2000 before it moved to Broadway, where it played for nearly a year.

Lapine and I met in the former living room of legendary Broadway producer J. J. Jacobs—now the home of the Shubert Organization, which provided Lapine with an office and assistant from 1993 to 2005 (in exchange, Lapine provided nonexclusive development and consulting services). The opulent setting with its gold-leafed detail, rich paneling and two grand pianos overlooking Shubert Alley, was a far cry from the Open Space and Gertrude Stein. And as Lapine admitted, returning to one's roots can be extremely hard.

MAY 2003, OFFICES OF THE SHUBERT ORGANIZATION, NEW YORK CITY

You took a circuitous route to directing.

It was rather happenstance that I started in theater, because I was trained as a designer, photographer and graphic artist. I worked in architecture for several years, and also did freelance graphic design. My hope was to become a fine-art photographer. I worked in photography for a while, but didn't actually like making my living doing it.

The long and short of it is that when I was in my mid-twenties I got a design gig with Yale's *Theater* magazine, which was the journal that came out of the Yale School of Drama, and after one year was invited to work full time doing all the graphics for the Yale Repertory Theatre. I also taught a little class to administrators, primarily in design and advertising for the theater.

Because it was a conservatory, there was a January work-month in which everyone worked in a discipline other than their own. My students encouraged me to direct a play, and that's how I began. One of my students found the play, I believe: "Photograph," by Gertrude Stein. I'd been a fan of the more visual kinds of theater, downtown artists of the Robert Wilson, Richard Foreman, Lee Breuer school. The Rep at the time was very conservative, so part of the impetus of directing this show was to do something more abstract. And it was an enjoyable experience. The actors were not professional, and the work was very much an art piece.

When we decided to try to do it in New York, a friend of mine who knows Jasper Johns said, "He's a great fan of Gertrude Stein, and he has a little foundation." I wrote the foundation a letter, and I got a check in the mail. That underwrote our production.

Lyn Austin and Mary Silverman from the Music-Theatre Group came to see the show, and they said, "We'll do something of yours." Gave me a slot, didn't even ask what it was. So I created *Twelve Dreams*. And then after that, somebody told me about a writers' colony, and I went there, just scribbled some scripts out, and sent one to Playwrights Horizons (which was just starting at the time). I believe it produced something like fourteen plays a season. It had two theaters running, and there was always a show going on. Again, I was given the opportunity to stage something that was essentially half-baked, on faith; and I was supported without pressure, I might add.

I don't think the way I got into the theater can be replicated, unfortunately. At the moment, it's a very different environment.

What do you think has changed?

Today money is so tight. I look at the Public Theater, and it's just appalling: there sit five theaters, and they're empty half of the time. I'm sure the theater is doing the best it can do, but when I was starting out in New York, you would go to the Public Theater like you would go to the Loews Cineplex, and you'd look up at the board and you'd see five plays (some of which you'd never heard of), and you just bought a ticket and saw whatever was going on.

Producing entities have become financially restrictive. They're very precious about what they can do, because they get to do so few productions.

Do you think audiences have changed as well?

Audiences have changed because it's so much more expensive to go to the theater. If you offered ten-dollar tickets to the Public Theater, you would fill it every night. You don't go on a whim anymore unless you have a disposable income, and unfortunately that's not a younger audience. I think it's a pretty sad state of affairs.

What were some of the first things about directing that surprised you?

I didn't have any training, so I didn't really know what I was doing . . . which in some ways was a blessing, but in other ways was obviously a major liability! The first go-round wasn't so hard because they weren't professional actors. You could tell people, "Walk slowly across here," and nobody said to you, "Well, why?" They were making images; they didn't question the image.

But once I started working with professionals—that was a big shock! They started asking me, "Why?" I was writing something and wanting the lines delivered as I heard them in my head. I didn't know you weren't supposed to give line-readings.

So you had to change your style.

I don't think I *had* a directorial style. I thought visually; that was my strong suit. I knew what I wanted it to look like, and how I wanted it to feel. In that respect, the directing was easy.

But I had to teach myself how to get performances out of people. I learned a lot from actors. In some unfortunate ways, it became a game of psychology, and after several years I began to understand that I had to suss out certain personality traits; I had to understand the methodology of actors to know how to talk to them.

As time went on I also learned a valuable lesson: even if you don't know what you're doing, you have to *appear* to know what you're doing. Or at least present it in a way that's honest, so actors can feel confident that you're going to get them where they need to go. And create an environment with designers, as well, where you bring out the best in them.

How did you learn to accomplish that?

You learn to do that by giving up your vision, in a funny kind of way. It's a delicate balance. You obviously have to have a vision for the show. But if it's so narrow and so constrained that you don't allow for new ideas and creative alternatives, you run into problems. When I design shows now, I try to design them with a certain flexibility, so that if I change my mind, or other ideas come up, they can be accommodated.

Likewise, I used to start by trying to push actors into a very narrow perception of what I wanted the performance to be. Now I do the opposite: I give very little direction at the outset, because I like to see what people bring.

Bernadette Peters (front) and the cast of Into the Woods, *music and lyrics by Stephen Sondheim, book by James Lapine. Broadway, 1987. Credit: Martha Swope.*

So is the director an editor? Is direction an art or a craft?

I think it's both art and craft. There's a kind of craft in knowing how much time you have, how long it takes to accomplish x, y and z. There's a certain craft in knowing that an actor won't get where you need him to go, and you'll have to replace him.

But there's got to be an artistic vision that's personal and idiosyncratic and can't be taught. You have to have an individual aesthetic if you want in any way to create something that has originality to it. Otherwise, it's hard not to replicate other people's productions.

Especially in the case of revivals?

My revival of my own *Into the Woods* [2002 on Broadway] was instructive because I had imagined I was going to improve all the things I wasn't able to accomplish before, and I was going to see it anew. And I didn't see it anew, and I didn't improve anything. I mean, I made *some* improvements. For example, there was a song, "Last Midnight," that I could never quite make work in the first production. In rehearsals for the revival, I discovered that if the evil character, the witch, held the baby during the song, it gave it a whole different tension. The moments that don't work, that you can't make work, that you suddenly *make work,* are the most exciting. But I still think the show has some very basic flaws that we were unable to address.

I usually have ambitious visual concepts that don't get realized, because when you work on a Broadway scale, it gets really scary to take huge risks. You're talking about millions of dollars of people's money. If I had done *The Diary of Anne Frank* at a not-for-profit theater, it probably would have been a more interesting production in many ways.

On the other hand, I had all these abstract ideas at first, but then I went off to Amsterdam and visited the Anne Frank house. And I just thought, "Oh God, this isn't material you should be 'arty-farty' with." It just wasn't that kind of a show. I thought the best I could do—and the challenge of it—was to make people *live the moment* that these people lived. So I ended up going with a very literal re-creation of the attic. I would have loved to see the other production (the one in my head), but that would have been about me. Because I also write, I try not to overshadow the writing. Instead I try to highlight it, support it.

Have there been watershed moments in your development as an artist?

Sure. The first Shakespeare I did, *A Midsummer Night's Dream,* was kind of a mess. First of all, the idea of doing your first Shakespeare *in Central Park* is nuts; it's impossible to work in the park! I made a lot of mistakes. I was very tight [with my budget] because I'd spent a lot of money on costumes. Sometimes just one thing can completely sink a production. The next time in Central Park, I did *The Winter's Tale* [1989], and, again—the costumes! The costumes were bad! But I had a great costume designer, Franne Lee, and when I said to her, "Gee, they're not working," she said, "Let's throw 'em out." And we did a completely different take on them, which freed me up a lot. Those moments when I could toss things out, and not be afraid of making bold graphic choices at the last minute, have always been exciting and have served the pieces well. That's part of the craft: the more you do it, the more you realize the world is not going to come apart if you change x, y or z.

That's why you like doing extensive workshops?

Well, workshops are fun; I don't like the audience. If I could do shows without an audience I'd be really happy. Even though workshops are great, I don't really even like *those* audiences. However, at least you don't have critics to worry about.

When you get to a certain point in your career, there's an expectation; your work is compared to past productions. You can't think about it too much.

That sounds like it comes from a man who thinks about it too much.

Well, you think about it. You can't avoid it. It's not a generous business; colleagues often are not kind to one another. I find writers are far more supportive of one another than directors. As a director, you have a kind of critical mindset when you go see a show. I can't help but be aware of the lights and the set and the performances. I know something's really great when I can finally let go of that and not be looking around the theater to see how they hung the lights.

Playwrights, because they're writing from a very personal place, don't feel so competitive. If a playwright is writing about his mother, his mother wasn't my mother, you know what I mean? Or if he's writing about a historical event—well, *his* take on it isn't going to be *my* take on it. Also, it's so miserably difficult to sit and write, and you're so exposed. Directors aren't exposed in the same way that writers are. So I think there's a kind of kindred spirit that writers have with one another.

You once said, "The only reason to write the book of a musical is to have something to direct."

I was being facetious.

Are you a writer more than you are a director, then?

I just say, "I work in the theater"! I don't really make a distinction.

Book writing is a thankless task, in certain respects. *That* is a form that really requires a great deal of craft. I love it, I really, really love it, but you're rarely singled out as a librettist. People go to a musical to hear the music.

But what I meant by that statement was that part of the fun of writing is to give yourself a challenge visually as a director. Even if I'm writing for other directors, I want to inspire them visually.

Given how visual you are, is it difficult for you to let a set designer work?

Not at all, I'm totally collaborative. Their work is my work, and my work is their work. I have such a sense of how I want things to move that it's fun to solve the problems with someone else. If you have two creative minds working, theoretically, you're going to come up with something better than just one.

Did you ever start a design process and end up somewhere completely unexpected?

Sometimes. I can't say that all of my "design shows" have been successes. I've made a lot of boo-boos along the way. With the last show I did [*Amour*, by French pop composer Michel Legrand, on Broadway in 2002], I wasn't on top of certain aspects of it. Sometimes you end up making choices that hamstring you when you get on the stage. Though I have an image, it doesn't mean I have the answer.

What mistakes have you made that taught you good lessons?

I don't know if "mistakes" is the right word; there are things I'd rather do differently.

For instance, the first *Into the Woods* had a large raked piece that was at the center of the stage, and it rotated 360 degrees. The downside of that was that it *never went away*, and it ate up a huge amount of stage space, which ended up constraining me. When it worked, it worked great. There are a number of instances when I've designed moments that are great, but I paid a price for these moments throughout the rest of the piece.

It's ironic I ended up on Broadway because I really had a downtown sensibility. Once you move uptown, you can't go back. I would love to do another Gertrude Stein play, but you know what? It would seem ridiculous. I would enjoy doing it, but I have an uptown sensibility now.

Let's say that the Culture Project on Bleecker Street called you up and said, "We've got a slot for you." With all that you've done, now that you've had a chance to play with all the toys—

Oh sure, the minimal, the simple, I can work on small scales. I prefer working on small scales. I just meant I don't think I could work in an abstract way anymore like the Gertrude Stein or the first *Twelve Dreams* [at the Public in 1981; the second was at Lincoln Center Theater in 2005]. I think my mind's become more literal.

What's happened to that abstract kind of work?

I don't feel there are many directors who are working that way now. I guess in Europe they are. It may be a result of economics, and it may be a result of aesthetics. Anne Bogart's been teaching a lot; I don't know whether her students are following her example. But maybe it's just where I'm sitting now, that I don't have a chance to see or meet a lot of people working in fringier forms. The world has just changed so much. There's such a glut of entertainment. When I came to New York in the early 1970s, it felt like live performance was thriving. It was all around you, and it was affordable.

And media things were not. I used projections in the Gertrude Stein, but that was expensive and difficult. Now, of course, you can generate media much more cheaply than getting a group of actors together in a space. A lot of creative minds are choosing to work in film and video and more abstract forms like animation.

Are you lured by opportunities in film?

Sadly, the film work I've done has been about making a living. I would love to explore something filmically that is more abstract, but I haven't gone that route. I'm not sure I think that way anymore. And films are *very* story driven; theater allows you a bit more freedom visually. You can't *punt* when you're making a movie. You pretty much have to know where you are, what you're shooting, what kind of lighting you need, what kind of equipment you need. You have *this* day and *only this day* and this particular location, and you've got to tell the story. You can't go, "Oh, wouldn't it be cool if . . . ?" I get bogged down in the storytelling.

Is that storytelling-versus-visual issue particularly hard for you with Shakespeare?

Well, Shakespeare's really hard! Costumes tell you where you are in a Shakespeare play. In Shakespeare, it really says the director doesn't know what he's doing if it's not rooted in some kind of period look. It's tricky. Shakespeare *always* seems better in the rehearsal hall!

I think we can say that exploring the mind of the artist is a common theme in your work; you also seem to be attracted to dark pieces and mindscapes. Do you see links in your work?

I'm totally nonanalytical about what I do. I have no interest in being analytical, I think it's death the minute you start; I think it's dangerous. You have to work at a certain level from the unconscious. Let it be what it is.

Can you be analytical about your career, then? Where are you headed?

I would like to think that I'm leaving the world of the theater to do something else, but I don't know what that something else is. I never set out to work in the theater. I would like to do an opera one day. I would like to do a really great movie one day. I love doing musicals, and I like writing. I'm sort of at a crossroads at the moment, not sure where I'm going to go, what I'm going to do.

I have a play that I've written that I'm doing in the fall, directing it as well [*Fran's Bed*, at the Long Wharf Theatre in Connecticut]. It'll be fun to do it out of town. I don't think I've ever done a play out of town; I've almost always opened them straight into New York. I'm looking forward to that.

Let's talk about process. How do you work with actors to build character?

Every actor has his or her own kind of process. Some come in and they've memorized their parts; some don't get off book for weeks, some are Method, some have no method, some have craft, some have no craft. Basically I take the first week to learn how everyone works and how they relate to each other. I tend to do runthroughs of one act after the first week. I'll just tell people to get up: "Move wherever you want to move; carry your script around, and let's just listen to the play." There are other people, like Des McAnuff, who sit around the table for days, really analyzing the text. And if you're doing Shakespeare, you definitely have to do that. But I'm a little ADD. Actors think I'm joking when I say that we're going to have a runthrough after the first week, but I think they like it. And it allows me to step back and listen and see the whole act.

The second week is about bringing everyone together, starting to focus everyone. The person who comes in very prepared is often the hardest to deal with, because he or she gets very stuck in what he or she is doing. It's an interesting balance, and it depends on the piece. Some things need more structure than others.

The weird thing in theater is that it takes as much time as you have. If you have three weeks, you'll get the show up in three weeks; if you've got six, you'll get it up in six. The terrible thing about the American process is having the whole show designed before you start rehearsing. In Europe, they start on the stage, they have the lights there, and they build around it. It's a more organic process, but they have lots more time and money.

Was that your experience in Europe with Disney's *Hunchback of Notre Dame* [Berlin, 1999]?

It was ridiculous, one of the stupidest things I've ever done. I don't know what I was thinking; I take full responsibility. It was fun, but it was *really dumb*.

Because of the language barrier?

Well, first of all, I was writing the book [for a score by Alan Menken and Stephen Schwartz], and then it was being translated. (It apparently wasn't a great translation, but I didn't find out until opening night, when some German man of letters said, "This is terrible! Why are they talking that way?") And I was directing people first in English (because I had to hear it in English) and then putting it into German. I didn't realize I was casting twelve different nationalities, so German wasn't even the native tongue for more than half the people.

But where I *really* was stupid was the first preview, when I realized I didn't know *anybody* in the audience! So there was no one to talk to, you know what I mean? Everything would have been fine if I'd had people to ask at the end of the night, "Did you understand this?"

So you make use of preview audiences in specific ways?

I've gotten really good at reading an audience: when they're bored, when they're involved, when things land. I usually ask people I know how they felt about certain relationships or performances. There are very few people I *listen to*. Certain people's opinions I don't care about. I think it was Mike Nichols who said something like, "When somebody says something to you, you can basically ignore it. When the second person says the same thing, you want to perk up. By the third time you get the same remark, you'd better really listen." But it's hard to keep open to criticism. You get defensive, you are so close to what you are doing, it's like you can't hear it. You're exhausted, so it's very hard to have any objectivity.

Let me take you back to the acting process. You talked about over-prepared actors, actors who have difficulty finding new choices because of all the prep-work they've done. How do you get such an actor onto the right track?

You have to be careful because people get confused: "Well, you told me this," or, "You told me that." So I always tell the actors at the beginning of the process that I'm trying to take chances and explore. You have to be willing to make poor choices in order to find the interesting ones. You have to create an environment where people feel free. And then, after a while, it is what it is, and you have to just leave it alone. Sometimes I won't rehearse certain people or certain moments; I'll just let it go until the last week: then they'll be desperate for direction and they'll listen.

Again, it's group psychology. Not just *an* actor, it's a bunch of people together. Sometimes you have to be the bad guy, like with children.

The cast of Sunday in the Park with George, *music and lyrics by Stephen Sondheim, book by James Lapine. Playwrights Horizons, 1983. Credit: Martha Swope.*

It helps if there's a common enemy, and usually it's you. It's really hard to have a production where someone isn't demonized. It unites people in a bizarre way.

Sometimes happy companies make happy shows; other times it's the reverse.

Often the best experiences have been the least successful productions . . . and sometimes the worst experiences turn out to be unbelievably wonderful shows. I always get worried when things go too well.

When that happens, are you afraid you're not pushing yourself enough?

No, it means somebody'll get strep throat. You'll have an understudy for the first preview. You're waiting for the disasters to happen. I like to get them out of the way sooner rather than later!

Talk to me about how the process differs with actors in a musical as opposed to a straight play.

I don't see a lot of difference in the medium, because I always approach songs like scenes. I always rehearse them without music, just lyrics. The nice thing about a musical is that you have a conductor who keeps the rhythm of the show consistent. Sometimes in a play I wish I had a conductor.

When I did the Shakespeare plays, I would make the actors paraphrase each scene in their own language. Same thing with songs. The dramatic action can't stop with a song; it helps to rehearse it like a scene, a monologue, a soliloquy.

Is that more for the actor or the audience?

You do it for the actor. I don't worry too much about the audience until they show up. When actors sing a song, they often forget about what they're singing. They're worrying about the note, they're worrying about the measures, they're worrying about the tempo. You have to remind them that they're actually *saying something.*

Sometimes with good actors you just *leave them alone.* I used to be very paranoid at the beginning when actors would talk to each other, or to this friend or that one, or to the writer. But I don't have any of that worry anymore. I sometimes *see* people changing their performances after they speak with someone. As long as the performances are good, I don't care *how* they get good. If the cleaning lady tells them, "You know, Jean darling, you should really put down the napkin here," and it works: great! I don't have to be the source of everything. Whatever works. Sometimes I'll tell them, "I wouldn't listen to so-and-so; I don't think that's the sensibility of this show. If they were directing it, then that would be fine." You know, good, smart actors realize that they have to serve your vision.

It's hard to keep focused on the vision sometimes, isn't it?

Well, you get so caught up in the little things. How often has it happened that you haven't liked an actor or performance, and then he or she is the one who gets the rave reviews? Like racehorses, people peak at different times. If you admired actors in another show, you can pretty much rest assured they're going to get to that place for you, even if they don't initially. It's just hard to keep your eye on the big picture. I try to take a few days off when I start previews. Producers get freaked out because they think I'm walking away from the show, and actors get nervous that I'm leaving. But I think it's useful to get a show on its feet, and then if you have the luxury, go away for a long weekend and come back and see it fresh.

Also, I almost always write out a little spiel to the actors at the first rehearsal, and often I'll go back to it before the first preview and read it again, so they can remind themselves of what our intentions were, and what we were trying to accomplish.

But your ideas change, right?

Oh, certainly. I'll go through it and say, "Oh, we certainly didn't do *that*," or, "That was a bad idea." If you don't keep it open, you're fucked.

What's the biggest challenge in mounting new work for you?

It's the writer; it always comes down to the writer. If it fundamentally isn't there, all the pyrotechnics in the world aren't going to hide it. Sometimes you can get away with pyrotechnics, but I don't think *those* are the things that are going to last.

What kind of notes are useful for an actor?

"Please don't step out of your light." "Please don't do this." "Please don't do that." I'll try to step back. It's about finding as many shades of color as you can in performance. That to me is the most important thing: to give people ways to accomplish things in a different way.

Let's talk about collaborations, because you're so well known for them: you and William Finn, you and Stephen Sondheim . . . what makes for the right kind of collaboration?

I think they're good collaborations because our egos are well-placed. They can be passionate about things, and you obviously want to listen carefully, but I don't remember anyone being insistent upon anything, you know what I mean? It was just a good chemistry. I can't put my finger on it other than to say that our strengths complemented each other.

Bill is very idiosyncratic. Bill writes very much from his own kind of creative world, and Steve writes very much from outside of himself. Bill's shows always have Bill front and center. Steve really writes in other characters' voices; he likes to get into the head of the character; he likes to put himself *in* the character.

Of the three collaborations with Sondheim—*Sunday in the Park with George, Into the Woods* and *Passion*—which was the easiest?

Well, none of them were *easy*. The Finn musicals were easier somehow. *Sunday* was not well received when we started previewing it. And *Passion* was received with hostility in previews.

Passion was incredibly difficult. Just trying to get the show *written* and *up*. And Steve was amazing, I have to say. Just remarkably calm and analytical, and unemotional, in a good way. Steve does a good job remaining clear about what the intention of the show is, and not necessarily getting swayed by its reception. It's not that we don't keep working on it, trying to get the audience more behind it, but you can't pander to the audience. You can't write the show for the audience.

Into the Woods was of course a little more "user-friendly," but *Into the Woods* was and is still unwieldy in its ambition and size. We had a lot of producers' input with *Woods,* which we did not have on the other two shows, and that was stressful.

So they're all hard. It's like a marriage, or being a war buddy, when you collaborate, particularly on a Broadway show. You'd better get along, because you're going to be stuck in that trench together for a stretch. I can't imagine doing it with people I didn't like.

Can you talk a little about that process with *Sunday in the Park with George*? You brought the idea to Sondheim?

You mean the writing of it? Yes, I generated the idea, but it certainly became our idea. Oh God, do people really *care* about this?

Everybody wants to know about the creation of that work—

Yeah, they're calling you up daily.

Would you go back to working with Sondheim or Finn?

Sure. We're very close friends and have a great working relationship.

Would you say you've got any mentors?

No, because I never worked with another director. There are directors whose work I love: Bob Wilson, Hal Prince. [Prince's] *Sweeney Todd* was the first Sondheim show I ever saw, and I thought, "This is really interesting, really well directed."

What do you think about young directors in the theater? Do you feel a responsibility toward them?

No. I mean, I'm happy to help. But I don't feel a responsibility. I always have assistants on everything I do, and I try to let them in on the whole process. But teaching directing? At Yale I tried to tell Bob Brustein that the directors there didn't understand fundamental visual tools. I thought they should teach a course on *looking*. You know, go look at paintings, look at buildings, look at the whole manner of visual stimuli: where the eye goes, how color and motion play in.

So do you think teaching directing is possible?

Sure, [in the form of] a master class, by watching something that someone directed and talking about what you see. In master classes, I ask the directors a lot of questions: what the intention was, why did they choose this to direct? And then they give the answers, and I say, "Gee, I thought it was *this,* and here's *why* I thought it was *this.* And if you don't want it to be this, you might try another approach."

Do you find young directors make the same mistakes?

Probably the biggest problem with directors who go to theater all the time is that their judgment is so clouded by their knowledge that it gets in the way of finding their own voice. You want to get people to think outside the box. I have to try to get myself to do that, too.

ELIZABETH LECOMPTE

Crashing the Pieces Together

UNLIKE HER LEGENDARY EXPERIMENTAL theater work, Elizabeth LeCompte is straightforward, if very shy of the press. As one of her longtime company members said to me, "Liz is very careful about the company she keeps." And for good reason: the company she's kept—literally and figuratively—has helped her carve out a definitive niche in the history of twentieth-century, and now twenty-first-century, theater.

LeCompte's body of work is inextricably tied to the Wooster Group, which she cofounded and has led for more than thirty years. Named for the SoHo street in New York that serves as its home base, the Wooster Group is possibly the most celebrated force in experimental theater this country has produced. The company's technology-infused fantasias on familiar texts are the subject of virtually numberless scholarly articles, conferences, awards and passionate encomiums. In fact, many of the directors in this volume point to the Wooster Group as a vital influence in their own evolutions.

Yet most of those directors have abandoned the experimental in favor of more populist fare in the new century. Not LeCompte. In what sometimes sounds like a backhanded compliment, LeCompte is considered a stalwart of the downtown theater scene . . . as if "downtown theater" had any specific meaning anymore. Worse (or better) yet, she's been designated as a keeper of the experimental theater flame, even as many traditional theatergoers still regard the label "experimental" with suspicion.

So, despite the fact that the Wooster Group and LeCompte travel all the time, they travel in a very tight circle. From their home in SoHo's Performing Garage to St. Ann's Warehouse in Brooklyn to the European festivals that prize her contribution to world theater, LeCompte is very careful about the company she keeps in terms of audience as well. Apart from one foray in 1997 to the Broadway district with *The Hairy Ape*, starring then company member (and LeCompte's ex) Willem Dafoe, the general populace needs to seek out the Wooster Group like a speakeasy. Its open rehearsals—which seem to outnumber its actual performances downtown—aren't advertised. The adventurous already know where LeCompte is.

Adventurous theatergoers have long been enamored of the Wooster Group, but classifying what LeCompte has created over her decades with the company is devilishly difficult in so limited a space (a must-read for those interested is David Savran's innovative 1986 study, *Breaking the Rules*, published by TCG). LeCompte is most famous (and notorious) for juxtaposing classic texts with unexpected elements in performances that include spoken word, dance, highly deconstructed design ideas and a heavy mix of technology. Multiple layers of performance mediate the audience's reception of the source text to such a degree that often it's hard to discern anything other than flashes of the original. It could be said that LeCompte *directs juxtaposition*: of one text against another, of one performative idea against another, of one design idea against another. The deconstruction is so complete that delineating the performance's point of view is almost impossible. Savran notes the irony of a clearly politically committed theater that refuses to be pinned down: "Eschewing the certitude of the liberal critic or the authoritarianism of the proselyte, it questions from a position of doubt."

A Wooster Group show might splice together Thornton Wilder's *Our Town* with a party scene based on Pigmeat Markham routines ("Here come da judge!"), performed by white actors in blackface *(Route 1 & 9 [The Last Act]*, which premiered in 1981). Or Arthur Miller's *The Crucible* will be wedged against Timothy Leary's writings on the drug culture of the 1960s *(L.S.D. [. . . Just the High Points . . .]*, 1984). Or the love triangle in Racine's *Phèdre* finds illumination (or obfuscation) through a badminton match without a birdie, just MIDI-created sound effects *(To You, The Birdie! [Phedre]*, 2002). Audiences are left with a series of impressions, and each viewer reconstructs the event differently in his or her mind.

As surprising as these juxtapositions are for audiences, LeCompte makes sure her actors also work with the unexpected to keep their performances as live as possible. Beyond changing the work nearly every time it's presented (from night to night, as well as in the pieces' different incarnations from year to year), LeCompte builds performative elements that cannot be rehearsed into most of her productions, often with the use of technology. In many productions, actors must gauge their performances to video projections that change nightly, or respond to audio cues (rather than the other way around). In one of the most notorious bits from *Route 1 & 9,* characters at the blackface party ordered takeout live (the calls were projected through the sound system), often from Harlem, as a way of emphasizing the racial and geographic distance between downtown and uptown. That production, with its brutal confrontation of liberal views about race, prompted widespread allegations of racism in the critical community and a 40 percent cut in funding from the New York State Council on the Arts.

Barely two years later, in October 1983, LeCompte's dramaturgical experiments again drew fire. During open rehearsals for their juxtaposition of excerpts from *The Crucible* and Timothy Leary's writings (then simply called *L.S.D.*), Arthur Miller himself visited the Performance Garage and watched a performance. Fearing the piece would be seen as a parody of his work and discourage a major revival of it, Miller instructed his agents to deny the Wooster Group the right to use any part of his play. LeCompte reworked the piece, reducing the amount of Miller's text and adding the subtitle (. . . *Just the High Points . . .*). Almost a year to the day after Miller's first visit, the revised production opened in New York to a pan from the *New York Times,* and ten days later, a "cease-and-desist" letter from Miller's lawyers. LeCompte twice attempted to get around the copyright issues (first by inserting gibberish where Miller's text once was, and three months later by using the text of Michael Kirby's original play *The Hearing,* based itself on Miller's work); both times the controversy halted production of the play.

LeCompte's use of recordings has ignited firestorms about authorship and authenticity as well. In preparation for her shows, she and the other members of the Wooster Group often conduct audio-recorded interviews of figures relevant to the work at hand. LeCompte then builds those recordings into the performance—a practice that has prompted reactions ranging from moral indignation to legal action. In one early instance, in *Rumstick Road* (1977, with a 1980 revival), LeCompte used an interview conducted by Spalding Gray with his mother's psychiatrist about her depression. Gray performed his half of the conversation live. In the same piece, Gray played a recording of his grandmother reading from the works of Mary Baker Eddy; at the top of the recording, she explicitly asks him not to play it in performance. He played it entirely. In the *Village Voice* in 1980, Michael Feingold wrote:

Gray obviously thinks he's found a terrific way to rivet the audience's attention. So, obviously he has. But I feel cheapened by having been made to participate in this violation of a stranger's privacy . . . To make a point of including dishonorable transactions like this . . . is to brutalize the audience, implicating them in the artist's pain instead of offering them a share in its transcendence.

"Violation" is a word that springs up frequently when people speak of the Wooster Group, yet LeCompte simply says, "I'm not in it to hurt people's feelings, but [people's feelings are] also not my primary concern." She just passionately believes that theater must abjure convention at all costs to remain relevant and visceral.

And so LeCompte uses her unique approach to explore realms of the American psyche that conventional theater either avoids or deals with from a simplistic, patronizing perspective. Not content, for example, to let Eugene O'Neill's *Emperor Jones* explore the subjects of race and colonialism as it is, she casts the formidable white actress Kate Valk as the black Brutus Jones, complete with blackface—and wearing a kimono, infusing a kabuki-like tone to the entire performance. The multiple layers were a never-ending feast for the intellect. As the *New York Times*'s Charles Isherwood wrote of its 2006 revival:

> We remain at all times powerfully aware that we are witnessing an actress fashioning, with superb precision, a simulacrum of a stereotype. And this heightened awareness of Ms. Valk's performance as an artificial construct shapes our perception of her character as a man spouting words and attitudes that destiny has forced him to emit. We see Brutus Jones himself as an actor helplessly playing a role written by the savage errors of American history.

LeCompte was born in Summit, New Jersey in 1944 and studied painting and photography at Skidmore College, where she received a B.S. in Fine Arts in 1967. She met Spaulding Gray in 1965, and after her graduation the two moved in together in New York's East Village. She first immersed herself in the world of postmodern theater theory by assisting Richard Schechner in his noted (and notorious) Performance Group in the early 1970s. Influenced by the experimental ferment of the Vietnam era, Schechner had rejected the commercial theater model of the time and formed a company in which the director was the auteur, in charge of design, writing and more traditional direction. LeCompte soon became frustrated by what she perceived as a lack of discipline in Schechner's methods. In 1974, she and Gray began to work on their own pieces created through improvisation (these would eventually become the trilogy *Three Places in Rhode Island,* of which *Rumstick Road* was a part). When Schechner left the Performance Group in 1980, LeCompte took over as director and renamed it the Wooster Group.

The rest, as they say, is history—though in the Wooster Group's work, "history" is a slippery term: who owns it, who tells it, how is it constructed? Through the years, the Wooster Group has forged ahead with experimentation as institutional theater has grown ever more conservative, and has been very careful to avoid easy classification.

Nonetheless, the time of the 1970s and 1980s when its productions would prompt outrage, disgust or legal action are, for the most part, behind it. The Wooster Group's experimentation has now been accepted as an almost institutionalized alternative to institutional theater itself—to the point that in his 2005 review of *Poor Theater, New York Times* chief critic Ben Brantley could refer without irony to the company's "wit, warmth and humility," in paying tribute to Jerzy Grotowski.

I spoke to LeCompte in May 2004, about two months after Gray's body was pulled from the East River. For any student of theater in the 1980s and 1990s, Gray and his autobiographical monologues were icons of experiment at the intersection of performance, theater and popular entertainment. LeCompte and Gray were romantically involved for over a decade, but their artistic relationship lasted even longer and shaped both of their careers. The loss of Gray to presumed depression and suicide—a subject he examined so forcefully in his monologues, especially the ones he created with LeCompte—was potent as we discussed their early work together. His death certainly altered the perspective through which LeCompte now viewed her artistic path.

MAY 2004, VIA PHONE FROM THE WOOSTER GROUP OFFICES, NEW YORK CITY

You have a background as a visual artist. When did you turn to directing?

It was pretty gradual, because I did theater and continued to paint and draw and photograph, one medium next to the other, for many years. In school I was an art major, but on the weekends I worked at a café that had a theater, where I got involved. So those two things kind of vied with each other, or joined each other, for a long time.

I got involved with Spalding Gray at the theater company there. It was 1965. He had already graduated, and he would often go to different resident theater companies. So whenever I had time off from school, I would go visit him and see conventional repertory theater.

I joined the Performance Group as an assistant director to Richard Schechner, and I did a lot of the photography. I also helped with the design of the sets; I was an all-around visual person with the Performance Group. Richard would say to me, "You should direct," because I would help a lot when he went away for months at a time. I would take over and keep the pieces together. Sort of an avant-garde stage manager, I suppose you'd call it. I just kept the pieces together.

Sometime around 1973 or so, Spalding and I both got interested in new dance. We'd been watching Grand Union; Robert Wilson was working a lot with movement; we saw Richard Foreman. We decided to do a piece on our own—*Sakonnet Point* [1975], which was mostly a dance piece. I designed the set and a sound score for it. And I thought really that was just about helping out Spalding. It was the beginning of the trilogy, *Three Places in Rhode Island*.

Did you know at that point it would be a trilogy?

No. I think Spalding had an idea that he was going to do several pieces, but he didn't articulate it until later. After that first showing, he had his first really bad mental breakdown. We did *Sakonnet Point* again, with him still quite sick, to try to find something for him to do. And I began collecting material for *Rumstick Road* to keep him busy.

Then gradually, as he was performing in *Sakonnet Point*, he began to feel better, and so we began work on *Rumstick Road*. I realized I liked this process, and I would continue to do it.

So your process on *Rumstick Road* was less about facilitating Spalding's work, and more about uniting your vision with his words?

Yes, I'd say so. I designed the set, which put Spalding directly in front of the audience, speaking to them. That was the first time he had spoken directly to the audience. That was the first monologue, really. He was *right* in front of the audience, with this set behind that I could animate, not necessarily illustrating anything he said, but animating certain things that I took from the monologue. Sometimes the images were directly from his past, because I knew his family pretty well. And sometimes they were my own, and sometimes they were [Wooster Group founding members] Ron Vawter's or Libby Howes's stuff.

So we began to blend generalized themes behind his monologue. I suppose you could say I still have that sense of frontal narrative in most of my pieces; it developed there. Though it began to fragment into many different voices.

Of the later work, *To You, The Birdie!* perhaps has that frame, but then I think of *The Emperor Jones* and *The Hairy Ape*, which were visually different, denser, thicker.

Yes, I think the last real frontal narrative pieces that I did were *Brace Up!* [1991, revived in 2003] and *To You, The Birdie!* After that, I did those two O'Neill plays for Katie [Valk] and for Willem [Dafoe]; they're full plays, so I really followed more what the play needed than what I had been doing.

Your aesthetic changed so much with the O'Neill plays. There's certainly a lot of mediation in your *Emperor Jones*—the gender-switching, the Asian costume, the blackface—but it's so different from your earlier work, which seemed to be about the act of mediating text. Were your encounters with O'Neill a turning point for you?

What happened to me with those two pieces was this: I could take all the things that I learned, that I liked to do in the earlier pieces, and I could apply them to a text that was already done. The process was so much easier, so much less stressful, because it wasn't so personal.

I used the same set for *Brace Up!* and *To You, The Birdie!* as for both of the O'Neill plays. It was just a new way of using the set, really. In

Left to right: Eric Moskowitz, Ursula Easton, Ron Vawter, Tena Cohen and Spalding Gray in Nayatt School. *The Wooster Group, 1978. Credit: Nancy Campbell.*

Brace Up! I was using a lot of Japanese forms, noh theater forms, patterns on the floor for movement and eye alignment. And I think I carried that over into both pieces in different ways. In *The Emperor Jones,* Katie was really following the score of a noh theater performer. She picked out her favorite noh performers and she was looking at the TV all the time and following their scores, back and forth, improvising off of them. So I don't see a great deal of difference. I think that people tend to see a difference because it's one spoken voice. *Rumstick* was really conventional because it was one voice, with other images coming in and out. *The Emperor Jones* was a throwback to *Rumstick Road.*

Another big difference is that you left the text alone. When you first encountered *The Hairy Ape*, did you make a conscious decision not to play around with the text (unlike, of course, your revisions of *The Crucible* or *Our Town*)?

For some reason, they just didn't call for anything internally for me. Whereas with the other pieces, I just always wanted to *break in* and *say something*! Maybe [the O'Neill plays] felt like a closed system, which was very attractive. [In the O'Neill plays] we used a lot of television imagery, and Willem was lip-synching to his own voice, and Katie was working off TVs. I had a lot of things in there that were fragmenting. So it was really nice to have something that was *absolutely secure.*

And also [with the O'Neill plays] there wasn't the problem of casting, that I had, for instance, with *Brace Up!* I loved every word that was in the Chekhov text [*Three Sisters*, on which *Brace Up!* was based], in the translation by Paul Schmidt. But I didn't have all the people who could actually play those parts, so I had to come up with strategies to tell Chekhov's stories the way Chekhov would have wanted it, without a lot of traditional actors. I didn't have a lot of people who could *carry* the roles. So I had to find different ways the roles could be carried. Sometimes I would have to use a strategy like Katie coming in and telling what had happened—we didn't have an old character actor that could come on stage, but she could introduce somebody I could get on tape. Or take Anna Kohler: she had trouble walking on stage; she wasn't comfortable. So I could put her on a TV.

But that was all in the process to try to make it as close to what I felt Chekhov was saying. Whereas with both the O'Neill plays, I had all the characters and everyone was exactly right, including Kate, even though she was a woman; she was exactly right for the Emperor Jones. And Willem did the best possible Hairy Ape that I could imagine in my whole life. So with these shows I didn't need to do so much mediating with TV; I didn't need to fragment as much.

You added a complex layer of fragmentation to your work in 1991 with *Brace Up!*, in which you placed live actors alongside live video of themselves on stage for the first time. It even prompted you to create a set of rules—I would call it a manifesto—about how actors work with technology ("Performers on TV develop relationships with stage performer through the aural sense"; "Performers on TV develop all relationships through a language of vocal and spatial displacements," etc.). What attracts you to fragmentation?

I don't think I encounter the text as a fragmentation, and I don't think I try to fragment it. I think I try with what I have—my abilities, and my performers—to make it whole. I use the TVs to try to *unify* performance styles, because I'm not attracted to performance and acting as it's taught in most acting schools. It's a kind of mask that feels old to me. It feels like the 1950s or something. It doesn't feel like we're talking to each other, it doesn't feel *filmic*. I love the stage—but I love the immediacy of film.

I'm always trying to find some way that you can imagine on stage that *this* was the first time, this was the first take: take one, that's done, print it! But that's very, very difficult to do over and over again on the stage. I think I use the televisions to *set off*, so that actors are not thinking inside what their next move will be. They have the text, but they have to surprise themselves with where they'll be looking and how they'll be feeling. Once they do that, then they can *choose* when to use that, and when not. It's not so much that I want to fragment it. I think I'm trying to find some clearer way of speaking on the stage that's more immediate, that has a sense of film.

Let's take *To You, The Birdie!*. You created an almost uncomfortable intimacy in the staging by splitting up our view of bodies on stage: an actor's body topped by a close-up video of his face, or the locker room scene in which we see the live torsos of Hippolytus and Theramenes above very intimate video displays of what's happening below the waist, under the towel.

That's a good example of a way to fragment the speech. If you listen to the two men speaking and don't have the visual image, it's very uneven; the rhythms are uneven, it doesn't sound like a play. What we did works because they're taking their actions off of the video. And the video changes: there's a video guy who's manipulating the images.

I hadn't realized that.

Well, you don't need to. I'm trying to get to that intimacy that you feel, I'm trying to get it without it being a funny process in which the audience goes, "Oh, wow, what are they doing?" For me, it makes it more real-time. Without that process of what they have to do with their legs, or where they interface with the TV, it would be stilted. What they have to do physically sometimes has to take precedence over what they're saying. And sometimes what they're saying has to override what they have to do. It's more the way we really talk. So the combination of the two things is for me *more real*. And yet it's still a stage performance, which I love; it's still in the space.

Let's jump to process: how do you begin working on a show? You're currently working on *Poor Theater*. I asked one of your performers, Scott Shepherd, what you're doing, and he said, "Oh, we're just talking . . ." Is each show's genesis different?

It kind of is. With *Poor Theater,* we had two or three things I was interested in a couple of years ago. One of them was Hopalong Cassidy. Some of those cowboy movies were real morality fables for America. There was always the good man on the white horse, there was always the bad guy, and there was always a moral lesson that was very healthy; it was a "healthy culture," in quotes. Everyone understood: there wasn't any ambiguity about what was good and what was bad. It didn't have the moral ambiguity that *High Noon* had.

Why was I interested in them? It was probably because it was after 9/11. We started collecting these movies and listening to their commentary tracks. That was one area of work; we would do that for a couple of days. We were fooling around, making our own commentary track for one of our shows, too. And I got the news that Billy Forsythe's company in Frankfurt [Ballet Frankfurt, known for its radical interpretations of contemporary ballet] was going to be disbanded. Well, I was very affected by it, because it felt like the end of an era in some way for me. I even sensed with us that it was the end of an era. So we started collecting every interview we could find with Billy, and collecting every videotape we could get of his dances.

We slowly started improvising off his dances, and off his interviews, to see where it was taking us.

This was with how big an ensemble?

It's always going to be a small ensemble. This was just me, Katie, Sheena [See], Ari [Fliakos] and Scott, and then two or three of our technical people, and Ken Kobland was going to do some filming. We originally thought Willem was going to come into it, because I had an idea for a track that I could put him through, but he was going to be away for many, many months. And we had to have this piece for our grants. [laughs] So that's what we started with.

I thought about Billy, I thought about the beginning of my work, I thought about the first time I saw the Polish Laboratory Theater when I'd just been hired by Richard Schechner to be his assistant director, and he said, "I've got these tickets to see this guy, Jerzy Grotowski." I still remember it; it was huge.

What do you remember from it?

Pretty much what I tried [in *Poor Theater*] to get on the stage. I remember a tremendous sound, a tremendous amount of commitment to some kind of verbal and physical task that was a total mystery to me. But it was incredibly affecting.

Certainly the commitment of Grotowski's performers and the Wooster Group's are similar: textual, technical, physical, all together. You can't see a Wooster Group performance without sensing that commitment.

Perhaps that's something I took from him. Though he was so narrow in his idea of what technology was. He saw it as "the evil one." For me, technology was always a friend, a lover, something that made the performers more powerful and better. It didn't seem to be a negative, ever.

So you're watching and reading material . . . there's a lot of discussion involved?

We don't do a lot of discussion. I free-associate a lot in trying to put these things together. The only reason that shows that don't have a single text hang together is because there's one mind, and my mind is the one mind. Now, mind you, *mind* you, [laughs] I try to incorporate everyone else's mind into *my* mind when I'm working, by free-associating, and saying, "What does that mean to you?"

I tend to be the one to direct the conversation. If I'm trying to do something and I don't know why, I'll talk in front of the company and they'll ask me questions to try to help me clarify. They'll say something that I don't agree with, and that will clarify *me*. And it's a back-and-forth conversation; it's not really discussions. It's like they're trying to elicit from me what the hell I want to do!

But they're not saying, "Well, *I* want to do this," and I'm not saying, "I have an idea, and it's gonna be *this*." We discover it in this process. "I love this Grotowski piece here, I don't know, I just want to hear it in the space, but how can we hear it, *how*?"

And they'll say, "Well, why don't we just turn on the television?" And then I'll say, "Because I don't *want* a television to be seen here." And by that process, *they* lead me inexorably to what makes me happy . . . and usually what makes them happy. Because I have to incorporate so much of who they are to fill in my own gaps. And I have huge gaps.

And in that process, I'll watch them, and see they love to do it. And that becomes a part of it, because I love to see performers do what they *love* to do. I'm not so interested in what performers want to do for *me*. That makes me very nervous. I try to lead them toward something that really excites them.

So it's a very complex process. If anybody watched, it would be like watching the inside of someone's mind trying to make decisions about a painting. When it works, we're one mind. When it doesn't, then nothing happens. It's not a wasted day, but it's a slower process.

When you're working together, are there rules, spoken or unspoken, about things that will happen on stage? For example, you wrote of *Brace Up!*: "Stage performers do not look at each other."

That was only for those years of working on *Brace Up!* And that was after the fact: that's when I looked and realized what I'd done!

I try to change the rules for every piece, because it gets pretty boring otherwise. If we like the rule, we keep it; if we don't like it, we throw

Roy Faudree, Willem Dafoe (front), Dave Shelley and Paul Lazar in The Hairy Ape *by Eugene O'Neill. The Wooster Group, 1995. Credit: Mary Gearhart.*

it away. Or, I make them keep a rule they don't like, because that makes me see them struggle, and that's fun! Watching people struggle with something they don't understand usually creates something good.

What do you call yourself? What does a director do, in your mind?

I would call myself an artist. I call myself a "director" because I'm in the theater, and I have to conform when I'm applying for grants. But I wouldn't necessarily call myself a director in the strict sense of the word, because often I come up with the constructions. For example, I really enjoy working on the sound constructions, but that's not a director's job.

But as a director, I am the one who says, "I really need to see *this.*" And that doesn't mean material. Katie brought in *Phèdre*. I didn't even like it. She would do it one way, and I would go, "I need to see it some other way." So as a director, I'm the person who finally has the overall vision of the piece.

And when I say "overall vision," I mean the overall vision in terms of set and sound and lighting—everything—and the story. It's a little bigger than what a normal director does. That's why it takes me longer to do it, and that's why I stay with a piece all the time. I don't just do it and leave. I'm too involved in everything. By the end, it's *me.*

Even after pieces are done, you often remount them, sometimes years later. What do you get out of that process?

They adapt to every new person that comes in. And I learn more. Picasso returned over and over again to several themes in his life; and each time, in each place, it would alter and be altered. I suppose for me, it's the same. I don't think of myself as remounting pieces so much as reconstructing them. I'll use what I like and throw away what I didn't like, or what didn't work, or what wasn't interesting before.

Also, I try to remount pieces because that's a really good way to give me time to develop new work. If I can play an older piece in repertory, I can work during the day on the new one. I'm not forced to work as fast, to have something as quickly.

So is the directing part of your job a craft or an art?

I suppose it's a little of both. Craft comes in keeping the pieces together. I'm the ultimate stage manager once it's done. But making it is an art. There's no craft.

Does being a woman complicate your ability to produce your art? The last time I spoke with JoAnne Akalaitis, she told me that being a woman makes it difficult to access opportunities.

Oh, yes, I think that's very true. Now I don't experience that so much, because I don't work outside, and I've never accepted a job outside of the Wooster Group.

Is there a reason for that?

Why would I want to? I have everything I want here except money! I have no desire. But when I tour, I know how difficult it still is to be taken seriously as a woman.

Also, you have to realize, there's a reason why it's *Robert Wilson*, it's *Richard Foreman's* Ontological-Hysteric, it's *Peter Brook's* . . . but it's not "Elizabeth LeCompte's Wooster Group." It's just the Wooster Group. Because if it were "Elizabeth LeCompte's Wooster Group," we would probably have a little more trouble. It's not so easy to sell a woman's vision. So I try to make it not seem like a woman's vision, and a lot of people don't realize that they're actually seeing a woman's vision.

It's a scary little trick, because there's a downside to it. A lot of people don't realize what I actually do. I've had to go into places where people have asked me if they could speak with one of the men about the piece, because I couldn't possibly be the director—and that's only in the past three or four years.

But a part of that's mine: I don't put my name up above, and I try to hide in the middle of it. And I don't only do that because it's easier for people to think *maybe* it's a man's vision, or maybe it's a neuter vision . . . I also do it because I'm a voyeur, and I like to be invisible. I don't want the performers to think that it's only my vision; I want them to know that I'm willing to get lost in them if they get lost in me. That's a tacit agreement we have that allows very strong men to work with us.

I remember reading in David Savran's book about you, *Breaking the Rules*, that many people didn't realize your contribution to the Spalding Gray trilogy.

They still don't! Which is fine with me. That shows you where my ego is.

You were talking about the end of an era regarding William Forsythe's company. I'm sure that Spalding's passing has made you feel that as well. Can you talk about that?

I wouldn't be able to describe it. For me, it's always a feeling. And it'll show up. *Poor Theater* has a lot of those issues in it, and I'm working on an epilogue. There's one four- or five-minute piece that hasn't been finished. When we open it next fall, hopefully that'll be finished. And that maybe will be a little clearer: how I see the future.

For me, it's like, "What does an avant-garde theater *do* in this time?" That's the question Grotowski's people were asking in 1962; we're still asking the same question. I'm just asking it again. I got lost a little bit in some Greek tragedies, some O'Neill . . . but I'm asking that question again.

Do you ask yourself why it's so easy for the Wooster Group to find accolades and audiences on the other side of the Atlantic?

Yes! [laughs] But that's probably because we can play to a bigger audience there. Here it's really hard to play to a bigger audience [the Performing Garage seats ninety-nine]. We've done so much better since we've been able to go out to St. Ann's Warehouse in Brooklyn. It's three hundred. And that's what we do in Europe.

And you don't like to play bigger than that?

No I can't really, unless I change to something that uses more projections. And I don't like projections so much; I'm not attracted to the surface of them.

You moved to a larger house in 1997 with *The Hairy Ape*—the Selwyn [now the Roundabout Theatre's American Airlines Theatre], an old falling-apart theater on 42nd Street that, in its Broadway heyday, was home to Noel Coward, Cole Porter and George S. Kaufman. But then you went right back to the Performing Garage in SoHo. What did you learn?

The production at the Selwyn really helped us; it gave us a profile right away. It didn't mean that more people were going to come down here to see us; it just meant that more people had heard of us, which helps with grants. Now mind you, we were squatting in an old theater. It was much more funky than the Performing Garage! So it felt very comfortable that way, especially for *The Hairy Ape*. But we played for four hundred people. That's when I knew it was too much. But we had to do it in order to make our nut.

The Wooster Group comes to Broadway, but in a dilapidated out-of-use house that couldn't be farther from the tourist crowd, philosophically speaking. Is it important that you don't get accepted by the mainstream, that you remain on the fringes?

No, because I feel like I'm at the center. I have to! If I felt I was an outsider, I'd be making things that were angry or defensive. And I don't feel angry or defensive; I feel I'm at the very center of the culture. I just feel that I'm tiny. But tiny things are powerful. No, I never think about that; I always think we're right at the center.

Do you feel you've got a particular responsibility as an artist?

Everybody's always asking that. I think your intentions are really important when you work. But I don't think you always know your intentions. And that's what's risky about avant-garde art. We take a risk: that our intention is good, that it's not toward evil. But you never know.

Whereas in the mainstream, you *have* to know. You do know it; you've tested it. And anything that has any ambiguity would be excised from the piece.

For us, if we don't know whether something's risky, if we're not sure, we'll take a chance to put it in front of the audience, and we'll see. That's where the risk comes in. Sometimes we take a risk because we won't know what it means until the audience is there. Because for me, it's so much about a dialogue between the performer and the spectator.

That's why you do so many open rehearsals before opening a piece?

Yes. I had a lot of people talking to me about being offended at rehearsals for *Poor Theater* and *To You, The Birdie!* I had to test each time: "Why am I doing it, then?" And sometimes I was able to say, "It isn't important enough, what I'm doing there," and I was able to reinvent whatever that section would be, until I could say to someone, "It has to be there." I know it has to be there if I take it out and the play isn't there, or the purpose of doing it isn't there. It's not something I can always articulate in words until a long time after.

Can you cite an example of something you had to leave in?

Oh, sure. In *Poor Theater*, I had to leave in this woman we videotaped, Margaret Croyden. She'd heard we were doing a piece about Grotowski, and she came down here and said she wanted to talk to us about him. "I knew him well," she said. And we videotape all of our rehearsals. We're wired for sound; it's just something that turns on when we turn on the lights! And anyone who comes down to the Garage has to know it.

So she had spent a long time talking with us, two or three hours. And I put the tapes away, and we didn't hear from her again. And then, as I was working on the piece, I remembered something she had asked me: "Why did you have to do this again? It was *done*."

And I thought, "I have to put that in there." Because that was the question I was asking myself the whole time. I need the *other* person asking me that, and I need for there to be no answer, because I *still don't know why*. I didn't need it as a rhetorical question. I needed it from someone who had *seen the piece*. From someone who was an authority.

So I left it in, only we changed her voice, and I put my own face in for her. I'm playing Margaret Croyden. We don't use her name anymore because she's asked us not to. She was horrified by it. She hated it. She said, "You have to take it out. I do not want my presence in this piece."

We did the best we could. We altered her. But I couldn't take the words out: I needed a person who had seen Grotowski.

If you didn't want it to be a rhetorical question, why did you use your face?

I only chose it to be my face because I'm the only one who knows how to quickly lip-synch as I'm listening on an earplug, so that it looks like it's coming from my mouth. It's very difficult to do; it's a skill that we develop. And I was the oldest person in the company!

Another example is that in *Rumstick Road*, people objected to the voice of the doctor saying that he had given electric shock treatment to Spalding's mother. I mean, all those things were *legal*. It's legal to record one-way in New York if one person agrees. There are problems with privacy if you don't change the name and all that kind of stuff. So we changed his name, but some reviewers from the *Village Voice* were horrified.

But that was a time when both Spalding and I thought, "This just has to be here." We didn't want to go out at the time and find someone with that New England voice; it was so important to have the authority in the voice, and to get an actor to do that could take *months*! It's not easy!

But wasn't it also important to know that it was authentic?

I don't think that's important. We could have had a really good actor and have said it was the actual person, and that'd be just as good.

Perhaps it's only in retrospect that the intimacy feels like a violation of privacy—and I don't mean it derogatorily. But "violation" has always been something critics and audiences have latched onto with your work. Changing all the lines of *The Crucible* for your piece *L.S.D. (... Just the High Points ...)* for example—

Oh, we had to. That was just so painful for me.

Did you really think that Arthur Miller was going to say, "Go ahead, change all the lines of my play and make up your own"?

Yes, I sure did! [peals of laughter] Now mind you, it worked out rather well. [Professor of Drama at New York University] Michael Kirby went back to the original transcripts [of the Salem witch trials]. There were whole sentences that Arthur Miller had pulled from the original transcripts. So we were able to have our cake and eat it, too. We were able to put a modern thing on top of it, and then occasionally dip in so people would remember that it was *The Crucible,* which was kind of lovely. And that wouldn't have happened without Arthur Miller saying, "No, you can't do that!"

You've mentioned grants a number of times. Do you ever worry that the grant process can lead to censorship, or censoring yourself?

Yes, yes! But that happened so early for us. With the first *Route 1 & 9,* it was our colleagues, not the government, who censored us. People we were familiar with said, "You can't do that; it's bad taste," or "It's racist."

What threat did they perceive, do you think?

I think the threat was hurting people's feelings. Which is a real thing. I'm not in it to hurt people's feelings, but it's also not my primary concern. I don't think there's any way that anyone could say our intention was racist. You couldn't say that unless you believe all white people are implicitly racist—which is a possible stance. But in terms of intent, we were trying to make a statement about art and performance and masks, and a statement about culture in New York. About uptown and downtown, and the distance between the two.

So what had you hoped?

I never think about it. What I hoped? I hoped people would see how beautiful the piece was! Visually, aurally, psychically.

To me that piece was: you see a beautiful black and white couple going down the street, and you go, "Oh my God, that's the most perfect world! That's two *others* who are together." I saw that as a beautiful world. And I was trying to intimate it and trying to say how far away we were from it. I hoped people would see that possibility.

EMILY MANN

Listening for the Truth

EMILY MANN IS OBSESSED WITH UNCOVERING history. From the gently nuanced honesty of her Chekhov productions at New Jersey's McCarter Theatre Center (where she has been artistic director since 1990), to the riveting "Theater of Testimony" she's written (a genre of plays that many credit her with creating), Mann's directing and writing pursues the truth of how things were, in order to understand how things might be.

The historian's drive lies deep within her bones. Her father, Arthur, taught history at the University of Chicago, and gave his daughter the idea for her first documentary play. When Emily was in college (she graduated from Harvard in 1974), her father shared the riveting story of a Holocaust survivor told to him as part of an oral history project. She wanted to dramatize it, but her father told her to find her own interview subject—a direction that led her to another woman with another story. Mann took her words and crafted a dramatic tour de force; she directed its premiere in 1977 at Minneapolis's Guthrie Theater as *Annulla Allen: Autobiography of a Survivor*, while serving as that company's first Resident Director.

Annulla was followed shortly by a new play, *Still Life*, which she directed in its premiere at Goodman Theatre in Chicago in 1980. The play, starring John Spencer as a troubled Vietnam veteran, moved Off

Broadway to the American Place Theatre the following year, and sparked a revolution in American docudrama.

While the courtroom drama and stage biography were common enough forms when Mann started, her inventive dramaturgy, provocative editing and incisive research catapulted her subjects beyond the facts to much larger, cultural truths. Most of her "Theater of Testimony" is based on interviews, with which she sculpts tiny windows of experience to illuminate an entire generation's struggle, or a whole country's rage. Perhaps it's her director's eye working in close concert with the dramatist's (she has directed all but one of her own works), shaping narrative to compound the viewer's responses to the facts. Mann's continuing influence can be seen in the works of Anna Deavere Smith (whose *Twilight: Los Angeles, 1992* Mann directed in its premiere at Center Theatre Group's Mark Taper Forum), Moisés Kaufman and many others. That history lives, breathes, and has the power to change the future is a central tenet of her beliefs.

Still Life was based on actual interviews with a Vietnam veteran, his wife and his mistress. To tell their stories, Mann created a stark and simple setting: sitting at a conference table with his wife to one side and his mistress on the other, the veteran narrates a slideshow for the audience and trades direct address with the other characters, leading up to a gut-wrenching, achingly honest confession, a scene Mann counts among her greatest achievements in theater. The production garnered six OBIE Awards—including ones for direction, playwriting and production—and propelled Mann's career. She freelanced out of New York for the next ten years, writing two more plays, including the docudrama *Execution of Justice* (recounting the trial following the murders of San Francisco's Harvey Milk and Mayor George Moscone in 1978) which played on Broadway under her direction in 1986.

Ascending to the directorship at the McCarter in 1990, Mann saw an opportunity to return to the classics. After a near-disastrous first season in which subscriptions dipped dangerously low, Mann rebounded in 1992 with a production of Chekhov's *Three Sisters* starring Linda Hunt, Mary Stuart Masterson and Frances McDormand, drawing record crowds. Chekhov, Shakespeare, Williams, Molière—many of the great classic writers in the Western canon—have become staples of her tenure at the McCarter and her work outside it (including a multiracial *Streetcar Named Desire* on Broadway in 2012). The theater received the regional Tony Award in 1994.

Even while running a theater (and fighting the multiple sclerosis diagnosis she received the year of the Tony Award), Mann has continued both writing and directing. The 1990s saw her last two major docudramas: *Having Our Say: The Delany Sisters' First Hundred Years* (based on the book about two African-American women coming of age under

Jim Crow and living well beyond it), which moved to Broadway from the McCarter in 1995 and was nominated for three Tony Awards; and *Greensboro: A Requiem* (about the aftermath of a 1979 Ku Klux Klan rally, where anti-Klan protesters were shot and killed), at the McCarter in 1996. Since then, Mann has not been able to write another docudrama (*Mrs. Packard*, her 2007 play about a woman wrongfully committed to an asylum, was based on historical events but not technically a docudrama).

Perhaps it's because the classics have consumed her imagination. Making realist standards even more truthful to a contemporary audience (as well as the directorial impulse to get as close to a writer as possible) led Mann down a different writing path: adaptation. Mann has now adapted works by Strindberg, Lorca and Chekhov—and, you might say, Shakespeare, by directing such unconventional productions as a controversial 2003 *Tempest* starring the actress Blair Brown as Prospero.

Given Mann's outspoken liberal views, one might expect these productions to turn the tables on the patriarchal literature she's adapted in some radical way. Not so. Despite the gender-bending of her *Tempest,* her take on the classic heroines (Nora, Miss Julie, even Juliet) colors them in shades of very deep gray. Her directorial interpretations of the classics are noted for their fluidity, honesty and directness—not for a revisionist stance. Shaping history is one thing; tampering with it, another.

This isn't to say that Mann has little interest in new plays or new stories written by others. Much of her long career had been built on them, and she has frequently used the McCarter as a platform to launch them into the wider American canon. Her production of Nilo Cruz's Pulitzer-winning *Anna in the Tropics* went to Broadway after its 2003 McCarter run; she directed the world premieres of Christopher Durang's *Miss Witherspoon* (2005) and Edward Albee's *Me, Myself & I* (2008), later directing both Off Broadway at Playwright's Horizons; and her production of Danai Gurira's *The Convert* (2012) traveled from the McCarter to the Goodman in Chicago to Center Theatre Group in Los Angeles as a shared world premiere.

Nonetheless, Mann owes her national reputation to her interview-based work, and after meeting her it's easy to understand why she's found success with this genre. Her presence is energizing, and she speaks with an engagement, vigor and self-confidence that inspire the mind of the listener. Mann sets you instantly at ease, yet makes you eager for her approval. It's no wonder this woman, with her deep respect for all those she encounters, could locate the truth inside such complex personae as a Vietnam veteran who'd killed innocents, a World War II survivor and a Klansman.

One only need imagine Mann conducting an interview for *Greensboro* with a white supremacist to understand the power of her listening skills. Despite ample evidence against him, her interview subject had gone free. "It was one of the most difficult things I've ever done," she told National Public Radio in 1996. "I suffer from multiple sclerosis . . . [I was] sitting with people who have admitted that they're responsible for the deaths of some extraordinary people, and who believe in everything I disagree with. When the interview was over three and a half hours later, he didn't want to leave. He was having a grand time, and I couldn't walk."

Mann is a masterful listener, even in the toughest of circumstances, and that ability drives her success as a director, writer and producer. Whether she's listening to an interview subject or the soul of Anton Chekhov, she's paying careful attention to what history has to tell her.

MARCH 2003, MCCARTER THEATRE CENTER, PRINCETON

You built your reputation through documentary drama, putting extraordinary—or ordinary—people's voices on tape.

Annulla was my first documentary play. She was a survivor of the Second World War. She got out, and much of her family did not. She was a very interesting person to meet when I was twenty years old, trying to figure out who I was as a Jew, and why or how some people survived, and some did not. There has been a big question in my mind much of my life: "Would I have been one who did or didn't, and at what cost if I did?" All these huge identity questions, and questions of strength and moral decision-making, came up very early in my life. I needed to come to grips with that, and I did a lot of that in my first play. It's a lifelong struggle, and I hope never to recover! I hope I'll be questioning all the way to the grave!

Still Life was the second such play. Why did you want to put the voice of the Vietnam veteran on stage? What moral quandary were you considering at that point?

I was trying to justify and defend being against the war to my father. He had been a liberal all my life, and then when the Vietnam War hit, and the late sixties hit, he took a turn to the right, as did many of his very intelligent colleagues and friends. And I remember saying to him, "If I were a boy, I would definitely *not* go to serve in Vietnam: I would do whatever it took, whether it meant avoiding the draft through conscientious objection, or going to Canada; I would *not* go to war."

And he said, "*Oh yes you would.* I would make sure you did. You would serve your country."

And I said, "Well then, you would lose a son. I wouldn't do it."

We had a terrible, terrible argument over it. And I respected him so much—morally, intellectually, in every way. And he respected me. He was desperately disappointed, but I thought I needed to make him understand. *Still Life* came out of that need. I didn't really know until I was in the middle of it. I went to the opening with my father; he held my hand and watched. And at the end of it, he looked at me and said, "I utterly disagree with you, but I respect your position. We have to agree to disagree." And we made a truce.

That's an amazing strain in your work: people making a truce with themselves or others over intractable issues. This seemed especially true in the interview process for *Greensboro*, your play about the murder of anti-Klan protesters.

That's an interesting piece. I don't feel I completed it to my satisfaction because I didn't direct the premiere. I had recently been diagnosed with multiple sclerosis; I'm in great shape now, but at that point in time I wasn't feeling well, and I thought, "Well, I can't direct *and* write this huge piece on my own." So I asked another director whom I greatly admired, but had never worked with. Now I understand why playwrights get so nuts with directors. I didn't get to do the rewrites I thought needed to be done—normally, I finish my writing in the room with actors.

And then it was all about the set: it was overdesigned and difficult, and what I wanted was those fabulous actors to be engaged with the text. So it didn't ultimately communicate all that I wanted to say. It is a very passionate, loving piece, even though it's about terrible pain and murder. The survivors are amazing, warm, beautiful people, and I wanted it to *rock*. And it almost did; it was an inch away. I never had the opportunity to comb through it the way I've had with all the other plays, you know, where every moment counts—I do that as a director. I even do it with Shakespeare: you change a word here, you change a word there, you reshape a scene.

I'm always fiddling, whether it's writing, directing, acting or design, and then I take the necessary steps. But when you're just the writer, in a lot of ways, you're powerless in the room. You shouldn't be, but you are.

So now you wouldn't premiere a new work of yours unless you're directing?

If I did, I would have to have an *amazing* relationship with the director. If I could direct a workshop as the playwright, and was then happy with the text, I could let someone direct it. But yes, I need to have my hands on it, working with actors in the room.

In a completely different direction, Chekhov has been a big hit for you at the McCarter. Now you're taking on *Uncle Vanya*, which you're adapting. Are you shaping that task more as a writer or as a director?

I don't know if I make those distinctions: I make theater. And I don't think, "Oh, I'm a playwright. Oh, I'm a director." I'm always using both those skills. Yesterday I was sitting in the room with the designers. Directors have to have acute visual skills as well.

I make theater with people, and theater is collaborative. If I'm working with this genius set designer, it doesn't mean I don't question the floor plan. We just stripped away half the set yesterday, and we're both thrilled. It's a collaboration; it's a partnership.

So when you ask if the adaptation is directorial or writerly, I guess it's writerly. I know Chekhov wanted things to be utterly simple, and in their perfectly shaped simplicity, all the complexities of life come out.

What I find in most adaptations of Chekhov, including David Mamet's . . . well, he's written another play there! What I'm trying to do is be transparent, let it shine through. I think the *Vanya* is my best. It's about twenty percent shorter than anyone else's in English that I've seen. The Russian scholars who've been reading it are saying, "Oh my God, it's like he was writing in English. This is how it sounds in Russian."

So now as a director I look at that script, and I know it syllable by syllable. That's what a director really should know going into rehearsal. You should know a script as well as if you'd written it. Now, given that sensibility of that script which I know so well, and all the moment-to-moment work I *know* is in there (I haven't staged it in my head, I haven't placed some huge *concept* all over it), I'm trying to reveal Chekhov. And from there, taking what my sensibility is as a director, trying to meet Chekhov.

I've fallen madly in love with him, of course: I wish he were alive and in the room with me. I'm trying to simply stage that beautiful vision of life. What chair Vanya's mother is sitting in is as important as the words coming out of her mouth, as to whom she's talking, and whether she's stage left or stage right, and what light there is, and . . . all of it, all of it combines to make a series of moments that are purely what Chekhov envisioned.

How do you know that what you've gotten to is what he envisioned?

Well, I don't know, because I can't talk to him. And I don't know if there's any production of it that could serve as a guide. We know he didn't like Stanislavski's; we know he had mixed feelings about the one in St. Petersburg. I think he was on the verge of an *absolutely new scenography*—I found that out doing *The Cherry Orchard* [2000]. He was beginning to envision a theater that really looked into the eternal, that was on a spiritual and a psychic level beyond anything his theater had seen. At the very end of his life, he was really a precursor to Beckett. In fact, we know from his notes that the play he was going to write before he died was very much like Beckett: it was people on board a freighter in the Arctic Sea, and the fog was enveloping them and they were about to hit an iceberg. Like, *hello*! No drawing room here! He was going off to someplace very interesting. And you feel it in everything, in *Cherry Orchard,* but the seeds of that are in *Vanya.*

Why do you think you're so attuned to this work?

I always have been. It's Chekhov, Williams, Ibsen: I approach them *terribly humanly.* I was perhaps a hypersensitive child! Most theater people were, don't you think? You just have no skin. I remember one time going with my mother to a garden show, and I touched a plant and it curled up, and I said, "Oh, I wonder what that is?" I don't think she

Mary McDonnell, John Spencer and Timothy Near in Still Life *by Emily Mann. American Place Theatre, 1981. Credit: Martha Holmes.*

knew a thing about plants, so she said, "It's a sensitive plant," and she looked at me and said, "much like you!" [laughs] I was one of those kids: my feelings were always hurt, I was always crying, afraid of saying things to people because I might hurt *their* feelings. It must have been impossible to be my parents!

So I'm just very attuned to human beings, and the emotional life of human beings. I resonate to the sensibility of Tennessee Williams. We met and thought we were long-lost family members. I have that *feeling* about Chekhov. I feel like I know him. It's very arrogant to say this, and presumptuous, I realize. But having immersed myself in the *language* of two of his plays, I feel very close to him.

What would he say about you?

Oh, he was *awful* to many women, I hear, so I don't know! [laughs] Perhaps it's arrogant, but I think I'm doing what he had talked about wanting to see. It's a stagecraft of utter simplicity. I actually think we would have gotten on.

How do you talk to actors about that simplicity?

I'm simple but specific. I'm after what's completely human and very funny, the way people are funny when they're very much themselves. Add to that a *slight* understanding of vaudeville. But it has to be done very slyly—you can't perform the four great Chekhov plays in a vaudeville style. Always, the humor has to come from people being utterly themselves.

You know when Waffles [in *Uncle Vanya*] goes through his rigma-role about his wife? That is sheer stand-up! When I auditioned that role, the people who tried to *make* it funny were not funny. The ones who truly understood it knew that the only way to make it work was to get more and more and more upset, and play the intention deeper and deeper, of *why* it's clear that *he* had done the right thing and he was a happy man. It was screamingly funny. But that's a very tricky thing with Chekhov, and it's true of any comedy; it's got to have reality to it. Chekhov understood how you could just about wet your pants from laughing at who people really are. He was wonderful with comedy. I can't believe the number of Chekhov performances I've seen that don't understand that.

Where do those directors go wrong with Chekhov?

Maybe they don't believe him when he said he wrote comedies. It's understandable. He says *The Seagull* is a comedy and yet it ends in a suicide. Still, until the fourth act, it is hilarious.

So how do you ensure that you go "right" with a cast, and keep them from playing tragedy when they should be playing comedy? Do you stop them when you see they're off track?

I never make an actor feel wrong. The whole cast of *Tempest* came to me at the end of the run last Sunday night, and said they had never enjoyed working on a play so much, that they had done their best work. One of the reasons for that is that they knew they were safe. If they don't have an idea, *I* do. Though of course I'm dying to hear their ideas because that's why I cast them. And if they're about to go over the precipice, I catch them and stop them and bring them back. It's about never making anyone feel wrong, yet never letting anyone go off in the wrong direction either. There's always a sense of emotional safety, combined with a demand from the get-go of working from absolute truth. I don't let anything else happen in the rehearsal room.

Do you think actors generally want to be directed, to contribute only within a limited sphere, or do you think they want to play all the time?

It's different from one actor to another. Everyone works differently. You have to get the performance out of some actors by directing the person they're opposite, which is a very good trick. If it's directed at them, a wall immediately goes up. But if you give the adjustment for the scene to the other person, they understand where they enter into that adjustment. So they make their own adjustment, but they've done it on their own, and think it was their idea.

Ultimately the best directing is when you're saying the least and the actors feel what they've gotten came all from them. You've got to put your ego aside when you're a director and do what's best for the work. And each actor needs different things.

Knowing about acting is the best thing a director can know, by the way. If you have someone who's worked mainly with internal technique as opposed to external technique, and you're working with another actor who's mainly about external technique, you've got to find a way for the two of them to be in the same world, and create the scene together.

That difference of approach isn't something you try to avoid in casting?

I just cast the best actors, and how they get there is up to them. It's exciting to have people with different techniques in the same room. People learn from each other. But you'll make your points with each one differently.

I just had that situation in *Tempest* with the clowns. Ultimately you couldn't tell the difference on stage. But one of them [John Keating] was one of the most precise physical comic actors I've ever come across—his Stephano was hysterically funny, in every way built for the stage. He could take apart some of those really hard Shakespeare clown moments, and understand exactly what they were, and it all relied on a certain kind of timing and placement on the stage. The other, Trinculo—brilliant, funny, great actor [Cameron Folmar]—with him everything has to work internally. He had to get all of his emotion going to understand what was happening. To get them both in sync was a really fun challenge, because each one informed the scene from different directions.

I'm thinking of a *Tempest* I saw recently in which the same dynamic was at work, but the director couldn't resolve the distinction. Why do you think you were able to do it?

I'm a listener. Which serves me as a director. After a while you just have an instinct, you know what makes people tick. And I must say, you learn to leave judgment at the door. If you say you'll only work with people who work from an internal state, you're going to lose a lot of brilliant people.

At the end of the day, we all work the same way. Because we're all after the same thing. You couldn't just do everything saying, "I'm going to wait for the end of his line, come right in on it, turn here, take my hat off and sit." You still have to *fill it*. The actor still has to be real, utterly real; he's telling a story, a human story. And of course he knows what his intentions are all the time, and uses all this to build exactly what he wants. It's all really the same, whether you're going from the inside out or the outside in. So as a director you just need to know the right language to help the person.

Whatever "technique" you use—whether you believe in Viewpoints, whether you believe in Meisner . . . ?

All the same. I've worked with a lot of people who studied with Anne Bogart. There's Jefferson Mays: he's a sheer Viewpoints product.

So you need to know his vocabulary.

Or not . . . Maybe they need to know yours. You have to find a way to work together, because at the end of the day, I know the basic idea that I want for the whole. I know what the world is, I know what the arcs are, and I'm open to every kind of discovery in rehearsal.

If the actors come up with something better than what's in my head, I'm thrilled, and I edit and shape that. The foundation is all there. It's always coming from something that's part of the world: the needs of the characters, finding layer after layer after layer of all those things, and putting it together. Eventually it evolves into an extremely rigorous, disciplined piece.

When did you know who you were as a director?

I've just grown and grown as a human being directing plays. Garland Wright [the artistic director of Minneapolis's Guthrie Theater from 1986 to 1995] once said a beautiful thing: "Theater was my university," and it's true for me, too. It's how I learned about life and how to live. I've gone through phases. My first professional Shakespeare was *Romeo and Juliet* last year: no one can believe it, but it's true. I was trained in Shakespeare at the Guthrie. But I thought Shakespeare productions all that time were extremely false—people acting badly, musty and crusty and fake and Anglophile, and I hated that.

After about twenty-five professional years of work, and with the Middle East situation so distressing, I thought, "I need to look at this again." I don't know why; it just came to me in a flash. I reread it and it blew my mind. And I thought, "I know how to do this." It was like finding a new play of genius!

You rediscovered something essential in Shakespeare for you.

You're dealing with a fellow theater person in Shakespeare. You're getting rid of these academic, priggish ideas about how to do these plays . . . he was not someone who thought it was literature. If you didn't get your laugh, he'd rewrite the line or fire the actor or change a word and make it better. If it wasn't funny—it was written to be funny—then cut it! I cut all those four-hundred-year-old jokes that don't work, or that we couldn't make work. Others I gave little shifts and changes.

You know that wonderful line when Trinculo comes out from beneath Caliban: "How cam'st thou to be the siege of this moon-calf?" I figured the people in the audience would need a dictionary. So we changed it to, "How cam'st thou to be the shite of this moon-calf?" And there were screams of laughter from the audience. You have to have an amazing amount of confidence to do that, I suppose—or chutzpah, really, to do direction of any sort.

It's become a common theme in these interviews. The directors in this book all trust their instincts implicitly.

You've got to trust yourself in order to trust others; it's that simple. Then it's ironclad, unshakeable and everyone's work is in a very positive place. And then you can really argue about a moment and know an actor isn't going to say, "I'm going to quit!" or any of that nonsense. It's always about the work. You're free to go places that you would not go in any other situation. What we're after in directing is finding a unique combustion between two actors. I'm an actor's director, but I also hope I'm a writer's director, and that I'm a designer's director, too, because I adore all the elements of the theater. And I've gotten better at them.

How have you gotten better?

Doing more writing has helped my directing. And doing more directing has helped my writing. And working with actors has helped my design sense. And doing so much as a producer for other people's shows— working with all the people that come through this theater. I'm such a maniac about the fact that nothing on the stage can be anything but ter-rific. We can't afford it. The bar is very high, so I'm in there slogging away with everyone.

When you work at something every day, you simply get better at it. I was speaking about this yesterday with Michael Yeargan [scenic designer for her production of *Uncle Vanya*]. We did *Three Sisters* together, and we'd never had our schedules work out since: now that's twelve years ago. I realized how much I've grown as an artist. I'm faster. This time, in four hours we had redesigned the set with the basic ele-ments, and now it worked, *and* it's cheaper *and* it's simpler, and I know exactly where the pipes are, I know exactly how the drops are working, and I know exactly how we want to deal with the masking.

He started to place a chair and I said, "I could not *cast* a woman who would sit in a chair that's facing in that direction. I wouldn't be able to find her anywhere!" [laughs] I couldn't have said that twelve years ago; I wouldn't have known it then.

How will I know that I'm seeing an Emily Mann play? Is there an Emily Mann aesthetic?

I would think so, but I don't know what it would be. I don't throw myself all over things. I suppose simplicity of design, completely truthful act-ing. And usually some quietly radical point of view. But what's radical about it usually is that *it's true*. It's never the external, it's always the internal truth.

So in directing *A Doll's House*, I thought that Torvald's tragedy is as big as Nora's. Pretty simple, but the whole play comes to life. She is a very silly woman, you know? Maybe it takes a woman to tell the truth about another woman. I *loved* her. But she is in fact revealed as someone who has played all these silly games because she doesn't know what else to do; she is trapped within her own world and her own society, of course, but at the end of the day, the choice that she makes is so desperate, to leave her children. So sad, so crushing to her husband ... and there was another alternative. *He's* woken up, *she's* waking up. Those children need her, and there's another way to come back through that door and deal with the real tough stuff. She's not going to do it, though, and she doesn't know what's going to happen to her. But *that's* an interesting play because it's not a flat polemic, it's a very interesting human dilemma. And I've directed it three times.

Three times? Why?

The first time I was about to get married. The second time, I'd had a child. And the third time I directed it I'd had a divorce. Those events informed each production. I always use what I know.

Just the other day, the artistic staff had all just gone to see *Vanya* at BAM [directed by Sam Mendes for London's Donmar Warehouse]. Half of them thought Simon Russell Beale was good; the others thought he was awful. But they said, "You know, in your productions, everyone has a full life and a story—but in this production, *they don't*. You sort of remember Simon Russell Beale, and that's it, and you liked him or you didn't like him."

What I meant out of all of this is not to put down someone else's work, but in the type of work I try to do, every single actor in my productions—each and every character down to the extras—has a full, full life.

Which directors do you admire?

There are lots of directors whose work I love. David Leveaux at his best (everyone has their ups and downs); Stephen Wadsworth at his best, especially his Marivaux productions, which were spectacular.

What makes Wadsworth so good at plays by Marivaux, do you think? Because he adapted them?

It's partly that. And his brilliant, near revolutionary work in opera. He completely understands style. From the inside out. His first professional direction of a play was *The Triumph of Love* here at the McCarter [in 1992], and it was such a relief for him not to be dealing with opera singers and people who can't act. It was fresh and new. Because it was so acclaimed, he's had to work very hard not to be made to direct everything in "the Wadsworth style." All artists have to deal with that, not letting themselves get into their own bag of tricks, the thing that they've been most lauded for.

Have you ever gotten into a rut?

Yeah. Not for long . . . Yeah.

Well, I haven't found the next piece I want to write. So rather than trying to force it, I've been writing through my directing: the Shakespeare plays, and the Chekhov, too, and Lorca, another artist I'm madly in love with. I've adapted *Bernarda Alba*, one of the greatest plays ever written. Lorca's last one, of course, before he was brutally murdered.

But I think I got into a bit of a grind with not having the time to do a documentary from scratch the way I wanted to, so I haven't. I don't think that's a *rut*: I'm on a hiatus of sorts.

The other thing is, there was a period when I was directing new plays that were *not quite great*. And using my skills to try to get a play to work that I knew didn't quite work was very debilitating. Working with writers who wouldn't rewrite, who wouldn't look at it, you know? The frustration grew because I wasn't being satisfied as an artist, plus I wasn't helping. I was neither making a play better for another writer, nor enjoying the process as a director.

That's why I started to work in the classic repertoire again: because I want to do plays that are *brilliant* again. And not to say that I don't want to do new work; I do—but not a steady diet of it. I think that was the rut I got into. I need a balance. For a while, I was not getting fed by artists of great magnitude. I had to submerge so much for the writer, and often the writer was wrong, or if not wrong, unable to make the necessary changes to make it right. It was just okay—a well-done production of a promising piece—what a worthy enterprise, right? *Ugh!* I don't have the heart for it anymore.

Let's go back to rehearsal process. What's the first day with the actors like?

It used to be just sitting there, talking about the whole idea, why I love the play, why we're here, why it's new, why it's the time for it, look at the clothes, look at the set . . . And we'd sit around the table and tear it apart, and do very challenging tablework, which I still think is often very useful.

But for the first time, with *The Tempest,* I did something else. We had a four-day workshop before rehearsals began, and at that workshop I never let anyone sit down for one moment.

I said: "Look, I have designed this, I have a basic floor plan. Here's why I love this play, here's what it's about: it's a woman at the center, it's Blair [Brown as Prospero]. You can see why you're cast this way. She's a queen instead of a king. I've done the requisite changing of the words, I've cut about twenty percent of the play, it's got a shape that

I think works. You can do *nothing wrong*—we're going to get up on our feet now!"

We had the time of our lives! Playing, doing crazy stuff, and by the end of the fourth day we did a runthrough on our feet, holding books, and we had the staff of the McCarter come over. Everyone was like, "You could *open* this." My God, it was so thrilling! We had a temporary score, so there was music, everything except the lighting, the clothes and a high balcony.

Everyone loved it so much that they couldn't *wait* to get into rehearsal. We had a three-month break and they had parties with each other! I did not lose one actor in three months. I could not believe that good fortune. No one took another job. People turned down work.

Did you know that's how it would work when you started?

I didn't. Isn't that interesting? I knew I wanted to get up on our feet a little bit, just to make sure the design was right, and talk about the big things of the play. I got in there and it just came to me in a flash!

It was right for this play. Everyone in the cast *loved* it. They said, "I never want to do tablework again!" But I don't think I can do that with *Vanya*. I'll have to decide what those first days are going to be like.

Tell me about some challenging times with actors, ones you've had trouble getting through.

[much laughter]

Here's one thing I can talk about. We were doing a new play, with a very interesting cast, and a certain star actress was in it. And this actress can be very challenging, but we adore each other and love working with each other. Thank God, I had enough confidence to do what I did.

She would often come into the room late, even in the first week, and as the young people were working, she would just start *scowling*, watching them, making little noises. They got so rattled because they wanted this great actor to approve of them. They were young! They were in their twenties, so vulnerable, and they just couldn't do the work! I finally took her aside and said, "Look, you're a very powerful person. And your presence in the room can either be a force of great unity and love and harmony for the cast, or you can pull us apart. And what you're doing right now is very detrimental to the other actors."

"What, me?" she said.

I said, "Yes, you!"

She said, "I didn't say a word!"

I said, "No, you didn't need to. That's what I mean by saying you're a very powerful person. Use your power for the positive and not the negative." And she *changed,* and it was beautiful.

David Zayas, Jimmy Smits, John Ortiz, Daphne Rubin-Vega and Vanessa Aspillaga in Anna in the Tropics *by Nilo Cruz. McCarter Theatre Center, 2003. Credit: T. Charles Erickson.*

Now, a few years earlier I would have sat there feeling devastated and not knowing what to do. Being semi-aware, I would see that the kids were feeling that way and I wouldn't know what to do with that. I'd be a little bit intimidated by the great actress myself, right?

Instead, I said, "Don't do that! We're not having that!" And she was so grateful. No one ever talks to her like that, you know: *cut the shit!*

What I've learned is that there is always someone who is a center of a company. If that person is deeply neurotic, or unable to work in a harmonious way, the entire company will feel it, and it will not be a harmonious company. If on the other hand you have a Blair Brown at the center, or a Jane Alexander, or a John Glover, or a Rosemary Harris—actors who love and know "company," and help to build a company, and give great joy and positive energy inside the room—you as the director don't have to be the center. That part of it is done for you, and you just really jump on for the ride.

It's interesting that when I asked you about challenges with actors, you didn't pick something about process, but instead chose to talk about company psychology.

I don't work well in chaos; I work well in harmony. I need a harmonious situation in the rehearsal process for me to do my best work and thus for everyone else to do their best work. I do a half hour of yoga with my casts every day before we start the rehearsal. I haven't had a personality problem in a rehearsal room since I started to do that. Some people *thrive* on chaos; they make it happen. I am the opposite. I told you that story because I've had to learn over the years how to make a harmonious room. Sometimes it can't be done unless you fire someone. And sometimes, producers won't let you fire the *problem*. "The problem" is the box office money, and they're not going to give up that name actor, even if that person is tearing the room and every other actor apart. And that is something you have to learn how to deal with. I've gotten burned by that fire a number of times. You live with it: it's not fun, but you make it work.

You may have two characters, as I did (the actors in the roles will remain nameless; one of them has passed to the other side) who are supposed to love each other dearly. The whole play was just the two of them. And the actors were both *crazed,* and could not work harmoniously with each other, the text, the director, any of it.

And so I had to choreograph "love": "On this word you look at each other." "On this word you put your hand out as if you were feeling a sensation of warmth between the two of you." *I'm not kidding.*

Let's look at the other side of the coin. When you achieve harmony, what can you create?

The balcony scene in *Romeo and Juliet.* One critic said in his review, "You may think you've seen the balcony scene in *Romeo and Juliet* many times, but let me tell you, *you never have* till you've seen . . ." [laughs with glee] It was one of my best.

I think it was when I realized they didn't have to be *on* the balcony. And so I had her come down to say, "Do you love me?" Once I made that discovery, the whole scene had a shape and architecture that was glorious. The chemistry between Sarah Drew and Jeffrey Carlson was fantastic. And the great, unmistakably unforgettable moment was her deciding to race down to the courtyard to be with him. Stop, kiss for a beat of about five, and then ask, "Do you love me?" And the *whole theater rocks.*

Did you figure that out in the moment?

I knew before rehearsal started. I didn't know how to do it, but I had a sense that she should come down and be able to go back to him on that line. I didn't know how to build the scene to make that happen, but

I had a sense that was the moment. Again, that's a writerly thing. I just said, "Okay, take away all of the stage history that you've been told—the balcony scene, she's up there, that's what you know—just forget that! What if that's not true? What if you didn't have the height?" I asked all of these questions, and I finally read it as a writer. I just read the scene, and I went, "Oh! 'Do you love me?' She's there, with him."

I had to figure out all the things Juliet had to overcome. Sarah knew about it. She *was* Juliet in a lot of ways. Very young; she was a minister's daughter. She's not like a typical American girl. Sarah understood and *shared* a lot of the inhibitions or moral limitations of religion and family. She could understand what chastity meant.

I had to get Jeffrey to the point where he understood what he wanted, what rules he was breaking. And then all three of us determined together how we could make the language and the moment all build. And we did that not intellectually, but by going through huge intentional changes. There were lots of layers by the time we got to the point one day in rehearsal when she turned to Jeffrey, and she just had to go to him. She had to.

There was a Donna Murphy moment when I directed *Miss Julie* [in 1993, with Kim Cattrall as the count's daughter, Miss Julie, and Peter Francis James as Jean, the footman and fiancé to Murphy's Kristin, a cook in the household]. You know that interlude in the middle that's usually dreadful and comical? The peasants do that jolly dance and then do that awful "I'm sexually turned on" thing, and then run out, and Jean comes out of the bedroom with Julie—he's shtupped her, right? That is *so dreary* to think about.

My entrance into the play was actually through the character of Kristin. From my view of it, Kristin turned the play on its head. My feeling was that Kristin had a very good thing going with Jean, and Jean had a good thing going with her, and they were happy. And then his fantasy got the better of him, and *he* had to go and see what could happen with Miss Julie. And it's midsummer, Miss Julie's feeling crazed, she's never had *this*. She wants to find out what sex is, and it is the most amazing thing that's ever happened to her in her life. It's not that she was *raped,* it's not that it was bad, it's not like she came out throwing up like in Bergman's production: *oh no no no no.* It was *so good,* she wanted more . . . and more . . . and more . . .

When you are having a marriage or an affair with somebody, you know what your partner's doing; you know him or her very well. So here's what I had in the interlude: first, two peasants come on, and they're looking around for where they can get laid, basically. They finally end up on the kitchen table. Kristin, who is sleeping in her room, hears something. She comes out, and she's just, "Uh, excuse me! Not on my kitchen table!" and they leave.

So she's left alone, and she realizes Jean isn't there. Then she realizes that his door is closed. Then she thinks, "Oh . . . my . . . he's in there . . . with Miss Julie . . ." She puts the kettle on the stove, and watches the door. Then she pours herself some coffee, takes the sugar bowl to the table. There's music going on all through this. As the lights start to change, she is dipping a big lump of sugar in the coffee and sucking it . . . with one eye on that door, knowing *every move he's making.* It was *so sexy*—I cannot tell you. Then at a certain point she decides to get up, and she *slams* down the plate. Hard. Loud. She goes into her room and shuts the door, really loud. The light completely shifts—it had all been very erotic, the lighting, the lilacs outside—now everything goes to a quick gray.

And Jean comes out of his room, and Miss Julie comes out after him, trying to keep it up—and he's like, "No, no, no." He knows he's in deep trouble. It wasn't as amazing for him as it was for *her!* She's been awakened sexually. He's been there, it was fine, but it wasn't his fantasy. The scene was really fantastic.

How did you get to those dueling realities for those characters? Do you hold private conversations with each actor?

No, I don't do that anymore as much. I think a lot of it changed when I was ill, because I couldn't run up on stage and have private conversations. Sometimes I'd have people come to me, and I could say what I had to say.

There are times when you want to say private things, but it's not that I'm telling an actor one thing that is a completely conflicting reality for somebody else.

What is a good reason for a private conversation?

When the discussion has something to do with technique, when the actor may feel it puts her down in the eyes of the rest of the cast. Or if it's something sexual, "I'm losing the eroticism of the scene," for example. And the actor needs it to be private. In fact, the only time I've allowed conflicting realities was in this last show [*The Tempest*], in a partnership with two actors. I think they each needed to believe what *they believed*, and it made absolutely no difference to the story of the play, because there was an ambiguity that was very exciting to watch. One did not have to succumb to the other's idea of what was going on.

But it can backfire. It won't backfire if the *truth* of the scene is that each character has a different agenda. But once you get to a certain level, it doesn't work. If the actors figure out that there's been a manipulation that's directorial, that doesn't have to do with the truth of the scene, the scene will never grow. I'm very careful about not doing that.

Sure, there are some things the other character *doesn't* know and *shouldn't* know, and if you want to keep actors from not knowing certain things, that's great. I just did it when I was doing the auditions for Yelena [in *Uncle Vanya*], and they were all playing very flat. With each woman I did the same thing: I took them aside, and said very quietly, so no one else could hear, "Do you think your marriage has been consummated?" And they all went, "Ohhhh! Thank you!" And then the whole scene had a reality and an urgency and a need it never had before. But I would never say that in the room so the actor playing her husband would hear it, because it would not be useful.

Let's jump to aesthetics and writing. Your work can be said to have started a trend in documentary theater in this country. What accounts for the popularity of this form in a medium that traditionally trades, at least in the U.S., on metaphor and domestic fiction?

Because good documentary pieces, if they're any good as plays, are *all about metaphor*. You can't just put up a raw dialogue and call it a play. Also, I think there's a great hunger in America for "truth"—and people get fooled by what that is all the time, like with reality television, which is so unnerving and annoying and altogether heartbreaking.

But it's all part of the whole for me. I told you the story about my father and *Still Life*. I could not have made my point to him except from the point of view of a Vietnam vet. My father was an historian, a believer in the record and the truth. You can argue about whether or not Mark [the vet character in *Still Life*] was telling the truth, but he was telling the truth *as he knew it*. He was reporting *what he had done,* as was his wife, as was his girlfriend. At the end of the day, their testimonies cannot be dismissed as the fevered imagination of a playwright, a person who writes fiction, who can make any story fit his or her own needs of what he or she wants to say. On that level, documentary theater takes off because it is *real people talking, real stories, real events*, and an audience feels it's authentic, dispatches from the front, you know?

And you cannot present that without metaphor, without artistic craft. You're forming a work of art out of found objects, if you will, out of the shards of testimony, or history.

If you could distill what an Emily Mann production is, I would hope you'd say: it's acting on a level that is as truthful as one can get. I like to work with actors who *do not lie* on stage. And I require and I expect and I demand the highest level of truth from them. One of the great moments in theater I've created is John Spencer doing the confession in *Still Life*, night after night after night, tears streaming out of his eyes. And it was different every night, and it was better every night. It was a great, great artist at work. He spoke Mark's real words, and they made him tell the truth as an actor. He couldn't lie. There's no place to hide in a documentary.

But I think that's true of all great writing. There's no place to hide in Chekhov. There's no real place to hide in *The Tempest*. You've *got to tell the truth* as an actor. It's got to be real and alive and truthful every moment. And that's what I demand. Documentary-style acting, no matter what it is, whether it's heightened language like Shakespeare or Chekhov or *Still Life*.

Audiences for both theater and mass media are interested in authenticity—though, of course, the authenticity Hollywood sells through reality television is a thoroughly manufactured construction of the truth.

I do think Hollywood culture has underestimated the American people. And I think Hollywood culture has infected the news, which has turned into entertainment and is implicated in the dumbing down of America. And the universities have not done their jobs. We are not challenging people to use their brains. And we are going to see a potential sink in American power globally. But given that, or perhaps because of that, I find that our audiences at the McCarter are growing and growing and growing. People are starved for challenging work.

I remain optimistic.

It's a very wide net that we cast at the McCarter. And it helps that we don't just play to a liberal, centrist viewpoint. We have a lot of very conservative people in our house; they write to me a lot, and I like what I hear. I hear that they've changed in interesting ways.

You said in an interview about *Having Our Say* that one reason the play was so popular is that the sisters, at their advanced ages, are "loving and funny, old and harmless . . . so people hear them without feeling threatened." Is that sugarcoating a point of view?

That's not quite it. Bill Cosby [whose wife, Camille, coproduced *Having Our Say* on Broadway] said if the same words were coming out of very dark-skinned African-American males in their early twenties, people would not be able to hear it. On that level, I know what he's talking about, and I completely agree. On the other hand, the Delany sisters are not sugarcoated at all, they are the *real thing*, they tell the hard truths about race in America, and what is fantastic about them is that they open their arms to anyone who sees them as *people*. Not only as black women, but as human beings.

My favorite letter came from a white woman in Princeton, who said, "Thank you so much for introducing me to the Delany sisters. I have never known a black person before who did not work for us. Now

I feel a black person could be part of my family, or my very good friend." That's huge—that she would admit that. She never thought of black people that way? If I can do that to one life, I feel happy.

You're someone who could clearly survive and live comfortably as a free-lance playwright and director. So why have you chosen to take on the added burden of running an institution?

That's a good question: I feel like I'm in here with a shrink! These are questions I ask myself every day.

I think it is not a burden to me. Not to say there isn't some burdensome stuff, and a lot of slogging work. But it actually gives me complete freedom as an artist to direct what I want to direct, for the most part. Of course I still have to look at things in terms of all the other duties I have at the theater, plus the finances, and balancing the season.

But there's the activist side of me that is very, very gratified by this work. We serve a community, and it's very multicultural, multiracial, and it goes across class and age and gender. And we are able to have a conversation with people of all different kinds.

When I was thinking about taking this job, Peter Hall [the British stage director, who ran both the Royal Shakespeare Company and the National Theatre in the course of his career] said to me, "If you take it, you have to make sure that every single thing you put on that stage is an event." And that's been our motto.

And also, I get to build a body of work in one place, and I get to give work to other people I greatly admire. I get to learn from them, and watch them, and see what they have to give to this community. That's the pro side. On the con side there's only one thing, which is that I haven't had the mental space in a while to write a new piece. And that's sort of nagging at me.

I'm thinking about writing a play from *Antigone* [the result premiered at Ten Thousand Things in Minneapolis in November 2005]. I'm back to the ancients. The thing about taking one of the ancient texts is that, although they change with the times, they're *always true*.

But you're not thinking about a new documentary piece?

If I could find a documentary piece that is so clearly, profoundly *unto itself* that its specificity would have universal meaning, and it wouldn't date, that would interest me. That's what I'm looking for. If I can find that project, I will write it.

Can directing be taught?

Yes; I'm a big believer in apprenticeship. In fact, we're changing the name of our internship program to the apprenticeship program. I believe in learning through apprenticing yourself to a mentor or master. And I think that it's not just for the artisans but for the artists as well. As I said to you, I don't think you can become a good director unless you're good at a whole lot of things. You have to understand how plays are put together, and you have to know about acting. Whether you take acting classes, or observe them, or watch a director who's brilliant with actors, you've got to learn. And you've got to know about design; you should really be in on all of those design meetings.

Another good way of apprenticing is to stage manage, because you get to watch the process. That's the old British model. That's how I was trained when I apprenticed at the Guthrie: I was an assistant stage manager. Boy, was that hard! You were there at eight-thirty in the morning and didn't leave the building till midnight.

So I believe in that, though some people get that through drama school. I went to a year of drama school. I was on a Bush Fellowship, which covered a year at the University of Minnesota and a year at the Guthrie. Drama school might be good for other people [but a traditional three-year MFA program] wouldn't have been that good for me.

Why?

I have problems being graded; I like learning from professional artists whom I deeply admire. I chafe against academic authority figures. It's my own problem. You have to know your own kind of personality; you have to know yourself. Where are you the most free? Where do you learn the most? How do you stretch yourself? Apprenticing was right for *me*. It's been right for a lot of people. There was a long time when there weren't drama schools, especially for directors.

What's good for some people about drama schools is that they get to see some really good teachers at work, and then, in their spare time, they can do their own directing. If you approach it as a paid-for, safe environment in which to do your work, it might be great. But often you come out brainwashed, and you're in debt, and you can never get out of it! $35,000 a year for three years? And you're not going to earn more than seven or eight thousand for a while.

Finish this sentence for me: I'm a director because . . .

I love the theater. Being a director gives me the opportunity to connect with all levels of the theater. It's my life. I can't imagine my life without it. My son, my husband, my mother and the theater!

MICHAEL MAYER

Undesigned Career

MICHAEL MAYER IS EAGER TO PLEASE in a restless, ninety-mile-an-hour way. It's a mark of his rapid imagination that he is always directing himself as well as the room around him, solving a problem and moving on. His loft in the West Twenties in New York City is decorated in a vast array of styles with an equally vast array of media, from Krazy Kat to Miró, and the table where we sit holds set plans for an upcoming project, four novels, dozens of magazines, scripts and the odd flyer for a neighborhood gym. If any of these objects—with the possible exception of the flyer—is lucky to get his attention for a while, it's likely to become a highly praised production. Throughout our conversation in March 2003, the phone rang a dozen times, the dog walker came in and out tending to the numerous needs of Rufus, Mayer's prized Kerry Blue Terrier, and with all the hullabaloo, Mayer managed to devote his attention completely to each interruption—if only for about twenty seconds.

"Who are you talking to next? I am *not* going to sound as smart as Moisés Kaufman . . . I sound like a chorus boy!" Mayer is funny, refreshing and surprisingly not disingenuous. His appealing combination of jolly swagger and witty self-deprecation reminds one of the Groucho Marx joke about not joining any club that might have him as a member.

Indeed, there was a period in Mayer's rapid-rise career that suggested he wasn't a "serious artist": the Broadway runs of *You're a Good Man, Charlie Brown* (1999) and *Thoroughly Modern Millie* (2002–2004) brought him a great deal of celebrity, and a reputation for crowd-pleasing fare. But to trivialize these accomplishments (which both garnered Tony nominations for his direction) would misunderstand their vital place in the rest of his challenging, politically sophisticated career.

Mayer's start in the early 1980s coincided with a rage in postmodern critique relative to identity politics and gender questions. The plays of Jean Genet and Oscar Wilde were getting renewed attention, feminist criticism was essential to the academic's toolbox, and this scholarly zeitgeist filtered into theater productions, culminating in the 1990s with Tony Kushner's epic *Angels in America*. In the midst of this conversation, Michael Mayer's career began. His early audience-pleasing success rested on a foundation of extremely challenging plays about sexuality by writers such as Genet, Kushner, Caryl Churchill, Arthur Miller and John C. Russell. The two threads came together in a big, Tony-winning way for Mayer with *Spring Awakening*, the unlikely Broadway hit musical based on Frank Wedekind's 1891 Expressionist play about teen sexual angst. From the commercial to the rarefied, few directors have done more to explore issues of sexual identity on stage than Michael Mayer.

Mayer grew up in Rockville, Maryland, and began his career as an actor (his charismatic presence is a clue that acting still lives within him, as a person and a professional). Completing New York University's graduate acting program in 1983 (where his classmates included a couple of directing students named Tony Kushner and David Esbjornson), he found his way into directing in the 1980s in part by creating his own shows to perform in ("I guess you'd call it performance art"), and a fortuitous opportunity: assistant directing for Kushner on the playwright's *Hydriotaphia* in 1987 at HOME for Contemporary Theater and Art in New York City. His interest in controlling the entire stage event was sparked. His directing career began shortly thereafter in 1988 with Genet's *The Maids*, and then in the same year a revelatory *Cloud Nine* by Churchill—its first New York staging in seven years.

Churchill's play—a story linking colonial and sexual repression, told through the absurd filter of cross-gender casting—was the first of many successes for Mayer in the constantly evolving genre of plays at the nexus of sexuality and cultural politics. Six years of relatively small projects followed before his first really big break came in 1994 with *Angels in America*. As George C. Wolfe was opening part one of *Angels* on Broadway, Mayer was directing part two downtown at NYU. When Wolfe took over the Public Theater and became too busy to direct the national tour, Mayer's name rose to the top of the list.

From there, another epic parable of sexuality and culture—Arthur Miller's *A View from the Bridge*—brought the director his first Tony nomination in 1998, and the attention of every not-for-profit theater in town. It also brought him incredible loyalty from the Roundabout Theatre and its artistic director, Todd Haimes, who produced *View* and has since brought him back frequently to helm a diverse selection of plays, from *The Lion in Winter* (1999, starring Laurence Fishburne and Stockard Channing) to the Broadway incarnation of *Everyday Rapture* (2010).

Despite any number of high-profile projects he could have pursued after *View*, Mayer instead directed John C. Russell's sly and subversive *Stupid Kids* in 1998 at WPA Theater—four years after the young playwright's death from AIDS. The play is a postmodern, super-smart version of *Rebel Without a Cause*, mixing two gay and two straight high schoolers looking for love while stuck in detention. With its off-kilter portrayal of teen angst and slippery sexuality, the play helped spark a generation of similarly themed plays and similarly engaged playwrights: think of the work of Adam Rapp, Keith Bunin and Kenneth Lonergan, or the United States Theatre Project's widely toured *Columbinus*, about the 1999 school shootings in Colorado. Though Mayer took on *Stupid Kids* in part to fulfill a promise to the dying Russell, his prescience in choosing the script speaks volumes about the historical moment, and how attuned he was to it.

While directing *Stupid Kids*, Mayer was attaching himself to another important project: Warren Leight's lyrical drama *Side Man*. Transferring quickly under the auspices of the Roundabout to Broadway (where it won the best play Tony in 1998), *Side Man* ended Mayer's own career as a theatrical side man—the reliable Off-Broadway director—and cemented his place in the spotlight. Mayer's work with the actors on that play was as detailed, smart and devastatingly emotional as his work on musicals is exuberant, sexy and riotous. Indeed, what's thrilling about a Mayer production is that each one draws on a different set of stylistic conventions, and follows them through with absolute commitment. Is the director of *Thoroughly Modern Millie*—with its ingratiating cheer and 1920s razzle-dazzle—the same guy who put Miller's Brooklyn longshoremen in the searing crucible of a Greek amphitheater? It's no wonder he credits both *The Wizard of Oz* and Bertolt Brecht as two of his major influences.

After *A View from the Bridge, Side Man* and *Thoroughly Modern Millie*, Mayer was a bona fide star director. But the projects that followed in the next four years (with the exception of the national tour of *Millie*, which he directed) were neither as successful in the mainstream nor as revelatory as his Off-Broadway work had been. His longstanding relationship with the Roundabout brought a number of tepidly received revivals, and he took a break to work on two films (*A Home at the End of the World* in 2004 and *Flicka* in 2006), both of which opened to mixed reviews. Was Mayer's high profile making it impossible to take on the more serious work of his earlier career? Had he succumbed to the lure of more commercial interests? Where was Michael Mayer?

The answer came in 2006, when *Spring Awakening* opened Off Broadway. Mayer had been working with composer Duncan Sheik and bookwriter/lyricist Steven Sater for eight years behind the scenes to bring *Spring Awakening* to the stage. Workshops with revisions all across the country, changes in Mayer's availability and, most significantly, the Roundabout's withdrawal from the project following 9/11, delayed what for years seemed New York's most promising experimental musical.

Though agonizing to the show's creators, the delay gave Sater and Sheik (with Mayer's heavy involvement) the opportunity to make major revisions. When the production finally opened at Off Broadway's Atlantic Theater Company in June of 2006, the explosive, rock-infused tale of adolescent sexuality was immediately an enormous hit. Six months later, the production opened on Broadway at the Eugene O'Neill Theater, and the *New York Times* declared that "Broadway, with its often puerile sophistication and its sterile romanticism, may never be the same."

According to Mayer, the musical's long gestation period also allowed for the times to catch up to its message. After *Spring Awakening* opened on Broadway, Mayer told me:

> By the time we opened at the Atlantic, the musical was speaking with terrifying clarity to an audience of Americans who have watched the clock of social progress turn back hour by hour, year by year, so that Frank Wedekind's text feels as relevant today 120 years after he wrote it. Any fears that I'd had about the subject of how we talk to our children about sex being dated were sadly put to rest. It's the odd thing about political art. You sort of wish that it wasn't needed. You want to be living in a progressive society where plays like *Spring Awakening* seem like problem plays written for a troubled world that no longer exists.

Any fears Mayer had about sounding like a chorus boy in a roomful of Brecht scholars must have vanished with the success of *Spring Awakening*. And he's taken that freedom to explore the musical form more deeply, and more broadly. *American Idiot* (2009, Berkeley Rep), the pop-punk rock opera he cocreated with Green Day front man Billie Joe Armstrong, picks up where *Spring Awakening* left off: smashing contemporary rock with traditional musical form to explore disaffected, disconnected youth a hundred years later. That same year, he directed Sherie Rene Scott and Dick Scanlan's *Everyday Rapture* (at Off Broadway's Second Stage), a musical that slyly subverts the "Broadway Baby" mythology that's been cultural currency since the 1933 movie *42nd Street*. (In *Rapture*, a girl from the Midwest gets seduced by the lure of Broadway, but only manages to become a "semi-semi-semi-star.") Both shows moved to Broadway under Mayer's direction in 2010.

To cap it off, in 2012 Mayer directed perhaps the most widely seen musical about musicals since *A Chorus Line*: *Smash*, the NBC television show about the development of a fictional (at least for now) Broadway musical based on the life of Marilyn Monroe. Mayer directed the pilot, which was seen by more than 11 million viewers. He's following that mega commercial success with what might be considered its cultural opposite: Verdi's *Rigoletto* for the Metropolitan Opera in 2013.

That's a long, complicated trajectory, and it would take a prophetic eye to figure out where Mayer is going next. It's been undesigned, for sure; but it also feels somehow inevitable. Michael Mayer, pursuing his passions, is reimagining musical performance with every unplanned step.

MARCH 2003, MAYER'S LOFT, NEW YORK CITY

When did you decide to stop acting?

It must have been so long ago because I'm so old! I'll be forty-three in June! I studied acting at New York University in the graduate acting program, and I got my degree in 1983. Ron Van Lieu and Olympia Dukakis were my acting teachers. At the time there was a directing program that was run by Carl Weber (he had worked with Brecht at the Berliner Ensemble), and David Esbjornson and Tony Kushner were both directing students in it. I worked with them and was friendly with them, in particular with Tony. And shortly thereafter, I was a frequent actor in the theater company that he founded called 3P Productions.

As I was pursuing my acting career, I found myself so frustrated with the lack of opportunities, and I had a growing realization of my limitations. Concurrent with those realizations came a recognition that I had a greater interest in the big picture of the play than I had initially realized. The tunnel vision required of great acting was outside the realm of my abilities, because the story and the way the story was told were of increasingly greater interest to me. As a response to the lack of work coming my way as an actor, I started writing my own performance material.

How would you classify the work you were doing?

I guess it was performance art. They were these long, neurotic rants, and I would also sing songs; I rewrote the lyrics to standards and pop songs. I called it *The True Confessions of a Neurotic Manic-Depressive on the Verge of a Major Anxiety Attack*. Looking back on it, I was trying to exploit what I imagined my gifts as an actor were; I was trying to distill and consolidate the elements of my most successful performances prior to that. And it was successful on its own terms. Eventually it was called *The Katatonic Kabaret*. I wrote all the material and directed and produced it, and my very dear friend Julie Cohen and I performed it at a bunch of different clubs—Gusto House on Fourth Street, way east between Avenues B and C, Dixon Place, La MaMa. We finally ended up with a full-length performance at the old Duplex on Grove Street, where we had a very successful run.

Tony Kushner came to see it. He was lovely and generous about it: "You know, it's beautifully staged, and the writing is great." He was working at the Repertory Theatre of St. Louis at the time and he commissioned me to cowrite a play for their educational theater program. So Kimberly Flynn [his frequent collaborator and dramaturg] and I wrote a play together called *Gendervisions*, about gender and television and the way they intersect.

Then Tony asked me to assistant direct his latest play, *Hydriotaphia*. That was the first play of his I wasn't actually *in*. It's huge, a monster play, so he was rewriting it constantly, and a lot of the scenes had to be rehearsed without him. I was really inspired by the directorial process and felt I was connecting to the acting in a way that I hadn't really as an actor. My understanding of the acting process somehow had deepened by looking at it from the other side.

After that I directed a production of *The Maids* by Jean Genet; my friend Julie coproduced. One of the actors in that show had his own theater company, and he hired me in 1988 to direct *Cloud Nine,* a Caryl Churchill play that I had read and loved (and I'd never seen a production of it). It turned out this was the first New York revival since the Tommy Tune production in 1981. I cast Camryn Manheim in it (she had been in *Hydriotaphia* and we had become great friends) and a couple of other former and current NYU kids that I knew. Marcia Gay Harden was my lighting-board operator!

We performed *Cloud Nine* for one week at the Sanford Meisner Theater on Eleventh Avenue at Twenty-Second Street. Completely sold out right away. I hadn't given any thought to the fact that it was such a popular play—anyway, I did a good job on it.

Casey Nicholaw, Sutton Foster and Noah Racey in Thoroughly Modern Millie, *music by Jeanine Tesori, lyrics by Dick Scanlan, book by Richard Morris and Dick Scanlan. Broadway, 2002. Credit: Carol Rosegg.*

How do you define that for yourself?

I thought it was an elegant staging, and a clear reading of the play. I thought that I got good performances from the actors for the most part. And I thought it was funny and political and ultimately very moving. It was a damn good production, considering that I had three weeks to rehearse it and we teched it in four hours or something like that.

And a bunch of people came to see it. New York Theatre Workshop people came. Jim Nicola [NYTW artistic director] was there and Morgan Jenness [then dramaturg at the Public Theater] became a fantastic early supporter of mine.

Next I did *Baby with the Bathwater* by Christopher Durang, *J.B.* by Archibald MacLeish and *Bent* by Martin Sherman . . .

Were you thinking of acting anymore at this point?

Oh no, no, no. At this point I was just about directing. I wasn't performing anymore. The transition happened very quickly. And because I had all of these opportunities, I was very fortunate to try my hand at a bunch of different styles and different texts.

Meanwhile, I was working full-time at the U.N. Plaza Hotel as a switchboard operator. Then I worked at a company where we'd sell information from building permits to vendors, who would then prey on innocent people to sell them carpeting and phone systems. It was really skeevy. I didn't like it at all, but it paid the rent. Then I got a dreamy job at the North American Conference on Ethiopian Jewry, which my cousin founded. For the first time, I thought I was actually contributing something to the world with my day job. My days were quite full—I'd help send missions to hilltop villages in Ethiopia, and at night I'd be rehearsing and casting and designing these plays. It was a nutty, nutty time.

That takes us to 1989, when I was assisting David Warren at the Public Theater on [the William Finn musical] *Romance in Hard Times*. And then, I got into the Drama League summer program at the Hangar Theatre and New York Theatre Workshop's New Directors Project.

Up to this point, I hadn't studied directing. I'd sat in on a few directing courses in my life without ever thinking about directing as an option for myself. But at the Hangar that summer, I was a director full-time, and it felt like graduate school. I got to spend twenty-four hours a day as a director, which was a new and fantastic experience . . . because I wasn't sneaking. I didn't feel like I was pretending to be a director when my real life was saving Jews, or selling telephone systems, or answering phones for rich people in a hotel. I woke up in the morning and I didn't have to think about anything but the play I was doing. The only problems I had to solve that whole summer were problems about the dramaturgy of a scene, or about how the costumes were going to be designed, or how I was going to stage something.

Did your background as an actor help you with these challenges?

Because I spent so many years acting and studying it and thinking about it and talking about it, I definitely have an experiential relationship to acting. And because I was also a singer, I've had experience as a performer, which I think of as different from experience as an actor; the task is very different, the relationship to the audience is very different. Musical theater performers, cabaret, something where your primary relationship is with the audience as opposed to another character—it's almost Brechtian—you bring so much of yourself to the performance. It's more like you are *you,* not the character. With those experiences so available to me and in my memory, in my body, it's easier for me to communicate what I'm looking for from an actor.

Because I never studied directing, I never knew the way you were *supposed* to do something. I made it up. And honestly, to this day, if it's more expedient for me to act out a moment badly than it is for me to talk about it, that's what I'll do. If it's better to show it, I'll show it. And if it's better to talk about it, I'll talk about it. I don't have a voice in my head that says, "The way to direct a scene from Tennessee Williams is this." No one ever told me that "upstage right" means something different from "down left." I don't know the rules.

And you don't mind that?

No, I don't mind that I don't know that. You know all those lightbulb jokes?

> How many stage managers does it take to change a lightbulb?
>> One.
>
> How many designers does it take to change a lightbulb?
>> Does it have to be a lightbulb?
>
> How many directors does it take to change a lightbulb?
>> I dunno, what do *you* think?

I'm very open to revealing my ignorance about a moment. I've never been one to feel like I have to have the answer, as long as I know the *question*. Then I don't care where the answer comes from. I don't have an ego about that, I really don't. I don't have a problem sharing that credit. Loath as I am to discuss any great strength about my directing, it seems to me that I get great results creating a lively debate in the rehearsal room. The trust of my actors and sense of group ownership over the production . . . everyone feels invested.

Let's talk about creating that room. What do you do to prepare for a production, and what do you bring into the room?

It really depends on the project. Sometimes I just spend an enormous amount of time reading the play, over and over again, listening to music, looking at paintings or reading related material. I sometimes surround myself with images that have resonance for me, more emotional research than literal research, though I don't necessarily bring that into the rehearsal room.

I directed a production of *Hay Fever* at NYU, and I brought in a ton of research. We played music from the twenties, had vast picture galleries. We played around with adopting poses, using the research to get into the period feel. I thought that was extremely successful. But as you start working with more experienced and professional actors, often it's understood that the actors will do that on their own.

If there's a visual image that's important to me, I certainly have no compunction about asking everyone to look at it. On *Thoroughly Modern Millie,* we did a lot of dramaturgical work with the cast—reading material, period-related visual images. I think it even helped the ensemble members, who don't necessarily have roles to be explored in complicated ways. By reading some of F. Scott Fitzgerald's short stories, or looking at old *Vanity Fair* pictures—the way the clothes were, the way the bodies carve out space—all that stuff is *gold* for performers, because they begin to imagine themselves inhabiting that world.

You've said your method, if you have one, has to do with "getting out of the way of the play."

Musicals have a very specific process, because at the end of the day, the staging of the scenes almost always has to take a backseat to the musical numbers that the scenes inevitably lead into or follow. When there's song and dance, the music absolutely dictates the shape the performance takes. But in a play, the shape is much more subtle and elusive, and I feel like the actors and I are on a journey to figure it out: to probe the text, and find the clues within it. It's not as explicit as the notes in a melody, or the time signature of a piece of choreography. The intimacy of that relationship is very specific to a play, and almost impossible to find in the course of doing a musical—one doesn't have the time.

In other words, you can afford to find the shape of a play in rehearsal, whereas creating the environment for a musical must be done beforehand.

Yes. In fact, my preference is to have an empty stage, to find the best visual metaphor for the play's theme, but in the *emptiest possible venue*. *Stupid Kids* is a perfect example. It was literally two empty spaces: a dance space and an empty space. *View from the Bridge* was virtually an empty space; *Side Man* was almost an empty space. Everything happened in one place; it was all about the addition of props.

Uncle Vanya [Roundabout, 2000] was a real exception . . . and it's tricky to talk about regrets here, but let's put it this way: the next time I direct Chekhov (which I want very much to do in my life), I will approach it very differently. It will probably more resemble my approach to those other plays. It's not going to have so much stuff!

So, the empty space and the world within it: is that how I know I'm watching a Michael Mayer production?

I would ask whether it's important that you know that. I've never given much thought to putting my signature on something. I would hope that you would recognize that whoever directed it had a passion for the story being told. That the actors seemed genuinely connected to the characters. That there was a musicality to the way the scenes transitioned.

That where there were opportunities for humor, those were celebrated. That where the dramatic events of the play occurred, there was adequate space and time given to let those moments resonate as completely as possible with the audience, without stopping the energy, giving us a sense of a real journey.

Is that the same answer you would have given ten years ago? You might have said then, "A Michael Mayer production deals with politics and sexuality . . ."

That's a passion of mine. *A View from the Bridge, Stupid Kids* . . . I would say those politics represent the lion's share of my work. It's certainly the work that I'm most attracted to, the work I'm most imaginatively engaged by. I think the truth of my experience as a gay man in his early forties in the United States of America at the beginning of a new century is very much informed by sexual politics, gender politics and identity politics. And insofar as those themes emerge organically in a piece of material, I'm going to read that with much more investment than something that doesn't address them. Any script that suggests the need for, or proposes the possibility of, a better way of doing things than we've historically done them is going to be of interest to me.

Even something as innocuous on the surface as *You're a Good Man, Charlie Brown*—on a very basic level, that show proposes that happiness is two kinds of ice cream, not one, right? For a little kid to receive that information from a multiracial cast is a *good thing.* You're putting something good in the world that way.

By the same token, if I can bust racial stereotypes in a musical comedy as ostensibly cheerful and harmless as *Thoroughly Modern Millie,* how fabulous is that? For an audience coming in and expecting just to have a good time, to have just a tiny dose of politics in there—I'm all for it.

Do you think your process in musicals informs your work in straight plays? You mentioned rhythms and musicality . . .

I've directed many more plays than musicals. But as a performer, my gifts were more musical than not. I'm a musical person. I hear music, I listen to it a lot. I'm interested in it as an art form. I'm the kind of person who walks down the street singing.

Are there favorite moments you've directed from musicals or plays? Tell me about a moment you created in a rehearsal of which you're really proud.

I remember directing *Side Man* at New York Stage and Film, an early version. I just loved the play; I thought Warren [Leight] had written something so beautiful and personal, and I was so honored to be working on it with him. And we were rehearsing a scene in which Terry [the role played by Edie Falco] was expressing her rage at Gene [her husband, played by Frank Wood] in the presence of their young son [played at the time by Geoffrey Nauffts]. I remember we didn't know what to do. We knew that at some point Gene's trumpet needed to be endangered. And he needed to demonstrate that his connection was so much more to his instrument than it was to any member of his family.

And I remember standing there with Edie, and being in the moment, and I guess this is where my actor-training came into play, because I became Terry in that moment. And I knew exactly how Edie needed to deal with it: she was going to look right at Frank, and pick up the trumpet, and *drop it on the ground*. This absolute moment of defiance. I knew it in my bones.

Edie got it right away. And from that rehearsal, on through the run of the play on Broadway, that moment never failed to shut the audience up. You could hear a pin drop. And that awful silence when Frank's character goes to the trumpet, picks it up to make sure it's okay, gently packs up the case, and walks out of the apartment, was *devastating* every time. Every time I saw that scene, I had a little moment of pride, because I knew that I had imagined it.

I sound like a chorus boy, don't I? Who are you talking to next?

Moisés Kaufman.

I am *not* going to sound as smart as Moisés Kaufman.

Do you really feel like that?

I always feel like a fraud. I didn't go to Yale, I didn't study directing, and I didn't study design with Ming Cho Lee and lighting with Jennifer Tipton, you know what I mean? I don't have an MFA, I don't have all the things a director is supposed to have. Yet I have a wonderful, rich, thrilling career that I couldn't be happier about. How'd I get so lucky?

Does that fear, or gratitude, inform your work?

I really don't know. If you're an artist, everything's a tax write-off, everything informs your work.

Since you started off as an actor, do you think you're particularly good at casting? Or have you run into problems there?

Sometimes it takes me longer to figure out an actor's process. But I like to think most of the actors with whom I've worked would want to work with me again. I walk into the room without too many preconceptions. I like to think that my actors have the kind of freedom to fail and figure things out and not have to come up with all the results immediately, that it's a pleasurable experience and a learning process. Look, I can be a "result queen" as much as the next fellow can, but when those cases arise, at least there's a sense of fun about it. So if we can all agree that it should be green, and this particular shade of green, the fun will be how to fulfill that, and make that grounded and connected and truthful. "You know what, I really need you to do *this* here, and I don't know how to tell you to get there." And they say, "Well, let me try it." If it's open, then it's not manipulative—I really don't like to manipulate, and I really don't like passive aggression.

That seems to be a mistake some young directors make.

Here's the thing: directors don't really work with each other! I've assisted a couple of directors in my life. But generally, directors don't get to watch each other work. I can't really say what most directors do. I can say what most *actors* do; I have a real hunch about that. I've been in enough auditions and rehearsals at this point that I *feel* like I've seen it all. But other directors? I don't feel qualified to say something about their process.

I can look at a show when it's up and running, and I can get a sense of the director's contribution, and appreciate elements (or not) that are there. But I just feel like my own process is unique. I'm not following a particular school—I don't do Viewpoints, I don't do Meisner. I don't have a system with a name, so I'd be loath to comment on someone who does.

Are there things that consistently challenge you as a director? Places you get to in the process that are always hard?

I'm a wildly insecure person. I'm obsessive, not a good sleeper, everything keeps me up at night. But I've learned over the years to embrace my own craziness and enjoy it (to the extent that it's possible to enjoy that kind of torture).

There's a crisis in every production, there's always an insurmountable problem. Eventually I find a solution for it. And it either works brilliantly, or it works well enough, or it doesn't work. That's Samuel Beckett: oh well, no matter; try again, fail again, fail better.

Talk to me about the difference between your early experiences in the not-for-profit world—*Stupid Kids, Triumph of Love* at Classic Stage Company [1994], etc.—and your more recent commercial-world experience. Is there a difference as a director?

In terms of the work, not really. The work is the same. If it's Broadway, there's more money, more toys to play with, you can get more famous people to be in your plays. Sometimes you can do things on a grander scale. Obviously you can reach more people, because more people sit in the theater.

If it's a commercial venture, then you have a certain obligation to fulfill the financial transaction. If people are gonna spend a hundred dollars on your show, and spend two and a half hours of their time, they better have a *really good experience*. So the pressure of pleasing an audience is much greater in that case.

A piece that develops in the not-for-profit arena and moves to Broadway does so because it *is* successful on those terms already. It's gotten the critical or commercial support for such a transfer.

When I'm working at the Roundabout (which is Broadway, but still a subscription, not-for-profit theater), my obligation is to be true to the play and my vision. That's it. I don't feel like I have an obligation to . . . Well you know, that's just a lie, because I do care about the audience. I want to communicate and connect to an audience. That's what makes it work. But in terms of giving audiences their dollar value, that's the realm of the commercial theater.

So what's the nature of the transaction in the not-for-profit world? Why is the hundred dollars that the Broadway audience spends more important than the fifty dollars that the not-for-profit audience spends? Clearly, in either case, you want to deliver something they want to buy.

There's a pact that you make with your audience from the moment they walk in and the play begins. You're telling them, "This is the kind of evening that I'm promising you." They invest their time and their energy and their intelligence and their sensibility and you do the same. And you hope those two forces come together and agree with each other: "Yes, you delivered what I wanted, even if I didn't know that's what I wanted when the evening began." It's not like saying, "I'm going to make you cry tonight," and then you do. I'm just saying, "I'm going to bring you on a journey," and the audience says, "I'm going to go on this journey; I *trust* you." When the journey is completed, hopefully the audience and performers can both say, "That was a really satisfying journey."

Can you be more surprising with the journey in a not-for-profit theater?

I think that is the case. It should be the case.

There are other relationships to consider on the not-for-profit side: the audience has a relationship with the theater, they've seen the plays, they know what to expect, they have a sense of the artistic director's taste. So, at the Roundabout—where I have a real relationship with that audience—they have some context when they come to see a play I'm directing, because they also saw x, y and z of mine. But I can't predict what that relationship is; I just know that they have it. I'm not an unknown quantity.

You successfully straddle the commercial and not-for-profit worlds.

I remember when I had a Career Development fellowship from TCG in 1991–1992. One of the people I observed was Richard Foreman. I have such admiration for him as an artist and as a director of plays other than his own. I love to see everything he does, whether he's written it or not. But I'm not an edgy avant-garde director. Richard Foreman *is*, and I can learn so much from him, watching what he does, the commitment he makes, the specificity and singularity of his vision. But you know what? My mom is not going to like his work. It's nothing against my mom and it's nothing against Richard. It's just that his work isn't for everyone.

True avant-garde work benefits other practitioners. The trickle-down effect is that people like me can see the Wooster Group and Richard Foreman and Anne Bogart and Peter Brook and Ariane Mnouchkine—the great visionary directors—and maybe take something of that and translate it into a more accessible form. I'll never do the kind of work that Richard Foreman does, but he can inspire me in a way that changes my work, and my work—which is innately more accessible to a general audience—can then perhaps push its own envelope.

Can you give me an example?

I did a one-man play called *An Almost Holy Picture* by Heather McDonald. I first staged it at La Jolla Playhouse with David Morse [in 1995], and subsequently at McCarter Theatre Center [in 1996]. Then I restaged it at the Roundabout with Kevin Bacon [in 2002]. And I can tell you that there were certain elements of my productions that were less realistic, that were stylized in terms of design, performance, staging, energy. And they were completely inspired by the work I've seen by some of my heroes, like Richard Foreman—I never could have done it without that exposure.

Is the production of *Spring Awakening* you're preparing going to draw on other things in your background?

I'd say the major inspiration for that comes from the late Tadeusz Kantor and his Polish theater company, Cricot 2. I remember seeing *The*

Skylar Astin, Jonathan Groff (seated) and John Gallagher, Jr. in Spring Awakening, *music by Duncan Sheik, book and lyrics by Steven Sater. Broadway, 2006. Credit: Joan Marcus.*

Dead Class and *Wielopole, Wielopole* at La MaMa. The work that he did is completely informing my approach to *Spring Awakening,* even though it's a rock musical.

Talk to me about going into film. How does the fact that you're a theater and music-theater director affect your journey into this new medium?

It certainly gives me a great deal of comfort to know that I've been relatively successful moving from genre to genre, and that moving to a completely new form might not feel as strange as it would otherwise.

What draws you to film as opposed to theater?

I've always loved film, and I have to say that my work has often been called cinematic. I'm not sure exactly what that means, but it gives me comfort. I never really thought of myself as a film director, but I did know that this story, *A Home at the End of the World* [Michael Cunningham's 1990 gay coming-of-age novel] should be a movie. I didn't think I was going to be the one to make the movie. I thought, "I hope they don't fuck it up when they turn it into a movie!"

What about the story drew you to it?

The reality of it. Theater lives best in the realm of metaphor. The minute something is real on stage, I always think it should be a movie instead, because movies do realism better. Something can be very truthful and not at all real. Directing theater, I always aim to be true, I almost never aim to be real—reality's too small and mundane for the theater. And I don't think reality is ever holy, and I think that the theater *ought* to be. Film, however, can be at its most magical when it is at its most real. *A Home at the End of the World* is a real story.

Both film and commercial theater demand stars. What's good and bad about that?

Most stars really know what they do well. So there's a huge amount of trust that you can give to a star. For instance, you know that Stockard Channing is going to deliver an Eleanor of Aquitaine for you in spades. It offers you the chance to relax when you have a star in a star vehicle.

The downside? Some stars haven't spent a lot of time on stage, or it's been a while for them. And sometimes they forget the kind of stamina that's required. Sometimes they have been protected by a system, a fawning "yes ma'am" kind of thing. They don't remember what it is to *not* be told constantly: "Fabulous, fabulous, fabulous!"

But for the most part I've been lucky. Most of the famous people with whom I've worked are real artists. It's rare I come across someone who wants to phone it in, or rest on his or her laurels.

What about designers? You use many of the same designers over and over again.

Talking about design is difficult for me—maybe this is why I should have gone to Yale!—because it's so abstract. To figure out how to talk to someone in those terms is such a complicated process. Once you find someone with whom you can communicate, you just want to repeat that experience. So although I do love working with new designers, I feel a loyalty and obligation to work with those who have worked so hard for me in the past, and there's a comfort level about the communication, an understanding of the process.

Let's go back to the arc of your career. Notwithstanding what you've said about the subversion of stereotypes in _Charlie Brown_ or _Millie_, your early work was more politically committed than what we've seen recently. I suspect that the larger the venue (whether commercial or not-for-profit) the more seats you have to fill and the less risk you're able to take.

The larger venues have, to a degree, dictated what I'm doing. But my career is completely undesigned. It's like an English garden, you just let it go.

You know, _Millie_ happened almost three years ago. I thought it would be long over by now, and here it's just beginning a national tour. [The production was mounted at La Jolla Playhouse in 2000; it opened on Broadway in 2002, where it ran for more than two years; the original team mounted a production of it in London's West End in 2003, where it ran for eight months.] Likewise, _Stupid Kids_, you know how long it took for me to get that on. [Mayer promised John C. Russell that he'd direct the show when the playwright was dying of AIDS in 1994; it took Mayer four years to find a theater—the WPA Theatre Off Broadway—to take the risk in 1998.] And _Triumph of Love_ at CSC: I had been trying to get someone to let me direct that play for years by the time I finally got to do it in 1994.

It's really just about when these things end up coming to fruition. And with a musical, which is such a huge enterprise, by the time you can finally bring one of those into port, everything else has to stop for the moment.

Why are you doing the _Millie_ tour?

Well, it's my production, and it'd be a shame not to do it. This is the national tour of a Tony-winning musical, and although I don't think audiences give a shit that I directed it, I do think they're expecting the version of _Millie_ that was on Broadway, and I'm the one to deliver that.

What kind of joy will you get out of it?

Millie was a hard, long process. We fought a lot along the way, in terms of the production and the writing as well. But what was beautiful about _Millie_ is that all of the artists involved really went through _something_, and came out the other side even more connected. And that's a rare thing after you go through a difficult process. At La Jolla, where we tried it out, it didn't work the way we wanted it to.

Why not?

I think we made some basic mistakes. We had a visual idea that had to be seriously adapted because of the venue's limitations, money and time-wise. We ended up with a pale version of something that was actually not correct in the first place.

Can you be more specific?

Basically, the design for the production at La Jolla looked like it would have been appropriate for the operas *Lulu* or *Wozzeck*. It was very German Expressionist–looking, very dark, one set. The whole thing had a darkness to it that was just inappropriate to the material.

When did you realize you had to fix it?

First act of the first preview, it was pretty clear. It was frightening! Every one of us—choreographer, writers, designers—we all looked at this thing and were like, "Oh my God, what have we done? We're doing a different show than it wants to be."

So there was a long process figuring out what the show wanted to be. And we went back to page one. And I have to tell you, that's a very scary and hard thing to do. But we did learn that the story wanted to be told as a *stage musical*. And that was the saving grace of the experience. That little fucker of a story was going to be told on stage as a musical, despite every effort we made to stop it from happening!

Do you mean that the piece was too dark for Broadway, its hoped-for home after La Jolla? Was it about lightening the material?

It would be reductive to say that. The change was holistic. I think it was about reorienting the show completely. Because that audience wanted it to succeed. They could see this thing struggling for life, the critics wanted it to be alive, the actors wanted it. Even though it was a hit at La Jolla, it wasn't the show we wanted to do. [Bookwriter] Dick Scanlan, [composer] Jeanine Tesori, [choreographer] Rob Ashford and I were sitting there going, "Okay, this is a hit, but *we don't like it.*"

So Dick and Jeanine did one of the most courageous acts in the theater that I've ever seen. They went back and rewrote the show from page one. They wrote all new songs. A huge chunk of the second act at La Jolla was successful, and one number in the first act really worked.

Otherwise, we rethought the whole thing and the way it all worked. The set was different, different costumes, different lighting, different choreography, different numbers, different staging—new characters even! By the time we started rehearsing in New York, it was another animal altogether. We'd all been on the same page at La Jolla—it was just the wrong page. In New York, again, we were all on the same page, and it was the *right* page.

So you reoriented the show to have a more traditional musical-theater feel. How did you find the right tone?

When we found our Millie, Sutton Foster, at La Jolla, we found the show. [Foster was famously plucked from the chorus to take over the lead role from Erin Dilly during rehearsals.] We suddenly realized that we needed to have that character at the center of something. At La Jolla, I felt she was at the center of nothing.

So for New York, we filled the world around her. Suddenly she had a relationship to a world as opposed to a void, which would have been appropriate to characters in *Lulu* or *Wozzeck*. Those characters are lost in a nightmare, not of their own creation. But Millie is at the center of the universe she always wanted to be in, and she is going to transform herself and, in turn, her world. It became a much more dynamic show. And we made huge changes from the first rehearsal in New York through opening night. We were absolutely ruthless.

What advice do you have for directors wanting careers in the theater?

Seize every opportunity that you can. I did my theater work after my regular work. Find a job you can live with that hopefully feeds your soul while you're making your work, and do your work *wherever you can*. Find new writers, do readings, hook yourself up in any situation you can to assist, to observe. I've seen young directors focus on a career rather than their work, and they may end up with certain opportunities that they can't really fulfill because they never stop hustling long enough to focus on making the work in front of them the best it can be.

But I also would say, find work that you *love* to do. Whatever it is, find something in it that you really can connect to and be passionate about. Your passion will translate to your collaborators and to your audience. And if the best you can do is find something that you like, like it as much as you can. Find a way in so that it can be as personal as it can be, and, in doing so, be as honest with yourself as you can.

MARION MCCLINTON

Blowin' Jazz

IN 1959, LLOYD RICHARDS BECAME THE FIRST African American to direct on Broadway, with Lorraine Hansberry's *A Raisin in the Sun*. Later, as dean of the Yale School of Drama, artistic director of Yale Repertory Theatre and head of the National Playwrights Conference at the Eugene O'Neill Theater Center, Richards discovered the talent of playwright August Wilson. He mounted *Ma Rainey's Black Bottom* first in New Haven, Connecticut, and then on Broadway in 1984. Thereafter, Richards and Wilson were an astonishing team: Richards directed five more installments of the writer's ten-play cycle on the African-American experience in the twentieth century—including *Fences*, which in 1987 won Wilson a Tony and a Pulitzer. Their enduring partnership—like that of director Marshall Mason and playwright Lanford Wilson, or James Lapine and Stephen Sondheim—made their two names nearly inseparable.

But Wilson was twenty-six years Richards's junior, and the venerable director was slowing down while Wilson's career was still on the rise. After their final Broadway collaboration—*Seven Guitars* in 1996—Wilson needed a new partner to bring his words to life. Eager for a new production of his play *Jitney* (which he'd been rewriting on and off for many years), Wilson tapped an old friend: Marion McClinton. The result (at Off Broadway's Second Stage in 2000) was an enormous hit; McClinton also premiered Wilson's subsequent works, *King Hedley II* (which earned the director a Tony nomination in 2001) and *Gem of the Ocean.*

McClinton was primarily an actor in 1977 when he first met Wilson at a CETA (Comprehensive Employment and Training Act) orientation in McClinton's native St. Paul, Minnesota. (Wilson claimed they met at a poetry reading a year later, but McClinton swears he's got the history right.) In fact, he had left college in 1975 to focus solely on acting, and joined St. Paul's Penumbra Theatre Company, where he remains a member to this day. It was there that McClinton performed under the directorial hand of Claude Purdy in Melvin Van Peebles's *Ain't Supposed to Die a Natural Death,* and McClinton points to Purdy (and Penumbra founder Lou Bellamy) as his biggest directorial influences.

It was also at Penumbra that McClinton played the role of the Narrator in August Wilson's first professional production, *Black Bart and the Sacred Hills,* in 1983. Two years later, McClinton played Fielding in the first incarnation of *Jitney.*

But with the success of *Ma Rainey* on the East Coast in 1985, Wilson went in one direction as McClinton went in another. The two would not reunite professionally for more than a decade. In the meantime, McClinton acted and wrote plays, and he had begun directing in 1981 with a production of *Waiting for Godot* at St. Paul's Park Square Theatre. (He returned there in his twenty-seventh year as a director with a production of Lanie Robertson's *Lady Day at Emerson's Bar & Grill.*)

But it was his first production of an August Wilson play—an untraditional revival of *The Piano Lesson* at Penumbra in 1993—that turned directing for McClinton from an interest into a profession. McClinton's production was a departure from the stark naturalism of Richards's original mounting, in which "the cooking of eggs, the washing of dishes, and the comings and goings from an audibly flushed toilet . . . became subliminal beats in the rhythm of a self-contained universe" (according to the *New York Times*). The beats and rhythms in McClinton's production came not only from Wilson's words, but from McClinton's own emotional response to the text—a staging full of musicality, muscularity and intimate performances. According to Penumbra, Wilson later called it his favorite production of the play, and a "model of style and eloquence that would inspire my future work."

McClinton's staging represented a changing of the directorial guard, from the postwar realism that had dominated serious theater for decades to direction with intimacy, immediacy and the personality of the director at work.

McClinton was terrified that Wilson would object to his unusual staging; the playwright, after all, was notoriously demanding with directors, in a way nearly unheard of in the profession. But Wilson was hugely impressed.

McClinton's style, if he has one, seems a combination of Method acting and jazz. Through the Strasberg Method, actors in this country are trained to make use of their deepest, darkest memories to enliven their characters' journeys. McClinton can be said to use this sense-memory technique as a director. No detail of his life—challenges in his marriage, the trials of raising children, his illness—is too dear or personal if, in the retelling, it helps get his actors as deep as they need to go.

Jazz is a potent metaphor for McClinton, who uses it to discuss the work of his favorite playwrights (among them Wilson, Beckett and Chekhov); to discuss the rhythm of a scene; to examine the position of black theater in America; really, to analyze just about anything. Watching his work makes this inspiration clear. The proudest moment of his directing career, he told me, was a long, wordless transition at the conclusion of *Jitney*. Those fortunate to see it experienced what was, indeed, theatrical jazz. A dozen actors, each seeming to represent a different tone on the horn, or note in the bass line, marched on stage one after another to share a riff and then grab a wordless solo of human action, joined next by another actor who riffed off them and went into his own silent, fully musical moment.

McClinton has frequently been asked to mount revivals of Wilson's work across the country (at CENTERSTAGE in Baltimore, Maryland; Missouri Repertory Theatre [now Kansas City Repertory Theatre]; the Pittsburgh Public Theater; and even on Broadway with a revival of *Ma Rainey*). His own work as a playwright and actor has also made him a natural fit for challenging new works, especially by emerging African-American writers. His production of *Jar the Floor* by Cheryl West (Second Stage, 1999) was closely followed by New York City productions of new plays by Kia Corthron (*Breath, Boom,* at Playwrights Horizons, 2001), Carl Hancock Rux (*Talk,* produced by the Foundry Theatre at the Public Theater, 2002) and Regina Taylor (*Drowning Crow,* at Manhattan Theatre Club, 2004). Along the way, McClinton's own plays have gotten produced, often with him in the director's seat.

August Wilson died in 2005, having completed the last of the ten plays in his cycle of the African-American experience. Richards died one year later. And though it looked like McClinton might be the one to inherit Richards's mantle, his career hit an unexpected speed bump.

I first spoke with McClinton in 2003 while he was preparing the world premiere of *Gem of the Ocean* at Chicago's Goodman Theatre. Shortly thereafter he took the production to the Mark Taper Forum in Los Angeles. He was rehearsing the pre-Broadway tryout of the play at Boston's Huntington Theatre Company a year later when illness—polycystic kidney disease, a hereditary condition ("I got it from my father; it's the only thing he left me")—forced him to resign from the production. (He was replaced by Kenny Leon, who took the work through to Broadway.) Recuperating for nearly two years, McClinton was able to take little work, but when I spoke to him again in the fall of 2006, he was about to open only his second professional production since the onset of his illness: Dael Orlandersmith's *Yellowman* at a company dedicated to multicultural work, Mixed Blood, back in the Twin Cities.

Just prior, McClinton had directed the American premiere of Kwame Kwei-Armah's deeply felt play about London's African-Caribbean community, *Elmina's Kitchen*, at CENTERSTAGE in Baltimore (2005). That McClinton would return to the theater by introducing American audiences to a writer with similarities to August Wilson is hardly surprising. But far more significant for McClinton is the fact that six years later, Kwei-Armah ascended to the artistic directorship of that Baltimore theater, becoming one of the very few people of color (and even fewer, of playwrights) to run a LORT theater. Kwei-Armah repaid the favor in 2012, enlisting McClinton to direct Bonnie Lee Moss Rattner's *Gleam* in his first season.

The Orlandersmith play, with its dense musicality and lyricism, was another pitch-perfect project for the director. McClinton found deep resonance in Orlandersmith's world of painful memories and intraracial conflict. The jazz soared, and the audience listened intently: his production swept four local newspapers' "Ten Best" lists for 2006.

His illness keeps him closer to home these days, and the theaters of the Twin Cities have reaped substantial benefit. Since 2005, McClinton has helmed productions at most of the area's major companies: the Guthrie, Children's Theatre Company, Pillsbury House Theatre, Ten Thousand Things and Mixed Blood Theatre. He's even performed—as Jim Bono in Penumbra's 2008 staging of *Fences*, directed by his mentor Lou Bellamy.

Our original interview had felt rather businesslike and a bit uninspired about its topic: McClinton had told me that directing was his least favorite of the theatrical disciplines. Two years later, his faith in theater had been revived with stunning intensity. He spoke, at age fifty-two, with an enhanced appreciation of what it means to be in the rehearsal room. And he told me he'd never say he didn't like directing again.

Setting up that second interview, McClinton wrote a remarkable e-mail to me:

> A lot of life has come and gone since we talked and as somebody must have said somewhere, sometime, with a bit of wit, life has a way of fucking things perfectly up. And it is the perfect fuck-up that fuels the artistic passion to understand that which confuses God. Without the fanfare, the politics, the game, one gets slammed right up face to face with oneself, and

you must decide who the fuck is looking back at you with your own eyes in the mirror. A forced epiphany becomes a great moment of clarity. When all that is left is the work without the hoopla, one finds one's art in the pit of one's soul, and it takes on a stunning new meaning. In this nation, especially in the commercial times that dominate all aspects of the American condition (and have shrunk not only the audience's attention span but the vision of a lot of our so-called artists in the time it takes a silent fart to escape), no one is hypnotize-proof. Me included. But my illness (which sometimes feels like an artistic divine intervention) has left me alone in a room with my art, my life and what it truly means to me, sans hype . . .

I have become spiritually reborn in the secular religion of the theater, a religion that predates Christianity and Islam both, and although I wouldn't say that a lot of what I said before has changed much, the reasons I would say those things now have become intensely personal.

APRIL 2003, THE OFFICES OF GOODMAN THEATRE, CHICAGO

You've been a playwright and an actor. When did you decide directing was right for you?

I haven't yet! Probably out of those three disciplines, directing is the one that I enjoy the least. But it's the one that, right now, takes care of most of the bills and gives me time to spend with my son. When I acted I was gone three to four months at a time, easily; it's not the same with directing.

To me, directing is kind of like being secretary of state, you know? You're responsible for diplomacy, sometimes getting warring factions together—but you're not the president! Especially when working on a new play, you don't have the final seal of authority. It's a tricky kind of job in the theater. Theater is about collaboration, and I think the director has to be the biggest collaborator of all, because you're the only person who really deals with everybody else.

With a new play, especially with a new play by a writer like August Wilson or Kia Corthron, writers who have very specific ideas about their work and a very distinct vision, your job is to interpret and enhance that vision, not to challenge it or change it. That requires a certain kind of skill.

When you work with a play by somebody who is no longer alive, then your job is to find something personal and distinctly different from what's gone on before, while still serving the playwright. You're not going to be more brilliant than William Shakespeare; you have to give up that idea from the very beginning. What you have to do, though, is see whether there is a new interpretation that peels another layer of skin away from the onion.

I believe that the best directors are the ones who have the least active egos, in order to deal with different factions—but you have to be the one who eventually shapes the picture. You're the one who sees the vision, perhaps not how the playwright first saw it, but how it's going to end up physically, better than anybody else. The ability to move, talk, excite, to get the cast and playwright revved up, is an important part of the job. And the director has to find the emotional connection between what happens on stage and what happens in the audience.

That's why previews are so helpful.

Very much so. But that process starts way in the beginning. One thing a director has to make clear with his or her collaborators is that the audience is not privy to all the discussions that we have. What we discuss at tablework, or at a restaurant, or outside the hotel—for hours—needs to be completely clear in two or three seconds to an audience who has never seen the play before. When you think to yourself at previews, "Why didn't they get that?" you have to sit back and realize, "It's because they didn't have that five-hour conversation that we had!"

So the director has to be the eyes and ears, the emotional center and intellectual center of the audience at rehearsal. You have to see exactly what they will see. You have to ask the questions they're going to ask.

And the first task is to be sure there is clarity. Then people can decide whether they like the production or not, whether they like the play or not, or whether they have problems with some of the issues in the play. But if clarity has not been achieved, then none of that's possible. No audience comes in to hate a play; they're not going to spend that money to do something they're not going to enjoy, right? I've always said, "All we can do is lose 'em." They've come in on our side to begin with.

Why do you say that directing is your least favorite discipline?

Because the imagination and creativity of the director is all interpretive. Even though an actor is an interpretive instrument, the actor gets the audience. When the lights go up, the connection between the actors and the audience is akin to that which a musician has with his audience.

As far as they're concerned, *you're* the play. You're the live element that they're going to connect to, or not connect to. All the other elements can be wonderful, but if the live element doesn't work, it doesn't matter how good or how bad the play is.

As an actor, I thrived on that connection, that energy I got from them, that I could give to them. Lights going up on opening night is one of the three most fantastic sensations that I've ever gone through in my life. I miss that connection.

And the other two?

Orgasm . . . and, I think, the perfect meal!

How do you feel about playwriting?

For me, it's a very private relationship between me and the play: me and the characters, me and the story. It's the only thing that I own *completely and totally*. I don't own my son—he's thirteen, and he's got a mind of his own, and he's supposed to have that. My own play is the closest thing to a child that will always be obedient and exactly what I want it to be.

Sometimes it's hard to share that. A lot of times when a play of mine is produced, I go into the green room and listen to it, so I can keep the connection that I have to the play from the beginning. I can still see it as I see it in my head.

The director does what I call "grown-up work." It's a hell of a responsibility: if the play works beautifully (especially if it's a new play), rarely does the director get more than one line of credit in a review. If it bombs horribly, you'll get your paragraph in! So you have to walk into it without a lot of ego.

Theater is not the director's medium. Film is, because the story is told with images, and a performance can be stitched together on film. In film, you can save a bad performance, and you can also take a good performance and mess it up.

But the theater director's job is like playing a game of pool. Your touch has to be very gentle, and how you leave things to be built upon is more important sometimes than how you succeed. I find I enjoy directing a lot in the rehearsal hall when things are popping and being discovered. As it gets closer to production, I enjoy it less and less, because I have to give up control.

What's that light touch, the technique that "leaves things to be built upon"?

Mine is basically a style that reflects the rhythm I live inside of the world. The art form that speaks best to me in that regard is jazz. So I try to duplicate and replicate patterns of jazz in directing—particularly the art of improvisation.

Now, you can't improvise lines in theater. But what I've found that you *can* do, if knowledge of the character and story is clear and strong, you *can* improvise emotions. That's the thing that will keep it fresh from night to night. You can change rhythm inside of monologues, inside of scenes, based on the emotional moment.

My style is about finding the emotional center. In classes I've talked to, I've said there are two basic ways of acting: there's the show-and-tell, and there's the emotionally centered and honest interpretation. A show-and-tell can be anything, from Brecht's presentational whatnot to the style of Grotowski, in which the emotional truth or center of the character is not as important as the visual and physical statement of the director or playwright. For me, the emotionally centered and honest performance is where the feelings of the actors, the feelings of the characters, are complete and very honest.

In classes I say, "Let me show you two things; you tell me what's going on." First, I walk in and I start throwing papers in the air, and kicking a chair, and screaming at the top of my lungs, and I ask, "Well, what was that?" And they say, "That was someone who appeared to be mad."

And then I leave and come back in, and I *am* very upset and angry, but I don't talk. I sit down at the table and just pour a glass of water, and hold it for a while, then drink it. And I ask, "What was that?" And they say, "That person was very upset about something that just happened."

"Oh, really?" I say. "Now whose anger did you believe the most?" And they say, "Well, the second guy. The other guy threw stuff all over the room, but I believe the second guy was more angry."

When you *show* the audience your emotions, you stand outside the character. They have the capacity to believe or disbelieve. And they might say, "I'm not feeling it, because the actor's not feeling it." Now, the second actor who walked in the room and just sat: they believed that one pretty wholeheartedly, because the actor was feeling it. The character was feeling it. And that doesn't give them the opportunity to decide about its authenticity. It just *is*.

You can tell when somebody walks into the room if they're not happy; you know it immediately because of the aura they give off. That is the thing I try to get the actor to feel, in performance. I don't want the audience to have the opportunity to *choose* whether they believe what you're telling them or not. I want them to buy it from the minute the actor's on stage. They already *know* all of this is not real: that's not a real

The cast of Police Boys *by Marion McClinton. CENTERSTAGE, 1992. Credit: Richard Anderson.*

kitchen, or a real bedroom. What makes it real? It's only the person that's real on the stage.

My style is basically trying to find that honest moment in performance.

How do you do that? Do you suggest blocking and vocal inflection, or do you let it happen organically?

I call it the "kitchen sink" technique! Throw everything, including the kitchen sink, up on stage and see what lands. I'll never give a line-reading because if I do that, the actor has to step out of character.

The most important thing is to cast good actors. That *Jitney* cast, it was like having the Lakers and Magic Johnson and Kareem Abdul-Jabbar—just roll the ball out on the court and let 'em run. I couldn't fuck that up!

I live and die by my collaborators. I like working with the same actors, like Steve Henderson, Paul Butler and Viola Davis. These actors have trouble making false moves. So if they question something, it's because something doesn't read true about it.

I also like having the writer in the room, though some directors don't. I find it very relaxing, because it stops all conversation about what's happening in the scene. Instead of arguing about it, I'll just ask,

"August, what did you mean this to be?" And since he doesn't write anything by accident, I'll get the answer and then go, "Good, it's what we're working toward." It saves credit for me. A lot of the writers I work with are very sure of themselves and what they're writing about.

Sometimes, if we're going after an emotional moment and we're not connecting in the play, I have no problem taking the next two hours for us to talk about our lives. My marriage has been an interesting little play by itself the last four years—it was falling apart, coming together, falling apart—so sometimes I use *that* in talking with them. "Here's something emotionally very much the same." When actors know I'm not shy about using anything I can to help them, they'll listen more. And sometimes it will open something up for them.

It is organic, although usually I'll stay up until four in the morning the night before, reading the play, and have a completely mapped-out plan . . . which rarely ever gets used. Because the actors will often do something and I'll go, "Oh! Let's go with that; that seems to be better." But in case nobody comes up with something, I have something to fall back on. Some directors found me to be a difficult actor to work with because I would connect honestly with characters, and if I was asked to move just for the sake of how I looked or something, I would resist. When I cast actors, I cast them because I want to see what they have to say. I love smart actors. A smart actor will get you out of more trouble than you can find to put yourself in.

So my style is pretty organic. A lot of times I'll improvise on the spot. I'll come up with a plan, but don't hold onto it if something better happens.

Like jazz improvisation.

Yeah. You have your notes; how are you going to play them? We use honesty as the base. This is one thing I picked up from August. No matter what style the play is, I don't want the actors to be aware of the audience. Your character isn't aware there's an audience watching them. They're only aware that people are on stage with them. The more we make this world self-sufficient, the more the audience will enter it.

Does research play a big role?

I'll look at the period, I'll look at the things August gives me about Pittsburgh, or read certain articles and books. Kia Corthron gave me research for a play she's writing that I'm directing. My biggest resource is the playwright: I'm much more interested in picking their psyche as far as why they wrote the play. The better playwrights all know why they wrote the play. And the not-so-good playwrights don't know, and in that case it's anarchy. I don't know if theater's a democracy, but it definitely shouldn't be anarchy!

So I research the writer more than I research the topic of the play. I'm more interested in what the writer finds important in the world. Because I'll find the kernel of why they wrote the play there. And a lot of times it doesn't matter the setting or the year.

In *Seven Guitars,* August has set a Joe Louis fight in 1948, but that fight actually happened some years earlier. So it had nothing to do with the time, but it had a lot to do with the *moment.* I find out about that moment more from talking to August than from researching the time period.

What about other plays? You've done Shakespeare, Genet, Beckett . . .

There's where I do research. I research the time of the playwright, and get as much as I can on the playwright. With Shakespeare, it's a great mystery, but I read about his life, the influence of the time period; I'll read Marlowe, I'll read Jonson. I want to get a sense of the world he was creating his work in. Because he was such a master of understanding the human condition, but he understood the human condition based on the world in which he was living. So let me immerse myself into that. And that gives me insight into the great passion in his writing.

With Beckett, I'll read his interviews, his plays. There's a little story about Beckett I remember whenever I direct his work, just to remind me of his outlook on life. Beckett was walking with a friend and the friend said, "It's such a beautiful day."

Beckett went, "Yes, it is."

And the friend said, "Doesn't it make you feel glad that you're alive?"

And Beckett said, "Well, I wouldn't go *that* far."

And in that statement is all of Sam Beckett's plays. So whenever I find myself getting cute or whatever, I remember, Beckett didn't enjoy any of this! He wrote about the incredible task of living day-to-day.

How do you translate that into directing a performance?

By looking at the struggle of the characters. In *Godot,* you have Didi and Gogo just trying to get through the boredom of their existence. Even planning their suicide is difficult. And as a director, you need to understand why Beckett tells the story in this particular way. I use the personality of the writer to help me understand why this story is being told and the way it's being told.

Are there playwrights you've not directed who excite you?

One writer I've not directed but studied a lot is Chekhov. In studying Chekhov's own life—that he was a doctor and a great short-story writer, and all that—it relates to a certain diligence in his writing, a diligence focused toward honesty and toward enduring. Life was to be endured. Whether it's comedy or drama is immaterial. He endured his life, and he saw the value and the heroism in that. In a lot of ways, Chekhov and August Wilson are very similar in how they see the world and how they see people living in it. Heroism is living through your life, day in, day out.

Can you give me an example of a moment you directed of which you're particularly proud?

The moment that I'm most proud of had to do with a simple problem. At the end of *Jitney,* there are two scenes: where the son finds out his father is dead, and the next scene after the funeral. But we had a problem: everybody's on stage at the end of one scene, and then they're all in their funeral clothes at the beginning of the next scene, so everybody had to change costumes. A transition was needed to buy them time to change. And the transition had to keep the story moving.

So what do we have? We have Philmore, the doorman, who just walks across the stage. Once Philmore's done, let's have Rena—she can already be dressed in her funeral clothes—put funeral flags on each of the cars. And by that time Philmore can get out of his doorman's coat and be in *his* black suit. And he can meet her, and they can walk up. And we've played Jimmy Smith music about as far as we can, so what do we do? Well, whenever you're in danger, go to Sam Cooke! So we took a song by Sam Cooke, "Any Day Now," and we said, "Who's ready first?" Turnbo, he's dressed first, so send him out. We'll have Turnbo come in and start to erase the names on the chalkboard. But he can't erase Becker's name.

So now who's next? Youngblood? Oh, great, bring Youngblood down; let him see Turnbo's not able to erase Becker's name. They've been battling contestants the whole play. They come together at the end, and start playing checkers. Who do we have next? Shealy. Well, have Shealy see this, and have him give Youngblood the high-sign: "That's a good thing to do, young man . . ." The whole transition was based on when I had people available, and how long it was going to take for people to change.

The transitions were partly credited in making *Jitney* what some have called August's most "audience-friendly" play.

And I am more proud of that than any other thing I've done on stage, because I had to find the moment of transition *in the story*. I think *Jitney* is a magical play, and it was the magic of the play that helped me tell that story. A lot of people told me that the transition was their favorite part of the play, and we came up with it in tech rehearsal.

Are there points in the process when you doubt yourself?

Daily.

How do you surmount those?

By realizing I'm not going to solve everything. I am convinced (and I'm usually correct) that when opening night happens, if I've done the best job I can possibly do, there's still probably going to be one very simple thing I didn't get. So I've stopped watching opening night, because I can't enjoy it: "Oh, *shit! There it is!*" It's also a nice way of giving the play over to the actors. They'll say, "Did you see the show tonight?" and I'll go, "No, I didn't see it, how'd it go?" *I* ask *them,* and they can tell me. By that time, it *is* theirs. The play always belongs to the playwright, but the production, once the audience walks in, belongs to the audience and the actors.

Which are you best at—playwriting, directing or acting?

Probably directing. I enjoy acting more, but I have a terrible sinus condition, and I have a bad lisp, so technically there are certain things I'm not good at as an actor. Sam Shepard plays, I can tear 'em up. But you'd never have me doing the opening soliloquy of *Richard III*: too many "s" sounds!

And playwriting is so personal to me. I've not allowed anything to be published. I think I'm going to change that next year. But it's hard for me to let them go out into the world.

Do you want to direct them?

Not particularly, but most of the places that commission me expect me to. One, because they're familiar with me as a director, and two, it saves them a plane fare and hotel room!

Directing is the job that I've always felt the least prepared as an artist to do, so I work much harder at it. As a playwright I let certain things happen in my plays that may not be technically sound, but I don't care, and that's okay because it's my play. And as an actor I can be completely responsible for what I want to do, but not responsible for anything else. My responsibilities as a director have forced me to become a better artist. And I think that I *do* that better than anything else; I just enjoy it less.

How did you get to this point in your career as a director, then? If you like it so much less?

The first play I directed was *Waiting for Godot*. I wanted to do it because I loved the play. I'd heard of a production set in South Africa, and I wanted to do a production like that.

Claude Purdy was probably my biggest influence. Claude had great vision as a director. His plays were like movies, and I was more interested in movies at the time. Lou Bellamy and Horace Bond are also influences. Lou Bellamy is a wonderful actor's director. I learned from him that you must have patience, and I had *none* as an actor. But I learned from Lou that a director has to be the coolest person in the room. Because they're going to look to you if anything's messed up. And especially if everything *is* messed up, you have to look calm! And you can get through it.

Where did you direct *Godot*?

In Minnesota, at Park Square Theatre. But most of the plays I directed at the beginning were at Penumbra Theatre Company; and I still think the best production I ever directed was *The Piano Lesson* at Penumbra.

You talk a lot about keeping true and honest to the playwright, and yet with that production you took a much bolder approach, certainly different from Lloyd Richards's watershed production, which most people thought was what August wanted. What made it great for you?

Fear!

It was the first play of August's that I'd directed. We're very good friends, but I also know that his plays are *his children*. So friend or not, you fuck it up, you're not going to get another one!

So I kept going over and over what was happening in the play. Everything I pulled, I pulled from the text of the play. He saw it and he loved it. The boldness was really the boldness of the writer. I didn't create anything that wasn't there. I think there's an incredible muscularity to a lot of his work, I just went after it.

What does that mean to you, muscularity?

That these are not sedate people: these are people who are full of life, full of dreams, full of energy to manifest that life and manifest those dreams. He writes about people who do not take a step backwards. As a director you can have a lot of fun, because you can have conflict anywhere on stage at any time. These people speak their minds. These people are courageous and refuse to back down. They're bold, and the muscularity comes out of the characters' refusal to have society dictate to them who they're going to be or what they're worth. I just let that manifest itself more physically in some of his plays.

That works for some and not for others. I find that *Gem of the Ocean* is very different in that regard, because the characters are dealing with an intense loneliness after slavery, and there is a yearning and a searching in that play that's very different from some of the other plays. I find I have people seated in this play much more than in any of his other plays. Because it's the honest thing to do. When a character says, "Sit down and talk to me," what are you going to do?

It's the subtlest play that he's written. And so I'm finding that I have to use a different vocabulary.

Specifically?

It's not so much about the muscularity as it is about the soulfulness of it. That time period was a very highly politicized time period for black America. It was the beginning of a new century and people were getting stopped from leaving the South. A new life was being born in the North that didn't look a lot different from the one in the South. So there was a lot of radical feeling among the people.

It's finding what that center is, and in this play, I find it in the women characters. So *their* physicality, *their* muscularity is much more important in this play.

Do you talk about that "center" in the first rehearsal? Do you make a big first speech?

Yes. It lets the company know why *I'm* there and what my reasons for doing this particular play are. Ever since my mother passed and six weeks later my son was born, I find that I have a responsibility to give to my son what my mother gave to me. And so everything I do is part of that responsibility.

The speeches usually run about fifteen to twenty minutes. There'll be a speech at the beginning, and there will usually be one on the last day I give notes. It's what some of the actors and August have come to call "the State of the Union address." The last note session isn't really about notes; it's about what we did here, and the importance of what we're doing, the importance of being artists in a country and at a time that doesn't respect the spirituality of the human being, of the human condition. There is a lot of gas in the mine shaft and we're the canaries, and we've got to be screaming right now.

The speech at the beginning of the process is about why I'm at the table with them, and the importance of the project to me. The actors who know me know what I'll do in rehearsal. For the brand-new actors, it's their introduction to me. I'll tell them pretty much where I am at that point in my life so they know who they're dealing with.

At the end it's a celebration, giving over the play to them. We *did* this. We took this journey and we survived this journey and we're going to share it with an audience, and it has value. Some will like it, some will love it, some will hate it . . . Doesn't matter. What's important is that we attempted the journey and we completed it. And now it's up to the ages to decide what its importance is.

I personally don't care much about reviews. If I cared about the reviewers' opinions, I'd have them in rehearsals. (Probably only a few of them: Michael Feingold, because Feingold has *been* in rehearsals.) But I *do* care what they say about the people I work with, because my job is to protect them. So if my actors and my playwright come off great and the reviewers hit *me*, that's fine: mission accomplished. Because these people basically put their artistic integrity and their careers in my hands. And it's a hell of a responsibility and I don't take it lightly. They don't put their careers in my hands so I can masturbate my shit on stage. They say, "We trust you; take care of us, and we'll go everywhere for you." So I read reviews because I want my folks to be protected.

I feel the worst when somebody has given everything they've had to give, and the press doesn't respond favorably to it. I loved Roc Dutton's performance in *Ma Rainey's Black Bottom* in our revival. The *New York Times* took exception to it; I think they took exception to a lot of pre-show stuff, and three-quarters of that was bullshit, it wasn't even true. That bothered me, because I saw what that actor was willing to give every night, and it's not what your normal actor can give. Even if they *could* give it, they wouldn't want to. So I felt very depressed about that. I can't even remember what they wrote about *me*.

So what do you do?

I tell the actor, if they've read the review, that I totally disagree. And that if I cared what that critic had said, they'd have been in the rehearsal hall. I let them know that the support is the same and my opinion of their work has not changed, is not affected by that.

It doesn't sound like you're the same director you were when you started years ago.

No, I think I'm better. Working with August has improved me as a director because of his strict adherence to honesty. Like with *Two Trains Running*. I sort of put a director's stamp on it. The audience loved it, and it worked, but it wasn't the play.

How do you mean?

I had some of the monologues as direct addresses to the audience. The end I embellished by having the community give money to West to get a better casket for Hambone, and then Hambone shows up in a white suit in the window, and the lights go down. The audience loved it. The brilliance of great writers is that you can have all kinds of interpretations, and they work. But in working with Wilson, I realized I had dissipated his metaphor for the rise of the sixties at the end of the play.

I've learned to listen more to the playwright; I've learned that the success of the production depends on whether or not the playwright can say at the end of it, "I'm proud of that production." I'd rather have August be proud of it than Ben Brantley. No slam on Brantley; I think he's a decent critic. But my job is to take this person's vision and put it on stage so they like it. It's like giving your kid to someone and saying, "Teach him." Well, I better teach the hell out of that class, because that matters to somebody.

I've learned to be more patient. I don't blow up as much as I did when I started directing: too much youthful exuberance, too many Otto Preminger movies about how you're supposed to be a director. Now I listen more to the actors, to the playwright, to my design collaborators. I've actually found one of my most important collaborators is the stage manager: I really only work now with two: Diane DiVita or Narda Alcorn. And I will have some of my most important conversations about the play and the production with them. I find it utterly amazing that there's no award for best stage manager, when there's no way you can have a production without them.

Keith Glover and Rosalyn Coleman in Two Trains Running *by August Wilson. CENTERSTAGE, 1994. Credit: Richard Anderson.*

SEPTEMBER 2006, VIA PHONE FROM MINNEAPOLIS

Tell me about the return to work for you.

I was someone who had always pushed the envelope as far as fitting many projects into my schedule. My style was to be pulled from one project to the other and let them inform each other. But this had stopped me and placed me in a position with no work and no money for a while. I had to figure out: what is it I really was expecting to get from this? And what did I want at age fifty? I had to sit down and think about what it all really meant to me *without* the money, *without* Broadway, *without* all of those things that can be very alluring and addictive and like crack cocaine. What was the thing that was the most important to me? What was the thing I'd really be able to carry from it? Because the rest of the stuff is fleeting—it can be here today and gone tomorrow.

And it really came down to a project I did at Juilliard last year, a workshop of a play by a third-year student, with second year students acting. You know when you say you live for certain things? That was the thing that I lived to do. It was for next-to-no money. The important thing was that I came out of intensive care to get into that rehearsal hall, and how much a part of me it was *without* all the rest of the stuff . . . you know, *without* Tony nominations, *without* the *New York Times*, *without* any press—without all of that stuff that can help feed your ego and your arrogance. The bottom line was that magical and spiritual thing about it was the work itself, trying to push the form, working with these students who are going to be major actors.

The audience in the workshop was literally *screaming* like they were at a rock concert. The thing that I think was contagious was the *joy* and *love* of doing what we were doing. All the other stuff hadn't gotten in there yet: that's coming for those students down the line. But at that moment, there was a purity like you find in jazz musicians. They're never gonna make a ton of money at this thing, but that ain't the issue—they're going to be practicing sixteen hours a day anyway. Because there's something about their particular art form that compels them to keep going, to keep trying to find that interior thing that pushes them into a fuller understanding of their own humanity, and something which they can share, which gets us to that secular, spiritual relationship between the audience and the people on stage.

Originally when we spoke, you said directing was your least favorite discipline in the theater. But now it sounds as if the camaraderie and collaboration in the rehearsal room is the greatest source of joy for you.

You have to have it taken away from you, sometimes, to realize how much it's a part of you, and how much you actually love it. Getting sick gave me a lot of time to realize how compelled I am to do all this. It's not just my job—even though not doing it caused a lot of financial problems which I'm going to be trying to dig out of for the next few years. The thing that was more important was that there was this compulsion in me to work in the rehearsal hall, to delve.

While I was recuperating, I started writing again, and started practicing acting again, but the thing I *couldn't* do by myself was direct. I needed the other people to do that. The things I'm working on as a writer, I don't know if they're going to work; I need to get in a room and work with actors to see if these theories really hold water.

So it's not being able to do it that really showed me how much it was a part of who I am. It's the same thing with artists and sculptors and musicians: the work is *who you are*. It goes beyond the stuff that drives us crazy—the politics and whatnot. The thing that keeps us in it (because it sure as hell ain't the money) is that we're *compelled* to do this. There's something powerful about being part of this tradition that's been going on for millennia.

Today was the second day of rehearsal for *Yellowman*, which I'm working on with [actors] Regina Williams and Thomas W. Jones II. And I'm playing once again with the jazz rhythms—

That's a perfect project for your directorial style.

Hey, we got some stuff that was just beautiful, where Regina and Tom just *took* off. Once we jumped on Dael's rhythms, it was like a jam session. It was all there. They didn't have to figure out what they were doing, they were doing it on the *moment,* they were doing it on the *fly.* And the *excitement* of that . . .

In theater, we don't just hold up a mirror for people to look at. I think what we really do is we take our soul and teach people how to dance with their own by getting them to feel. And especially in this time, when everything seems to be pushing you in the opposite direction—not to feel, but to be distant. But that's not why people over the centuries have come to theater. It's the same reason they go to church: they come to experience something with other people that tells them they're alive, and that being human is valuable—even though there are things that are tragic about it, even though there are things that are comic about it—that it's valuable to *be* that. That there's a reason that we live, that we have life.

All the stuff that I was talking to you about beforehand was theory. I've been rereading the things I said then, and thinking, "You're being esoteric about this, but you found out when it got taken away from you that this wasn't what you thought about *theater*, this is what you actually thought about *living*, about life." And being able to share this with actors, designers, made all the difference in the world to me as a human being, and the value of doing this art form, the value of doing theater, the value of being in that rehearsal hall just grew larger and larger and larger.

I was actually surprised, because I thought I wouldn't miss directing. And I didn't miss directing, I missed *church*; I missed the congregation. I missed what those prayers that night were going to be, and how we were going to try to write a better prayer, and how we were going to try to understand what prayer actually is. We need to get in touch with that, and I think the theater is the one place that does it without the baggage that religion can bring in.

With the passing of Lloyd Richards and August Wilson, what's ahead for the new generation of African-American theater artists?

It ain't pretty, you know? Particularly with the absence of August, I don't know of an African-American theater artist who is in control of his own work. August was in control of his work. He was also a producer of his work. You could not force August to cast anybody he didn't want to cast; you couldn't force him to have a director he didn't want to have; which means you couldn't tell him *how to tell the story he wanted to tell.* I don't believe there's that kind of African-American artist right now, with that kind of respect from the mainstream theater. I believe that everybody else is being asked to compromise, especially if you're going into the larger arena.

August was brought into the larger arena by Lloyd, who was in a position to shepherd him in and to say, "*This* one, *this* voice is really something different. Other people might not pick up on it, but I do. I understand it, I know how to direct it, I know how to cast it, and I know how to produce it."

That Lloyd Richards doesn't exist for that next August Wilson right now. . . . Put it this way: it's like asking Glenn Miller to find the next Charlie Parker. What *he's* going to find is somebody who sounds more like Glenn Miller, because that's what he understands, that's where he lives artistically. There *are* writers out there—I just worked with that young writer Brian Tucker at Juilliard, who's a monster of talent, and young, and he's somebody who eventually can't be denied. And there's a young artistic director out in Chicago, Derrick Sanders [of Congo Square Theatre Company], from whom I really believe big and great things are going to come, because he has vision, he has passion, and he doesn't just want to get a seat on the gravy train, he wants his own locomotive. He wants it to be his own railroad!

They're *there*, but to be in the position that August and Lloyd were in? That's different. Because August and Lloyd affected the entire American theater. They opened it up so that a lot of people could get work throughout mainstream American theater. I think that it's going to go backwards now. You already see more and more white directors directing plays by black writers. I'm not saying there's anything wrong with that, in theory: a good director is a good director. But when you start seeing good black directors not working, you have to wonder, "Are they actually better for that play than *this* person would be?"

I wouldn't put myself in to direct [Sean O'Casey's] *The Plow and the Stars* or *Juno and the Paycock* over [Guthrie artistic director and former artistic director of Ireland's national theater] Joe Dowling. Joe Dowling knows that better than me. He has a personal connection to that. The stuff that would have been called "institutional racism" in the twentieth century is just absence of knowledge now. People just don't think about it. They don't see August as the Louis Armstrong of a movement in theater that was akin to the jazz movement in American music. Black theater is not looked at as that kind of an art form. It's looked at as a subsidiary of the art form that's already there. Jazz music is not looked at as a subsidiary of classical music; it's looked at as its own entity, inside of which you have black artists, white artists, Asian artists, all playing that music.

People were beginning to see this thing August was starting *wasn't* just a subsidiary of American theater. It was actually becoming its own *kind* of American theater. This man really was in the same caliber as Shakespeare and Chekhov and Ibsen and Beckett, because of the effect that he had on the theater that surrounded him. He didn't just write great plays, he *completely changed the landscape,* like Armstrong changed jazz, like Brando changed acting. The American theater ain't the same since August Wilson and Lloyd Richards.

At a forum a few years ago, you argued along with Wilson that for black theater to survive it must find its own support network and nurture its own. You said, "Michael Jordan could make sure the Crossroads Theater didn't go down, with the money he'd bet on a golf game." It has to do with that mentorship issue you're talking about.

Michael Jordan needs to get out of his pocket and give Derrick his money! He could take care of Derrick, and all the theaters out there! And I believe he should—he needs to give to the community in that way. I feel even stronger about this than I did before. I'd get in his face about it! I think the theater is the most important thing in the country right now, cause we'll tell the fuckin' truth. And those theaters need to be supported financially, because that's where that next Lloyd is going to come from, that next August is going to come from.

Without places like Congo Square being financially supported, these artists are gonna have to go to classical musicians to play their jazz. And who's going to suffer in that is not just the artists, but the American theater itself, and more importantly, the American audience. Because the American audience is already *there,* they're already wanting to get past what is being done on the American stage now.

The young kids—like my kid, who's almost seventeen—they *love* theater; they just don't care for a lot of what is classified as *mainstream* theater. They talk about hip-hop theater, but they haven't seen that in New York, because it's going on underground . . . The way people are playing with language, playing with character, playing with rhythm, playing with music—they're really tearing it up, but they have no place to play. We need a place where these guys can sit down and jam.

The people who like classical music don't have that big of a problem with Sonny Rollins and John Coltrane and Louis Armstrong, because if the form is being pushed, it's good for everybody. The twentieth century gave us Brecht and Beckett—that's what kept the ball up in the air. It didn't die; it got more interesting. Well, what are we going to do with that in the twenty-first century? In America, we usually wait for somebody else to do it. But look at the things we brought to the world musically. There's stuff like that going right now in the American theater.

So what's the difference between doing an August Wilson play at Penumbra versus doing an August Wilson play at CENTERSTAGE? Isn't the latter a classical musician playing jazz?

It depends on who's doing the play, and what they've learned about doing the play. Charlie Parker is always going to play "Now's the Time" different than Phil Woods. Phil Woods plays the hell out of it, but you shouldn't get his version at the expense of losing Parker's, which is where his came from. I see *that* happening more; I see there being a rolling back. I was talking to a noted black director today, who said, "Sometimes when you notice that people have rolled back in the hiring of you, you felt that maybe you were being *studied,* and not really being appreciated for what you were bringing as an individual artist." That they saw "black director," not individual artist. That's why I call it *jazz* theater, because you put "black" in front of it, and people are like, "Oh, oh, oh, oh, why does it have to be black?" It's rooted in a different aesthetic. But it connects not just with those of a similar culture, but with people in Arizona, in Idaho, in Montana . . . Bottom line, the human story is the human story.

I love Chekhov. I find my story in all of Chekhov's plays and in his letters and stories. And sometimes you need to see that thing that is *different* from you to actually see yourself. Which is why I say the power of Shakespeare is what it is over all these years: the truth is the truth, genius is genius, brilliance is brilliance. When the honesty of a human being is put before you, it doesn't matter if it's from the sixth century, the sixteenth century, or the twenty-first; if it's on a street in Harlem, or on the south side of Philly, on a cowboy ranch in California, or in medieval England. Hamlet's condition and problem would be the same no matter where Hamlet was. Seeing *Fences,* people say, "That's the relationship between my father and me." If we continue to try to homogenize the theater, then we're going to lose its power. The theater is *about* diversity, about taking diverse stories and placing them in front of you to show you who you are, to show you yourself, to get you to think and ask questions.

Somebody said to me about *Yellowman,* "Should we be airing our dirty laundry?" And I said, "You're just worried about airing *your* dirty laundry! I don't care if it's *your* dirty laundry I'm airing, but I'm airing mine—my personal laundry." Being in the room, doing that again . . . I didn't realize how vital that was to everything I did: how I raised my son, how I get along with my family, how I look at a sunny day. It's such a glorious thing that we do, and it's been going on since the Greeks—that's amazing! It's been going on that long . . . and it's going to hell real quick.

The thing that scares me the most is that we are letting the red-staters and the Bushers dictate what we should show our audience.

Anybody who does something like *Yellowman,* I have to applaud. Dael's honesty is so brutal. It indicts you. The audience wants that. And for that same reason that they want it, I'll never say I hate directing again.

I am writing more now, because with August gone, I'm trying to figure out artistically what I need to be doing. Seeing all the people we've lost over the past year . . . Well, maybe I'm on that last third of the journey myself, so it's very important what I do with it. There's been the Tony nomination, there's been Broadway, but what I've learned over the past year is what all this stuff really meant for me.

So you might be on Broadway, you might be at Congo Square . . .

Wherever I'll be, it'll be something that I believe wholeheartedly in, and something that I'd be willing to spill blood over. Because I realize not just how important it is to me, but how important it is to our audience that we keep doing that. Because when we give them a *Yellowman,* they thank us; they're not getting it anywhere else.

BILL RAUCH

Building on the Cornerstone

IN THE MID-1980S, A HARVARD UNDERGRAD-
uate named Bill Rauch heard a dispirit-
ing statistic: only two percent of Americans attended professional theater
regularly. With the kind of blind, wild
ambition common to students at elite
liberal-arts colleges, Rauch and close
friend Alison Carey cofounded Cornerstone Theater Company to make theater
with and for the other ninety-eight percent. On June 30, 1986, they set out on
a bus tour with ten friends to do it, managing to change the American
theater along the way.

In the decades since then, Cornerstone ensemble members have visited
rural communities across the United States and underserved segments of
their home community, Los Angeles, staying long enough to create plays.
Some of the plays are new, many are adaptations of classics, but they all
strive to respond directly to the challenges those communities face. The
plays are usually produced with a combination of professional artists from
the ensemble and amateurs (whom they call "community collaborators"),
and the effect of the work is a combination of traditional theater outcomes
(such as the firing of the imagination) and community activism. Success
stories of the latter kind are legion: one Cornerstone play directly caused
an African-American clergyman in Los Angeles to finally confront the
AIDS crisis from his pulpit; another in Port Gibson, Mississippi, a town

with a history of race division, led to the most racially integrated commerce board in the country; a third paved the way for the creation of a
community-based theater in Maine.

In the spirit of Augusto Boal's Theater of the Oppressed, and in the
tradition of Luis Valdez's Teatro Campesino, Cornerstone is now recognized as the country's foremost community-based, civic-engaged theater. Other companies with similar missions, such as Sojourn Theatre
in Oregon and Albany Park Theatre Project in Chicago, have risen in its
wake; untold numbers of other theaters across the country now
embrace Cornerstone theory and methodology in their outreach work.
By focusing on small and underserved communities, Cornerstone has
paradoxically become a national force.

From 1986 to 1991, Cornerstone mounted twelve productions in
different rural communities across the nation, from Long Creek,
Oregon (*The Good Person of Long Creek,* 1988), to Eastport, Maine (*Pier
Gynt,* 1990), and ten towns in between. Cornerstone hunkered down to
adapt classics with members of these communities, celebrating each
town's people and showing itself *to itself,* much like the way Greek theater functioned as a rite of purgation for the citizens of Athens. Rauch
directed all these plays, and they form the aesthetic and theoretical
basis for the company's further work.

In 1992 the company settled in Los Angeles, in part because its
members felt L.A.'s diverse population would provide ample opportunities for new kinds of residencies. As it had done elsewhere, Cornerstone
created plays in neglected L.A. communities such as Watts, Chinatown
and Pacoima. But somewhere along the way, Rauch and his ensemble
decided to broaden their notion of the word "community," and began
making plays that united diverse Angelenos under other rubrics. With
the move to L.A., Cornerstone was not only strengthening communities, but creating new ones. The company began creating "bridge
shows," in which collaborators from previous projects come together to
create a play that serves as a kind of summary of the past several shows.

Rauch's last community-based project at Cornerstone was a five-
year investigation of communities of faith, culminating in 2005 with
the bridge show *A Long Bridge Over Deep Waters,* written by James Still.
Synthesizing aspects of the plays Cornerstone had made in a slew of
communities (Catholic, African-American Christian, Buddhist, Baha'i,
Hindu, Jewish, Muslim, GLBT people of faith), *Long Bridge* was an emotional ordeal for Rauch and the ensemble.

In order to connect these very diverse communities, Still and Rauch
decided to model the play after Arthur Schnitzler's *La Ronde* (in which a
character leaves one scene and encounters a different character, who leaves
that scene to encounter yet another character, passing the baton like that
for ten scenes). The order they decided on dictated that the scene about the

Muslim community conjoin with the scene about the GLBT community of faith—which meant including a scene with a gay Muslim character.

Cornerstone had been down this difficult road before, and had alienated a number of its Muslim community partners by presenting an adaptation of *You Can't Take It with You* (2003) featuring a gay Muslim character. *Long Bridge* reopened wounds that had not yet healed; an administrator left the company, and two Muslim members of the project bowed out of the production. Rauch and the ensemble met repeatedly to try to resolve the issue, or at least get a clearer understanding of where everyone stood. In the end, the production went on, and many of the Muslims who were angered by the play nonetheless found ways to support it. As Still said later, "For eight nights on a stage on the planet Earth, there was a gay Muslim in a scene."

Rauch served as artistic director of Cornerstone for the bulk of its existence, directing most of its productions until 2003, when he took a sabbatical that resulted in his decision shortly after *Long Bridge* to leave the company. And after a single, busy year of freelancing, he was appointed artistic director of Oregon Shakespeare Festival in Ashland. Almost exactly twenty years after cofounding Cornerstone, the forty-three-year old director was taking a job at a company with a budget nearly twenty times that of Cornerstone, and with a seventy-year history of making excellent theater for the traditional two percent of Americans who regularly attend plays.

I was fortunate to interview Rauch a couple of times for this book: first in 2003, as he was about to embark on the life-changing sabbatical that took him away from Cornerstone, and again in 2006, just days before he learned of his appointment at OSF. So this interview serves a twofold purpose: it not only tells the story of the development of the country's most influential civic-engaged theater through the words of its visionary cofounder, but it also serves as a document about what the theater industry calls "founder issues"—how a company with a founder transitions into a new phase, and how that founder himself or herself creates a life separate from the institution he or she created.

While building Cornerstone, Rauch was also building his own reputation internationally as a theater artist and visionary. But after about fifteen years with the company, he was unsettled that he was regarded primarily as a "community-theater guy." That's not a bad thing (especially if you're the most important "community-theater guy" in the country), but if you're looking to fashion your own identity—especially if you've been leading the same ensemble for so many years—there's always the nagging question: am I an artist in my own right? Rauch often tells the story of a call he got from Arena Stage in Washington, D.C., in the early 1990s, asking if he'd like to interview about doing a project there. He was convinced he was finally being asked to exercise his own artistic muscles as a freelance director. But the artistic director wanted Rauch to bring Cornerstone methodology to Arena to create a "Cornerstone-type play."

In some way, that fateful meeting paved the way for Rauch's eventual departure. In the years that followed—especially the early 2000s—he directed more and more outside Cornerstone, entrusting the company's work to a growing pool of ensemble members, artistic associates and far-flung colleagues and commissionees. His relationship with OSF began in 2002 when he directed Robert Schenkkan's *Handler*, and he was invited back every year after that. Some directing work happened close to his home base in L.A. (at South Coast Repertory and the Mark Taper Forum), but he also worked at the Guthrie Theater in Minneapolis, Yale Repertory Theatre in Connecticut and Lincoln Center Theater in New York City.

The Cornerstone methodology Rauch created has definitely informed his leadership at OSF, which has shed any reputation for stodginess it might have had before he came along. At Cornerstone, collaboration was the name of the game at every step, and Rauch is exceptionally capable of making every person in the room feel included, valued and part of the process. That skill is vital, as he is now leading the nation's largest longstanding ensemble of actors (there are more than one hundred of them). He's also managing to insert Cornerstone's community-minded, non-traditional outlook into OSF's more traditional programming. His first production as artistic director, *Romeo and Juliet* (2007), was designed specifically to explore the ongoing debate between traditionalists and revisionists at the company by staging part of the production in period style, part in contemporary style. His programming has included work outside the Western canon, like the Sanskrit tale *The Clay Cart* (2008) and the work of Ping Chong (*Throne of Blood*, 2010).

But it is his devotion to new work that has brought the most fundamental changes to Ashland. In 2009, Rauch initiated the Black Swan Lab as an in-house new-work incubator, using the ensemble's talents to develop new plays with hundreds of hours of workshop time each year. And most importantly, he tapped Cornerstone cofounder Alison Carey to join him at OSF as director of the American Revolutions project, which aims to create 37 new plays (the number of plays in the Shakespeare canon) about significant moments in American history.

Before he made the move to Oregon, though, Rauch's conversation was marked, explicitly and implicitly, by the tension of an artist struggling to emerge from the overpowering shell of the institution he created. Cornerstone's buzzwords and mission invariably crept into his discussion of his personal aesthetic. It's true that OSF once epitomized what Rauch was rebelling against when he cofounded Cornerstone. But in the years since he started his career, American theater has changed significantly. Thanks in great part to his work, the field's concept of whom it serves, or could serve, continues to expand.

How did your journey into theater begin?

The thing I remember most strongly was a life-changing third-grade skit in which I got to perform. Seeing older students in elementary school put on plays was influential, too. My parents took me to theater—they had a subscription to Westport Country Playhouse—and I became a volunteer usher there. Then I became the head usher, and then the "playhouse beautifier," which is their fancy name for "janitor." I had two shifts, beautifier by day and head usher by night, and it meant that I got to see everything multiple times.

I acted in junior high, high school and in my freshman year of college. But then I applied for a slot to direct a play in my second semester. Although I had experimented a bit in high school, that was my first real experience with directing. It was *The Visit* by Dürrenmatt, and it was like turning on a light switch. It was so immediate and clear that I wanted to direct. If I had anything to bring to the world, maybe it was through this medium, this discipline. So I stopped acting. I was a pretty bad actor anyway!

What turned the light on?

I loved the whole process, but there was an electric connection between the piece and the audience, especially that first night. And there was something about being in the room, and also outside of it; I wasn't up on the stage, but I had been connected to all the people who had made the piece.

I was so overwhelmed by it emotionally that I went into the bathroom, because I needed to get away from people. I took a minute by myself, because it really felt like a life-changing moment. Something sacred had happened in the room, and I was part of that sacred thing in a way that made sense to me.

So give me the general journey of how you got from *The Visit* at Harvard to Cornerstone.

I've taught now at a lot of different universities, ones with much more structured programs than Harvard, which has no theater major. And although I have tremendous respect for the programs in which I've taught, I've come to appreciate the fact that I started working without a structured environment. At one college where I taught, there were theater majors about to graduate who had never done a play, because there were more majors than there were opportunities.

I directed twenty-six shows as an undergraduate! Because it was all extracurricular, there were no limits. You could do as much work as you had hunger for. Some of that was in official theater spaces and some of that was in the basement of my dorm, or outdoors. Immediately afterwards, I was very self-conscious that I didn't have formal training, and now I realize that there were things I missed out on by not having that. But I was able to learn so much by doing. Those of us who started Cornerstone joked about how Cornerstone was our graduate school.

During those years at school, a group of my closest friends and colleagues started talking about launching a theater company after graduation in 1984 and nicknamed it "Truck Theater," because the impulse was to get in a truck and drive to places where there weren't professional theaters and do plays there.

I had founded a little company in my second semester of senior year. Instead of going through the usual, "I'm doing a show, let's have auditions," I invited a group of people that I had worked with to start a company and spend the whole semester just making plays together. We called it the Kronauer Group, because the acting master of my dorm was named Kronauer, and he said we could use the basement space. And we jokingly called it the Kronauer Center for the Performing Arts, and did shows in there until the three women in the dorm room above this basement corner insisted that we leave. That's where *Medea/Macbeth/Cinderella*—which is a piece that has been part of my life for a long time—was born. [He directed it for OSF in 2012.]

I had just been introduced to the work of the Wooster Group, its play *L.S.D. (. . . Just the High Points . . .)*, and it was a really pivotal event. I thought, "If this level of excellence can be achieved by an ensemble . . ." I focused even more on ensemble than on Liz LeCompte's brilliance. I knew from that moment that I wanted to work within an ensemble context.

So I invited a number of people to make plays with me for that last semester. Lynn Jeffries, David Reiffel, Chris Moore, Peter Howard, Amy Brenneman—there were at least five founding members of Cornerstone in that group. And then that summer, I was hired to do a project at a mental health center, working with residential patients, and with that same group of friends I did Molière's *Sganarelle*. The guy who played Sganarelle was illiterate. He couldn't read, and he was the lead in this rhyming verse, classic piece! Obviously that was a dry run for Cornerstone, without us realizing it at the time.

After college I stayed in Cambridge for a year because I had fallen in love with my partner, Chris, and I didn't want to leave him. The second year out of school, I went to Washington, D.C., and was Peter Sellars's assistant director at the American National Theatre at the Kennedy Center on three productions. And during that year, we built Cornerstone in earnest.

I visited Alison Carey, the company's cofounder. She was one of my college friends, and her boyfriend at the time had bought and renovated a building, and was selling it as a commercial real estate venture. I was blown away that someone our age had done this thing that seemed to belong to people much older than us. And this guy said, "Just go for it—what are you waiting for? If you have a vision of starting a theater company, just do it." That was the inspiration, this for-profit young real estate mogul! And somewhere in and around all of this, the notion of involving the community in making the work had come up.

How did that happen?

By the time Alison and I sat down to write our first plan for the company, the idea of involving local residents in the work was locked in. I don't know when it happened. I so wish that I had kept journals, so that I could find out when that idea dropped in. When did it go from "Truck Theater" to "We're not just going to drive the truck and perform and leave the next morning; we're going to stay long enough to build a play *there*"?

How did you even get to "Truck Theater," and the idea of bringing theater to underserved communities? Did you study sociology at Harvard?

I was an English major, and I was woefully ignorant of the community theater tradition in this country. I had never heard of the WPA Federal Theatre Project until Cornerstone was just about to start. I stumbled upon Roadside Theater, and other organizations that are community-based. I wish that I had been educated about those things. But there was a total purity of impulse, inventing what we wanted to do. Only afterwards did we realize that we were part of a much larger movement with a long history and long future.

I remember being interviewed for a college paper, when I was a senior. I reread it recently, and it was fascinating. I said I was interested in making theater for the "lowest common denominator." I find that phrase, obviously, extremely problematic now, both politically and socially.

But I really cared about that idea from when I first got started in theater. My first musical in high school was *The Music Man*. I had just moved to Haddonfield, New Jersey, and I was told by a lot of my friends that the auditorium didn't fill up for the high school musical. And I thought, "There's an *injustice* there! Every seat should be filled!" So a bunch of us went to *every door of every home* in Haddonfield, New Jersey, and asked, "When's the last time you saw a play at the high school? Well, we believe you'll really be moved by our play." And we packed the house.

I guess I've always had this hunger to reach people who don't normally go to theater, and a dissatisfaction with work that only performs for people who do. I mean, God bless traditional theatergoers! I'm not taking anything away from them. But I felt a hunger to reach people who didn't already go to theater. And I would say that hunger was shared by all the founding members of Cornerstone.

Alison and I started planning in earnest in the fall of 1985. Alison had a connection through a former boyfriend to Manny Azenberg, the commercial theater producer. And around that time, apparently, he had said something about building bridges between not-for-profit and commercial theater. So Alison and I spent a weekend in November 1985 writing a three-page letter to Manny Azenberg, asking him to give us a couple hundred thousand dollars to start a theater company, because we had all these great ideas! We were going to go off for two years, and work in ten communities around the country, and create ten fantastic new American plays. Then we'd come back and be done with that adventure.

Manny Azenberg never wrote back. But we had articulated our vision on paper.

How did that vision change?

We knew we wanted to involve people from the community in the work when we started. But it was only over the course of the first season that the aesthetic of adapting a classic text set in the community developed, and it developed very organically. Working in our third community, when we did Noël Coward's *Hay Fever* [1987] in Marfa, Texas, we realized something important: we were interested in not only adapting the language but adapting the setting, so that the play was set in the community in which we were producing. That was a major aesthetic shift.

After we'd worked in a dozen communities, in the summer of 1991, we brought people together from all twelve of those communities in our first bridge show, which is a project designed to build bridges between communities, both artistically (with who's on the stage), but also including the audience in experiencing a play together. And suddenly: "Oh I see, *this* is what we're on this earth to do as a theater company."

Other grassroots community-based organizations grow up out of one community, and serve that community, but we are nomadic by design. There are all sorts of problems about being nomadic by design, but one of the advantages is that we can invite communities we've worked *with* to work *together*. So now we don't think about a single project without thinking about what cycle it is part of, which will culminate in a bridge show.

Introducing playwrights into the mix was another huge shift. Originally, we just adapted everything ourselves, and it was me and Alison, Mary-Ann Greanier and two or three others in the company who loved to write. But there was never a playwright credited, it was always: "Adapted by Cornerstone Theater Company and the people of . . ." whatever the town was.

So when we moved to L.A., involving the playwright's voice in the process became a goal. And as we hired a greater diversity of playwrights with a greater diversity of aesthetic, they began to introduce original work, oral-history-based work and adaptations of very different kinds.

Me not directing everything was also a huge shift in the company's life. That happened after a couple of years in L.A., and that's obviously gotten more and more extreme as the years have passed. Now I direct a minority of the company's productions.

And we began defining community differently: originally, it was always geographically defined, that it was the residents of a town. Now

Amy Brenneman and Edret Brinston in Romeo and Juliet *by William Shakespeare. Produced by Cornerstone Theater Company in Port Gibson, Mississippi, 1989. Credit: Benajah Cobb.*

we have defined community by shared birthday, by occupation, by culture and language and by faith and religion.

How does it all work? From deciding on the community, to the project, to opening night—what comes first?

Everything follows from the community. Some of my colleagues and I taught a course on community-based theater at the University of Southern California, and we posited that you can ask three questions of a work of art: Who is communicating? To whom is it being communicated? And what is being communicated? And different artists or different organizations ask those questions in different orders. For Cornerstone, "To whom?" is always first. We start with the audience, with "Where are we doing the play? With whom are we doing the play?"

Our methodology has become much more complex. In those early traveling days, for example, we arrived in Marmarth, North Dakota, and we cast, adapted, rehearsed, performed and closed *Hamlet* [1986]—all in eight weeks. I can tell you now that we will be working with a Hindu community in two years, the winter of 2005. And we are building relationships in the Hindu community, building community partnerships *now,* two years ahead.

In those early days, when you showed up, did you know anyone?

Well, we never went anywhere uninvited. We'd have to get somebody to agree to host us, and the things we would ask for from a community were a place to rehearse and perform, and housing: private bedrooms for each company member in otherwise unoccupied buildings. We considered ourselves professionals and not exchange students, so we needed to have our own space to live in. And that was sometimes really easy to find, and sometimes it was the deal-breaker with a community.

What made you think a community would do such a thing?

You know, to this day, it always starts with one person who *gets it,* and who makes the leap of faith. And that one person becomes an advocate and convinces other people. It's sparking the imagination of that person. More often than not, we would make the initial contact, although occasionally it's been that someone has asked us to come in to do something.

With *Steelbound* [1999] in Bethlehem, Pennsylvania, we were invited by Touchstone Theatre. Or in Watts, for instance [for Bernardo Solano's *Los Faustinos,* 1994], we had a board member at the time who had started a Latino organization there.

Los Faustinos was based on *Faust,* and *Steelbound* on *Prometheus Unbound.* **Why do you start with the classics?**

In the company's first five years, we did only adaptations of the Western canon. We did only one original piece; everything else was an adaptation. Today in L.A., it's fifty-fifty, whether we're adapting a classic or doing an original piece—and if we're adapting a classic, whether that classic is from the Western canon or from another part of the world.

There's a struggle for me in talking to you: how much am I talking as Bill Rauch the director, and how much as a representative of Cornerstone?

I'm happy to answer the question, but I just want to underscore— because Cornerstone's early traveling years were so romantic and mythic, a bunch of artists getting into a van and driving to remote places—that the artistic identity of the company is still wrapped up in that early methodology.

I don't want to misrepresent the company's work. Obviously, it was originally the primary thing we did, and it still is part of what we do.

Much of who you are is indeed wrapped up in your career as a theater revolutionary leading Cornerstone. Many of the ideas in those early years originated at least in part with you. So don't dodge the question!

Okay! Why classic texts? There was the practical aspect: we hit the ground running. There wasn't time to write a play from scratch. There was the aesthetic. For me and for a lot of my colleagues, we loved the aesthetic *clashing* of the old and the new. A very crass but clear example is from *Romeo and Juliet* [1989, in Port Gibson, Mississippi]. The insult that Tybalt gives to Romeo, when Romeo turns the other cheek but Mercutio can't stand it and responds with violence, is, "The love that I bear thee can afford no better term than this: thou art a villain." In Cornerstone's adaptation in Mississippi, it was, "Thou art a nigger."

So aesthetically, it's not, "You're a nigger," and it's not, "Thou art a villain." It's, "Thou art a nigger." That is a very particular aesthetic. And it's energizing. It was Shakespeare, that icon; it was that classic story; and it was the reality of racial segregation in this country, and in that particular town. It was those things coming together and creating something new.

I would also say politically there's a power (in terms of theater being, often rightly, perceived as an elitist art from) in taking the very texts that have been used to make people feel shut out, and turning those over to a community. "This is not just a thing to make you feel stupid in your high school English class; this is your community's story." Transferring ownership of the story has incredible political power.

I don't see clear boundaries between your personal aesthetic and Cornerstone's.

You're going right to the white-hot topic!

You chose to work with an ensemble. You chose that as a way to make your career and to develop your own aesthetic. You've clearly articulated that questions of community and personal ownership are important to you as an artist. Even with *The Visit*, you've talked about transferring ownership of it to the people who came to watch it.

That's true!

Cornerstone is an ensemble-based company. And I struggle on a daily basis with my role as a *founding* artistic director who is the primary company spokesperson, and also *one* member of a consensus-run ensemble of artists, administrators and technicians. I've got a thousand stories about why it's hard, and a thousand stories of why, for seventeen years, it's been worth it to continue to live in that struggle. But I've been working outside Cornerstone professionally at an accelerated rate in the last two years. That complicates the dynamic further.

I'm going on sabbatical for eight months in July in part to catch my breath, and to really reflect on those questions. God forbid, if Cornerstone ceased to exist tomorrow, I know that I would still be a theater director. And if I stepped away from Cornerstone tomorrow, I believe that Cornerstone would continue to flourish, and do just fine without me. But all those dynamics about founders' identities being wrapped up in company aesthetics, and vice versa, exist.

Tell me about the outside directing you've been doing. It's very much at theaters that are in opposition to the Cornerstone audience model.

Cornerstone was founded in many ways in negative reaction to the regional theater movement. At the time we were young, we were naive to a degree, and we didn't fully understand the power of the regional theater movement as its own negative response to centralized professional theater. But we were reacting against this sense that if you were plopped down in any regional theater in the country, you wouldn't be able to tell what city you were in based on what was happening on stage and who was in the audience. So we had a hunger for work to be more locally responsive. And for the work to attract people who didn't normally go to theater.

But we started forging connections with regional theaters as we got larger. In 1993, Doug Wager [then the artistic director of Arena Stage], after being moved by a Cornerstone piece, invited us to create a community-based piece on his mainstage as part of his subscription series. He wanted us to combine Cornerstone's professional actors, Arena's professional actors and an equal number of community-based actors—most of whom had never acted before—into something that would be part of Arena's subscription. So I came to directing at larger institutional theaters through Cornerstone.

Honestly, when I met with Doug, I had a list of dream projects I wanted to direct on my own, and I thought maybe we were talking about me doing something as a freelance director. But it became clear in the first couple of minutes that he was really interested in doing a Cornerstone community-based project. And there was a moment when my heart sank, because I thought, "Ah. I can only be 'community-based' guy." There was an ego thing, that I couldn't be an artist outside of a community-based context.

But as I reflected on it, I thought, "What is a bigger event in my life and in the life of Arena Stage? Me coming in and directing a play, or Arena twisting itself into a completely new shape institutionally to adopt the mission and the methodology of our little theater company that was one-twentieth the size and budget?" And that began a series of similar projects. The Long Wharf project [*The Good Person of New Haven*, 2000] was one in that series; and we did one at Great Lakes Theater Festival [*Peter Pan*, 2001] with James Bundy, who had been Cornerstone's managing director.

It was actually James who gave me the chance to start my freelance career. James called me when he took over Great Lakes Theater Festival as artistic director, and he said, "Like lots of regional theaters, I want Cornerstone to come and do an epic, community-based project with my community. But first of all, I want you to pick any play you want to direct. And the season after that, we'll do a Cornerstone project." As my friend, James knew that was something that I needed as an artist.

And it was incredibly powerful to me. Ironically, we commissioned Anthony Clarvoe to do a new adaptation of *The Wild Duck*, set in contemporary Cleveland, and we ended up having all the party guests in the first scene played by Cleveland community leaders—clergy, TV personalities, newscasters, and on and on and on. So, of course, it was a community-based project despite the invitation to do anything I wanted!

What's different about your process with community collaborators versus your aesthetic with trained professionals?

I remember in an early Cornerstone project, there was a woman who was very excited to work with us. She'd had some professional experience, but she lived in a small town. In the middle of a very tense tech, I stopped because a ten-year-old boy had an idea he wanted to share, and I listened to the idea. And she cited that of an example of how disappointed she was in Cornerstone: we did not live up to her expectations, because we were not imparting professional standards. I was allowing precious moments of tech to be taken up listening to a ten-year-old. Obviously, she had her own definition of being professional that I don't share. But that was a very telling moment for me.

I really believe a director's main job is to listen to and help edit everybody else's ideas. It's so scary to go into a rehearsal room and start a process. To start every day of rehearsal. What allows me to overcome the fear is that the room's going to be full of interesting, smart people to whom I can turn and say, "What do you think? Do you have any ideas?"

It's too glib to say, but at its core, I believe there's no difference between directing community-based actors and seasoned professional actors. It's just that each person brings a different expertise into a room.

You have to approach community-based work with an absolutely sincere sense that everyone in that room has something to offer that has to be respected equally. If you've had the privilege in your life to become a professional artist, whatever you bring to the table as a professional is no more important than what somebody else brings to the table in terms of life experience. If someone is bringing the firsthand experience of what it is to be on welfare to playing somebody who is on welfare, that is an expertise that is unbelievably valuable to have in that room. And if somebody has transformed himself or herself successfully over a forty-year career, and knows a ton of shorthand about how to create something in a rehearsal room, that is an incredible expertise, too. The art of directing a Cornerstone play is honoring both those expertises, and finding a way to balance them, and not allowing there to be a hierarchy.

But of course there are huge differences; especially in trying to find a vocabulary that can be shared by everybody in the room. Issues like, why do you want to open your body so that the audience can see your mouth? And trying to get at that from the essence of the character and the essence of the story, rather than [in a mock British accent], "In the theater, we keep our bodies open!"

In Cornerstone's case, the plays wouldn't *exist* without the community. The story wouldn't exist; the audience wouldn't exist; the cast wouldn't exist. We are constantly humbled by that fact. The colonial, imperialist model is a huge danger. We made blunders early on, when we would fall into language . . . I remember one of my colleagues once said in front of a huge gathering of community folks, "We go to places where they don't have any culture." And rightfully, she was booed and hissed.

Lowest common denominator.

Exactly. I feel like I'm so much more enlightened about these issues, but if I'm still doing this work in twenty years, I'll look back at where I am right now and reconsider the depth of understanding I have.

How does one kind of work feed the other?

I know my seventeen years with Cornerstone is feeding my freelance work in a *huge* way. I know I could not have directed Robert Schenkkan's *Handler* at Oregon Shakespeare Festival in the way that I did; that we could not have collectively built the production we built if I did not bring my Cornerstone experiences to the table. And yes, I do believe those outside experiences are helping to shape who I am as I go back to Cornerstone. They're helping to feed me.

But I fear that I'm slipping into an identity crisis. Everyone wants to put me in a box as an artist, as if I am only the person who does this kind of work in this way. You spend so much of your career defending why you would choose to do that, or talking to people about it because it's so interesting, that you lose track of the artist who exists outside of that work.

Well, *there is no outside,* that's the thing, right? There's no way to separate it. So it has been nice, sometimes, to direct a play outside of Cornerstone, because it reminds me more than anything that being an artist is being an artist. And creating a work of art is creating a work of art. And if I have only veteran actors in the room, or if the majority of people in the room have never set foot on stage before, we still have to figure out: what's the story we're telling; how are we telling it; and can this process be as inclusive, loving and gentle as possible to create work that is dangerous and ferocious and earth-shattering and life-changing? Whether I'm in the community center basement or on the mainstage of some large institutional theater, that's still the task.

You've said, "Most of the plays I direct don't happen in theaters. They happen in malls, in barns, in closed factories, in public and private spaces that are transformed into sacred spaces through the highly political ritual of live performance." Can you talk to me about what that means?

I'm really interested, especially since *Steelbound,* in this notion of what is politically radical. What is politically and aesthetically progressive?

In terms of productions I've directed, joy is important to me—there being joy in the room during the creative process, and in the exchange between the audience and the performers. That does not mean that I'm interested in everything being warm and fuzzy and sweet and sentimental. We use the noun "celebration" a lot about Corner-stone's work. And yet, if you look at the history of our source texts, we've probably done more tragedies than comedies, and more plays with a lot of bodies on the floor at the end. So we celebrate a community with a play about a bunch of people who end up killing themselves or each other!

It sounds like you're talking about catharsis with "celebration."

But I'm also interested in the Augusto Boal thing, right? My interpreta-tion of what he says is that catharsis is a way to anaesthetize the audi-ence, to keep them from going out and changing the world. You want to move people to action. Piss people off enough to want to go out and change the world. That interests me a lot. I guess the most deadly response to anything I direct would be apathy. I'd rather people be angry, or ecstatic.

When you go into a room with non-ensemble members, is there an expec-tation about how you're going to work?

Every actor is different; every artist is different, and has his or her own process. But I do believe that a lot of the great work in world theater comes out of ensembles, because there is a depth that can be achieved with a group of people who know and trust each other, and push each other to take new risks. I'm a believer in ensemble.

I think it's not surprising that I'm finding a second artistic home at Oregon Shakespeare Festival. In so many ways, OSF and Cornerstone could not be more different. But OSF is driven by a huge acting company that appears in rotating rep, and that sense of "company," which others might see as a painful limitation (you have to cast out of the company, you don't get all your first choices in casting), to me is a measure of great strength.

For a director, it's partly about finding your artistic soulmate in every person in the room. No matter how different your process may be, you're going to go on a journey together. So how can you inspire each other, learn from each other?

You announced your departure from Cornerstone last year, and a month ago it was reported you're a candidate for the artistic director position at OSF. So maybe now's a good time to ask: will traditional and non-traditional audiences ever really meet?

I have seen those audiences meet time and time again in Cornerstone productions.

Does a dialogue happen between them?

Sometimes. Certainly not always, but sometimes. And it's interesting that you use the word "dialogue," because at Cornerstone we've been more and more proactive about creating opportunities for dialogue. Not only in the making of the art (which we've always done), but in the processing of the art for audience members. Sometimes professionally facilitated dialogue.

How does Cornerstone measure the success of that dialogue?

Well, measuring success for any work of art in general, and on a Cornerstone show in particular, is very tricky, and ultimately impossible. You have to try. Not only because the funders make you try, but because you wake up in the morning and you ask those questions: "Is my work making a difference in the world? Am I leaving the planet a better place than I found it?"

I think the most important measurements tend to be anecdotal. They tend to be stories about a person or a couple of people, and what their journey has been since they were part of a project or simply experienced a project. We've got a lot of those anecdotes. But trying to turn success into something statistical? In Cornerstone's case, when the work is so handmade and homemade, it's very, very tricky.

Absolutely, anecdotes can be very potent. I just think sometimes our society, and even our field, and certainly funders, look for measurements that go beyond anecdote. I'm even falling into it, aren't I? Saying "*beyond* anecdote," as if "anecdote" is insufficient, and that somehow data is more meaningful.

Cristofer Jean and Miriam A. Laube in The Clay Cart *by Śūdraka, translated by J. A. B. van Buitenen. Oregon Shakespeare Festival, 2008. Credit: David Cooper.*

But it's true that I can do a poor job on a production and still get one person excited enough to provide an anecdote, whereas I can do a great job on a production and get twenty-five people excited. Surely statistics have a place in measuring success.

I'm being stubborn in my answers because it's such an ongoing battle for Cornerstone in terms of the impact of the work . . . But yes, there are many things that are clearly measurable. Based on audience surveys, for example, we can tell you that during a certain two productions, the audience demographics—racially and ethnically—almost exactly mirrored the racial and ethnic demographics of Los Angeles County. That's a very clear, hard picture of who is seeing the work.

Or I can talk about the Port Gibson, Mississippi, experience, the biracial production of *Romeo and Juliet*. A couple of years after we left, the community had only done one more biracial play. And at that point in our evolution, we measured ongoing success based on how much theater communities created after we left. If communities did a lot of theater, we had been successful; if communities didn't, we had somehow failed.

And in Port Gibson, that *Romeo and Juliet* was a big media event for Cornerstone, and led to an increase in our national profile, but the community had only done their one play, so I thought we had failed in some profound way.

When we were back in town on the *Winter's Tale* national tour a couple of years later, Alison Carey and I were pulled aside by fifteen to twenty different people, black and white, who all told us the same story: that Port Gibson had been named a Main Street town by the National Trust for Historic Preservation. This was a federally subsidized program for small towns to get business back on the main streets and away from the fast-food strips. And Port Gibson had recently been honored at a national convening of more than four hundred Main Street towns for having the most racially integrated board in the United States.

And everyone ended the story with: "Don't you see? It's because of the play. We all met; we all learned to trust one another, and we all learned to work together through the play." And that was a *seismic* shift for me in how I thought about measuring success. Because obviously that national honor for that community—and the role that Cornerstone had played in it—was something, first of all, that I would not have known about, and second, was not how I was measuring success up until then.

Does Cornerstone now have an ongoing presence in communities where it has worked?

As the years have gone on—and as the majority of our work now takes place in our home city of Los Angeles—we talk as much or more about our relationships to individuals as we do to communities. Individuals and individual community partners, rather than communities in the blanket sense of the word. For instance, I can talk a lot about our relationship to the Watts Village Theater Company, a small professional theater that got started out of our fifteen-month residency in Watts. And that, in a way, is a more concrete and productive thing to talk about than our relationship with the community of Watts. Because our relationship with the community of Watts is really about our relationship with a whole bunch of individuals, a whole bunch of different community organizations. We've gone back and we've performed in Watts; we've had all sorts of collaborations with different organizations and individuals within Watts; but I think we've learned over the years that being more specific, not generalizing about "the community," is more accurate and ultimately more helpful.

So, why did you finally leave Cornerstone?

[long pause]

That's where you script "long pause."

It's not as if you didn't know it was coming!

I left Cornerstone because my curiosity about what a professional life without Cornerstone would be began to overtake my curiosity about what lay ahead for me and Cornerstone.

And you learned that on your sabbatical?

I think I had a little seed about whether or not that was a question I should even be asking before the sabbatical; the sabbatical confirmed it. The sabbatical also confirmed that the company would be able to not only survive but thrive in my absence, and that in fact I had things that I wanted to do as an artist that were outside the confines of Cornerstone.

It was not an uncomplicated decision, obviously, because I can safely say that Cornerstone has the most intense purity of mission of any theater company in this country. And to walk away from that as an artistic director was hard to do.

Because Cornerstone was part of my life for twenty years, I am always going to try to put myself as an artist in the position of having the type of conversations I had during my time at Cornerstone. It so shaped who I am, and how I think, and how I move through the world. Of course I'm going to try to seek out those opportunities.

But the particular aesthetic strategy that Cornerstone uses, of making a work of art about community, on that community's own ground in every sense of the word, leads to a certain type of magic that I know I won't be able to re-create elsewhere. I hope I'll be able to create a lot of different kinds of magic.

The good news is that Cornerstone is still going strong, and has a wonderful new artistic director [Michael John Garcés], and hopefully I can return in years to come as a guest artist.

What kind of challenges were you curious about that you couldn't have at Cornerstone? Doing a show on the scale you're going to do *The Clean House* at Lincoln Center [2006]? Working with specific actors?

Over the last five years, I've been directing a lot of new work as a free-lance director. And being there for the birthing of a new play—a new play that may not be in collaboration or celebration with one specific community, but a new play that may go on and be produced across the country—that's been really fun and exciting. And I want to do more of that.

What about new plays excites you now? Is it the collaboration with the playwright, the solving of new challenges that have never been solved before . . . ?

It's all of the above and more. There is always a charge working on a Cornerstone show that's about being there for the beginning of something new—something new in peoples' lives, something new in a community's life. I think I feel a similar charge out of working on a new play that may go on to other productions. There's an essential joy in the act of telling a story for the first time. At the same time, of course, I love to work on classic texts, and have had some wonderful experiences working on classics, especially at Oregon Shakespeare Festival.

I've talked to a lot of new-play directors for this book, and others who are mainly classics directors. And most of them agree that each pursuit takes a different set of muscles, and often they say that a director is more present on stage with a classic than with a new play.

For me that's an oversimplification. Obviously I would be having a different dialogue with Sarah Ruhl about how to put her play [*The Clean House*] on stage for the very first time at Yale [in 2004] than I'd be having in my head with William Shakespeare when doing *The Two Gentlemen of Verona* [OSF, 2006]. But essentially, those two conversations are the same. Both are me trying to interpret what the playwright's intentions are. I am a big believer in the director's role being an interpretive one. No matter how aggressive the aesthetic approach is, when we're talking about text-based work, it's an interpretive art form. And I *agonize* over what William Shakespeare was trying to get at, because I deeply, deeply trust William Shakespeare as a writer. So it's not about whether he would approve of any choice. It's whether the choice that I'm making is imaginative enough, and yet rooted enough in the emotional complexity and reality that he's created, or the social reality that he's painted a possibility of. Is my work rising to the level of the words?

But surely, there's an additional dialogue you're having when directing a classic, with all its previous productions.

Absolutely, that's really well put. It's about a dialogue with the entire production history of the play, rather than a dialogue with a playwright who might also be sitting in the room.

And that entails a slightly different approach to an audience, right? They've seen it before, so you need to prove yourself as a director with it—

Part of the dialogue with the audience is either the fact that this is a play they've seen many times before, or this is the very first time they're entering that world. Even with a classic, you have to assume that there are audience members who *are* entering that world for the first time.

In the past five years, what have you particularly enjoyed working on outside of Cornerstone?

Working on Lisa Loomer's *Living Out* at the Taper [2003] was a particular thrill. I felt that the racial dynamics, and more importantly the class dynamics, were so dangerous and so fascinating. As Lisa kept rewriting through the rehearsal process and deepening it, *lying* came to the forefront as a theme, how everybody was lying across class boundaries—it was exquisite and surprising and funny and upsetting.

How did you as a director help guide those rewrites?

I do think I play a strong dramaturgical role as a director, absolutely; but in a way, that's a question you have to ask the playwrights I work with.

When working on a new play, I find that I like the writer to be around as much as possible. Inevitably the writer can't be there every minute of every rehearsal, and that's good: to have some time for the writer to go away and then come back to see things with fresh eyes. But I'd rather err on the side of having the playwright around more than less.

Any instances recently directing a new play when you couldn't make a scene work?

I did a new Robert Schenkkan play called *By the Waters of Babylon* [2005] at Oregon Shakespeare Festival. There is a character, a Cuban gardener who, you eventually learn, was a renowned writer in his own country. He has very little to say for the whole first movement of the play, and then finally the language comes pouring out of him. And I was struggling as a director with how to treat some of his monologues, to keep them from being political lectures to the other characters and to the audience. That was something that Robert and I talked about very openly. He did some rewrites, and he had a lot of great insights for me and the actor about what was underneath—what may on the surface seem to be stating facts, but actually came out of a much deeper emotional place, and was revealing more than we realized it was revealing.

Did you just plainly say, "Robert, this feels too political?" or did you approach it differently?

You're getting at a question of trust. How does a director establish a trusting relationship with a writer? What kind of communication would violate that trust? And how do you nurture that relationship? Robert and I had worked together once before on *Handler*, so there was already a lot of trust and mutual respect, and that allowed us to communicate openly.

Another interesting example was *The Further Adventures of Hedda Gabler* at South Coast Rep [2006], by Jeff Whitty. It's a very funny, very deep play in which a lot of different fictional characters coexist in another dimension. There's one scene in which several fictional versions of Jesus interact with the title character. And the issue started from other artists in the room; we really had to embark on some serious discussion of what the scene was saying. Was Jeff ultimately saying Jesus was a fictional character? No, that was not Jeff's ultimate point. How do we make sure that the audience doesn't walk away thinking that was the ultimate point, or at least that it's open-ended enough that people can impose on it what they want to believe?

Jeff went through a lot of rewrites on that section, trying to take in the input, trying to be true to what he had in his heart and what he wanted to express, and trying to not kill the comedy that's such a delicate balance in the piece. It was a really beautiful process.

Has your process changed since you've left Cornerstone?

Well, the funny thing is, I directed a Cornerstone ensemble show this past spring; I'm currently codirecting a Cornerstone show at the Guthrie; and that faith-based bridge show is only a little over a year ago. I'm actually still right in the thick of intermingling Cornerstone projects and freelance projects. So I don't know if I have the distance to answer that question.

But that said, my curiosity, my hunger, about how to most effectively create a world on stage and to interpret the playwright's words is pretty constant. So it just feels like each project is this great new adventure with its own incredible challenges. The main feeling when I'm not doing a Cornerstone show is relief that I don't have to schedule around the conflicts that a first-time actor brings to the table, as opposed to a professional actor who's contracted to be there! I know that sounds silly, but it really is quite profound. The amount of hours and emotional energy that goes into scheduling a Cornerstone community-based show is immeasurable, indescribable! Stage managers are the great unsung heroes of Cornerstone.

Design-wise, is the process different when you're freelancing?

Yes and no. Working on a lot of different scales as a director in recent years has made me appreciate what can be done with a lot of money and a lot of technology, but it's also made me wary. I feel like I've seen—hopefully not too often in my own work—technology overwhelm a show. Great work can happen on a shoestring, and great work can happen with millions of dollars spent, and bad work can happen in both contexts; and I think I've learned that very profoundly in recent years.

I'm really interested lately in the relationship between casting and design. In some theaters, casting happens long before the design process, and in other theaters that flips. I realize they've grown to become somewhat interdependent for me. If one has gotten ahead, I need to get cracking with the other.

Can you be more specific about that interdependency?

You start making major decisions as a director about the world of the play by who's going to be playing these characters. And you start making major decisions as a director by designing, especially the set, but every other element as well. And I've found that if I don't know who the actors are, but I'm starting to design the set, I feel lost—and vice versa. So, for instance, Chris Acebo is a set designer I've been working a lot with lately, and Chris and I will talk about casting, as well as about set design: what roles are cast, what aren't. What we're essentially talking about is the world of the play. It's not like, "Let's create a physical environment and plug in some people later," or, "Let's cast a bunch of people, and then figure out what kind of physical world they're going to inhabit." For me, I do better when those two things go hand in hand. And I don't think I ever realized this so strongly until you asked that question.

Structure is really important to me; I like to take apart the structure of the play. And I'm really interested through the design process—set, costume, lights, music, all of it—in how we can *separate* worlds within a play as strongly as possible. How can we most fully explore what keeps groups of characters distinct from one another? Maybe that's just part of who I am; exploring our common humanity through our differences.

A very clear example of that is *The Two Gentlemen of Verona* that I just directed at OSF. Five of the main characters leave one place, Verona, to go to another place, Milan, and the entire arc of the play comprises this journey. I felt completely adrift when we were discussing choices that kept the worlds similar. So we decided to explore worlds that were as unlike one another as possible. We ended up embracing two choices that are quite different: Verona is Amish, and

Milan is kind of a country-club-style estate. And as we kicked them around, the choices seemed almost cartoonishly absurd. But in practice, as we began to work on the design process and work on the text and work on the casting, the rightness of the choices really fell into place.

Is your shorthand changing with professional actors?

I think I'm a patient director, and as I mature as a director, the main person I have to be patient with is myself. If I don't have some brilliant blocking solution, if I can't articulate what the needs are for a character in a given moment, I'm learning to avoid going to that place that we all go to as directors, which is: we beat ourselves up for not having those answers. Instead, I try to remember that I do theater because it's a collaborative art form, and I'm surrounded by lots of smart, caring people. And all I need to do is pose a question and the answers will come flooding in, and then I have the privilege of sifting through the brilliance of all my colleagues, and then picking a direction.

Is "To whom are we communicating?" still the most important question you ask as an artist? Or as a freelance artist, are you asking those questions you mentioned earlier in a different order?

I definitely don't think I'm asking those questions in a particular order anymore. "To whom?" is still *really* important to me. In other words, when I thought about *Two Gentlemen,* I wanted to come up with two worlds, two cultural contexts that had resonance for our audience right now. So in many ways I was driven by the "To whom?" But the "What are we communicating?" and "Who's doing that communicating?" are also pretty darn important. Especially with new work, I'm starting with "What are we communicating?"

So the pithy answer would be, I'm enjoying switching around the order in which I ask those questions.

How do you feel about making work for a smaller, more traditionally theatergoing segment of the population—"the two percent," as you've referred to it—which is now much more often what you're doing?

That quote comes from the mid-1980s, when we started the company. But I'm still really interested in the full spectrum of society being in the theater for plays I direct. And I think that one of the reasons that I'm beginning to feel I should become an artistic director again, and not remain a freelance director for the next chunk of my life, is that as an artistic director I can be more reflective and strategic about how to reach that full spectrum of society than I can as a freelance artist.

As a freelance director, I've been connecting to these long buried impulses to be an artist, and to tell stories, that I had when I first became a director—when I was nineteen, twenty, twenty-one, before Cornerstone ever existed . . . just that joy of telling a story as well as you and your colleagues possibly can. I really felt connected to that, and it's been great, and it's been liberating. But even in this short time of being away from Cornerstone, I'm coming to learn that I am an artistic director at heart, and that is what I want to end up doing again.

On a very practical level, in terms of my family, I want to be home; I want to sleep in my own bed. I want to wake up and have breakfast with my kids. I don't want to be on the road. And I don't think there's a city in this country where I could be a freelance director and make the kind of living that I would like to make in terms of supporting my family, and sleep at home at night.

On the artistic level and on the life-mission level, I feel like running a theater is part of what I want to do. And I'm surprised that I feel it so quickly after leaving Cornerstone, but I feel it with great clarity.

Are you worried about finding artistic satisfaction at a large institution?

Running an institution is in itself a work of art. I become completely energized about the challenges that face the organization and that face me. And I am no more or less energized by those than I am by the shows I direct.

What about OSF has drawn you to that particular job, as opposed to others?

I was thinking about the theaters that have been my artistic homes. And it suddenly was so striking: Cornerstone, all about an ongoing ensemble at the heart of the operation; Oregon Shakespeare Festival, all about an actor-centered company, the largest acting company in the country; Yale Rep, where I'm an associate artist and have worked three times in the last four years, and where although there's not a company, there's a very intimate relationship with the Yale School of Drama, with its students in a way becoming a company; and South Coast Rep, which had for many years a resident company and still has founding members in the majority of productions in any given season. So it suddenly dawned on me that there's a throughline, which is *company*, and in particular acting companies.

So what are your thoughts about the future of companies, and in particular collectives? Did you leave Cornerstone in part because you weren't sure the collective, consensus-run model worked anymore?

My decision to leave Cornerstone in part rested in a fork in the road for me and the company: I realized that what I needed to do next if I was going to lead an institution was to *not* run a consensus-led institution any more.

Ah—so you were already thinking about your next institution?

You caught me. [laughs]

But yes, I felt that I needed to make decisions as an artist outside a consensus-making body. At the same time, I believed an ensemble-based decision process was best for Cornerstone. And the company agreed. I said, "I think consensus is right for the company, but it's not right for me." It was not the only reason, but it was a potent reason.

My stepping down was part of a long-term process in deciding in what direction the company needed to head. We drew up a list of hard questions, of "undiscussables." Starting with, "Should Cornerstone continue to exist?" and including, "Should Cornerstone have an ensemble? Should that ensemble govern itself by consensus? Does Cornerstone need an artistic director?" Pretty much every hard question we could think of. We tackled one topic every two weeks at company meetings over the course of several months. And the group confirmed that consensus was really the way it wanted to operate. And we specifically looked for a new artistic director who was hungry to work within that context.

I do feel like I'm excited in this new chapter to have more freedom to make my own mistakes. But as we've said, no matter the institution, that spirit is deeply a part of the fabric of who I am. I'm a collaborator, and I wither without collaboration.

BARTLETT SHER

Missionary Zeal

THE LATE GARLAND WRIGHT, ARTISTIC DIREC-tor of Minneapolis's celebrated Guthrie Theater from 1986 to 1995, was well known for establishing one of the country's foremost resident acting companies. Fewer know of the resident director program he started there, in which emerging professionals worked for two years alongside him watching, listening and absorbing all they could. It was an institutional mentorship program without contemporary parallel, and many of the country's best directors now working passed through it. But none has achieved as much success—or so prominently inherited Wright's gift for elegance with the classics—as Bartlett Sher.

The artistic director of Seattle's Intiman Theatre for ten seasons (beginning in 2000), Sher is best known nationally for his Tony-winning productions of *The Light in the Piazza* (Intiman 2003, Goodman 2004, Broadway 2005), *Awake and Sing!* (2006) and *South Pacific* (2008). But before his Broadway success, Sher was known regionally as a director of twenty Shakespeare plays in twenty-five years, an institutional leader with near-missionary optimism about the regional theater movement, and a deep interpreter of texts.

Born in 1959 in San Francisco, with six brothers and sisters, Sher never thought about his future career. Instead, he spent time going to

Grateful Dead concerts, attended an elite Jesuit prep school (where, he says, everything was about forging connections) and got wrapped up in the sociocultural frisson of late-sixties/early-seventies San Francisco. By the time he left college, he felt completely unprepared to live anywhere else in America.

Nonetheless, in 1981 Sher started the San Diego Public Theatre with a number of friends, and soon found himself assistant directing at Des McAnuff's revitalized La Jolla Playhouse with some of the country's most progressive directors, Robert Woodruff and Peter Sellars among them. A detour to the University of Leeds in England (where he earned a master's in 1986) cemented Sher's belief in the inherent connectivity of art, culture and politics. He and his then-girlfriend Carla Kirkwood were the only Americans in the program, and Sher absorbed new ideas from the Asian, African and European artists around him. By the time he came to the Guthrie in 1990, Sher was an amalgam of unusual influences: the Grateful Dead, Woodruff, Jesuit schooling, African and Asian theater traditions, and the theater theorist he credits with forming the aesthetic backbone of all his work: Tadeusz Kantor.

Kantor, who died in 1990, was a Polish painter, set designer and theater director who broke ranks with the Eastern European avant-garde in 1955 to form his own theater company, Cricot 2. His plays and "happenings" never gained a popular reputation, but his theories melding the physical and the visual had tremendous influence on theater artists in the 1970s and 1980s—and certainly on Sher throughout his entire career. For example, when Sher created a *Cymbeline* for Theatre for a New Audience in 2001 (it became the first American Shakespeare production to play England's Royal Shakespeare Company before landing Off Broadway) featuring a palette of samurai warriors, American cowboys and Renaissance Italians, he was creating what Kantor would have dubbed an "autonomous work of art" that played within its own logic and rules. Sher's adherence to Kantor's theories, along with a heavy dose of biomechanics pioneer Vsevolod Meyerhold, lend a theatrical, neo-absurdist air to many of his productions.

Working with Wright, Sher tamed those influences and placed them in a distinctly American context when it came to the classics. Wright's gift for process-oriented stagings that fully incorporated design elements into every choice cemented Sher's visual and choreographic talents (he is rightly known for his engaging scene transitions), and gave him a deep and actorly understanding of text. It's a gift he shares with many of the other directors Wright mentored, including Emily Mann, Charles Newell and Risa Brainin.

Wright asked Sher to stay on in the permanent position of company director, and he did until the end of Wright's tenure, staging works including *Pericles* and *Many Colors Make the Thunder-King* by Nigerian playwright

Femi Osofisan. His freelance career had begun to blossom, and led him to serve as associate artistic director at Hartford Stage under the leadership of Mark Lamos until 1997. A hectic period of freelancing ensued, until he was appointed artistic director of Intiman three years later.

During his much-respected tenure at Intiman, Sher's adventuresome ambitions brought great notoriety to the theater. After transferring *Piazza* to Broadway, Sher's star was enough on the rise that his company earned the Special Tony Award for Outstanding Regional Theatre the following year, in 2006.

But the theater's fortunes did not rise in step with Sher's. As New York—both Broadway and opera—came calling more frequently, he spent less and less time in Seattle. (He moved with his family to Brooklyn in 2008.) And the theater itself, often rumored to be in financial trouble, was unable to turn the Tony Award or Sher's success into dollars. By the time Sher announced his departure in 2009, Intiman had maxed out a $900,000 line of credit and was borrowing heavily against its modest endowment. His handpicked successor, Kate Whoriskey, was forced to cancel the bulk of the 2011 season, and an unusually public round of finger-pointing began in the press and online: the managing director was blamed for withholding information, the board was blamed for not practicing appropriate oversight, and even Sher was blamed—for overspending on productions that were too ambitious, for snubbing Seattle-based artists in virtually appointing Whoriskey and for using the company as a springboard for his career while ignoring its own needs.

Reviewing his tenure at Intiman, the charges against Sher seem like so much sour grapes. The excellence of the work was never in question, and his investment in Seattle artists (like *Piazza* bookwriter Craig Lucas) paid huge dividends for them and the company. While Sher did spend much time away from Intiman for *Piazza*, that process reflected his interest in European models of play development—working and revising through repeated productions.

Written by his longtime collaborators, composer Adam Guettel and playwright Craig Lucas, *Piazza* went through a number of iterations before reaching Broadway, at Lincoln Center Theater's Vivian Beaumont Theater, and each time Sher and his collaborators worked feverishly to revise it. Designs changed substantially; songs were added and subtracted and added again. The work that finally opened on Broadway in 2005 earned eleven Tony nominations and six Tony Awards. Sher's return to Lincoln Center Theater (this time using the Belasco Theatre as a venue) with *Awake and Sing!* was also greeted with Tony enthusiasm—it was named best revival—and led to a gig at the Metropolitan Opera: a commedia dell'arte–influenced *Barber of Seville* in 2006. He delivered another best revival Tony (and took home his own for directing) when he opened *South Pacific* for Lincoln Center at the Beaumont in 2008.

Despite productions as theatrically vibrant as *Cymbeline* or *Barber of Seville*, Sher's artistry has been praised as often for its invisibility. Both *Piazza* and *Awake and Sing!* (as well as the 2006 *Uncle Vanya* I saw at Intiman) were productions in which his hand was barely noticeable. And that's the way he likes it: he's more interested in the audience falling into the unique worlds he creates, rather than "catching him" on some concept or abstract idea.

Following the success of *South Pacific,* Sher was named Lincoln Center Theater's resident director, with advising duties and a guaranteed slot to direct one show there per year. It was during that summer that he realized it was time to leave Intiman. He told the *Seattle Times,* "I was [directing an opera] in Salzburg, and commuting back and forth from Europe, and began wondering how I could balance everything. Given the way my schedule was lining up for the next three years, there was no way I could keep doing all this." He informed the board of his intentions that fall.

During that final 2009 season at Intiman, Sher managed to snag his fourth Tony nomination (for August Wilson's *Joe Turner's Come and Gone,* for Lincoln Center on Broadway) and direct his second opera at the Met, Offenbach's *Tales of Hoffman.* But his more recent large-scale projects—an overproduced and poorly received *Women on the Verge of a Nervous Breakdown* (Lincoln Center Theater on Broadway, 2010), Rossini's *Le Comte Ory* (Metropolitan Opera, 2011) staged as an opera-within-an-opera— were met with less success, perhaps because Sher's hand was so visible in both.

Nonetheless, Lincoln Center Theater's faith in Sher has remained steadfast, and the director returned to form with J. T. Rogers's *Blood and Gifts* at its smaller Mitzi E. Newhouse Theatre (2011). That production was vintage Sher, a boldly designed theatrical world in which the actors explored the text with intimacy, intensity and tremendous rigor. The company is betting on more of the same (and perhaps another Best Revival Tony), asking him to stage Clifford Odets's *Golden Boy* (1937) on Broadway for them in the fall of 2012.

Sher's success with the politically engaged *Blood and Gifts,* and his return to the left-leaning world of Odets, bring to mind Craig Lucas's 2005 comments about him for *American Theatre,* "[Sher] is the only one of his kind: he believes you can change the world with theater." Sher sees theater's creation of community dialogue as an essentially American—and democratic—function. That passion is another bequest he received from Wright at the Guthrie.

On the morning Intiman was notified of its Tony Award, Sher wrote to his audience:

> We are the contemporary equivalent of a long-bearded old one telling a tall tale around a campfire. The stories themselves are

both old and new, and we share them so that through this work our community can test itself, and process its change, and challenge itself to move ahead . . . it's all based on the same idea: that somehow we can make something that approximates life, only bigger in language and sound and aspiration . . . [so that] we may see another possible view of ourselves, and we feel connected, connected as people and families, and communities and citizens.

With institutional leadership behind him, one is tempted to see in Sher's latest freelance period a struggle to find that kind of passionate, community-based mission on the country's biggest stages. It's hard to imagine him or his work without it.

JUNE 2007, INTIMAN THEATRE, SEATTLE

You were born and raised in San Francisco in a big Catholic family, the fifth of seven children. How did you end up with a career in theater?

It's very simple. Growing up in the fairly chaotic environment of the early 1970s, I was dragged by my older brothers to Grateful Dead concerts. And as Joseph Campbell has said, a Grateful Dead concert at that time was the closest thing we've got to a contemporary Bacchanalian ritual.

So there I was, an eleven-year old boy walking into a room with five thousand people in the middle of a very connected community experience, where they knew the text and the history as well as the band knew it, with a shared experimentation going on (both in the art and in the chemical "productions" in the audience) . . . that was an extraordinary artistic experience for a kid. I didn't have any sense that an eleven-year-old boy shouldn't be in such an environment!

So you were heavily influenced by that communal, ritual experience.

Not only that; the *dramaturgical structure* of Grateful Dead concerts had a huge influence on me. The first set was always drawn from a particular group of songs—old bluegrass tunes, rockabilly songs, rock tunes. The second set always began with the same structure, but then transitioned into a more "open-form" exploration (it was very Aristotelian, actually). That's where it would propel into really deep experimentation—they'd *invent*.

And yet, no concert was the same as the one before. They were always selecting the songs differently, and exploring the relationships between them (much in the Grateful Dead was based on transition). That created a shared expectation in the audience: what might be different about this show? So all in all, this unmediated community cultural experience had a very deep impact on my sense of rhythm, my sense of how pieces connect, my sense of exploration and experimentation and my sense of community.

Now, jump forward forty or so years to doing an opera at the Met: that's probably the closest I've gotten to the same thing! There's an audience that knows the piece very well; they are coming at it cheering, waiting for both the musical and theatrical exploration of it; and there is *enormous* skill and experimentation and openness on the part of the performers.

Did you see a lot of theater as a kid, too?

We would occasionally go to American Conservatory Theater in San Francisco. I remember many incredible productions of classics that Bill Ball did. I didn't go because my family was particularly into cultural things; people just went to shows every now and then. My first experience of a major theatrical event with my family was going to see *Hair* on tour in the early 1970s. It was completely nuts, it was really fun, and it was connected to going to the Grateful Dead!

At the time, my oldest brother lived in France. In high school I earned enough money to visit him. In the course of that visit, I went to all the major museums in Europe, and saw so much art that had a very large impact on my visual sense, and my sense of Western cultural history. It adds up to this weird combination of the Grateful Dead, and going to Europe, and seeing stuff in the city, and being in the middle of the cultural and political explosion of peace marches and riots and transformation that was San Francisco at that time.

That environment meant a kind of engagement in the world, and in what was going on in the world. I remember sitting in the living room with my older brothers while they were in high school, watching the lottery to see who was going to Vietnam, waiting to see which number was going to be pulled up for the draft. That was just part of the universe growing up then. You didn't have any choice but to be engaged, to be out in the world.

You're obviously very politically engaged now, but it doesn't sound like the political performance of the time is what interested you the most as a kid.

It's because there was no separation. People didn't separate a *cultural* idea from a *political* idea—it was all part of the same universe. That separation never occurred to me. You never separated your ideas about the Vietnam War or César Chávez from going to a play, from going to the Grateful Dead. It was all a part of the same matrix.

It's also true and worth mentioning that Jesuit education (I went to both Jesuit high school and college) is fundamentally about *connecting*: connecting ideas to each other, connecting history with now, connecting religion with ideas. So in college I was working for the hunger action coalition and at a Catholic Worker house downtown while I was making plays, and going to Groton, Connecticut to be arrested at the submarine base. That was all part of what you did. I wrote plays in college that were about both my own experience and the political context. Politics are always buried in texts (even in the plays of Neil Simon, or boulevard comedies). All the political assumptions are in there. That's just a given for how I look at the world.

So why nowadays do audiences separate works of art from their political contexts?

Believe me, I think I'm lucky that I don't feel the difference. When I talk about politics now, I don't like to talk about the difference between Democrat and Republican. No one thinks about politics in an *American* context anymore; we don't *connect*. Those separations make everybody confused. In my family there was a lot of division, but we engaged in our differences. On my mother's side, there were Goldwater Republicans. And we were living and growing up in San Francisco, which was very liberal, and my dad was a capitalist, so . . .

Was there a lot of political discussion in your family?

Constant. Political discussion and engagement over ideas. And it was healthy. It was dangerous, sure, because it threatened the family structure in some ways, but it was also part of life.

That's important to you now as an artist and a community leader.

I don't see a separation. When I'm dealing with people now who talk about career or talk about what their kids are going to do, it is so different from how we talked when I grew up. Nobody had any idea what they were going to do. Nobody went to college because they thought they were going to get a job somewhere. I went to a liberal arts college because I wanted to study as many things as I could: I took physics and I was an English major and I studied a broad range of things, so now I feel like I connect.

That's *key* to being a person of the theater. We have to understand the political and social context of every character, plus the emotional context, plus the history . . . In my work, it's led me to become both a classicist and an experimentalist. I'm always balancing those two things.

You switched from writing to directing during college. What happened after that?

After teaching drama at my old high school, I went to San Diego with some friends from college, and helped start a small theater company for three or four years. We built a space and raised the money and put on plays. At the same time, I worked at a local contemporary art venue called Sushi Performance Space, where I was kind of the technical director. So I was able both to work at my own theater, and to work with crazy people like Eric Bogosian and Joe Chaikin and Kei Takei.

This also happened to be the first year that Des McAnuff was at the [La Jolla] Playhouse. I saw Peter Sellars's production of [Brecht's *The Visions of] Simone Machard,* and Des's work, and Jack O'Brien's work at the Old Globe. There was a lot to be seen in San Diego at the time, while I was downtown digging away in the pits.

It's one of the reasons that sometimes, when I'm sitting with a group of young people who want to know where they should start, I say, "Go to the most obscure city you can find in America with the cheapest rents, and work for ten years, and make something. Then everyone will come and find *you,* rather than you having spent your time building a career."

But you went to a place and made work where there were a lot of outside influences, influences that weren't at all provincial, influences you couldn't find in a truly obscure city.

That's true.

My largest exposure to that kind of thing came in 1984: the Olympic Arts Festival in Los Angeles, where Madeline Puzo was the arts consultant. I went up there and saw Tadeusz Kantor, Giorgio Strehler, Ariane Mnouchkine, Tadashi Suzuki . . . and that just blew my head open. Particularly Kantor. Kantor was the one who changed me the most.

Soon after, I went to Europe with this amazing woman, Carla Kirkwood, to study more of that stuff. I did almost nothing for a year but research Kantor. In the same year I was reading Kantor, I decided to read everything I could about directing. I read Meyerhold, [Adolphe] Appia, [Edward Gordon] Craig . . . everything I could.

We went to this great international program at Leeds in England. There were no Americans in it except for us. We met people from China, all over Africa, particularly Asia; I had people in my class from Beirut, the East Indies, Japan . . . That created a great spirit of connection with the rest of the world.

Kelli O'Hara and Victoria Clark in The Light in the Piazza, *music and lyrics by Adam Guettel, book by Craig Lucas. Lincoln Center Theater, 2005. Credit: Joan Marcus.*

Not long after I got back to the U.S., I went to New York to do a production of *The Nest* by [Franz Xaver] Kroetz. It was not a success. Not anyone's fault except my own. I wasn't ready for that kind of pressure and environment. I left that experience thinking, "Oh my God, I can't do this, I'm no good at this."

Was that your dark period?

I'd been teaching at San Diego State and doing theater downtown, and I was really exhausted. I was about thirty years old, and I was thinking, "I've got to figure out how to do this!" Then Madeline Puzo called me and asked, "Do you want to come to the Guthrie and be a resident director?" Madeline and I had met when I was assisting Robert Woodruff in San Diego. She became a good friend of mine and has had a huge influence on my whole career.

So I went to the Guthrie and met Garland, he loved me, and the next thing I knew I was sitting with him working on the history plays. That was my first exposure to Shakespeare. I had never really done much classical work because I was doing lots of experimental work. I was making pieces, wondering if I could *become* Kantor, have my own company, whether that was the route I should go. Then my time at the Guthrie started, and that was the end of the first phase.

From the Guthrie to Hartford Stage, then three or four years of freelancing, and then Intiman. But all unplanned.

Again, I grew up in an era when you couldn't talk about your "career." Nobody used the word. You just worked and tried to make stuff. It was a *blessing*.

That meant the first phase of life was all about experimenting, absorbing a lot of influences and developing a lot of ideas about what the theater was meant to be, or what it could be. I can't express enough how deeply influenced I was by pursuing one particular artist in the theater like Kantor.

You've said Kantor forms the aesthetic backbone of your work.

Do you know this book? [he holds up a dog-eared copy of Kantor's *A Journey Through Other Spaces*] You should get this book. It's the greatest book.

Look at all those Post-it Notes.

It's a mess. Twenty years old.

Looking back at your work, where do you see Kantor in it? I presume you don't direct a play and consciously ask, "How will I 'Kantor up' this piece?"

No, I don't. Well, I've done that a couple of times. But generally, no, I don't do that.

There are certain things about Kantor for me that last. First, each work of art is *autonomous* and lives by its own laws. If you have that as a point of view, you learn to pursue an idea through a piece, and make your own set of laws for how that idea works.

He had this sustained radicalism of painting, as he called it, in the theater. He was a visual artist, so he had a completely different point of view on the nature of poetics in theater—how objects operate in it, where human beings fit into it, how you respond to texts in theater. All these ideas are *completely different* in Kantor.

So when you get to this simple idea that every work of art has its own autonomous laws, has its own autonomous structure, you can do something like the *Cymbeline* I did at Theatre for a New Audience in New York, where it doesn't seem possible that cowboys and ancient Britain and Renaissance Italy can be in the same structure. But if you follow Kantor's point of view, those elements follow their own logic inside that work of art. You divorce them from their original structure, and place them all next to each other, and they only make sense inside of that world. You've made an autonomous work of art.

Kantor also brought principles of abstraction to art: what a straight line means, what a triangle means . . . These are ideas we use all the time in the theater. A triangle is the strongest shape of all in a thrust, right? When you move across a space, a straight line has certain properties, as does a point, when somebody doesn't move. All of these things are the territory of the painter, which he brought to the structure of the theater.

Sounds like an Aristotle of the twentieth century.

Exactly. I really think that if you were to spend your time looking at how he thought about what makes a work of theater and a work of art, you would learn more from Kantor than from anyone else in the twentieth century, except Brecht.

So I don't start with any idea of what a work is going to become. I just pick elements that I'm going to juggle in the poetics of the piece, and figure out how they go together. Then I have something that *only* makes sense to itself. The members of the audience get lost inside of the work, and they're transported; they're lost in the poetics of that individual piece, in the same way they're lost in a Jackson Pollock painting, which is an extraordinary, abstract approximation of cosmic internal life.

Let's talk about that in relation to your *Barber of Seville* at the Met last year, with its yellow doors, and orange trees, and a balcony. You worked with set designer Michael Yeargan, a longtime collaborator with whom you've obviously got a good shorthand. How did you get to that design?

The first idea that occurred to us was: it's a chamber piece. The orchestra pit holds only forty-five pieces. So we came up with the passerelle [a thirty-foot downstage extension of the Met stage, over the pit, putting the singers nearly on top of the first row].

That idea led to thoughts of Strehler, meaning commedia dell'arte. We knew it wasn't going to be a giant realistic design. It had to grow more out of the tradition of commedia, which demands simplicity of form: doors, the two towers and a curtain between them and you could do that opera. By having the curtain, we're paying some homage to the commedia tradition, and some homage to Brecht, too.

So I sat down with these ideas of size and commedia (which often also means a wood floor), along with the fact that Seville is dominated by the color yellow and is overwhelmingly rich in orange trees. We threw those elements in there, we knew the kind of environment we were in, and we began to form a design. The piece began to make its own rules.

A lot of it was built around the character of Bartolo, because he's the engine of the comedy. He's a mean old Pantalone character from the commedia tradition who wants to keep the woman in prison. If you don't get inside Bartolo, you'll never release the comedy of the piece. He has to be a big, horrible force.

So the idea for the opening was to put Bartolo, drunk out of his mind and asleep, in front of sixteen giant yellow doors. The curtain goes up and his servant comes in and wakes him up. Bartolo wants to lock the girl [Rosina] in, so he tries to lock all sixteen doors, but they move on him, and he runs out screaming. Now that's an abstract idea; it's not realistic. To stage this in the overture is immediately saying, "We're not in a realistic world."

All of the doors had people behind them, too, so nothing was mechanized in the way the Met might normally do it. The doors could dance and spin and form a new setting. From the balcony you're suddenly in a street in Seville. All very homey, and within its own logic. Plus some sense of Seville, plus a kind of "souped-up-as-if-John-Galliano-did-the-period" look to the costumes.

Why that?

Because the person of fashion today has the same level of influence as Figaro did in that world. Once we figured out who Figaro was, we realized he was like John Galliano. He's the entrepreneur who's actually running the city. He has a snood and striped pants; he's got this crazy look. It didn't want to be fancy or "period"—*I'm not making statements about the play that you can catch me on.* I'm not saying, "It's all set in 1950." That doesn't make sense to me; it's inside its own world. It only makes sense *inside of itself.* The audience has no choice but to disappear into that world, and in the course of the piece it slowly develops and becomes its own universe.

The same thing happened when it came to *Awake and Sing!*, which was very Kantor-based. I asked André [Bishop, artistic director of Lincoln Center Theater] specifically to do it at the Belasco Theatre, where it had been done originally with the Group Theatre in a very famous production in the 1930s. The Belasco still has the same bathroom fixtures, much of the same décor, so when you walk in there you're walking into the physical context of that period. It was almost like an art installation.

We did the original Boris Aronson set, almost to a "T," initially. And then, in the middle of the second act, the walls *flew.* When the walls flew, we were releasing the piece into a world of poetics, but only once the audience was inside of our logic. By the last act, there were no walls left, just doors; all the things had disappeared, all the color had changed, and now we were in a world that could only be its own. We'd taken it from 1935 all the way to 2006, and transformed it inside our own context.

That moment when the walls flew was very difficult for some people. Some people said, "You can't do that!" You're trying to restructure within the mind because you have a job to help audiences get back to a place of connectedness and poetics. You have to use the evening to take them back to the garden, to take them back to that place where they're open to transformation.

With your *Seville, Cymbeline*, even *Vanya*, audience members know the vocabulary nearly from the moment they walk in the door. *Awake and Sing!* was a switcheroo.

It was partly because we were sitting in such a realistic context, the context of Odets. Each piece is going to have not only its own logic, but its own history.

When I did *Cymbeline* with Theatre for a New Audience down at the Lucille Lortel Theatre, I had no history to build on. When the audience came into that space, they knew it wasn't going to be like a traditional Shakespeare anyway; the space doesn't allow that. It had a red floor and a bunch of doors and a yellow curtain, and that's all it needed. They were in Japanese dress and Renaissance dress. They sang "Sons of the Pioneers" songs at the end of the first act and second acts. Again, that only made sense inside of itself.

Your *Cymbeline* is a good example of the huge shift in Shakespeare productions that's been taking place over the last twenty years. Whereas setting your Shakespeare in a specific time period or motif (like Peter Brook's 1946 *Love's Labour's Lost* in the style of the painter Antoine Watteau) was de rigueur for many years, it's given way in the top Shakespeare companies to something much more Kantor-like: you're demanding the audience work with you to unravel the logic of the design.

If you look at the only extant drawing we have of a Shakespeare play in its own time—a drawing of *Titus Andronicus* that scholars think is from the original production—there are two interesting things about it. First, it can't be any one scene. It's like they drew three scenes in one picture. The other thing you notice is that some people are in Roman clothes, and some people are in Elizabethan clothes—in the same production of *Titus Andronicus*. Now you would *never* see a production that did that. But the Elizabethans were thinking of clothing and time in a completely different way than we do. Shakespeare's sense of time was so fluid. He could put his own time right next to ancient Rome, he could put a clock in Rome—and in a setting that was completely unspecific! He never changed the set. The set was a mechanism for operating the plays. It was a way of switching time quickly. You could come in above, come in below—it had a very cinematic structure. They didn't have that sense of unity and verisimilitude that came in with the Duke of Saxe-Meiningen in the late nineteenth century. That's the idea that controls how our plays go now.

Brecht cracked that later, once realism became deeply absorbed into the culture. He knew that all that stuff had to be changed. And Kantor pushes that further. With Brecht, you could have anything you want as long as it's based on economics or class. And then Kantor pushes it to ask: "What's an autonomous work of art, and what are the rules that belong to an autonomous work of art, and how do we live inside of that?"

Making the audience work harder today—is that advisable? Seems like we live in a pretty conservative climate.

In America, we have a very broad, chaotic cultural context, and don't all share the same background. You have regional differences that are *huge;* you can't rely on audiences having the same educational or historical backgrounds. There's an enormous diversity of points of view—not only ethnic diversity, but diversity in views about what makes a piece of theater at all. So the piece has to have all the information *in it* to transform you. It can't rely on preexisting information.

That's why I divide an evening into parts. The first twenty minutes are unbelievably critical to an audience. Especially now, with people subject to what's referred to as "continual partial awareness." They're completely absorbed by technology. That first twenty minutes is transition to the only time they're in a space of reflection, where they don't have electronic information, when they're not splitting their concentration and are just in a room. What's liable to happen in that first twenty minutes is like a breathing and deprogramming. That's a critical little period of adjustment. I also think it's great if they nap in the first twenty minutes.

You do?

I think it's fantastic, because it'll give them energy for the end of the piece. They can be in a dark room and finally stop their head going; they can fall into a bit of a dream space and revive and be present in the moment when they wake up. It's actually, literally, a biological transformation.

The middle of the play is when they fall into the story, things begin to shift and they're released into the poetics of the piece. And the last fifteen to twenty minutes is a *really golden time* when they may be open enough to experience a deeply poetic idea, one they would never have been prepared to experience in the first twenty minutes. It can return them to a state of connection to language, emotional truth, visual magic . . . to a lot of things.

And I'm talking about something very different from the experiences you get with giant musicals, which only *heighten* that sense of continual partial awareness by rattling the audience inside the cage for two hours, so that they come out of it even more zapped out than when they started. I'm talking about a more lasting and deeper experience. That section of time when the real poetics happens is after you've been pulled into the magic spell of sitting around the campfire, in a community, with a group of new friends, where you might actually be able to listen.

Do you think that kind of Dionysian ecstasy is possible in this world of "continual partial awareness"?

I have to believe that one of the purposes of theater is transcendence. Aesthetic transcendence, where you can be pulled out of yourself. I know it's true when I've seen Pina Bausch; I know it's true when I've seen William Forsythe; I know it's true if I go to a great opera. And people *don't know that's what they want*. You have to make that possible for them. It's what I'm searching for as an artist.

We all know that experience when you're working on something, when you're in the middle of rehearsal, and suddenly it comes into the room, and you know you're on to something deeper in the play. I do think you can, through poetics, through theater, be connected to the world. You can be connected to a deeper sense of the universe; you can be connected to something unnameable.

The audience at most regional theaters today is much more homogenized than the audience at a Grateful Dead concert, and has different cultural expectations. Does that worry you?

I'll use an old Jesuit term. I think people who run regional theaters have a different apostolic mission. We serve a certain section of the culture. There's no kidding anybody that, at least at Intiman, they're middle- and upper-middle-class people. They are as diverse as we can get them. They are often psychologists or lawyers or teachers, or they run small companies. They're all kinds of professionals who connect in their lives with a lot of other people. So we have the apostolic mission of keeping them energized, and connected, and filled with ideas of their own history, the history of who they are as Americans and as human beings.

One woman came up to me after a show at Intiman; she's a cancer care nurse. She goes every day into extreme situations in wards where she takes care of patients at the ends of their lives. She helps keep them comfortable, and monitors their care—she's got a very, very difficult job. And she told me, "I love to come to Intiman because, when I come and participate in these stories, whether they're classics or new plays, they fill me up and give me the spirit to go back to my job. I bring those stories back with me."

So she can see *Our Town,* or *Skin of Our Teeth,* or *Uncle Vanya,* or *To Kill a Mockingbird,* or *Singing Forest,* and have an engagement with other people in her community. She can learn something about her world, she can remember ideas that come from her past, she can have a little taste of transcendence and transformation. And that gives her energy to go back into the world to pass those stories on, to feel connected to other people.

I'm not trying to make it sound "ooky-spooky," but art has a real function in people's lives. It doesn't have to be at Intiman. It could be going down to the Seattle Art Museum. There's a larger way of looking at the world that we must constantly challenge ourselves to see, through art. To me, art and culture are as important as health care in terms of people's long-term sustenance.

The bigger challenge is getting the audience to feel that going to something with a sense of transcendence is as rewarding and enriching as escape. It's not the same as escape; it's not the same as "bread and circuses." It is a little richer, a higher level of adventure. And you have to be brave enough to come in and relax into that.

I always use myself as an example: when I'm tired and I get home, am I going to watch *Indochine* or the TV show "Entourage"? Sometimes I'm going to watch "Entourage." I love "Project Runway." I love all the garbage-can stuff. But at the same time, the really lasting things are, for example, seeing the Piccolo Teatro di Milano do *Servant of Two Masters* in Paris, which fucking *changed my life.*

Americans don't even realize: they spend *all of their time* seeking out artistic experiences. Over and over again. Whether it's watching Ichiro [Suzuki, center fielder for the Seattle Mariners] hit a baseball—which is like a samurai ritual—or watching "Entourage," or going to see *Vanya,* they're constantly engaged in this search. They're just not always connecting!

Let's get back to your personal aesthetic. How did working with Garland Wright alter it? You've said he taught you how to direct in a thrust. What did he tell you?

Garland was a complete artist when it came to directing plays. Being around Garland, one felt an extraordinarily rich mind pulling together a vision of the play from the design to the acting to the staging. He had the benefit of working on the original Guthrie stage, which was essentially the most difficult space I've ever been in. It's a very deep thrust, and it literally took me two years sitting with him, watching him direct plays, before it clicked in my head how these spaces work.

The critical tech-through-previews period is probably where I learned the most from him. He was wonderful at teching. He was efficient; he knew how to keep the movement, the acting and development of the piece moving forward; he had an elegance and a deep sense of how all the parts held together. And then he had a remarkable ability to edit and question himself through the process of previews.

You've said frequently that being mentored by Garland was a seminal experience.

The theater works best in a process of rich apprenticeship. It had begun with Woodruff—who was experimental and rich and rewarding—but Garland was really a true interpreter, a deep interpreter. He got inside the core of what a text and a writer was after, and he expressed it very originally for himself. Watching him, you understood how language and visual movement went together.

Without that experience, there's no way I'd be able to do what I do. Every director, every artist needs somebody they pass through, who's above them, who leads them, who mentors them, who they *watch*. So for me, to move from the crazy experimentation of my young days (and Kantor and Woodruff) into a period of two years to just watch Garland work, pushed me to a completely different place.

Nowadays, artists are tempted to move too quickly. People don't have the patience to really grow, to allow themselves to continue to learn; to step back and go for another period of learning, and see more work, and step back, and move ahead and step back and move ahead, until they really have their own voice. That voice takes decades to develop.

Some young artists are afraid that's going to harm their originality. But what's interesting about artists is that it still goes through the vehicle of who they are. You can imitate this, and look at that, and follow this, and absorb that, and by the time it passes through you it's going to change anyway. So it doesn't hurt for you to absorb as many different things as you can. You could be Picasso absorbing Braque, and then you become a different version of Braque, which leads to another part of you. Or Picasso absorbing African sculpture, and translating that into *Les Demoiselles d'Avignon*.

At what point in your mentorship did you realize what you'd learned?

It was about a year and a half into working with him. Often he would ask himself questions out loud about the piece he was directing, and we

The cast of The Barber of Seville (Il Barbiere di Siviglia) *by Gioachino Rossini, libretto by Cesare Sterbini. Metropolitan Opera, 2006. Credit: Ken Howard.*

would weigh in on them. We were working on a production of *Medea* when, somewhere in the middle, he turned to me quite stumped about what to do in the staging. I offered an idea that was just about as good as his and maybe a little better. And he leapt on that idea and it actually changed and opened up the piece. That was a gigantic day! I was prepared by then to see what he was doing: I processed it through my own developing technique and artistry, and I offered a suggestion that was connected to his but pushed his a little bit along.

All from watching, absorbing, learning.

Watching him give notes, listening to how he talked to actors, taking in the way he led an actor along, the way in which he asked questions of himself, what interested him about a play (which was often very personal, and sometimes quite secret, and you didn't always know). How he moved through rough drafts of scenes into more complete drafts, and then how he had the capacity at the very end to change something completely fundamental that would then rework the whole piece.

Would that change have come out of something he'd just learned?

Yes, some question he might have asked. And he knew how to build in all the textures—he was complete in how he used design through a piece; he was very precise about the relationship of movement to meaning.

Your work is well regarded for its integration of movement, especially in terms of transitions. I'm thinking of the fluidity of the staging of the movement in your *Cymbeline* . . .

Doing four productions of the damn thing gave us the equivalent of those European companies having six months on a show. In the regional theater, if you repeat a production in several places, it gives you that development process. You can get a grip on it, and continue to tweak and change it over time.

We did *Cymbeline* for the first time outdoors at the Idaho Shakespeare Festival, which had a huge impact on its development. Then we brought it to Intiman, reconceived it for the RSC, and when we moved it from the RSC to New York, even then we changed a couple of key costumes. I made major adjustments to the physical context of it, and we were able to deepen it each time.

American directors, by the way, are equivalent to all the great Europeans that I admire so much. Their only obstacles are time and the context in which to continue to work and shape and develop something. But if you can do one thing for a long period of time—put it away for a while, come back to it, reenergize it and go through it again . . . That same thing happened with *The Light in the Piazza*. It started in Seattle, it went to Chicago, it went to New York—it had time to grow. That made a great work of art. The Maly Theater in Moscow gets months to rehearse a play, and they do it all over the world and it gets *great*. It's not that the artists at the Maly Theater know more about theater—they just have more time, and more continuity of expression.

Speaking of *Piazza*, what do you think makes Craig Lucas trust you so much?

We both realize that long-term conversations between collaborators are the real gold of what we do. I've worked with many of the same designers, writers and actors for a long time.

I don't ever remember having a conversation with Craig—and I don't believe in this—in which I told him what his writing needed to do. I am not that kind of interpreter. I don't like to workshop anything. I take a classical approach to it. When you have a Shakespeare play, you don't have rewrites. There are a lot of dead ends, and you have to keep asking yourself questions about why those scenes are where they are. The writer just *goes* somewhere and you have to figure out where he is going.

So Craig gives me plays, I read them and I say, "Okay, let's go. Let's get into rehearsal." I don't say, "Okay, let's workshop it; we're nearly there; maybe after a workshop or two it'll come along." I never know what people mean when they say stuff like that. Because a play is a different thing to me; it's like this expression that pours out of technique and intuitiveness, and when we get in to work with it, *I have to figure it out*. Then the writer comes in and watches, and goes, "Now I know what I need to change." It's not my job to do that.

So I think Craig trusts that he is at the center as a writer. We have very few people that are this gifted, and this experienced, in writing singularly for the theater. We have to honor what they do. I can only imagine that when Alan Schneider was working with Beckett, he didn't get much of a chance to tell him to rewrite. Or David Esbjornson working with Albee: when he gets *The Goat*, he doesn't say, "Oh, can I have a new scene here?"

Why did you decide to commission a new translation of *Vanya* from him?

First, I will never do the British ones. It's a different sound, a different rhythm. I do think there are some very good American ones. But when you have a writer like Craig, and you have a close association, you have to honor that by allowing him the opportunity to take a crack at Chekhov. If we were in England right now, there would be no question that we'd be doing David Hare's version, or Michael Frayn's, or some other contemporary English playwright's.

It was also something I wanted Craig to do for his own development; to get inside such a masterful writer, and see if it would have an impact on his writing. He's got a very good quality with Chekhov; he's got a great deal of his sense of humor, and he's got the brevity. It's very precise. It's very *spoken*: you feel like these are people talking to each other. That's not true of a lot of translations.

So you get that new script, and get into rehearsal—what, then, is the director's task?

In terms of working with actors, I call it "naming." There's a lot of conversation that goes on; some of it seems repetitive, but we're engaged in the effort to "name" *what it is* [whether it's an action, a movement, the world of the play, or the play's full meaning], to build a conversation in which everybody's trying to identify it, to name it.

With actors, specificity and action is the entire game. I try to make it so that the process of rehearsal is about naming the actions, naming all of the parts, naming the specificity, discussing all the history that leads to the moment they're working on, so they have nothing but information at their fingertips to be in the *doing* of the play, not in the *being* of the play.

It sounds exhaustive, and I might talk more than I need to in an effort to engage in the conditions of the play, to expand the conversation around those conditions. My work is often changing in incremental ways all the way along, as it deepens the ability to name what it is.

For example, in *Awake and Sing!*, we went through so many layers with that piece, with those actors, slowly deepening the naming of it, so that by the time I left the production, the movement absolutely supported the layers of specifics that had been named. When I left that production, it could do nothing but continue to deepen; there was no obstacle in the way to its improvement. A director can direct to a point where he actually *prevents* it from getting better.

How does that happen?

It can be as easy as the wrong kind of context. The deeper emotional moment has to be physically prepared for and arrived at in the space. For example, the build of the third act of *Vanya*: we discovered a moment yesterday when Vanya stands on a chair right at the moment when he says the most horrible thing about Serebryakov, to announce it to the world. That move onto the chair was a brand-new idea, and lifted the scene. Mark [Nelson, as Vanya] just found that in our rehearsal.

Now if you develop the whole shape of that scene correctly, all its structure is layered to build up as it goes, so that as Mark moves from the opening through the run and continues to discover things like that, the production will only support his growth. There will be no moment in which, if he comes upon something new, he can't continue to push forward. Part of my job is to create that situation: the confidence of the actors, their confidence in what the movement is, their sharing in the naming of what's going on, to the point where it continues to propel and deepen and get better. That's one layer of what I do.

The other layer is creating context in terms of design, in terms of all of the visual and physical elements of a production. You need to create a context in which those elements are trying to express something in the deeper substructure of the piece. Kantor would say it's not the table, it's the grain of the wood of the table. The table has its own shape, but you're trying to get at the actual grain of the wood.

When a design is at its best, we've created a physical environment that allows the *grain*, the substructure, to emerge above and beyond the external surfaces. Because a lot of design is often very external. You're in the right living room, you're in the right beautiful piazza . . . but that design may not completely open up into the deeper layers of the piece.

For example, take *Piazza*. After Chicago, we made it a *moving* piazza, so all of these towers moved and spun. That was something we discovered in Chicago, in thinking about the journey for Clara when she finds out in the hotel room that there may be something wrong with her, and she runs to Fabrizio to tell him she can't marry him. Adam [Guettel] and I wondered what it was like to run from that hotel room, through the streets of Florence. What was the panic of that like? So we built the swirling design of moving towers. He wrote a beautiful piece of music, and we created a completely open space where it was light, pure light, and her running in a circle. So the piece cracked open into the pure metaphor of light in the piazza for the trauma of this girl trying to make a decision about who she was.

A director can help most with the *space* of a play, and space is not only physical—space is internal. Kantor used to talk about space in many different contexts: space of the imagination, space of childhood, space of memory, space of prison . . . When I first sit down to work, I think, "What's the space where I'm working?"

Last night [in *Vanya*], for example, I changed an entrance from stage right to stage left (to bring the professor in for the big scene), and it had a huge impact. The entrance was shorter, it had a little more pop to it, it pulled him into the space more effectively, and laid the groundwork, in a very quiet way, for the scene.

Things like that are *constantly* my job. I'm allowing the actors to move along; I'm developing a space or a design for the piece; and I'm creating this movement context in which I'm allowing the storytelling to evolve, and asking myself what are the ways that I'm cracking through the crevasses buried deep in the play. It goes back to watching a Grateful Dead concert. What are the ways that I can play, or have them play, that are going to open us into that special territory where we haven't been before?

I can't talk about this in concrete ways, I can't teach this, or explain how I came upon this, but between the influences of Garland's technique, and Kantor's sense of abstraction and painting, and [Wole] Soyinka's sense of ritual, you arrive at a place where you're juggling all the different entrance points to the magic of the theater.

So you begin with all these abstractions, and turn to actors who are looking for something utterly specific.

Yes. Acting can only be built on relationships and questions and specifics. There is a physical life that's required of them, and a layering of the physical life, but the specifics and the context have to be there all the time.

Probably the best example is with opera singers. The more you give them specifics, the better the singing gets. If the aria is given a context in which I can emotionally understand it, that aria *has* to be there at that moment. I've gotten to a place where I'm connecting both the incredibly rich and ethereal pure nature of the singing with specifics of the human situation. That creates the need for an aria.

How do you run your rehearsals?

I'm pretty organic. I don't start with an image of the character that I'm going to lead the actor to. I don't work that way; I don't think that far ahead. When I audition, I spend a lot of time making sure I'm going to have a decent collaborator as well as a perfect person for the part. Often I will build a role around a person rather than make them get to the role. I'm not about cracking them and opening them up and getting them to a new place in their work. There may be great acting teachers who know how to do that, but I can't do that.

I don't spend a lot of time at the table either. I find that tablework becomes a lot of conversations with people telling other people what they know about something that nobody needs to hear about. Even in the case of Shakespeare, I'll spend time getting everyone on the same page when it comes to the language, and I'll make sure we have a certain number of assumptions, but really, the deeper information isn't going to come until you get on your feet and struggle with it.

So we're on our feet usually quite quickly, stumbling around in the dark, building a shape—at least a beginning shape that gives me information about the physical life of the piece. People have to trust that the first two or three weeks—and particularly the first runthrough—are liable to be the most excruciating experiences in their lives. You've got to have patience. One will *always* panic at some point in the middle of a production—that you haven't got it, that you're not any good, that it'll never work. But those first runthroughs are like "source points" for identifying what questions you need to ask to go to the next place.

Even now—after four weeks and three previews—I'm just finding in *Vanya* that the scene in the second act between Astrov and Sonya is beginning to make sense.

What have you learned?

It has everything to do with obstacles.

If you can be very specific about the obstacle a character is pushing against—what *doesn't* allow them to do something, what *prevents* them from saying something, what gets them to *not* be able to express something—you create the context in which the actual conflict of the scene may start to release. In the case of Astrov and Sonya, I've been misreading where Astrov is when he enters the scene, in terms of how furious and fed up he is with the house. It's been sitting in a kind of reflective place, and I need to create a bigger obstacle for Sonya to overcome: convincing him that he's good. In a way, it's the lowest point in the play for him when he says, "I don't love anybody, I don't care about this stuff, I can't stand being in this house, I hate all of our friends, I don't know what the hell's going on!" He's in that mean, miserable state you get to late in being drunk. I haven't actually evaluated that properly. I've been sucked into the "poor boy who doesn't love anybody," what's wrong with him, and how she cares about him. If I don't create the right obstacle there, I'm finishing the play too early.

But that's not known at the beginning. When I do it the second time, I'll know—which is one of the reasons I like to do productions over again. I'm not hard on actors for not knowing, because I don't know half the time. It's an active pursuit. I get very uncomfortable with colleagues who talk about what they know about an actor, and leading them to something, like they're some Svengali.

It's been said you can be tough on actors . . . do you agree?

I come from a big family, so I'm really loud and not afraid of conflict. If we disagree, *I will keep fighting.* Conflict is a source of growth. I'm not warm and fuzzy; I'm not good at slowly bringing them along. I talk a lot, we bang ourselves against it, we screw stuff up and I let people know it's not going so well . . . I'm very straightforward about where we are in the process. If an actor has a meltdown, and we start screaming at each other, and we get somewhere difficult, I don't mind that. I don't *enjoy* it. But I don't think that's bad for the process.

That may lead to why people think I'm hard on actors, because I will be straightforward about what isn't happening. But actors will always believe there's no buried agenda from me, because I'll keep it out on the surface.

Does running an institution help or hinder your artistry?

I don't think anyone who works in the theater over a long period of time can do it without a home. One of the other things I learned from Garland was how to be an artistic director. He made a choice in his life not to be a freelance director in New York (which he easily could have done with great success), and instead led an institution, and built a life in a community with his work.

We bring arts into a community, and people come into the theater to be energized and changed by stories that involve them, to have experiences of joy or sorrow or transcendence that are shared by the nine thousand people who are subscribers here. It is a community that loves to support the arts and in which I can experiment and develop as an artist, and into which I can bring other artists. We can use the resources of this home to have conversations, and to have an impact on the culture.

The elections in 2000 and 2004 were so bruising culturally that Laura Penn, my managing partner, and I came up with an initiative called the American Cycle, a series of great American stories and public programs over five years. It seemed to us that one of the things the theater can do is bring the stories that inform who we are (which was getting confusing) and put them on the stage to *remind* us. We did *Our Town* and *The Grapes of Wrath* and *Native Son,* and we're doing *To Kill a*

Mockingbird this year, as a way to keep people in an engaged conversation about what it means to be an American, to remind people of how kids learn about injustice—why fighting against injustice is an American value, and why we believe in it. When a bunch of schoolkids come in, they engage that question, and it becomes part of their story of what it means to be an American.

Another example of the way that theater can make a difference is *Nickel and Dimed*. I read the book *Nickel and Dimed* by Barbara Ehrenreich. As an old lefty, I thought I understood the conditions of living-wage workers. But this was something I just plain didn't know. I had gotten so bourgie and middle-class that I had lost track of what happens to a hotel worker, what the waitress is like at a Denny's, what might be true of maids who work at people's houses. I felt in some ways shamed by the book, and it seemed to me to make sense as a piece we could do in the theater. So we commissioned and developed it very quickly—Joan Holden wrote a marvelous adaptation—and it had an enormous impact on our theater and our community.

Now I only did that because *I* didn't get it, and I thought it had to be something we should talk about. That's something a theater can do. Theaters shouldn't just recycle what's happening Off Broadway, but actually look around and ask, "What is in my community, and what actually affects me? Maybe I can be in the world a little bit more."

Surely it wears you down running a not-for-profit, though.

I think you develop a lot of resilience and faith that it's going to be okay. And there are people who have a lot more faith in the arts than I do: boards of directors, subscribers, people who make small contributions, who are very valiant and courageous in their belief in this stuff. In a way I just have to believe in them: that they love the work enough, and they believe it's important to their community. Their sense of the missions of these places and what they want in their communities always embarrasses me because it's so much greater than mine in some ways. Because I can go into this incredibly dark artist place, where it's all going to come to an end and we're all going to die . . . but those people don't!

You told *Opera News* you would love to "assemble an example of American artists in a contemporary context in the theater making work as great as anyone can see in the world, right here. This is a political act." Why political?

Being an American is about democracy and ideas and expression, from Emerson to Hawthorne, from Wilder to Miller. So it's vital we keep alive the idea of great theater artists making great work, especially in our current context: the culture is shriveling up into a rampant, capitalist, individualistic, narcissistic universe. It is extremely critical to keep the idea alive that artists make vital cultural contributions. So in every community, whether it's Seattle or Chicago or Los Angeles, intelligent and expressive artistic accomplishment keeps democracy vibrant. And it keeps the citizenry engaged.

That engagement now is very much up in the air. Whether or not people want to stay engaged is a serious question. They're disappearing into all kinds of other opiates and opportunities to forget, or they get pulled in their minds into the logic of the extreme right wing, or the logic of the extreme left wing. Whatever it is, it doesn't allow them to continue to engage. So it's part of our job to keep them questioning, to keep them actively engaged in their culture and in their communities so there's belief in the future. That's an essentially American activity.

I don't think there's any guarantee that we'll survive as a function-ing culture. So artists have a responsibility for keeping our shared memory alive of whoever we think we were, and whoever we are going to become.

In previous articles, writers have spoken of your incredible optimism. Are you at a different place now? Are you more pessimistic?

I'm an enormous advocate of the potential of regional theater and its vibrant investments in communities. But I do think—and maybe it's recent—that there's an exhaustion in our communities about trying to identify who and what America is. They're exhausted by the struggle between the right and left; they see no clear sense of where we're going. More artists need to engage the question of who we are *right now* to take us to the next place. Theaters have to continue to believe they are a *source* of engagement and dialogue. They have to keep investing in that all the way across the country, because if that isn't maintained, we really will not survive. There just isn't a functioning apparatus in place to keep reminding us at a core level of what it means to be American. That question has to resurface because there has to be some sense of unity and connection. Artists are always the people asking the questions and taking fire and wondering aloud, either through the classics or new plays, "Who are we?" We don't know who we are because we've been so damaged by the struggle between right and left since 1990. In America (in which I believe deeply, deeply, deeply) the theater (in which I also believe deeply) has a major role to play in asking that question.

JULIE TAYMOR

Shaman of the Stage

MUCH HAS BEEN WRITTEN AT GREAT length about Julie Taymor. Putting such a peripatetic artist in context is dauntingly difficult: are we speaking about the Tony Award—winning director of *The Lion King* or the filmmaker of *Titus*, *Frida* and *Across the Universe*? Perhaps we want to look at the internationally regarded opera director or the Shakespeare revisionist? Or maybe we should start where she began—in Indonesia— with masks, dance and those fantastic puppets?

For one whose artistic journey has been so eclectic, Taymor has pursued her path with singular focus—and from a very young age. Born in the Boston suburbs in 1952 to progressive parents, the young Taymor exhibited an interest in performance that was much more professional, much earlier and more full of intellectual inquiry than anyone you're likely to meet. By age ten she was attending the culturally diverse and aesthetically adventurous Boston Children's Theatre. Her fascination with exploring other cultures started early, too, and was fed by a summer abroad to India and Sri Lanka during high school.

"Precocious" hardly begins to describe the young woman who graduated from high school at age fifteen and immediately joined an avant-garde theater troupe to delve into ensemble-created work (as was the rage in the late 1960s). "Driven" doesn't capture the quality of that same young woman who, a year later, decided she needed more rigorous physical training and headed to Paris because she'd heard about a French master of corporeal mime named Etienne Decroux. "Ambitious" doesn't explain the varied experiences of Taymor at Oberlin College, which included off-campus residencies in New York with Joseph Chaikin's Open Theater and Peter Schumann's Bread and Puppet Theater, and, finally, work with the ensemble of avant-garde director and theorist Herbert Blau, who himself had taken up residence at Oberlin.

Upon acceptance into Blau's troupe in 1972, Taymor was subjected to intense physical and mental training. The group made collective theater based on folklore and myth (*Electra* in the first year, the Donner Party story in the second), and in doing this work, Taymor encountered the "ideograph": a physicalization that metaphorically suggests the essence of a character, scene or story. Representing the childless Electra, for example, Taymor would repeatedly pat her belly and then hold out her hands. Pina Bausch's work is full of many such ideographs, as is JoAnne Akalaitis's, Anne Bogart's and Robert Wilson's; all of these artists use gestures as concentrated packages of meaning to direct the audience's dramaturgical reading of the play. Even commedia dell'arte works via a system of ideographs: the hunched-over, hook-nosed Pantalone character or the patch-clad Arlecchino with his slapstick and distinctive gait.

After her work with Blau, Taymor needed to put together all she'd learned as a director, and she found that opportunity in Indonesia. Four years (1974–1978) of nearly constant residence there (during which she apprenticed herself to W. S. Rendra and created her own company, Teatr Loh, a name that means "the source" in literary Balinese and "oh my God!" in everyday Indonesian) exposed Taymor to various performance forms in action: Javanese wayang golek [rod puppets]; topeng [masked] dance-drama; wayang kulit [shadow puppetry], many of which she'd studied while at college. The two major works she created in Indonesia (*Way of Snow* and *Tirai*, restaged in New York in 1980 and 1981, respectively) suggested, even in their raw exploration of these new worlds, a maturation of the ideograph form. Taymor's ideographs began to travel far beyond simple evocative gesture, and her staging displayed an overriding metaphorical intelligence. When Taymor says the ideograph of *The Lion King* is "the circle," she's speaking with a highly evolved sense of the word beyond what Blau taught her—to her, "ideograph" encompasses gesture, but also every element of design, performer movement, floor pattern and text.

Taymor's Indonesian accomplishments brought her to the attention of some important New York theaters when she returned in 1978, and led to a major design commission from the New York Shakespeare Festival: *Haggadah*, on which she collaborated with composer/director

Elizabeth Swados in 1980. In addition to garnering lots of press for Taymor, *Haggadah* introduced her to composer Elliot Goldenthal, who would become her creative and personal partner.

With *Haggadah*, Taymor's interest in controlling—or directing— the entire stage picture was reaching a critical mass. Her design and choreography work on Andrei Serban's *King Stag* at American Repertory Theater in Cambridge, Massachusetts, four years later (in 1984) would be the last time Taymor did not sit in the director's seat (though she now frequently collaborates with designers on her productions).

The success of *King Stag* finally brought her projects in New York City that allowed the kind of creative freedom she'd enjoyed in Indonesia: the musical *Liberty's Taken* at American Place Theatre in 1985 and the fantastical allegory *Juan Darién: A Carnival Mass* for Music Theatre Group in 1988, later revived at Lincoln Center (both were created with Goldenthal's music). A very important partnership with Theatre for a New Audience began in 1986 with *The Tempest, The Taming of the Shrew* a year later and, most significantly, *Titus Andronicus* in 1994. Taymor's love affair with that gruesome play resulted in her first feature film five years later, *Titus,* starring Anthony Hopkins.

In the meantime, the world of opera opened to Taymor in a huge way. While *Juan Darién* was a chamber work with operatic elements, it was nothing compared to *Oedipus Rex,* the Stravinsky oratorio that master conductor Seiji Ozawa asked Taymor to direct in 1992 for the Saito Kinen Festival in Japan. With a company of more than one hundred performers—including noted diva Jessye Norman—*Oedipus* provided a grand canvas for her vision; her film of the performance earned her an Emmy Award (for costume design) the following year. The opera's success paved the way for her to continue her innovative staging at major opera houses of more traditional repertoire, such as *The Magic Flute* at the Maggio Music Festival in Italy in 1993 and later at the Metropolitan Opera House, *Salome* at the Kirov Opera in 1995, *The Flying Dutchman* at the Los Angeles Opera in 1995, and the apex of this strand of her career, the two-city 2006 premiere at Los Angeles Opera and New York's Lincoln Center Festival of *Grendel,* which she and Goldenthal had been developing since 1988.

And then came *The Lion King* for Disney Theatricals on Broadway in 1997. The first woman to win the Tony for Best Direction of a Musical was suddenly empowered with overwhelming commercial success, a success clearly built upon decades of more rarified, avant-garde, intercultural exploration. Overnight, she became a hero to theater makers in the not-for-profit world; the wizard who succeeded in uniting art and commerce. Taymor recognizes *The Lion King* as a major turning point for her—not just for its artistry (which was prodigious and of which she is rightly proud), but because it allowed her access to the kinds of collaborators and producers that make truly epic productions possible.

More triumphs blending art and commerce followed for Taymor with film, which demands that the landscape partner with narrative to tell the story. Both *Titus* and *Frida* (her 2002 biopic about Mexican artist Frida Kahlo) possess incredibly tight visual palettes, yet Taymor seems to find a near-infinite variety of images, camera angles and shots, and spectacular worlds within each one. Taymor manipulates the medium to bring narrative to life in unexpected ways; the medium never manipulates her, as frequently happens when theater directors turn to filmmaking.

But Taymor was manipulated, and to disastrous effect, with *Spider-Man: Turn Off the Dark* in 2011. Any artist reading this volume likely knows the contours of the story: that Taymor began work on the musical in 2002 with U2's Bono and the Edge; that by the time Michael Cohl became lead producer in 2009, its budget was tens of millions of dollars beyond what was originally envisioned; that the piece had the longest preview period in Broadway history; that the previews were plagued by cast injuries and toxic early reviews, both in online gossip rooms and major newspapers; that Taymor was fired (or asked to leave, or left herself) in March 2011, four months after previews had begun; that the musical finally opened three months later, having cut some of Taymor's inventions (among them, a "geek chorus" framing the show and the central place of Arachne, a mythological figure from Ovid inserted by Taymor). Along the way, Taymor's production became the butt of late-night television jokes, gossip column fodder and even source material for a satirical *New Yorker* cover.

Taymor's artistic vision for the work was easily lost in the boorish avalanche of ink that was spilled about *Spider-Man*. "Why She Fell," an article in *The New York Review of Books* in May 2011 by Daniel Mendelsohn, tries to pick apart the threads of Taymor's past to understand it. He doesn't avoid the personal attacks, but at least he recognizes how Taymor's longstanding fascination with ritual transformation on stage (both narrative, like a jaguar turning into a boy in *Juan Darien*, and formal, like the blending of human body and mask in *The Lion King* and elsewhere) harmonized with *Spider-Man*'s archetypal roots: a geeky boy transforming—through a strange and theatrical magic—into a hero. Though he salutes many of her achievements, Mendelsohn finally concludes:

> At the heart of the *Spider-Man* disaster is the essential incompatibility of those two visions of physical transformation—the ancient and the modern, the redemptive and the punitive, visions that Taymor tried, heroically but futilely, to reconcile.

Notwithstanding *Spider-Man*, Taymor has succeeded in doing just that, over and over again, throughout her career. Her genius lies in uniting the power of ancient ritual with the possibilities of contemporary theater, and if she did not succeed with *Spider-Man*, it would be a grave disservice to forget how thoroughly her ambitions have changed the theatrical landscape around her. Broadway musicals may be forever influenced by her *Lion King*. Since its 2004 opening at the Metropolitan Opera, her *Magic Flute* has become part of its repertoire, and Western theater has opened itself up to the visual and the primal since she first brought what she learned in Indonesia back to the United States in the 1970s.

The landscape of these genres has been changed *literally* by Taymor's work because, for her, *the landscape itself tells the story.* She put it quite simply during the Metropolitan Opera telecast of *The Magic Flute* in 2007: "Design is storytelling. It's not something extra."

Historically, Western stage design has served the story at a remove (even the word "setting" suggests a secondary artistic element, in service to the primacy of spoken narrative). Some of Taymor's most thrilling and resonant work turns this idea on its head: the lush, vivid costume that turns the Dragon in *Grendel* into a tongue tells more about the character than the words; the visual repetition of circles in *The Lion King* (the gazelle puppets' gracefully circular forms, for example, or the oncoming wildebeest herd portrayed on rolling cylinders) does more to suggest a circle of life than does the show's most famous song.

Taymor's experience of Eastern cultures, her skilled artistry with physical forms and her ferocious intellect (which enables her to locate concise metaphor in a text with extreme precision) are what alchemize ordinary performance into the feasts of visual narration for which she is known. She's even created a word, "essencing," to describe the way she culls an idea or image from a variety of traditions and transports it to her unique performance culture. How did she know Stravinsky and butoh dance would form a greater whole in her *Oedipus Rex*? Or that a quasi-operatic score for her and Elliot Goldenthal's South American fantasia, *Juan Darién,* would be well served by Javanese shadow-puppet interjections?

I met Taymor for the first part of this interview in 2003 at the gold-leaf, white-glove Peninsula Hotel in Chicago, where she was staying for the launch of *The Lion King*'s national tour. With its colonialist symbols and stereotypically "Oriental" service, the Peninsula was a far, ironic cry from her accommodations in Indonesia as a young woman, where she spent her most formative theatrical years sleeping under banana trees, nursing various tropical diseases, while creating her first theatrical spectacles.

After I'd had a few hours of conversation with her, even the smallest of Taymor's artistic choices began to seem inevitable: "Of course," I thought, "The mustache on the Señor Toledo figure in *Juan Darién* mimics his whip," or, "Lavinia's hands become twigs—metaphorical 'stumps'—in *Titus* because the hand is that work's primary symbol." Spectacle and story become so intertwined in Taymor's work that one could not exist without the other.

But to watch a Taymor production is something else entirely: it is to be continually mystified and surprised. Nothing feels inevitable, because nothing is expected. Take the opening parade of *The Lion King* during the song "Circle of Life." Though influenced by many traditions and many cultures, the visual storytelling elicits a primal response, with many audience members moved to tears. As Taymor put it in our conversation: "It's not a sad moment; it's a joyous moment . . . *The Lion King* calls upon the power of the artist to create and identify beauty. That's the shamanistic function of artists."*

MAY 2003, PENINSULA HOTEL, CHICAGO

How did you know that you wanted to go study with Jacques Lecoq at age sixteen? That seems mighty precocious.

I started really young in the theater with the Boston Children's Theatre, and then with Theater Workshop of Boston, which was run at that time by Julie Portman and Barbara Linden, creating *Riot* and then *Creation*. It was the theater in the 1960s that was aligned most with Peter Brook and Jerzy Grotowski and the Living Theatre, and physicality was a huge part of it. I found then that I had a very good, strong sense of movement and dance. But I just felt we weren't getting any technique, any discipline. I had a vague idea that there was something called "mime," but I didn't know about Lecoq. I went over to study with Etienne Decroux; but when I got there, I heard through the grapevine that there was this guy Lecoq, and it seemed like I should just go with him.

What sparked your interest in other cultures? How did you know you had to leave Boston to learn what you needed?

By the time I graduated high school early, I'd already traveled. I'd already been to Sri Lanka, I had a real thirst for travel, and I had parents who were very liberal in letting me go at that young age. So I just did. It

---

*I am deeply indebted to Taymor's beautiful book about her work, *Playing with Fire* (Abrams, 1995), in the writing of this introduction. Cowritten with Eileen Blumenthal, the book was republished in 2007 with much new material.

wasn't that I knew a whole lot about it, but I thought, "I want to go and study and have a discipline."

Did you consciously realize you were packing your bag with so many different tools—which you obviously rely on in nearly everything you do—or did it just happen that way?

I don't think I thought about it that way. I think the curiosity was so great, and the desire for something solid. I wasn't interested in being an actress, in going the traditional route and playing in plays. I was already interested, indoctrinated, in the thirst for a new way to create theater— and in the way it took Meredith Monk or Robert Wilson or any of the artists at that time to places outside. Robert Wilson went to Shiraz, Iran; Meredith went to Japan; Ariane Mnouchkine went to India. There was an opening up of the minds of theater directors, the idea that Asia had a lot to offer in terms of theater styles. It was the first time we were seeing this work—not noh and kabuki and the classical, but [postwar performance like] butoh, and there was an amazement at the contemporary theater coming out of Japan. And the classical theater out of India and Indonesia was tremendously inspired and inspiring.

That summer, after I came back from Paris, I went to Oberlin and worked with Herbert Blau on a continuation of the Grotowski technique.

Where you primarily acted?

Yes, acted and designed. Then I studied at the American Society for Eastern Arts one summer in Seattle, which was an introduction to Javanese shadow puppetry and Balinese topeng [mask] dance, and that's when I really got a desire to go further and study Asian theater.

In *Playing with Fire* you say that it was W. S. Rendra in Indonesia who first encouraged you to become a "director" in the sense we understand it. What do you think he saw in you that made him suggest that?

Probably a self-directed individual. I was working in his company as a choreographer. I'd already done some directing work; I'd conceived and directed *Peer Gynt* at Oberlin. And I'd always been a director in my spirit, even if I was an actress. The thing with Blau's company is that all seven people were responsible for creating the piece. So it wasn't that I'd been someone who was just a tool, a musical instrument. I'd always been responsible for the content. I guess Rendra found out that I had these ideas for *Way of Snow* [which Taymor created in Indonesia in the late 1970s and brought to New York in 1980], and he just gave me the people and the space and the encouragement to do it.

Did you discover new talents in yourself on that production?

I think you find that on every single thing you do. If you're pushing boundaries and you're trying to do something you've never seen, you don't know what you're going to get. Almost every production surprises me. If I knew it already, I wouldn't do it. There are things I repeat, techniques I repeat, the flying birds and whatnot. But I enjoy going to places that I've never been. And then you find out what you can and cannot do.

Your journey has been so varied as an artist. Were there turns and surprises? Were there things you never expected to happen?

Opera. I wasn't looking for *Oedipus Rex*. To be asked to do that production [at the Saito Kinen Festival in Japan] without a whole lot of background: why would Seiji Ozawa take such a chance? *The Lion King* hadn't happened yet; all he knew was that I was a young woman who had lived in Asia for four years and worked with Asian theater forms. But Seiji took a humongous risk—much more than the producers of *The Lion King* took—in having me do a new festival with the greatest opera singers in the world: Bryn Terfel, Jessye Norman, Philip Langridge. And then I brought in Min Tanaka [a butoh choreographer]. Elliot [Goldenthal,

The cast of Juan Darien *by Julie Taymor and Elliot Goldenthal. Music-Theatre Group, 1988. Credit: Donna Gray.*

Taymor's longtime collaborator] would say that in many ways it's probably my best theater work.

I love *The Lion King*, I adore it, but as far as something almost perfect on almost every level, *Oedipus* is the one I would pick, because it's Stravinsky, it's Cocteau, it's *Oedipus Rex*! It's all those things, plus the greatest performers in the world! You can see the film of it, and I like the film, but the theatrical production was far superior to the film.

It was also amazing working with a diva for the first time. I've worked with great, great actors: Jessica Lange and Edward Norton and Geoffrey Rush, so I've gotten over that hump. But that was the first time, and I found that the convictions of my ideas were what got me through. A lot of people said, "Jessye's not going to wear a mask, and she's not going to go on that eight-foot platform that ascends fifty feet into the flies . . ." Just shut up already! If I believe in what I think is the right concept, then I'm sure she'll be inspired, which is *the way it was*. You know, good talent loves talent, so you can give talented performers the most outlandish and outrageous ideas. If the ideas are sound and good, they'll do them. And I think Jessye saw there was a good grounding in my concepts for *Oedipus* that were coming from the text, and from Cocteau and Stravinsky's original concept. It wasn't laying another gimmicky thing on top of them. It was really what their work was about. So she was very supportive and we had a wonderful time.

So the opera world was one surprise. I'd always wanted to do film, so that wasn't a surprise, but it was something I had to build and work toward at the right time. I grew up in the theater, so it's been easier and cheaper to do theater; film costs so much. But I'm doing films, and opera; I'm staying in all three.

What did you learn in your four years in Indonesia that you still carry with you in all those forms?

From Blau and Lecoq, the concept of the ideograph is pretty fundamental in the way I think and work. And that is about trying to get to an essence, often a set design concept—for *The Lion King* that is obviously "the circle"; in *The Magic Flute* we're playing with the Masonic symbols. With actors it's trying to get them to see themselves in *essences* and *abstraction*, even if you're doing naturalism.

Though my film *Titus* has a lot of style, the acting is very real. And yet there were moments when I worked with Anthony Hopkins in the same way I worked with Bob Stattel [who played the title role in her stage production of *Titus Andronicus*]: we found an ideograph. We talked about the image of hands. You go through the Shakespeare play, and you say, "What is the strongest motif that repeats itself over and over?" And it's the image of the hands.

What does a hand mean? It's the blessing, it's the power. And when you don't have your hands, what *do* you have? It goes into what Lavinia is about. Shakespeare's constantly using this imagery. Tony Hopkins had this hand gesture, an ideograph that you can see in the first scene with Lavinia. You watch him do this gesture with his hand, and it's an ideograph. Now, I saw Hopkins do this in other films; he does things with his hand, you can see he's a man who understands the power of gesture. But it's especially powerful throughout the movie *Titus*.

It is always tricky, to get the balance. In *The Lion King,* the biggest challenge for the actors is to balance the humanity of their characters with the physical ideograph. Like I keep telling the young men who play Simba, "You're a teenager, you're a rebellious teenager; I want that spirit . . . *with the movement of a lion* in stylized gesture and dance." (I got a lot of my movement information from my time in Indonesia, because mask work there is so good.) In the original production, we even had a wonderful Javanese dancer work with a few of the principals to help them understand the gestures of the body. There's a constant back-and-forth where you can have these movements, through which they tell the story without words, and then they break out of that. It's the dialogue back-and-forth that makes the performance so dynamic and interesting. If it's all stylized, it lacks direct human emotion. *The Lion King* is very much rooted in colloquial language; it's not poetic language. So you're dealing with human, real, familiar characters, but they're in the guise of something that's completely stylized.

The tradition in this country isn't about physicalizing and gesture. How do you talk about ideographs with the actors?

When we worked on the play *Titus Andronicus,* I spent a lot of time on that. Before we even started the table reading, we first opened up the ideas of the play. I let every actor be a part of the *whole* before he became the *singular,* his own part. So the issues of violence, vengeance, all of the themes of the piece are opened, and you're using your body as a landscape artist. You're not there to play it as a personal player in the story; you're there to explore. And that gives me as a director ideas for physical scenography.

The Transposed Heads [1984, as a play, at the Ark Theatre, New York; 1986, as a musical, at Philadelphia's American Music Theatre Festival and Lincoln Center, New York] was based on the most classic ideograph I've ever done. It's on friendship (it's hard to describe an ideograph in words). It came out of improvisation. The two best friends created an ideograph of two men whose arms were clasped together, with their feet close together, at the base . . . and it created the image of a heart, and a triangle. They're holding on to each other, but it's about balance, so if one pulls a little more, they fall. It's a brilliant visualization of what camaraderie and true friendship is. It's very fragile, because it's all about balance; and the way they got into it was very much like a high-five, a naturalistic moment. The ideograph evolved like a musical motif in an opera or symphony, over the course of the drama. Just like in film, images have a power to change how the audience *feels*.

I don't think people are doing this enough in film. I feel very strongly that there should be many more choices about how the camera tells the story in a scene. Why are you in a close-up when you should be in a long shot? What do you do when you're farther away? What is it when you just stay on a shot and don't have a lot of cutting back and forth? You look at my movie *Frida;* it's very, very deliberately conceived (*Titus,* too) in terms of camera movement.

In the theater, you remain in a long shot, for the most part. Of course in my theater, like *The Lion King,* there are little close-ups. You go from the big circle to the little circle, which focuses people on the intimacy, helps you get to the personal, the individual.

I came to that film equivalent in theater very naturally, because I was attracted to epic stories, whether it was *The Haggadah* with Elizabeth Swados, or *Juan Darién,* or Shakespeare. I'm not one who has done little, five-character plays. I'm interested in how you balance the intimacy of the story with its grand and epic nature. It's about *focus.*

With so many watershed moments in your career, which stand out for you the most?

The ones I love are *Oedipus, The Lion King, Juan Darién.* I was disappointed that *The Green Bird* [1996, Theatre for a New Audience, New Victory Theater and La Jolla Playhouse] didn't last longer on Broadway [in 2000]. It needed a lot more support to stay there, because people didn't know what it was, but it was really special. We had one producer who didn't want to spend the time and money to keep it going.

Elliot and I felt really strongly that with *The Green Bird* going to Broadway, you needed two stars in the two unmasked roles, because it's not a known thing like *The Lion King.* If there's no Antonio Banderas in *Nine,* or Bernadette Peters in *Gypsy,* or Nathan Lane in *The Producers,* people *will not go.* But the producer felt, "No, *you're* the star, you know, *The Lion King.*" Yeah, but it's *not The Lion King!* So that's what happened: people came expecting *The Lion King.* It was a very big mistake.

When I created *The Transposed Heads,* it was Off-Off Broadway! You know, spit and a dime and maximum $400. I had a novella and no script. And because I had experience making work from scratch with Blau (and even before that at the Theater Workshop of Boston, and with my own work [in the late 1970s] in Indonesia, *Tirai* and *Way of Snow),* it was comfortable starting without a script, with three or four actors. Even if they didn't have that experience, I could train them how to think conceptually with their bodies. A director is also a grand editor. You don't necessarily start with a script, but you start with a concept, a story, imagery, ideas.

That's a way I had worked with Blau: the writer didn't come first, but the actors' participation and involvement, what they brought to the table, was instrumental in telling the story. That really can't happen within a commercial and union-oriented environment. We don't have the money to pay for it. In the commercial six-week rehearsal period, it's just not possible.

What do you focus on in that rehearsal period?

I think this is kind of obvious, but often people play an *idea* of a character. As an example, let's take Scar, the evil brother in *The Lion King*. You can't play the *evil*, because he doesn't think he's evil. You have to play the full dimensionality. And this is something I think is very successful about *Titus:* that every single character, even Aaron the Moor and those two brothers, defined the *reasons*, the *fully three-dimensional reasons*, why he committed the crime, and how he felt about it.

I'm very much against playing the comedy, playing the *idea* of a character. Instead, find the vulnerability, and believe in your character's cause. You've got to see the larger picture. If you get bogged down in shtick—I'm really talking *The Lion King* right now, because I know all the pitfalls of doing that production—you undercut the power of the story, and there *is* a power to the story; it's not only sheer entertainment.

I think being a director is mostly being a psychiatrist—a psychiatrist who's got good ideas! Even on a film . . . I did three weeks of rehearsal on *Titus,* and two weeks of rehearsal with Salma Hayek and Fred Molina on *Frida*. And it was *absolutely fundamental* in both cases. Salma and Fred in particular, because he had a lot of experience, but she hadn't been given a role of this kind of weight—*no* woman, *no* actor's been given . . . it's an enormous role. When you have scenes like those in *Frida* between Frida and Diego, or Trotsky and Diego, you need more time. And it was an extraordinary thing to see Salma blossom as an actress and become confident. She's a tremendous improviser, and we did a lot of improvisation, and if I liked her dialogue, I actually wrote it down—it wasn't Shakespeare; we could really create new words.

But you do tailor to each actor. In *Titus* I had people who had never done Shakespeare or even live theater! The woman [Laura Fraser] who played Lavinia had never done theater, and neither had Jonathan Rhys Meyers. Jessica Lange had never done Shakespeare. We had a wonderful woman, Cicely Berry, working on text. Cicely was very important, especially for people like Hopkins, who really didn't want to do Shakespeare again: he loved working with her. Individually they would work with her on honoring the poetry, but letting it be language, *letting it just be dialogue*. And with me, they'd work on what was the heart of each scene.

In rehearsals, you get to a point when you just can't do it anymore because you need to be in the *real place*: the mud on the street, on the crossroads, has to inform what you do. But when young directors say they don't want to rehearse because they want spontaneity, they're full of bullshit. They're just terrified of actors, that's all *that* is. When you take the time, you've actually opened up a world; you've allowed the actors to experiment and to journey and to explore *without* the pressure of time and money, and they become more intimate with each other.

What kind of mistakes have you made as a director?

Well, it's hard to say. In film, you have such a lack of time, sometimes you make a mistake because you haven't really explored it in depth. You could have taken another tactic or track.

I find there are so many mistakes—the mistake of being too clear, having the camera work be too beautiful, of things being almost too thought-out sometimes. Film is much more spontaneous than theater, because you just have to act on your feet. If there are problems, you have to change it that day—*boom*—you do it, it's done. And that's a beautiful thing. Theater is so much about repetition in the process that the biggest danger is staleness for the company. Because you get it to be a certain way, and then you want it to remain that way, and it's just against human nature to repeat itself exactly.

And if an actor is not with you on the same page, that's a challenge. Even if I have a very strong idea about how I want it to sound, I try *not* to give line-readings, but to make it feel, even if it's not, as if it is coming from the actor. If they feel it's come from them, then they own it, and it's got a much more profound depth to it. If they're mimicking what they think you want, then I'm not sure you can trust it.

With Hopkins I went through a bit of a struggle, but I think our struggle was like two rocks: ultimately they rub against each other and make fire (as opposed to a dish rag and a rock, which make nothing). My mistake on that was that I had directed *Titus Andronicus* with Bob Stattel on the stage, and many of my ideas came from that collaboration. Even though I had a more in-depth understanding of *Titus* (because I had spent the time and Hopkins hadn't), I still had to be much more receptive to what Hopkins would bring. Sometimes I'd want too many specific things, because I'd heard them in my head too long. I had to really find a balance between what I wanted, and what I didn't know would come. And I think it's a great performance, because *he* got pushed and *I* got pushed. He took huge risks; we *both* did. He didn't get away with murder; a couple of times, he'd say, "That was really shitty today, can we do a reshoot?" It's very costly to do a reshoot. But I said, "You're right, because you were fighting this or that," so we'd go back and try to do it another way. People think actors give great takes every time, but they don't at all. Not if they're really experimenting and trying: they're looking for something.

Where does your thought process begin when you create imagery?

With the Shakespeare I've done, it comes from the language. Lavinia, whose "limbs are lopped and hewed and made thy body bare of her two branches." That's where you get the image of Lavinia as a broken tree. The stumps, the ravaged landscape; that metaphor of her in the swamp in the movie, or goddess on a pedestal in the play.

One of the reasons I adore Shakespeare is because it's all in the text. So some people say, "Then why do you do it visually?" Well, I believe profoundly that the images we hear in the language can be supported by images on the stage without being redundant. Our audiences don't listen as well as they see, and it supports the language to have the imagery be as poetic as possible. You need to match the power of the language with the power of movement and your imagery on stage. And that still can be very minimal. My *Titus Andronicus* was extremely minimal, and theatrical.

Sometimes the imagery comes through the music, if you're working on an opera or a piece of music-theater like *Juan Darién*, which was a short story that Elliot and I elaborated on. Elliot's "Gloria" sounded like thousands of butterflies. That's a beautiful image, but it's also an image of transformation. I'm always looking for images that have many levels of meaning, that on the one hand can be superficially appreciated, like in *The Lion King* when you see the circle of water disappearing at the top of Act Two: that's *drought*. But as the whole ideograph of *The Lion King* is the circle of life, it's better to do drought in a circle of silk, rather than in a realistic river on stage that goes dry.

Now the audience doesn't have to get all that, because they get it on a subliminal level when they see that circle over and over and over again . . . the circle of the gazelle wheels, or the circle of Mufasa's mask, or the set circling up out of the floor.

Theater doesn't come from ritual in this country in the same way that it does in older cultures, and ritual provides a kind of training for reading narrative through metaphor.

Tsidii Le Loka and the cast of The Lion King, *music by Elton John, lyrics by Tim Rice, book by Roger Allers and Irene Mecchi. Broadway, 1997. Credit: Joan Marcus.*

The idea of ritual is not the same here. I don't think we always use the word "ritual" correctly. Getting up and brushing your teeth: that's not ritual. That's just something you do all the time. But the way people celebrate Christmas or Hanukkah or Thanksgiving is, maybe. Because the coming together of a family, sitting at a communal table and the blessings and the prayers . . . that is more like the theater we're talking about, that came out of ritual, with all kinds of rules: what the women can see and can't see, what time of year, what stories are appropriate . . .

Going to the opera once every six months and getting dressed up isn't ritual. But it probably reflects the desire for a certain kind of formality that elevates you as a human being, because it goes beyond the mundane . . . which is something I'm always interested in. That play of the sacred against the profane or the mundane.

I know the success of *The Lion King* here has a lot to do with ritual. The beginning of it is particularly archetypal. That's what I've gotten more than anything over the past six years: "I cried at the opening!" Well, why are you crying? It's not a sad moment; it's a joyous moment. But I think that's going back to the origins and the essence of theater, the animation of the inanimate and emotion. When the audience sees people on stilts and hears the power of the human voice (without English language) to call the sunrise, and the sun is clearly built on battens of silk strips being held up by wires, *that's what causes people to cry*—the transparent act of transformation and imagination. Whether it's voodoo dolls or masks . . . they represent spirits. *The Lion King* calls upon something that people realize deep down, and it's not just the beauty of the images . . . it's the power of the artist to create and identify beauty. That's the shamanistic function of artists.

Do you see a lot of theater?

I have to be told to go! I'd rather see a bad movie than bad theater—that's so hard to watch.

What makes bad theater?

Lack of imagination. If I go into a theater and I see a whole house and a porch, I kinda know, Oh God, now here I am stuck for two hours on the front porch!

I had that immediate reaction when I went to see *Proof*, but I actually enjoyed it, so that went against my normal thinking. Usually, bad theater is when I go in and see that kind of set that they can't readily get off stage without burning it to the ground. Oh God, angst-ridden, talking heads!

So what do you need to be a good artist, to do good work?

I think you have to have something you want to say and a passion for the form. A desire to push the envelope and find ways of telling the story. You can tell an original story, or you can tell a story we know but in an original way—you've got to do one or the other. *The Lion King* is an old story, it's got all of the stock characters, but it's the way it's told that brings meaning to it. That's why musicals or opera are so interesting: it's not the story but often the quality of the music and the orchestration.

Do you think an artist has a responsibility to respond to the politics around her?

You don't have to, but I think you have the power, so you might want to. I don't think it means doing sociopolitical subject matter. I don't think there is a commercial show that has done more for race than *The Lion King*: a show that, for white people, is *not at all* about race, but transcends it; but for black people it *is all about race*. And yet it doesn't talk about racism. It's probably the only play with such a high percentage of nonwhite audience members that's not *about* American racism. It's not

Ragtime or *Jelly's Last Jam. The Lion King* celebrates the power of race without being about race. So in that way, it's an extremely sociopolitical piece. Mundane and naive and simplistic and clichéd as it may feel to a lot of people, it is also about something fundamental: the breakup of the American family. It speaks to black inner city life hugely, in this form. A child loses his father. How does that child—who runs away from a broken home, who is not a part of a community anymore—understand that he has a responsibility to his family and culture?

There is a lot of message in *The Lion King* without it being direct. It also takes people through the major passages of life and death. I'll tell you this one story. There was a family, it was told to me, that had a son and a daughter, and the daughter died. The parents brought their other child, a younger son, to see *The Lion King*. And there's that scene where the son says, "Daddy, are you going to be here forever?" And he answers, "Look at the stars. The great kings of the past look down on us from those stars. If you remember me, I will always be here with you." And the little boy in the audience turned to his parents and said, "Sarah is with us, isn't she?" And that's just incredible—that a moment in *The Lion King* could ease that family's pain, or make that child understand that his sister is in some way with him. Artists were originally the priests, the shamans, who took people through those great life passages.

I don't think an artist has an obligation to be overtly political. Stories that open your eyes to connections to the people around you are very important. But it's just wonderful to do plays like *The Green Bird*, which is about self-love and greed. I'm not particularly interested in doing the latest opera on, let's say, Harvey Milk; that kind of approach is valid for other people, but that doesn't make it more important than *Grendel*, which can feel completely mythic, but is really examining the human race in the twentieth century. Socially, it's extremely aware.

A few weeks before becoming the first woman to win the Tony Award for Best Direction of a Musical, you said in an interview,"It's just not acceptable [for women in this culture] to be powerhouse genius mavericks." Now that you're an undisputed leader in American theater, and a force to be reckoned with in film as well, do you still feel the same way? Do the battles get harder or easier?

The "male genius dictator" doesn't work in female form: strong women are just called "bitches." You know, things may change, but that's the way it *has* been—I think women still have to work twice as hard. You can't just have one success.

I think women have a tendency to be really good directors, because the history of women is to be very psychological, to try to get out of the other *without force* what they want! Women will be angry with this probably, but I think it's a big, positive thing. Obviously, the women have to be good at what they're doing—and that isn't to say there aren't women dictators, nasty-ass generals. But if you're making generalized statements (which I loathe, and that's what we're doing right now), if a woman is more psychological in the way that she gets what she wants, then that's not a bad thing.

Can directing be taught?

I don't think so. I've never studied it, so I don't know. To me you've got to have ideas, and an incredible understanding of human psychology. And it helps if you have a strong visual flair to be really special. I think theater has to be operatic; that doesn't mean grand, that doesn't mean big, but it requires the use of all of its potential *potential*. Not necessarily music, but sound and space and light and *acting form*. Sculptural form and space, and if you have that, it's just going to be *better*.

I like to think I came to being a director because I had a story to tell—and that was *Way of Snow*. A lot of first-time directors' work is very good (you see that a lot in movies) because it's personal, because they have a strong idea of what they want to say. But can they tell someone else's story, or is it the same story told over and over again? That's okay if you're a Scorsese, and you're better at telling mafia stories, and there may be enough stories in that world to tell. But I think it's great to see directors challenge themselves with different styles and media.

I put my first piece together out of desire to tell a story, period. And that's what I do: I tell stories. I'm interested in telling them in ways in which you can't just read them on the page. The meaning is in the form. The meaning is in the mask. It's not just there as a trick or a gimmick. I don't think my theater is about that at all.

When I said I wanted to stay and work with Bread and Puppet Theater in Vermont [where she worked during college], Peter Schumann told me to go out and see as much as I could, and don't stay with one person too long. Don't become a sycophant. Don't become a student of one. And that's why those travels to Indonesia and Japan were very important. Because I absorbed a lot. Stepping out of my own culture has been the most important thing for me.

THEATRE DE LA JEUNE LUNE

Balancing Acts

IN 2003, I ASKED THE FIVE CO-artistic directors of Minneapolis-based Theatre de la Jeune Lune—Barbra Berlovitz, Steven Epp, Vincent Gracieux, Robert Rosen and Dominique Serrand—whether they considered themselves an ensemble.

SERRAND: We have a new word. Now we say a "congress."
ROSEN: I think that sounds socialist.
GRACIEUX: No, it actually—
SERRAND: Now we call ourselves a "congress"!
BERLOVITZ: *You* call us a "congress"!
SERRAND: No!
BERLOVITZ: I know, I know it's in the [artistic statement] . . . I [she sighs] . . . well.

In the end, the terminology didn't matter. Three years later, the company jettisoned 28 years of collective governance, appointing Dominique Serrand as sole artistic director. And two years after that, in 2008, the company sold its building and closed its doors. Even a 2005 Special Tony Award for Outstanding Regional Theatre for their visionary body of devised work—from circus-inspired, movement-based evenings of comic lunacy to visually lush and imaginative revisions of the classics—wasn't enough to save Jeune Lune. As Serrand prophetically told me in 2006, "You always get the award on your tomb."

Although the company's precarious financial position—a reported debt in excess of $1 million against an annual budget of only $1.5 million—was the reason for the sale of their magnificent home in a former Allied Van Lines warehouse, the reason the artists did not remain together to create work was far more prosaic: after thirty years, the collective simply fell apart.

But to dwell on the company's demise would deny its extraordinary accomplishments and longevity. The seeds of Jeune Lune were planted in the early 1970s, when Parisian actor Dominique Serrand and Minneapolis native Barbra Berlovitz met while studying with French movement, mask and clowning teacher Jacques Lecoq. They began performing together, and were soon joined by two other graduates of Lecoq's famous school: Vincent Gracieux, another Frenchman, and Robert Rosen, a childhood friend of Berlovitz's. In 1978, the four teamed up for a Parisian production of *A Midsummer Night's Dream,* and Theatre de la Jeune Lune ("theater of the young moon") was born. They began splitting their time between France and the United States, creating and performing work in French for the Parisians, and translating it to English for the Minneapolitans. Minneapolis actor Steven Epp joined the troupe in 1983, and the company settled there permanently in 1985, establishing themselves with what became a signature comic work (and frequent moneymaker), *Yang Zen Froggs.* The company purchased the cavernous warehouse in 1992, and through a process of creative demolition, turned it into a spare, beautiful and flexible six-thousand-square-foot performance space.

They opened the building with an extremely ambitious project, borne of an artistic yearning the four founders had long shared. That piece, *Children of Paradise: Shooting a Dream* (based on the making of the legendary French film *Les enfants du paradis*) put Jeune Lune on the map, winning the American Theatre Critics Association New Play Award for 1993. "No more extraordinary theater work will appear this season," crowed *Newsweek* when the play toured to Yale Repertory Theatre.

From then on, Jeune Lune's delirious, insightful and visually magnificent works toured nationally and internationally, and thrilled its home audience in Minneapolis. Though artistic and administrative decisions had been made collaboratively through its history, the arrangement was informal until the four founders asked Epp to join them in running the company. The five officially named themselves co-artistic directors in 2001.

Although all five artists share a background in movement-based performance, they each took a seat in the director's chair on occasion, and all five shared responsibility for generating new work in a way unlike that of any major theater in the country. Projects would germinate organically when one or another of the directors found an idea—usually a source text—intriguing. Weeks, months or years of conversation followed, with the others adding to a communal pot of knowledge around the source. When the idea finally achieved critical mass, it turned into workshop, then rehearsal, then performance.

"The Lunies" (as they were locally known) created three, four or even five works a year, most in this way. Some texts were written solely by one member of the congress; others were authored by some (or all) of them collectively. Of the classics they put on, they gravitated most to Molière, Mozart and Shakespeare, frequently revising texts or combining them. (It's no surprise the texts that most interested them were classics that provided opportunities for physical, textual and visual exploration.) Even when they produced plays in a more traditional manner (like scripts by 20th century luminaries Arnold Wesker, Bertolt Brecht, or Eugene Ionesco), those productions inhabited the kind of theatrically exuberant worlds that were their hallmark.

No matter the source material, a Jeune Lune production was graced by an intuitive and joyful melding of the physical and the intellectual, employing circus arts, rigorous physical performance, occasionally mask and mime, and always stunning visual metaphor. The acting embodied the kind of immediacy and clarity of vision you'd expect from long-time collaborators who rejoiced in risk and answered only to themselves and their collective vision. As they wrote in their 2003 artistic statement:

> What is common to all our work is its poetic gesture. Everything is sacred, and everything is on the move. Like the moon, we reflect and influence . . . Whether it's a novel, an opera, a circus, a classic, an invention, it is a Jeune Lune show because it comes about through us.

As their mentor Lecoq used to say, "everything moves." Through their collective imaginations, Mozart's *Magic Flute* (1999) became a raucous cabaret enveloping actor and spectator, Molière's *Don Juan* and Mozart's *Don Giovanni* meshed into a cross-country road trip called *Don Juan Giovanni* (1994) and the relationship between an author and his fictional subject morphed into a puppets-and-people performance called *Gulliver, a Swift Journey* (2001).

But by the time I first met them in 2003, the "congress" was working less and less collaboratively. Serrand was spending a large amount of time freelance directing with other regional theaters, and had fallen in love with opera directing. Projects would be taken up that only used one or two of them at home. And the institutional pressures of running a major regional theater began to change the aesthetic and process behind the work. For example, I watched a serious debate among them about whether productions needed to appear polished at first performance thanks to a long rehearsal process, or (as Serrand insisted) it was more important to do a couple of weeks of rehearsal and then just "show"—present what you've got, see if it has legs and then go back to work on it. Would the audience accept a play that previewed for six weeks and opened only on its closing night? Could such a system work in the 21st century for a theater the size and heft of Jeune Lune?

When Serrand was named sole artistic director in 2006, Rosen and Gracieux took "leaves of absence," while Berlovitz (still acting with the company) stepped away from institutional responsibilities. I asked Serrand whether they had dissolved the congress.

> No we haven't. I'm the head of the congress . . . I'm working with a congress of artists and right now I'm the leader . . . [but] people are looking in all kinds of directions to think and refocus about their own work. For years we were trying to work more individually on our own projects. And we got to a point where we realized we needed to find a sense of unity in the direction of the organization, and to readdress the position of each one of us as artists. It was a very courageous endeavor, for all of us to say, "let's relook at our work," and if people want to go . . .
>
> Obviously, our main preoccupation is to stay alive and healthy, but not at any cost. If the recipe to be successful means we have to change our artistic production, then there would be no reason for Jeune Lune to continue.

Not quite two years later, Jeune Lune announced imminent closure. Vincent had already moved back to France, where he now works primarily with an English company called Footsbarn. The other four retain their roots in Minneapolis and work to differing degrees and in different capacities there and around the country. Epp and Serrand founded a new performing venture, The Moving Company, in 2009, and have produced three shows together working with former Lunies. But the five artists have not worked collaboratively since 2006.

Despite the demise of Theatre de la Jeune Lune, we decided to include this interview not only as a salute to their rare artistry, but as a snapshot of a difficult moment for an artistic ensemble. I interviewed all five of them at once in an attempt to gain insight into their way of working. Nothing about how Jeune Lune operated fit the dominant American models of artistic creation. So why should their interview be any different?

SEPTEMBER 2003, THEATRE DE LA JEUNE LUNE, MINNEAPOLIS

Let's start with the obvious question—how do all five of you work together? How can five people possibly choose a play?

BERLOVITZ: I would start with the fact that we're twenty-five years old, and over the course of twenty-five years, we've had different experiences of how that's worked, and how that hasn't worked. Vincent, Dominique and I directed the first two or three shows as a threesome. We codirected. And that continued in different forms over the years. But most of the time, now, we have a single director.

Given that, how do you define the word "director"? None of you are trained as directors. Do you think you define the art of directing in the same way other people do?

BERLOVITZ: No, I don't. And we're going to have different opinions. But I think it depends on the project. We do creations from ideas that we have; we adapt novels; we work on classics—we do a wide range of work. I think ultimately it depends on what the work is, and who we're working with: do we want to have a lot of input from the people we're working with, or do we have a very strong idea? In general, we tend to demand a lot of the people who work with us in terms of their ideas and their input. Especially from the actors—they bring to the stage an awful lot of creativity, and their vision.

Let's take as a case study your *Magic Flute* [2000], which Dominique is credited with directing. How did that project come about?

EPP: We had already done *Don Juan Giovanni,* and we did *The Impresario* [1996] after that, so we'd begun this work with Mozart. In that sense it was a part of a continuum.

Well, how did *Don Juan Giovanni* come about?

ROSEN: I think a lot of those projects come from the person who has the idea. Dominique said he was interested in marrying the opera and the play, the text and the music, for *Don Juan Giovanni.*

SERRAND: It comes from a curiosity. Whenever we take a play, a script, a novel, we always look at what someone else has written. We couldn't look at *Don Juan* and not look at the Spanish *Don Juan Tenorio,* and then listen to the opera.

With *Carmen,* which I'm doing right now, I had to go and reread [Prosper] Mérimée [who wrote the original novel on which Bizet's opera is based]. Of course it goes back to Mérimée. This is the same thing with *Don Juan,* when we did *Don Juan Giovanni.* For that, it became obvious that it had to be a discourse between Mozart and Molière, the different sensibilities about the subject matter. The *dialogue* about the subject is what's important. The playfulness of Mozart is also an important element of Molière. That is particularly entrancing with *Giovanni,* because he uses the typical buffoon character, the *canaille,* a leading character out of commedia. And he's given a tragedy. The first time a commedia character is given a tragedy.

When you put the two together, you realize Mozart and Molière have a better dialogue than Mozart and his librettist, Da Ponte.

ROSEN: I was inspired by something Peter Brook wrote at the beginning of *The Shifting Point*: where he says you start out with a "formless hunch." And I think that's very much how we work. We have a hunch. It's a passion, it's that root seed that makes you want to pursue an idea.

He also says in that book that the actor must pursue what the *character* would pursue. Because the character's going to know more than the actor knows. If you always bring what the *actor* knows to the work, then you've got to live with it! But if you pursue what the character knows, you delve into something you don't know about.

For a director, it's the same thing. You pursue something you don't know, because otherwise you're limiting yourself to something you're good at—the same tricks. We trust ourselves to jump into that world of the unknown.

BERLOVITZ: I think that on a simpler level, with something like *The Magic Flute,* we've never been shy about embracing our influences. In that case, we were very moved by Ingmar Bergman's *Magic Flute.* And there was probably the desire long before to look at that work and develop something with it. So it became an organic decision, and once we had done the *Don Juan,* that was the right time and place to do it.

EPP: There's also a particular vision which sometimes comes collectively, but sometimes it's very individual. Again with *Magic Flute,* I don't remember how we realized it, but you see in the film *Amadeus* that [director Milos] Forman went back to this idea, too: *Magic Flute,* compared to Mozart's other pieces, was really written for a populist theater company run by Schikaneder, a kind of beer hall.

It has become part of the operatic repertoire—yet that's really about as far away as you can get from how it was first done. It was also done on a very intimate scale: very small orchestra, very different kind of singers than the opera singers you find now.

Seeing that inspired us to put it into an environment that creates that intimate relationship with the audience. Now, the show we ended up with . . . You have that idea, but you're not necessarily going to end up there. There are things to find out once you put the material next to that idea. It's not obvious how it's going to work. But having the vision for the show, suddenly all the questions are there before you get to work.

SERRAND: *Magic Flute* is also very interesting in terms of its radical roots. Look at what it meant at the time—nobody would produce a *Flute* the way it was produced then. But it *meant* to be something revolutionary, by the way it was produced. So going back to look at the original production is often very radical.

A very good example lies in the origins of our production of *Tartuffe* [1999]. Molière wrote three versions of *Tartuffe* [the first two versions greatly provoked the ire of the church]. The first one was censored; the second one was censored; the third one was authorized. Should we do the third one? Or should we try to reproduce the violence, or the effectiveness of the first version, by acknowledging it has a history?

In our version, we started with that question. Molière wrote *Don Juan* before he wrote the third version of *Tartuffe*. So when we looked at the third *Tartuffe*, we said, "Well, *Don Juan* is now *in it,* if you just look at the playwriting." That *Tartuffe* has a lot of *Don Juan* in it, and that is probably how it got to be authorized. So how about we do *Tartuffe,* the *Don Juan* [version]? Having some blood of the *Don Juan* completely changed the perspective on the play.

So with every project there are layers. I think we're at a point where we start to resemble ourselves. You have to embrace the mistake you've always made, and turn it into a successful mistake.

Is that why you're revisiting *The Ballroom*?

SERRAND: Well, that was a great original gesture. As a company, we were on the move; it was the last show before we were going into the new building [in 1992]. We wanted to do something that talked about the world at large. It was a perfect piece: it was done too fast, with too many people—that's great! You need to do those.

BERLOVITZ: The other side is that, aside from the people in this room, that cast is not the same cast, and so it's a new creation. Therefore, the way it comes across is completely different.

It may sound naive because you work in this process all the time, but all those voices in a single production seems daunting to me, especially

when you add the actors to the five of you. Is it like having five drama-turgs in the room?

SERRAND: Yes!

So one of you watches *Amadeus*, and someone else sees the Bergman, and everyone brings their thoughts into the room . . .

BERLOVITZ: Sometimes, but I think there's an enormous amount of trust. We know each other so well (and at the same time, not at all!), so if someone says, "Well, I want to do this show," we say, "Okay!"

Then the discussion is purely on a practical level: when can we do it, and how does it fit in with the other shows we want to be doing around that time? That's what we talk about. But at this point, we have that system of trust.

SERRAND: Or not.

What I mean by that is that I think it goes further. If someone brought an idea about doing *Don Juan,* we'd say, "Okay, can we talk about it?" I guess the titles and the ideas don't live very long. What lives is what starts as a curiosity, like you say—

ROSEN: The hunch.

SERRAND: The hunch, the tickle, the thing that starts making you [snaps his fingers rhythmically]. Why does he have this idea?

ROSEN: It's the why . . .

SERRAND: And then you don't necessarily need to explain. It comes to a place where it somehow, suddenly, wants to live. And I don't think you can define what that is. Because there's an assertion, there's a will. *Children of Paradise*: "Let's do that." We created this company because of *Children of Paradise*. We knew the movie; we knew it so well that no one would ever touch it. It was like touching perfection.

Eventually by reading about it, we realize that the story is the *making* of *Children of Paradise*. That was our story. Then we can start touching it. So there's never a "no" to anything; it just exists when it wants to.

EPP: And those conversations sometimes happen formally, in the sense that we have ongoing meetings. But sometimes the most important idea will emerge because you're running back to the dressing room between this scene and that scene, and you happen to say, "You know, if we were to do such-and-such. . ." Suddenly it's completely happenstance and accidental. It's just that it's *out,* the ideas are floating around in this atmosphere, and somebody will have some information to add: an article, a photo that suddenly makes sense of an idea.

And when it finally cycles into, "Now, we're going to start working on this project," it starts to shift into a different—

SERRAND: Ready to roll!

Left to right: Megan Grundy, Christopher Bayes, Dominique Serrand, Felicity Jones, Steven Epp, Vincent Gracieux and Robert Rosen in The 7 Dwarfs *by Kevin Kling. Theatre de la Jeune Lune, 1989. Credit: Gerald Gustafson. Used by permission of Larry Marcus.*

GRACIEUX: Because also it's the clarity of the concept. I don't remember who brought the idea of making the movie, or if we talked first about the idea of just the world of *Children of Paradise*, but the concept of the making of the movie immediately framed the project really well. You have a frame; you can work.

EPP: That's a key—

SERRAND: That the concept be well defined.

ROSEN: Sometimes we'll work in other ways, but—

EPP: And sometimes we've had problems, we've *floundered* more because we couldn't find that key frame which everyone can understand, and which defines it. You have to clear that up in the beginning.

So once you have the frame figured out, and the idea reaches critical mass, you have a practical meeting to decide who directs the play? Or not?

ROSEN: Or not! Often the person who brings the project ends up directing it, but not always. Somebody might bring a project and say, "I'm not at all interested in directing it, I just want to play a part, or design the set."

And often, when we get to that point, it doesn't mean it's time to produce the show. We may get to that point and say, "Now we need to find out more, but we need to find out more on our feet. So let's schedule two or three weeks of the season to play around with the idea," with the intent of doing the show the following year if we find out enough.

Do you have a standing company of actors to help you do that?

SERRAND: Up until about three years ago, we had a permanent company with an average of ten people. Three years ago we abandoned the idea, because we *were* the company. There is a larger ensemble of actors with whom we've worked for years. But there was, of course, a financial issue in keeping a company of that dimension. Also, we were at a point where we had to rethink who the people in the room *were*. What their place was.

BERLOVITZ: It would be wonderful to be under the Soviet system with thirty-five actors on staff. Now it's a difficulty, when we want to workshop something, to gather the people we want to work with, and have their schedules all coincide. As a company, everyone basically lives by the same schedule, and you can have those people when you want them. But in a practical sense, to give actors a permanent salary, for them to be able to live and do their work . . . We kind of have that system, but we're not able to employ those people all the time. There are about thirty or forty people in the area with whom we work a lot.

ROSEN: The five of us all used to be in all the productions, and that's really not the case anymore, either.

When did that start changing?

SERRAND: There had always been cases when one or two of us would not be in a show, or two of us if the production was smaller. But it's been more systematic in the past five years.

Because the company was maturing . . . ?

BERLOVITZ: With all our new ideas, the time issue became huge. It was very difficult to constantly be in shows, and have the mind free enough to be able to be working on ideas for new ones. I think we collectively said, "We have to stop this! We have to have other people play our parts."

SERRAND: There was also a danger. The company was getting older, and there were bad habits. There was a certain guarantee: you can just come in and, somehow, get a role. So it was time to reask those questions.

And it was interesting, because most of the actors we were working with all the time suddenly were going out to work with other theater companies. And they found out they were the only ones who could speak our language, a language they had developed with us. And that made them quite remarkable in those other companies, in those other shows, having an extraordinary talent which nobody could quite understand. So of course, they came back to us with a much greater power, because suddenly they realized their own importance, and their involvement in the artistic process. And they realized that this place is not a given. There's something extraordinary we need to preserve and continue to develop with great discipline, because it's a very rare thing. It has changed the dialogue of how we construct productions.

The people who have gone out and come back to us, they have acted, they've directed, they've taken complete responsibility for a production. They come back and they're informed in a very different way. So the muscle is much stronger.

So you're trying to bring back these people who have become more powerful artists away from Jeune Lune.

ROSEN: Well, they want to come back, and we want them to come back.
SERRAND: Right now they're in the building, rehearsing shows that they're doing on their own outside.

So you're using this facility as an incubator for other artists' work, too?

SERRAND: I think it's a responsibility for us.
ROSEN: It's a double-edged sword when you're working with young artists. Even on the administrative side, you get the chance to work with brilliant young people, and after a while they go away. You can't keep people in a company.
SERRAND: We *tell* them to go away—
ROSEN: Why should someone commit his or her *life,* you know? Someone comes out of school, shows something really brilliant, and you're going to keep them here for twenty years, *chained* as a company member? Because they're only going to learn a certain amount here. You have to send people away. Go direct, write, have other experiences . . . just come back, please! Come back with information, and be a richer person.

And that's why you're sending Dominique away? [Serrand was about to direct *The Miser* for American Repertory Theater in Cambridge, Massachusetts]

[laughter]

SERRAND: Well, there is the great danger of stagnation.

What are you able to give these actors? What makes your approach so powerful?

BERLOVITZ: Actors don't realize how free they are on stage. I'm on the stage, it's happening *right now,* and what can I do in this particular moment to make this exciting? And the most exciting thing is to be *free, open and ready.* And that's what we demand of our actors.

ROSEN: That is the joy of play! The joy of being tragic, the joy of being the most evil person in the world. The joy—that's what *we* bring actors.

BERLOVITZ: We very often talk about actors in this company as "actor-authors," which makes them responsible for what they bring to the stage. At this point in our careers we might have different opinions about it, but I still feel something that I felt early on: ultimately, what the audience sees is the actor in front of the audience. They don't see the director in the room, usually. Hopefully they don't see the director figuring out the lighting, or the costumes. They see the connection of the actor *to them*. And they feel the emotion in that, and they understand, or not, *through that actor*. So the actors have to be totally focused on the ideas behind what they are doing. And they can only do that if they take authorship and responsibility for what happens on stage.

Some directors say the opposite: that when you see a show, it's the director you're watching. The director is on the line every moment.

SERRAND: Who says that? They're full of bananas.

[laughter]

BERLOVITZ: I've had the luxury now of being able to watch more of the shows from the outside. And depending on the show, I more or less see huge influence by the director. With *Carmen*, Dominique is working with a group of people who in general are opera singers, not actors. So his job as a director had to be very different than if he were working with us as actors.

SERRAND: They're becoming stronger in terms of acting ability—it's unbelievable.

EPP: We're pushing them to take opera further than they've gone.

SERRAND: And because we took them out of the opera and put them into play for another project, they're working these muscles.

ROSEN: But it's true, the director has a very strong imprint on the production. The actors are living in that world, filling up that world. But it's not just a free-for-all for everybody to create.

When I think of productions of yours I've seen, I talk about them aesthetically. Your "signature" pieces from the earlier years share a multiplicity of voices, sources—from commedia to Charlie Chaplin to circus. I'd say that one of the directorial imprints of much of Jeune Lune's early work is a visual lyricism, a narrative playfulness and irreverence. The unity of the vision is its multiplicity. That's clearly directorial, whether it's individual, or a collective functioning as an individual. But now, especially with Dominique directing more, the vision is becoming more integrated, unified.

THEATRE DE LA JEUNE LUNE

SERRAND: Well, take Liviu Ciulei, or Garland Wright, or Andrei Serban: for twenty years there has been what is called the "dictatorship of the director," "director's theater." I remember Liviu Ciulei going to an actor and saying, [holding his coffee mug very strangely and specifically] *"Zee cup, like dees,"* and that's all he said. "No, no, no! *Like dees!"*

And that's a kind of directorial wizard; a man who has an incredible concept. He was an architect, a designer; the whole thing is complete, the production is complete, the dramaturgy is complete. You sit in rehearsal, and you see an application of what was prepared before.

That's a whole school of thought. And not one that I disagree with, necessarily; I think we've seen some gorgeous things. But if you look more at directors who were actors, or were very close to actors, or who went to acting school—which we all did—we understand that actors are human beings. They want to do the thing that they think will make them *look best*. The only way you're going to make them do something they don't feel makes them look best is if you know them very well, and you can trust them, and they know to trust you. And you can start creating particular relationships on the stage that you would never, never be able to get from a "concept."

The concept is a *culture*, not a box. Which is why our scenographies are much less decorated than scenographic. They're a space, a page, and sometimes a very precise page. The director is there to be the good "saucemaker"; to make sure that the whole kitchen functions well. And nothing else!

You count on extraordinary talents, but you have to empower those talents so they know exactly what their responsibility is in the whole thing. And then your role as a director is just to make sure that the whole thing keeps moving, keeps existing. There is very little concept, there is very little choice. The research is done; the rest is delivery.

Here's a quote from one of your actors, Bradley Greenwald: "When they first hired me for *Don Juan Giovanni*, it was terrifying. I had just done a tour of *Don Giovanni* with the Minnesota Opera, and I knew the score really well. Jeune Lune hired me as one of the opera singers, and they brought me in a week early to help me pick out what music to use. I showed up for the first day of rehearsal, and Luverne Seifert, Dominique and Steve just started improvising a scene around me. I had no idea where they were in the story or what they were doing—I felt like roadkill on a freeway of Porsches." Sounds like a remarkable shorthand you've got.

BERLOVITZ: You're talking to a group of people who are like an old married couple. What we can understand between us is not necessarily what someone coming into this culture is going to understand. Lots of times people are lost and don't know which end is up. Especially if we get somebody who has not seen our work.

EPP: One aspect of our shorthand is simply our whole body of work. We're looking for a moment, and we can put it into context: "It's kind of like what we were doing in that part of *Children of Paradise*."

Something I think we used to do more is all the root training from Lecoq [in commedia dell'arte character work]. You can refer to something with his shorthand: "It's like a Sganarelle," or "It's like an Arlecchino moment."

ROSEN: It's also the art of improvisation. We can talk about a scene, and then just go full steam ahead; we don't spend a lot of time thinking about it.

Say we're working on *Gulliver*. We need a scene about the Yahoos; we grab costumes, you stick a wad of paper in your stomach, wads of paper in your mouth. We grab the shop vac and some ammunition— and we wreak havoc for ten minutes! Everything in sight can become a prop, anything that's not tied down can be in the show. And that's the culture that we have: every object lives, every moment lives. I think we're just fast that way. People coming from the outside are used to a lot more direction.

BERLOVITZ: One thing we've done, too, even with shows that are written before we hit rehearsal, is to take a couple of actors and tell them to take a scene, go off to another room, rehearse it, and come back and show. I think most of us in this country are not trained that way. A lot of actors are used to having four weeks of rehearsal—what is *that*? [much laughter] Two weeks of which are rehearsal, one of which is tech, and one of which is previews. When an actor hits those rehearsals, he has to know the lines, have an idea of how to approach the character; maybe he had the luxury to talk to the director beforehand. So when the first day of rehearsal comes, all of the questions are answered! That's *not* the way we work.

SERRAND: Actually, that's the way we work. That's the way I've been working for the last two years in this company. With very, very little rehearsal.

BERLOVITZ: But—

SERRAND: And I think that it is a great thing. But we have very different opinions.

BERLOVITZ: Right—

SERRAND: I agree with Barbra in the long term, but in a way, the best thing that could happen to this company is to say, "Just do it, get it done!" Because then you have to throw yourself very quickly into a decision that has to be pretty hot. Outside, when you're directing on that schedule, it's *abominable*. Because you know that people are not coming to just *give* you the show: you're gonna *pull* the show out of them. But in *this* company, I wish we'd do a show every three weeks. No time for thinking, just do it!

BERLOVITZ: Absolutely, I don't disagree with that, but I *do* think—

SERRAND: I think this company suffers when it does shows that rehearse nine, ten, twelve weeks.

Why do you think that?

SERRAND: Because people rest on the director, or on the certain self-assurance that eventually you get deeper into it by going longer. Which is different than, say, you do it in twelve weeks, but after two weeks, *you show.* And you do three more weeks, and then *you show.* Because you're constantly using the performance muscle.

EPP: That's the thing that we've never been able to do: come up with a system for a show once it's opened. Once it's opened and reviewed, as much as we're able to fine-tune it, we're usually by necessity on to the next project. We've never really been in a system where you would rehearse something very quickly, but it would begin to live in front of an audience a certain number of performances a week, so you're constantly rehearsing it, and it's more *found* and *whole.*

GRACIEUX: Which is why it's great to revisit shows.

ROSEN: Or tour.

Like the original commedia dell'arte troupes, always touring, always tweaking, only "opening" a show community by community.

EPP: The systems of the world don't allow you that. Inevitably there's going to be failure involved, and you have to be this perfect thing on opening night. It's antithetical to how live theater really works.

SERRAND: How about we do three days of reading, talking through and getting into the part, and then after a week, just go in front of an audience? So as an actor, you're always at performance level. There's no, "How should I do this?" It's just, "This is it. Good luck." The most unnerving thing in American theater is when an actor asks you, the director, to *explain.* You say, "No. I can't explain to you. I can *guide* you to where I think it could go. But explain it? That's *your* work."

EPP: Essentially the actors should explain what *they're* doing—

ROSEN: Don't tell me, "I don't understand"—

So you work on the tough-love principle.

SERRAND: If you don't understand, it's your problem!

[all five of them erupt, and none of the directors gets the upper hand until Rosen is able to silence the insistent Serrand]

Dominique Serrand in Figaro, *adapted by Steven Epp and Dominique Serrand from the play by Pierre Beaumarchais. Theatre de la Jeune Lune, 2003. Credit: Michal Daniel.*

ROSEN: Think of Carlo Mazzone-Clementi, who founded the Dell'Arte school in California, and who just died a couple of years ago. Actors would not understand something, and Carlo would just sit and shake his head. And Carlo would say, [Rosen holds a cookie in his hand, palm up] "You see my hand? It's open. [Rosen flips his palm over, dropping the cookie, and the others laugh] You see my hand? It's still open."

It was totally discombobulating. And you go, "Carlo, why don't you just explain what the hell you want?" And then I realized, he *did* explain it.

BERLOVITZ: I'm reading Patsy Rodenburg's book on acting Shakespeare, and she said something we potentially agree with, about what's demanded of an actor. You have an actor go over to a wall, and behind the wall is someone you love, and they're in danger and you have to push the wall to get to them. So what is that doing to your body, to your breath, without even speaking? And what is that energy? That's the energy you need for Shakespeare. And I think you need that energy *all* the time on stage.

In a kinder, gentler way, I think that's what the audience wants. I think they want to be in a room with someone who's electrified, who's dynamic, who's primal, who is hooked up to their emotions and therefore can convey those emotions. I don't think we want to watch people standing around, like in the work of, *ahem*, some playwrights!

ROSEN: It's essentially the difference between going to a play and watching actors act, and going to a play and watching people *play*.

You've trained your audience here in Minneapolis. They know they're coming to watch people play. Given how revolutionary you've been in the way you do theater in this country, why not announce a show that runs six non-consecutive weekends, that always rehearses and never opens to the press?

SERRAND: I'm very tempted to do that! To say there will be sixty-five previews and one opening!

[uproarious laughter]

EPP: We've talked about it, but these are stupid realities of season tickets and box office and all that shit. The trick is to find a way to create another system.

SERRAND: I bet there is a way technically for the audience to think that the show runs from October 1 to December 31, but officially it's called a preview until December 31.

But we're talking about a *war,* and I don't think we're interested in being at war. We have to just educate, make people understand that there is a virtue to the process.

Do you mean a war with the press, or the audience?

SERRAND: Let me put it this way. The country has turned incredibly to the right in the last six years. The great assault on art has been done in the past fifteen or twenty years. It's within our walls. It touches on everything we do. Audiences are rarely exposed to anything that's daring in any theater, so of course, when they come to us they are less ready to see something daring. Fifteen years ago, the whole scene in Minneapolis was a hundred percent more daring than it is now.

ROSEN: That's true.

SERRAND: People laughed and applauded at what we used to do on stage; now we get, "Oh, my God!" And it's not even close to what we used to do.

I disagree with what Barbra said. I don't think audiences want to see an actor being daring; I think they want to see something very safe and untelling of anything. The reason why they used to like to see the fragility of the actor was because there was vision from lots of artists, communally, to push the envelope and invite the audience into a very privileged, poetic approach. And the audiences wanted to go in and touch on that fragility. That's not the case any more.

BERLOVITZ: But when they see something brilliant, they are really, truly amazed.

SERRAND: Oh, I agree with you.

BERLOVITZ: They go, "Whoa! Maybe I should see that more often!" They only think they want to see stuff that's more like pablum, because that's what they're being fed.

SERRAND: I agree, *totally*, with what she is saying, but it's a different battle than it used to be. If you work with an orchestra where everything is tuned, you start to hear some notes you never would have heard before. This is not the artists' scene in America today. We're not in the fine-tuning stage, trying to *dare* things. It exists, but not in theater.

Can we talk a little bit about some challenges you've worked through, perhaps when there's disagreement about how to proceed?

BERLOVITZ: When I have directed, if something's not happening, or if there's a disagreement, it's because I'm not being clear enough.

EPP: There is a problem when an actor just isn't getting it, where it becomes individual coaching. Sometimes a director will say to somebody else, "Coach that person a little bit, watch them." So the feedback might come from different places, which can also be problematic. Sometimes you have to be careful with younger or outside actors who need one clear person talking to them.

Other times, we're creating a piece and we just know that we haven't found how that scene develops, or where that scene lands. And it isn't so much about solving an actor problem, and I don't know that it's necessarily a directorial problem. It's more that we've identified that something's missing, something's not right. And the solution can come from any number of places. We can get out of those situations because people are invested, and people come with a large understanding of the project, of the material, and so they're able to help.

Once you've decided who's directing, is that person invested with all the authority to make the decisions?

ROSEN: Generally, yes. But sometimes a dramaturgical question comes up, and that's because other people are invested in the writing of the piece. You try to not have that happen, because what you don't want in the middle of rehearsal is suddenly to have to go back and rethink the writing.

SERRAND: I think that's where the word "explain" makes sense. I directed a Shakespeare play in another theater recently, and I was told I had to take actors who could really speak Shakespeare, so I was prevented from taking the actors I really wanted. I was stunned when I put the people in the room, and most of them would ask me *what this meant*. And I said, "I'm sorry, but I was hoping that you would be the one telling *me* what it means when I don't understand."

That's where we empower the director, who has a responsibility to explain what it means for them in the whole picture, not what it means on the page—which can sometimes be so intricate and so complicated. We can all have a very clear understanding of what this line *means*, yet it's different for all of us.

BERLOVITZ: I think, too, what we ask of the director is to tell us why we're doing the project. Someone has proposed a project because that *hunch* excited them. We want to be a part of that excitement.

SERRAND: And that translates into the explaining of, "I think I understand this line, I think I understand the gesture, but what am I to understand about it in *your* production?" That's your responsibility as a director to answer—

GRACIEUX/ROSEN: Exactly.

SERRAND: —to make very, very clear. To the point where the actor can say, "Oh! Easy!"

You don't call yourselves an "ensemble," do you?

SERRAND: We have a new word. Now we say a "congress."

ROSEN: I think that sounds socialist.

GRACIEUX: No, it actually—

SERRAND: Now we call ourselves a "congress"!

BERLOVITZ: *You* call us a "congress"!

SERRAND: No!

BERLOVITZ: I know, I know it's in the document . . . I . . . well.

So: there's the evidence, right? Disagreement happens.

SERRAND: In the democratic art of artistic participation (which is profoundly anti-democratic by nature), we have broken the systems by which we work together, in asking and demanding more of us than is usually demanded in a production system.

If I believe, for instance, that a show is a beautiful idea, but I'm not interested in it—and that's a purely tactile, sensual thing, whatever—I do think it's very important that it happens. But why force myself into it reluctantly in the name of a collective even though it doesn't click with me, for reasons that are very personal? It doesn't make sense. We have different desires.

The twenty-fifth anniversary season press release lists dozens of projects and you can't work on all of them. How do you . . .

[they all explode with laughter]

BERLOVITZ: No!

ROSEN: No!

EPP: No!

SERRAND: Oof!

BERLOVITZ: We try to do it less and less because meetings take so much time. We meet once a week, and that meeting tends to include a lot of logistical stuff.

SERRAND: Let's go back for a second to "explaining." It's very interesting working in and directing opera, which is a very "locked" world, because there are habits, because people have certain expectations.

It's good for me because I'm a foreigner in that country. As a foreigner, I can look at it with new eyes and question it. But at the same time, I would never argue the expertise of everyone in the room, who knows much better than I do whether there's a particular technique that applies musically.

Still, I find that I'll lean over to the music director and, for some intuitive reason, with a particular aria that is always sung with such muscle and bravado, and I'll say, "I know it's done this way, but there's got to be a reason to do it another way, because the muscle in the music is actually restrained, if you look at it right. And why don't we trust that, and see where it leads us?"

In the last ten years, I'm beginning to understand the second year of Lecoq's training, which is "confirm." Don't try to invent anything new, because nothing's new anyway. But try to confirm what you know, and let it be told to you that you actually don't know what you know. *That's* new.

BERLOVITZ: In general, the world of opera is very conservative, more locked into the notes on the page than actors tend to be with a word on the page. You hear phrases like, "Oh, it's never done that way. We can't cut that. You just don't do that." One thing that I love about what we do is that if somebody says, "Why?" we say, "Why not?"

Have you ever been in a situation where an actor or singer doesn't want to take the journey?

SERRAND: Oh yeah!

BERLOVITZ: Yes!

EPP: Absolutely.

BERLOVITZ: Even though the culture that we strive for is open and searching and questioning and curious, it's a particular culture, and some people do *not* want to enter into it. There are some people who aren't very brave and who just don't get it.

SERRAND: I agree with all the things you are saying, but let me put that into a different perspective.

Let's say you're going to involve an acrobat in the show: in that case, you're talking to a specialist who is never going to listen to you, because they're going to do it the way they want. It's the same with an opera singer—or a plumber—who decides they're going to do it *their* way.

Those people have such incredible discipline and muscle. They can be looked at as conservative, because the training is extremely demanding. The musicians in my family are the most leftist, politically; but they're the most conservative in the sense that these people find themselves rehearsing an instrument religiously every day. And it has method, and discipline, and exactitude.

So in a way, I'm more interested in the conservatism of the specialist, and trying to shape it and move it and question it, than in finding myself with a vague actor who is "inspired," but doesn't have the muscle.

BERLOVITZ: In an ideal world, what you're saying about musicians and acrobats, I think, should be absolutely true about actors.

SERRAND: But it's not true.

BERLOVITZ: It *can* be, and it is true sometimes.

SERRAND: Very rarely. My experience at the Guthrie was phenomenal, seeing a couple actors who were just monsters of work, I mean, amazing, where as a director you don't even dare to ask them to do something different because what comes at you is so full, so complete.

BERLOVITZ: I truly believe an actor should be an athlete.

SERRAND: I think we have to rebuild. We've spent more time on concepts; now we need to work more on the tools.

I sense a fair amount of disagreement amongst you in regards to your evolution. Can you identify how your aesthetics have now changed? Without Dominique answering: what do you think is the personality of a show that Dominique directs?

[after a long silence]

BERLOVITZ: I think he's a painter, in the direct sense of that statement, and in the more metaphorical sense of that statement. I also think he has an understanding of movement working when it is completely irrational, or seems to be completely irrational, and making it seem rational. So, whereas another director might direct someone standing still at a particular moment, he might have them running around the stage, climbing a ladder, and then jumping up and down. And the combination works.

ROSEN: I think of an incredible lyricism and poetry, and also an incredibly broad and deep viewpoint about the work. As an actor in a show he's directing, I know that in the first rehearsal or two, he's already ten levels ahead in his thinking of what the show's going to be.

EPP: There's a complete vision; every aspect of the production is functioning, moving toward a vision. The space, the lighting, the costuming, the choice of the language, the character, the movement—it's all so integrated. It's complete theater.

GRACIEUX: When I see Dominique's shows, especially the *Carmen*, his vision really interests me now. I've discovered that it's pretty clear what he wants to say. It's like entering a kind of captivating world.

Let's talk about Barbra's work.

SERRAND: She hasn't directed in a while, so I don't know how she would direct today, but she has a very grounded vision of humanity and social purpose, so there's always a demand of actors to participate in the social gesture. That's very clear.

ROSEN: I think Barbra has a very strong, direct, aggressive energy in that aspect of politics and society, especially approaching it from the level of Greek tragedy. She's always been attracted to Greek tragedy, because it's such a huge, powerful view of society.

BERLOVITZ: Yet some of my favorite things we've done have been just purely entertaining, very little direct or indirect message. I do think theater has to be entertaining; if it's too heavy-handed, it won't be for everybody. There has to be poetry in the performances or the language or the design of it, the overall image that you see on the stage. It has to be theater rather than TV.

EPP: Barbra's always very good in rehearsal. You feel like things are well attended, but there's an invitation of freedom for the actor, and that it's ultimately about what the actor brings to the story.

GRACIEUX: I agree with all that; she's great with people. But I've really enjoyed her as an actress in the last few years; playing with her, that's a lot of fun!

When's the last time you directed, Vincent?

GRACIEUX: It was a long time ago: five or six years.

Are you happy to not be directing?

GRACIEUX: No, I'm not! [laughs] I will be back to directing soon, but at the right time.

Does Vincent's work as a director have a personality?

SERRAND: Of course it does, as strong a personality as *he* is! It's a very rare species—

GRACIEUX: Thank you!

SERRAND: He has the most accurate judgments on human relationships, probably more than any of us in the room, in a very visceral way. At the same time, he is the worst one to explain how they function. So I've always enjoyed him as a non-director director. I think he's best when he's not directing.

ROSEN: He's very wise.

What have you directed that you're particularly proud of?

GRACIEUX: I'm proud of puppet shows; I'm proud of the last twenty minutes of the Goldoni piece [*Il Campiello*, 1990]. I never accomplish something I'm really proud of in total, but I'm proud of moments.

What moments or pieces are the rest of you particularly proud of, as a company?

BERLOVITZ: *Yang Zen Froggs*: the engine that got us to that performance was really quite amazing—how we worked together, how we pooled our resources, how we were driven to create something that *had* to work, that was *going* to work, even though we felt, "We don't have a clue what this is going to be like!"

And although I can look back and say, "Well, I wish that had been different," the experience I had directing *Germinal* [1993] was tremendous. There were thirty-five people on stage; it was *huge*! And the fact that this company embraced a project like that—you don't see that anyplace else.

Steven, when's the last time you directed?

EPP: I've directed twice. Once a long, long time ago, and *Medea* about two years ago.

SERRAND: I was amazed at seeing *Medea*. I was designing, so I was close—and *not* close—to what it was trying to become, and I thought it was superb. You just don't see that very often: the gesture was so large, so well-thought-out, so complete. It's fun to see Steven direct because you see a very frustrated master having to wrestle with something he could probably by now write better than the material that he's offered. But I don't encourage him to keep directing because I want to make sure he keeps acting!

ROSEN: Steve is such a strong actor that if you're not on the level that he is as an actor, it's difficult for him as a director. He just can't go where he needs to go, and then he just wants to kill everybody, or he wants to act all the parts himself!

BERLOVITZ: I think he's got an enormous sense of clarity, and is able to convey his ideas to anyone in the room in an understandable way. He has enormous patience. Because he is such a strong actor he can walk into a scene and know how it should be done (although he doesn't say that). That gives him the well of knowledge about how to guide an actor who's having difficulty. If he senses an actor is giving him a particular direction, he'll nourish that. He doesn't impose himself on the actors at all.

What about Bob?

GRACIEUX: I love Bob's mind—it just amuses me so much. I think we can go places I don't know with him, and sometimes I'm annoyed because he's too slow or doesn't decide, or whatever, but I really enjoy working with him. It's a discovery, working with Bob.

EPP: He's great at creating the playground that allows the actor to go in and just fuck around in the best sense of the word. And he has a patience to let it emerge, which is key for him; when Bob works best, he has the luxury of enough time to do that.

It sounds like the tension we were talking about earlier, but also the playfulness you all discuss.

BERLOVITZ: Oh, absolutely. He's born with a sense of *play*. I don't think I've ever seen anyone have such a sense of play on the stage (and in life) as he does. He has an ease in what he does physically that is truly poetic.

SERRAND: I would add just one word: iconoclast. Always trying to complicate everything possible, by any means possible, and all the time looking for the fly that's in the soup. That is very, very good; we constantly forget that what's more important than the soup is the fly that's in the soup. Once you realize that, then you follow him. Few actors know what he's looking for; it's very, very difficult.

Any last words about what you've learned about directing—whether as actors, directors or designers?

SERRAND: The more I know, the more I realize I don't.

BERLOVITZ: Ditto. Absolutely.

SERRAND: And it's great.

GEORGE C. WOLFE

Master Showman

ACCORDING TO GEORGE C. WOLFE, THE charismatic, controversial producer of New York City's Public Theater from 1993 to 2004, writing is an art, directing is a craft and producing is a job. Wolfe has managed, though, to bring his unique artistry to all three in a career that has spanned decades, growing the American canon of innovative new plays and changing the landscape of the country's musical theater.

Born in Frankfort, Kentucky, in 1954 (the same year Joseph Papp founded the Shakespeare Workshop, which later became the Public), Wolfe, a gay black man, fought discrimination in his childhood, and now feels an obligation to open doors to those who find them locked. All Americans are mongrels, he says, so while particular identity politics don't feature in his work (he's not always writing or directing to illuminate, say, the gay black experience), identity itself is nearly always an issue in the plays that excite him. From *Jelly's Last Jam* (1991), for which he wrote the book, to Tony Kushner's *Angels in America* (1993) to Suzan-Lori Parks's *Topdog/Underdog* (2001) to John Guare's *A Free Man of Color* (2010), the plays and musicals that capture Wolfe's imagination are the ones in which characters stand on the border between an alien culture and the mainstream, and the stories they tell illuminate both sides of the divide.

As a child, Wolfe was always directing—"I wasn't just *playing* house; I was *directing* house," he says—and in high school he became obsessed by the theater. A trip at age twelve to New York City, where he saw Pearl Bailey in *Hello, Dolly!*, was particularly influential, and when he went to Pomona College in Claremont, California, he studied theater and began writing plays. From Pomona he moved to Los Angeles, where he continued to write and direct until 1979, when he moved to New York City. From New York University, he received a master's in dramatic writing and musical theater in 1984.

Wolfe's play *The Colored Museum* was his big break. First produced in 1986 at the Crossroads Theatre Company in New Jersey, the play is a provocative satire about race in American culture, told through a series of inflammatory and artful vignettes. It opens, for example, with a stewardess welcoming people aboard "Celebrity Slaveship, departing the Gold Coast and making short stops at Bahia, Port-au-Prince and Havana, before our final destination of Savannah . . . We will be crossing the Atlantic at an altitude that's pretty high, so you must wear your shackles at all times." Although the play was criticized by many in the African-American community (who felt it was anti-black), it caught the attention of Papp, who transferred it to the Public Theater later in the year.

Wolfe didn't direct *The Colored Museum,* but he did direct his next play, *Spunk,* an adaptation of short stories by Zora Neale Hurston. Developed at Center Theatre Group's Mark Taper Forum in L.A., the play was first produced at Crossroads and ended up at the Public in 1990. The production was a roaring success, and things began to happen for Wolfe in a big way. He won an OBIE Award for direction, and Papp brought him aboard as a resident director at the Public.

The OBIE also gave Wolfe the credentials nationwide to direct his own work. He'd been writing a book for a new musical for the Taper about the life of jazz musician Jelly Roll Morton (with music by Morton, Susan Birkenhead and Luther Henderson), and when director Jerry Zaks dropped out of the project, Wolfe was tapped to direct it. *Jelly's Last Jam* opened to raves in 1991, and transferred to Broadway in 1992, giving Wolfe his first credit there (and garnering eleven Tony nominations). Almost immediately after that, Wolfe was offered *Angels in America, Part One* on Broadway, which earned him his first Tony Award.

Meanwhile, Papp's short-lived successor at the Public, JoAnne Akalaitis, had been asked to leave by its board. In the middle of *Angels,* George C. Wolfe became the third artistic leader of the Public Theater, taking the title of producer, as Papp had before him.

Wolfe's eleven years at the Public were marked by phenomenal ups and staggering downs. A natural risk-taker, Wolfe gambled heavily on new musicals, some of which bore quite a bit of fruit. Of his own work, *Bring in 'Da Noise, Bring in 'Da Funk* (1995) was one of the phenomenal ups. Created with tap sensation Savion Glover, *Noise/Funk* transferred to Broadway in 1996 and earned Wolfe his second Tony Award. It played on Broadway for three years and over one thousand performances, ultimately touring the country under the Public's auspices and replenishing the theater's endowment. In this, Wolfe was thought by some to have earned his place as Joseph Papp's true successor: Papp's Public Theater production of *A Chorus Line*, which ran for fifteen years after moving to Broadway, earned the theater more than $35 million.

On the down side, Wolfe's Broadway transfers of his stagings of *On the Town* (1998) and *The Wild Party* (2000), financed primarily with the Public's funds, did not pay off, losing the Public an estimated eleven million dollars. *On the Town,* in particular, was a dark moment for Wolfe. On the heels of severe health problems (relieved by a kidney transplant), Wolfe's obsession with updating the 1944 Leonard Bernstein musical increased to a fever pitch, even after the production received mixed notices from its 1997 Central Park run. Without a commercial producer willing to take on the lead role, the Public stepped up as sole managing producer of the Broadway transfer. *On the Town* ran only sixty-nine performances there, and lost the Public $6 million.

The financial failure of *On the Town* brought gripes about Wolfe's institutional leadership to the fore. His erratic management style—unlike most not-for-profit theater leaders, Wolfe ran both the Public's artistic and management side for most of his tenure—was assailed in the press. His directorial style was criticized as dictatorial. The attacks became even more personal—for example, it was said that he only championed plays by writers of color—and gossip began to circulate that Wolfe would soon be leaving.

But he didn't, and his final four years at the Public were marked by a return to critical good graces. He directed three more plays that ended up on Broadway: *Elaine Stritch at Liberty* (2001), *Topdog/Underdog* (2001), and the Kushner and Jeanine Tesori musical *Caroline, or Change* (2003), all of which were well received. By the time he left the Public to pursue writing and film shortly after this interview in 2004, thirteen of the theater's productions had moved to Broadway on his watch, and it had embraced the kind of "cultural collisions" Wolfe wanted so much to present. New works by playwrights including Parks, Nilo Cruz, Lisa Kron, Oliver Mayer and even Arthur Miller brought audiences of every stripe through the doors. Shakespeare had fared well, too; Wolfe's own production of *The Tempest* played successfully on Broadway in 1995.

Since leaving the Public, Wolfe directed the 2005 high-profile HBO film of Ruben Santiago-Hudson's *Lackawanna Blues* (originally a play he produced at the Public in 2001, directed by Loretta Greco). That film won a number of awards, including a Directors Guild of America Award and an Independent Spirit nomination for Best First Feature. But this film success has, so far, been limited. Wolfe's follow-up project, the 2008 *Nights of Rodanthe* starring Richard Gere and Diane Lane, was roundly dismissed.

It may thus be no surprise that Wolfe has begun to tack back to theater. He reunited with his *Caroline, Or Change* partners Tony Kushner and Jeanine Tesori for a starry *Mother Courage and Her Children* in 2006 in Central Park, and tackled John Guare's ambitious *A Free Man of Color* for Lincoln Center Theater in 2010. Despite their artistic achievements, neither of those two productions fared particularly well with the critics. But his 2011 Broadway mounting of Larry Kramer's *The Normal Heart*, codirected by Joel Grey, has more than resuscitated his reputation. That production won three Tony Awards and a Drama Desk Award for Best Direction for Wolfe and Grey. Shortly after opening the production, the Stage Directors and Choreographers Foundation announced Wolfe as the 2011 winner of the Mr. Abbott Award, given to honor lifetime achievement in the field.

Meeting him in person, one is not surprised the man can be both revered and feared. Wolfe is an energetic fireball. Words fly out of his mouth more quickly than they can be digested, and still they travel too slowly for his own thoughts. Whereas other people may stress their modifiers to make a point ("I was *so* excited . . ."), Wolfe repeats them for effect, and then punches the verb ("I was *so so so so so EXCITED* . . ."). He never stays on a topic long enough for a listener to get comfortable with it. His hands dance as he speaks, and his living room is set up almost like a stage set, with him perching, catlike, on a settee in the very center. Wolfe's legendary charisma is seductive, to the point that you crave to stay on his good side. And you definitely don't want to be on the bad.

SEPTEMBER 2003, WOLFE'S APARTMENT, NEW YORK CITY

When did you fall in love with theater?

As long as I can remember I've been intrigued by theater. The school that I went to always did a "school-closing play." It was a small school, so everyone was in it, but being in it wasn't what excited me.

I remember watching rehearsals with what one might call my "director's eye." There was one production of *Babes in Toyland*—all the plays were directed by the principal, Minnie J. Hitch, and there was a number being rehearsed, somebody was singing, and she had blocked natural behavior: two boys sitting on a bench shoving each other. And

I remember watching that and thinking, "Oh wow, that's making the number seem real." That was incredibly *vivid* to me.

I didn't necessarily have that *language*, but that's what I was seeing, and I filed that away somewhere.

Also my cousins told me that when we played house, I would give them lines to say. I wasn't just *playing* house, I was *directing* house. I think I've always been less interested in being in it, and more interested in making it.

For as long as I can remember, it's always been about crafting space, and crafting bodies in space, which is what I think theater directing is: crafting space so that the language and ideas can soar. That impulse has always just been there . . . which is odd, because Kentucky is not exactly the cultural center of the universe. I don't think I ever saw any plays there, other than the ones that were done at my school. But when I came to New York and saw theater, I had the *tangibles* for that which had previously been *intangible*.

You've spoken in previous interviews about seeing *Hello, Dolly!*, *West Side Story* and other plays that were extremely influential—

Yes, and a production of *Hamlet* directed by Joe Papp, with Cleavon Little, by the mobile unit of the New York Shakespeare Festival, that was done in Washington Square Park. I was living right across the park. My mother was attending NYU that summer.

When you talk about yourself to somebody who doesn't know who you are, how do you identify yourself?

I sort of figure out how they're defining me, and go from there. If people say, "You direct, right?" I feel the compelling urge to say, "But I started out as a writer." Or if they say, "You're a producer," I go, "But for most of my career I was a director."

I don't know if this is a good thing to say in this book—

Say whatever you think.

I don't think directing is an art; I think directing is a craft. I think you can be an artist, and you can direct artfully, but by and large I believe directing is a craft. I believe acting in the right hands is an art, I think writing is an art, and I think producing is a job.

I think I am an artist, so I bring my artist sensibility to all of those jobs. The part of me that is very social, that likes to create structures whereby community can happen, and likes to make people feel safe, and likes to play—that's my director self. The side of me that is probably more subversive than anything else, and is really quiet, is the writer side of me. But since I've become a producer, I've had less opportunity to live in that head.

The producer side of me is really the *service* side of me. I grew up with a very strong sense of responsibility, very specifically from a racial context—I was taught that if you get into the room, you need to open the doors and windows so that others can get in as well. That thought process has spread to the rest of my work and life. It's not enough that you get yours; you must create structures so that other people, other artists, can do their work as well. So the side of myself that feels responsible—that's the producer side of me. It's a job that requires tremendous ego and energy, but I think has very limited ego satisfaction.

This past year I produced the Chicago premiere of Suzan-Lori Parks's *In the Blood*, but I didn't direct it. And I felt more satisfied producing that work than directing many plays I've done.

Ellen McLaughlin and Stephen Spinella in Angels in America, Part One: Millennium Approaches *by Tony Kushner. Broadway, 1993. Credit: Joan Marcus.*

Well, I think it's a sense of satisfaction that's more akin to parenting. Like, "Oh, that's a beautiful child that I helped nurture, but it's an entity separate from me." I feel very unterritorial as a producer. Mind you, I feel very territorial and competitive toward other theaters, but I don't ever feel territorial doing what I need to do to empower the artists working in my theater.

Our field can be suspicious of artists with multiple specialities—actor/ director, writer/director. Your career is the story of multiple journeys.

When I went to college on the West Coast, I went for acting and design. In my second year I switched to acting and directing. And all of a sudden, there was a whole side of me that felt instantly comfortable, and *loved* directing. And then in my last year there, I started writing. After college I moved to Los Angeles and worked at a theater called the Inner City Cultural Center where I wrote and directed my own plays. But then when I moved to New York, people told me, "Oh, you can't do that, they won't let you write and direct your own material," so I just focused on my writing.

And after many years, *The Colored Museum* happened, which established me as a writer. And then Crossroads Theatre wanted me to come back and do something else. And Gordon Davidson from the Mark Taper Forum called me up. They had a literary cabaret, and I said, "I have these three Zora Neale Hurston short stories that I've been thinking about developing," so I went out there and did this sort of readers' theater version of it and called it *Spunk*. It got a rave review from the *L.A. Times*, and people wanted to move it [to another theater in California for a longer run]. And I said, "No, I want to play around with it more." So I went to Crossroads and staged it. It ended up coming into New York, to the Public, where I won an OBIE for directing. Then people said, "Oh, okay, he *can* write and direct!"

In the middle of that, Joe Papp offered me a season at the Public. Also around that time, from the success of *The Colored Museum*, I got all these Hollywood offers to write. But I learned very quickly that when they say, "We love your vision," it means, "Surrender yours and do ours." Writers in Hollywood gave up their power a long time ago, and they'll never get it back. They get money, but they'll never, ever get that power back.

During this time I also was offered a bunch of other theater projects. Among them, I got asked to write the book for *Mr. Jelly Lord* (as it was then called). Jerry Zaks was the director, but he ended up leaving the project so that he could direct *Miss Saigon*—which never ended up happening, as we know from history. [In the end, Zaks turned it down and Nicholas Hytner directed the West End and Broadway productions.]

THE DIRECTOR'S VOICE, VOLUME 2

So the producers, Margo Lion and Pam Koslow, proceeded to try out every single director they could find for the project, but none of them were working out. In the interim, *Spunk* opened in New York and was a hit. That's how I ended up getting *Jelly's Last Jam* as a director. But fundamentally I came on board that show as a writer.

My career has been sort of *charmed*, and very blessed. *The Caucasian Chalk Circle* [at the Public Theater] was in 1990. And in the middle of all of that I was already working on *Jelly*. When *Jelly* was running, I met with Tony [Kushner] and got offered *Angels* to direct. And in the middle of *Angels*, I got offered the job at the Public, and it was like, *whooosh*! And now ten years later, my God, what happened? I'm a producer now.

And?

I really feel as though I need to go back and become a writer again! I want to take a break from directing, because it can *kind of* fulfill a lot of the same things that writing can—but not really. I figure if I stop directing for a while, it might give space for the writer in me to reemerge.

So much stuff has happened in the past ten to fifteen years, I just want to see how it would come out, what stories I have to tell.

When's the last time you wrote? The book for *The Wild Party* [together with Michael John LaChiusa]?

I also wrote the libretto and a lot of the lyrics for *Harlem Song* [in 2002]. But book writing is smart, craftful writing. Lately it's become writing that has *intimacy* removed.

What are you hoping to write next?

I have a couple of plays I've been working on, and a couple of screenplays too. It's odd because there is a very specific cinematographic sensibility to my directing that was always there, especially on the musicals, but that has sort of intensified in recent years, which tells me I'm about ready to direct a film.

Is that filmic impulse the driving sensibility behind your directing?

No, rhythm is. Everything is rhythm. It's the most primal force we respond to—not language, not even sound, but rhythm—it's the thing we surrender to most easily. And so for me everything about the theater is rhythm. From the time you pick up your ticket to the curtain call, there's a rhythm at play. At the beginning of the show, if the audience sits in the dark too long before the stage lights come up, it affects the *rhythm* of how they process every single thing.

But the most important rhythm is that which exists in the text. If you can locate that, then the audience can have a certain kind of experience. You have to do all kinds of text work to get the actors to feel free, so that they can surrender to this über-rhythm that you're creating. You can't just *shove* them into the rhythm. Otherwise it's not intimate.

Because ultimately I don't think theater's about *people*; I think theater is really about *ideas*. And that's one of the thrilling things about it. People are invited to be inside those ideas. If you have really brilliant playwrights, you're not aware that you're inside of them.

What you end up watching in the theater is an incredibly intimate exchange between an audience and actors. But what you take home is not that. You may take home "That was a brilliant performance," but if a play really affects you, it's generally the ideas, and the depth of those ideas; that is what you carry with you for the rest of your life if it's been an amazing experience. Theater can do that.

So it's coordinating all the elements—the designers, the actors, the playwright, everything—so that there is this rhythmic texture. Laughter is a part of that rhythm, and applause is part of that rhythm, and silence is a part of that rhythm.

What about a nonmusical play, like your *Macbeth* at the Public in 1998? How did you find its rhythm?

I don't know if I did. I found the rhythm in a *smart* way, but I don't think I ever penetrated the intimacy of that play. As a director, you have to penetrate the writer's rhythm. Anybody who writes anything, they write it with a sense of urgency. Shakespeare *had* to write *Much Ado*, when he wrote it. He had to, for whatever reason. Arthur Miller *had* to write *Death of a Salesman*. Albee *had* to write *Virginia Woolf*. If you can locate that level of intimacy, you can also locate the emotional urgency that's inside of it, and that begins to dictate the rhythm of the piece. The rhythm of the piece is not an external "one-two-three, turn, say-the-line" comprehension. The rhythm of the piece is connected to the intimacy and the urgency that is inside of every play that's ever been written.

Which you, as a director, have to locate.

You have to find it not only in the play but in *yourself*, so you can then illuminate it for all the artists working on it.

When you have playwrights that you champion at the Public, such as Suzan-Lori Parks or Lisa Kron, is it because the rhythm is immediately apparent to you as you read their work? Is it living on the page?

I only go on that kind of detailed journey if I am going to become intimately involved with that play, i.e., direct it. Otherwise it can be kind of dangerous. As a producer you can't want to date and marry the play, all the while inviting another director to come in, because it can contaminate your relationship with that director. It's one of the interesting things I've had to learn as a producer, because I'm a director who has a reputation. I have to make sure that I'm sending as many signals as I possibly can to directors that I'm giving them notes not on how *I* would do it, but on what I think *they're* doing, or what the *play* is doing.

How have you learned to do that?

I've had to develop a whole language. Sometimes it's not even a verbal language, it's a language of behavior. Fundamentally it's making yourself vulnerable to the state that the show is in, as opposed to judging what state the show is in. The directors know that my notes are coming from that place, instead of from a judgmental "do it my way" kind of place. Otherwise they'd shut down and nothing would be achieved.

What kind of language do you use with outside directors?

It changes per director. If I already have an evolved language with a director, I can just give clean, very direct notes. I was giving notes to a director on Saturday, and it was really interesting because I felt as though he had found the *order* of the play, and now he needed to find the *chaos*. He hadn't located, or he hadn't been able to empower his actors to find, the emotional chaos inside of the play. It was a very clear production (which is a valuable thing), but generally most people's lives aren't *very* clear. What are they thinking? What is the mess that's living inside of them which is driving them to make the strong choices they're making?

Very few people make strong choices from strong places. Most people make choices like, "I don't know what's going on in my life, but I hate you!" or, "I don't know what's happening next in my life; will you marry me?"

So my notes were about finding the combustion behind the clarity. Ultimately, you adjust the language so it's helpful to the current state of the work in process and the level of skill the director has. Because I think few directors are skilled in all the things they need to be skilled in. More often than not, directors who are incredibly into their relationships with designers are generally intolerant of the intimate process of actors, and therefore they want them to fit into the visual composition they are creating. They never learned to talk to actors. Then I think a lot of the time you find that directors who are really, really good with the intimacy of actors, and making them feel safe, have limited visual skills. They don't know how to make an event. Or you have people who are good with the visual event and are really good with actors, but have absolutely no language for working with playwrights. In theory, as a director, you should be able to speak the language of all three.

I think a director should live as an actor, a writer and a designer. You have to *live* in all three, not necessarily to see how good or how bad you are, but to gain insight into their process, which can in turn empower you to speak their language so you can get what you need.

You clearly have lived in all of those places—

It was ten long years between the time I graduated from college and *The Colored Museum,* so poverty and struggle forced me to live in all of those places! I did start out as a designer and decided I hated drafting. I don't like the details of it, but I love shaping space.

And acting. I think I was a *good* actor. But the idea that eight thousand people would have to make a decision before I could get a job was so *horrifying* to me. It so *horrified* me that a bunch of annoying people would be sitting behind a table after I'd gone into a room and poured my guts out, and would say, "Well, I don't know about him, he's kinda skinny." The idea that I would have to do that professionally so horrified me that I knew I would go in one day with an Uzi and kill everybody in the room.

The level of vulnerability that acting truly requires in an often brutal landscape is astonishing to me, so I have tremendous, tremendous respect and deep affection for actors. It's part of why I'm totally indulgent with them.

How do you mean that?

I'm very sensitive to how sensitive they are. I think it's very *hard* to be an actor. When *Angels, Part One* was performing, we were creating *Angels, Part Two.* There was this weird three-week period when the actors sort of lost their minds. Because when you rehearse, you have to make yourself *available* to everything, and when you perform, you've got to be in *command* of everything. Going from being forced to be available to everything in the afternoon, taking off all their clothes, if you will, and then having an hour-and-a-half dinner break, and then having to put all their clothes back on and perform for an audience, was *hateful*. It was such a brilliant distillation of the rigor of that process. Which is why you have to create such incredible safety in the room.

I believe there are fundamentally two styles of directing in terms of actors: you can stand where you are and demand that actors come to you, or you can go to where they are and woo them in the direction you want them to be. The first one is easier; the second is much harder, but I think the work ends up being more fulfilling for all parties involved. Your goal is to get them to utilize the intimate secrets they know from having lived on the planet for as long as they have, which is in turn going to enhance the work. If you brutalize them, they're less likely to reveal that vulnerability. It's that basic.

Sounds manipulative.

Unquestionably it is. So I always try to say on the first day of rehearsal why I think the project we're doing is important, because when actors believe what they're working on is important, they tend to let all (or most) of their potential bad behavior fall away. Actors are complicated people. The nature of their work requires them to bring their emotions into the room, and often enough, personal mess tends to follow that process. That's why it's very important you speak to the stakes at work in the material, because you're in essence saying, "Human-being mess is fine, and actor-monster mess is not." Naturally things are going to spill over a bit because it's all so intimate, but if everyone in the room senses what they are doing is important, I find everyone is much more responsible. They tend to check themselves when too much starts to spill.

In rehearsals I also tend to ask a lot of questions so as to shatter what they think they know so that they're available not only to the discoveries we're going to make collectively, but to their own private discoveries as well.

You mean questions characterwise?

Yes, but more than just that. "Why is that moment significant? What's going on at this moment? What do you think this is about?" It was really interesting working on *Angels*, especially with certain members of the cast who had done the show before at the Taper, where it had been very successful. They already knew the material very well. So my challenge was to make the material new for them.

In one scene I remember talking to the actors and saying, "Think of the lesion"—Prior's first lesion—"as if it were his new lover." Something he was obsessing about, something that was consuming all of his thoughts and feelings and that was causing Louis, his old lover, to feel

The cast of Bring in 'Da Noise, Bring in 'Da Funk, *book by Reg E. Gaines, music by Ann Duquesnay, Zane Mark and Daryl Waters, lyrics by Ann Duquesnay, Reg E. Gaines and George C. Wolfe, conceived by George C. Wolfe. The Public Theater, 1995. Credit: Michal Daniel.*

left out. AIDS is there, AIDS is there [gestures far off] . . . but this *thing* that's right here . . . what is it? What will make it *immediate*?

When I was working on *The Tempest,* all the actors were asking the usual questions: "Where's Miranda's mother?" "Is Caliban a beast?" And I said, "We'll find all of that, but first I want to know, *who owns our story?*" If you own your story, it gives you a certain kind of power. If somebody else owns your story, you're constantly fighting that person for the right to your story.

In their first scene together, Prospero tells Miranda her story, and in their second scene, she *defies him.* She defies him because she's miffed, instantly in love and all of that stuff . . . But I think the real reason she's able to defy him is because she now owns her story. Caliban stands in defiance of Prospero because he knows his own story, whereas Prospero tells Ariel her story. He has power over her.

If we can locate an intimate churning issue simmering underneath the text, it will not only activate the scene, but illuminate the ideas at work inside of the text. We're going back to what I said earlier about trying to find *why* this playwright had to write this play at this moment. What issues are going on other than the obvious ones?

For example, one of the stories in *Spunk* is about the abuse a husband inflicts on his wife while he's having an affair with another woman in town. Once upon a time, the husband and wife were a vital sexual couple. That's gone, but still present in the relationship is the desire to have a physical impact on the other person. The abuse is springing from the husband's desire to have an *impact* on his wife.

When you're talking to actors playing those roles, is this the language you use? Do you talk about objective?

I don't talk about objectives unless somebody needs it. I don't like to talk about all of that because I don't want to think of the material in such a clinical, distancing way. My normal working process is focused on empowering the actor to go on a journey of vulnerability. But by the time I get to previews, I will engage in talk like, "If you pause before you slam the door, that'll get a bigger laugh"—that kind of detailed, silly, but fun, technical work. But initially the work is much more intimate-slash-conceptual-slash-emotional.

Is there an art to knowing which questions to ask, and how to ask them?

I think I am an insightful person. I like to *watch*. When my career became whatever my career became, it was so disconcerting when people would watch *me*. I much prefer the other way around. Because I think you can just learn so much.

Like in auditions.

In an audition situation (which is fundamentally an awful construct), I'm much more interested in how an actor's brain works than in his or her talent. Because if I'm going to be in a room with these actors for five or six weeks, I want to have fun with them. I don't want to be annoyed if they are dull and have no opinions.

When I worked with Danitra Vance, I would say, "Danitra, I need you to jump off a cliff, swim through a river of alligators, go charging through the forest chopping down every single tree, and then you come to a barn and you walk inside."

And she'd go, "Wait a minute. What color's the barn?" [laughs] And we'd have to *obsess*.

I also like going into a room not knowing what the hell I'm doing so I can discover something. Because an audience can tell when they're in the presence of a stale truth. And an audience can tell when they're in the presence of a truth that was discovered *just for them*.

In the first scene of *Caroline, or Change*, Tony had the character of the washing machine speaking first—the washing machine being a manifestation of the maid Caroline's inner self—and then Caroline spoke. But for the life of me, I couldn't figure out how to stage the damn thing. In my head I saw the rest of the play, but this opening scene, I couldn't see it.

And then finally one day, I said to Tony, "We meet Dorothy before we meet the Munchkins." If Caroline sings the first line, and then the washing machine responds, I understand that. But if the washing machine sings before Caroline, I don't understand that. And he said, "Okay," and with that switch, I knew instantly how to do the scene.

Unquestionably there's a stylistic vocabulary that exists in all my work, but on every single project I do, I try to not know what I'm doing. I do tons and tons of research, but eventually I like to put myself in the exact same condition as an actor.

Being vulnerable—

Being vulnerable, yes. I remember working on *The Tempest,* after I'd staged practically the whole show, I found a notebook from almost eight months earlier in which I'd scribbled down a bunch of stuff, blocking notes and staging ideas I wanted to do, and had in fact ended up doing. I don't remember ever taking those notes. By being vulnerable to the room, I'd ended up back where I wanted to be, but I got there in a more organic, messy way, by discovering the play along with the actors.

Then you really have to trust actors as collaborators.

I was directing a project in college and learned an incredible lesson. It was a dark urban piece [written by Wolfe] called *Block Play,* we were on a break and I was over in one corner talking to the composer, and the actors were over in another corner making noise. And I was going, "It's just not working, it's just not working." And, "What about this?" And the actors were making more noise, and I was like, "Would you guys just be quiet? We're trying to solve something over here!"

I was just at the point when I was ready to scream at the actors to keep quiet when I suddenly realized they were playing around with the song we couldn't figure out how to solve. *They* had made it work. It was an incredibly valuable lesson, because you don't know where the solution is coming from. It could come from anybody.

It's been said you can be dictatorial in the rehearsal room. You believe you create an open and collaborative environment?

I'm so far from being dictatorial. As a matter of fact, my rehearsals more often than not feel like anarchy is about to erupt at any given moment. I like strong-willed people, I like opinionated people. I like people who feel comfortable being ridiculous. It just makes the work better. I'm a strong boy, and I have a very forceful personality, and if I have to assert my authority, I know I can. So I don't have to wear that. I'm not interested in wearing that, because then it inhibits people.

One time, very early in my career, I was doing a play in Texas and I yelled at an actor. And then two minutes later, that actor yelled at another actor. And then somebody else yelled at somebody else. And then I got it. Consequently, I work very hard to not spray my anger around the rehearsal room.

When you observe another director working at the Public—someone you've hired—how does that person's process differ from yours?

I generally don't watch rehearsals; I watch a runthrough. I have a rule that no one should be in the rehearsal room unless they have a job. They can be sharpening pencils, stage managing, moving scenery, be on promptbook, but I think everybody in the room should have a job, because that unused energy is going to have an impact.

Particularly as the producer at the Public Theater, I know that when I come into the room, I instantly contaminate something. So I don't let myself go into another director's rehearsal room. Perhaps twice in my entire time here, I have had to take over. Which after ten years is not bad at all.

What made you realize you had to go in and make a change?

In both cases, I knew it was a mistake to have those directors direct those plays.

Because?

One director was better at staging plays in which people sit around and talk. This play required a physical and visual virtuosity that was not this director's forte. After three or four weeks—this was very early in my tenure at the Public—*nothing* had been staged.

A lot of tablework?

Not even that. I just don't think he knew how to *enter* the piece. At one point, when he did get around to staging, he had somebody up on an elevated level one minute, and the next second they were down on a lower level. I asked him how they got down there and he said, "Oh, we haven't figured that out yet." He just didn't have the staging vocabulary essential to doing that play.

The other time it was a director who was used to working with actors who were his buddies, but we demanded that he cast the best, smartest possible people. And those people were more than he could handle. He was not in charge of the room. He sent out a signal: don't attack me, whatever you do. So all these actors started attacking each other. It was a situation where the room overwhelmed him, so I had to step in and tame the room, and then I gave the tamed room back to the director.

The actors were relieved in both cases because they instantly felt someone was taking care of them. On the second show, the designers thought I was an evil villain, but over time they recovered.

In one interview you talked about getting up from the table too soon for *Caucasian Chalk Circle.*

Yeah, the actors never performed that play with any true level of confidence because I panicked about my process and violated theirs.

I think sometimes I have a stupid kind of, "I just know I can make this idea work" impulse. I've been involved in a few situations where a collaborator was missing certain skills and I bravely-slash-foolishly thought, "If I throw my energy and my spirit and my intelligence at them *I can make it better.*" It's a Pollyanna brain that's working; it's not an "I'm all-powerful, and I can make everything brilliant" ego. Sometimes you can, but a lot of times you just can't. Some people from the outside could view it as egotistical, but in fact that's not what's going on at all.

I just did a show like that (which shall remain nameless), where I spent most of my time educating and compensating for a couple of the artists I was working with, instead of collaborating with them. The result was that, one, it made for a very draining experience; and, two, the work required a series of brutal decisions that I didn't make because I didn't have a clear, clean perspective—because I was overworking. The piece paid, in terms of what we were able to achieve. What I should have done was either replace one or two of the artists involved, or not done the piece. In fact the show grew significantly and got better, but not enough so, because I was *teaching*, I wasn't sharing and collaborating.

If actors are too young or haven't had enough experience but you put them in a situation with a certain kind of rigor, they will rise to the occasion if they have the talent and the aptitude. If you're doing that with a designer as part of a seasoned team, the same thing can happen. On this project, there were *too many* people not at the level of command of craft that the work required.

Can you tell me about a remarkable moment you created on stage, of which you are very proud?

It's probably because I just did it, but I'm really, really proud of *Harlem Song.* I wanted to create something that was as smart as it was populist, a new-century version of the "Living Newspapers" from the WPA era. I wanted to re-create a historical pageant, and infuse it with a linguistic and visceral showmanship. That was a fun challenge, and the end product felt stylish and really elegant and smart. Plus I did lots of lyric writing, which I love to do but hadn't really done since I was in the musical-theater program at NYU.

There were some really raw and exquisite moments in *The Wild Party* of which I'm very proud. Prior to directing it I watched tons of silent movies because I wanted to create that kind of visual stylization on the stage—a world of shadows and profiles and smoldering intensity. I'm also totally obsessed with New York in the 1920s; the black-slash-white-slash-sexual explosions that were taking place.

So while working on it I was thinking, as was Michael John, "How far can you smash a musical? How raw and intense can you make it and have it still fulfill the entertainment and buoyancy equation, which is essential to making a musical work?"

If the behind-the-scenes dramas that were happening on that show weren't so intense, we could have addressed and found the appropriate balance. As it was, the rawness of the piece was too much for what Broadway had become by then, which is a place where recycled emotions and images are celebrated, and erratic brilliance is punished for going against the status quo.

How about *Jelly's Last Jam*? That was a real turning point for you, and you managed to create a piece that both entertained and got to the heart of some serious social issues.

Working on *Jelly's Last Jam* was very interesting. Though I had never done a Broadway musical before, all of my work up to that point had a musical sensibility that was very specifically my own, and this show did as well. But right in the middle of it was Gregory Hines, fighting me *every step of the way* because he was coming at it from a very specific and very different Broadway musical sensibility. So there were lots of fights and showdowns, which were *painful* but ultimately very valuable, because they required that my language and vision be so clear, not only to him, but to the rest of the company, and in turn the audience.

I like things to look exquisitely beautiful while something very raw is happening underneath. That tension between the two really excites me. And that tension was also emblematic of my collaboration with Gregory, him being more attracted to the slick, with me being drawn to the raw underneath. It was hell fitting our two sensibilities together, but once I found a way of crafting it, it's what made the show work.

There was a really brilliant number that wasn't working during previews, called "Some Coons." It was one of those brilliant ideas that if we were out of town, we could have figured out how to make it work. There was a giant black lacquered box with a lid, and at one point it opened and there were actors inside with coon masks on, like chocolate candies. Jelly was leading the coons in a dance number with a lyric that went:

Some coons they dis and dat
Know where their place is at

in essence celebrating the fact that he was Creole and not black. But then the Chimney Man, Jelly's nemesis in the show, had a lyric:

Don't he know he's—yeah—just another coon!

And all the masked coons turned around and on the backs of their heads, they had on Jelly Roll Morton masks, i.e., Gregory's face. So Jelly went from being this unique thing to just one more "coon." It was conceptually a really fabulous, dark, edgy number, but we couldn't figure it out.

We ended up replacing it with a number called "Doctor Jazz," which was Gregory singing with a certain intensity. But that wasn't enough. The "Some Coons" number lumbered, but had bite. This number had the right energy, but no bite.

So I came up with the idea of the actors, the black dancers, putting white makeup around their lips—in essence making *their own faces* coon masks. When I informed the cast during rehearsals that I wanted to do that with the number that night, some of the dancers started to cry; there was all of this trauma backstage. It brought to the surface all of these racial demons that a lot of black people carry around. That night when they performed the number with *their own faces* as "coon masks," it added this other kind of edge, and that's what lifted the number.

The conceptual "Some Coons" number was too heavy-handed; the Dr. Jazz showbiz number was too easy; the white lips was the right combination and it made the point. And that was the result of the emotional violence of that collaboration, which then transformed it to a loving collaboration.

Speaking of *Jelly*, how does your identity as a black man directing, or my identity as a white man in the audience, function in your work?

All Americans are mongrels, fundamentally, and anytime anyone reaches for purity, more often than not, it exposes the falsity of that pursuit. With people of color, issues of identity live more overtly in our consciousness, but fractured identity is something everyone in this country can relate to. Consciously or unconsciously everyone brings their incomplete selves into the room. We bring into the room our incomplete childhoods; we bring into the room our fractured and oftentimes fabricated histories; everybody brings into the room our deepest fears when we come to see a play. And if the play pushes certain buttons, you laugh. And if the play pushes certain buttons, you cry. If the play pushes buttons you don't want pushed, you leave or you write a bad review about it! If the play pushes buttons you don't *like,* but you're willing to make yourself available to the process, then you can come out on the other side, hopefully, with another kind of perspective.

Specifically with *Harlem Song,* it was about a community coming together and dissolving, and coming together and dissolving, which was unquestionably informed not only by the historical work I'd done researching Harlem, but was also deeply informed by 9/11; the sense of fear and loss that I personally felt, and the reaching out to my circle of friends in the months following and how we needed, depended on, each other. So the show was about Harlem; it was about black people; it was about a riot here, a rent party there; a depression here, a war-torn world there; but it was very much about the *healing power* of community.

Speaking of community, I think when you direct a play, you have in your mind an ideal audience. There were things that happened with *Angels in America* when the Gay Games were in town that were astonishing. I know so many stories of young boys and girls who brought their parents to see the play as a way of coming out to them. There were times during *Colored Museum* when it first was in previews, when the white people in the audience would look to find the black person in the room to see if he or she was laughing. Then Frank Rich's review came out and said it was satire, and smart and daring, and then people started to trust their right to laugh. Toward the end of the run, when it was about seventy-percent black, it was like a football game in there.

But for me the most interesting audience (and in some respects my ideal audience) was when it was half black and half white, and that tension in the room was released through laughter. The word I probably use more than any other word when I describe theater is *visceral.* Because if you can create sensations inside of an audience, they're going to respond, regardless of their identity. There was this French woman I know who went to see *Harlem Song,* and she asked someone who worked in the theater, "Is it safe to bring my car?" But by the end of the show, she was jumping up and down and screaming, "I have to come back!"

Those are examples of people who already live on the border—gay people, blacks and whites together, the French woman in New York—

We're *all* living on the borders of our lives, *all the time*. And theater is a constructive way to go to the *danger.* It's a safer way to go to the danger.

Because you're there with a group—

Because you are part of a collective and you get to surrender together to the rhythm and ideas at work in a show.

I went to a Knicks game with a friend from the board of the Public and I was like, "I want to create a show where people *act like this*, this raw exchange of energy between spectators and participants, where *people cheer!*" And that show became *Noise/Funk!*

The energy on stage was so overwhelming with that show that people had no choice but to surrender to it. Savion [Glover] was the perfect collaborator for that. And tap, oddly enough, was the perfect medium, and Jules Fisher and Peggy Eisenhauer's lights . . . All the elements were right to have this really intense, raw event-slash-audience exchange.

And that's the kind of show I could have only made at the Public. Imagine if I had gone to a commercial producer and said, "I'm going to do this tap-dancing show with lynching in it—give me money!" That show went to dark places; and when it brought you back, the joy was even more empowering.

In every single play I work on, I try to find that place where you go, "I don't want to be here, take me away, this is awful, *this is hateful, oh my God* . . . okay. I passed through that, and I feel stronger." Or, "I know something about myself, about the world, that I didn't know." I reach for that every single time I do a play.

What are those dangerous places in today's culture?

I think the borders that are scary are where people have to surrender power. It's one thing to have gay people tell you the correct way to dress; it's another thing for gay people to say, "I want to marry." *Huge* difference. Power. When it's about power, when it's about people letting go of power so other people can have a little bit more, that's always dangerous. And it's harder and harder to get to a place of danger because of this horrible climate of commercialism you find.

Let's talk about maintaining that place of danger in a climate of instability. You've got a huge institution to run. How do you measure your responsibility to the institution with your responsibility as an artist?

I find that periodically you go through periods when you have to reconvince your board that they should keep supporting and raising funds for the adventurous work you believe in. To help them through those times you've got to put a blue ribbon on the box. You get Jeffrey Wright and Don Cheadle to do *Topdog/Underdog* so that audiences are fighting to come see fabulous famous actors, and the press is excited as well, and in the middle of all the hype you're also getting people to see and talk about an amazing, dangerous play. And then in the case of that play, it goes and wins the Pulitzer, so the board is reenergized and recommits to doing the kind of work you believe in.

But then don't you run the risk of getting your audience to expect celebrity with its art—that they will appreciate the glamour instead of the work?

Fundamentally we're not a celebrity theater; we're a writer's theater. That always comes first. If you're going to use stars, you'd better make sure that the material fits them. You run into trouble when you start choosing projects for glamour.

You, and historically the Public, seem to like running that risk with Shakespeare in the Park all the time.

The Park is an event; it's a whole big package. When you're paying $2.2 million for two plays, or $1.2 million for one play, it's the most amazing gift I can think of for a not-for-profit institution to give free to the people of New York City. So you must come up with creative ways to keep it free. Having productions with "fabulous famous people" attracts donors whose support helps to keep the "free" in free Shakespeare. Succinctly put, you have to bend to the dynamics of the world you're a part of without bowing to them, and that's the fundamental challenge of being a producer.

So why do it? You've spoken throughout this interview about having time for yourself as an artist. Why are you still at the Pubic Theater?

Because I believe in what the institution stands for, especially in light of the overt commercialization that seems to be flourishing in New York theater these days. And also because, as I stated earlier, it feeds the need in me to make sure other people get into the room. Also, I love helping to shape and define the cultural landscape. And I think Shakespeare in the Park is performing a great service for this city. I love the services the Public performs for its community, opening the building for groups to hold meetings and performances . . .

That's why I did it. That's why I took this job. Nothing else—not for glamour, not for money, not for power. Producing was Joe's art, unquestionably. For me, it's my service. I have a bunch of other places where my art can live.

MARY ZIMMERMAN

Mirroring the World

BACK IN THE 1980S AND EARLY 1990S, when American "auteur directors" like Richard Foreman and JoAnne Akalaitis eschewed narrative realism in favor of visual metaphor, and their international counterparts—Pina Bausch, Ariane Mnouchkine and Peter Brook among them—were at the height of their powers, Mary Zimmerman was paying close attention. Earning her BS, MA and PhD at Northwestern by studying their innovations, Zmmerman was poised to follow in their cerebral, postmodern footsteps.

She has, to a point. But Zimmerman's work has also embraced the opposite—an intuitive, almost childlike theatricality that is as comforting and traditional as listening to someone tell you a fairy tale. Some call it "story theater," this melding of visual theatricality and simple narration. But that sounds reductive in Zimmerman's case, because the juxtaposition of simple text and sophisticated, surprising image yields everdeepening layers of meaning in her work. Her best-known creation, *Metamorphoses*, operates in exactly this way, to potent, staggering effect. A collection of myths (primarily based on Ovid) presented episodically with seeming ease and theatrical simplicity, the stories amass such deep layers of meaning, the imagery is so inventive in its construction, that she was honored with the 2002 Tony Award for her direction.

With *Metamorphoses*, everyone remembers "the pool." Presented on a thrust stage and refined through at least six incarnations (the first in 1998, at Chicago's Lookingglass Theatre Company) before coming to Broadway in the wake of 9/11, the show had as its overwhelming scenic feature a nearly thirty-foot-long pool of water (about one and a half feet deep in the Broadway production), in which actors splashed about, or floated on rafts; they waded through its waves, gazed into them, or floated above them. Zimmerman's idea for it (refined into a set by frequent collaborator Daniel Ostling) came simultaneously with her idea to adapt Ovid, and she painted the surface of the water as if it were a canvas, using actors as brushstrokes, elaborate costumes as colors and magical lighting as tints. The phenomenon of watching *Metamorphoses* (especially for a spectator who had never before seen a Zimmerman production) was like a dose of theatrical adrenaline. The power of the simplest image to evoke emotion—a man turned into a bird, flying low over the water, watching its reflection—could be surprisingly overwhelming. Zimmerman's on-stage imagination taps into the same primal, ritual need that the work of Julie Taymor does. One is captured not so much by the overriding intellect that composed the image as by its innocence, its purity of meaning.

The Off-Broadway production of *Metamorphoses* opened at Second Stage Theatre on October 9, 2001, and the critics viewed that innocence as a celebration of life—and the perpetual grief of loss—in the shadow of the Twin Towers. Ben Brantley wrote in the *New York Times*:

> The images of loss repeat, distort, freeze and transform. Orpheus, a prisoner of his own memory, makes his famous mistake again and again, looking backward as his bride slips, unreclaimable, into the underworld. A sad, hopeful wife stands at the ocean's edge, scanning the horizon for the return of her long-dead husband, just as she did on the day his ship set sail. A girl, torn from her lover in the night, is evoked by words said softly three times by a narrator: "She's going to suffer."
>
> Sorrow is a fugue in Mary Zimmerman's heartfelt adaptation of Ovid's *Metamorphoses*. And though Ms. Zimmerman first produced the play in 1998 in Chicago, it could surely never have had the resonance it has acquired in the aftermath of 9/11.
>
> For New Yorkers today who encounter the same recorded visions of terrorist destruction whenever they turn on their televisions, Ms. Zimmerman's portrayal of tragic scenes repeated has an anxious and immediate familiarity. But there is balm in Ovid's world, as Ms. Zimmerman presents it. Those images from television stay the same; metamorphosis occurs in the human imagination. There can be artistry and solace in remembering.

Without their darker ruminations on loss (or the hefty intellect behind them), Zimmerman's theatrical fantasies would indeed warrant the simplistic (and, to some, condescending) label "story theater." But her visual meditations are much more eloquent and ultimately complex. Though she may be best known for *Metamorphoses*, her first work to achieve widespread notoriety was *The Notebooks of Leonardo da Vinci* (Goodman Theatre, 1993), a completely non-narrative visual feast of excerpts from the master's writings on anatomy, science and art. Her images may bring simple delight to the audience member in search of escape, but for the deeper thinker there are layers upon layers within those images, which accrue wells of meaning in the course of an evening. Thus the intellectual and innocent combine in Zimmerman's oeuvre, which spans the gulf between Ovid and da Vinci, between the children's fairy tales of *The Secret in the Wings* (Lookingglass, 1991) and a site-specific rumination on a legendary French novel in *Eleven Rooms of Proust* (coproduced by Lookingglass and About Face Theatre, 2000).

Zimmerman bounces back and forth now among her own adaptations, the works of Shakespeare, other classics (like *The Trojan Women* at the Goodman, 2003) and of late, opera. In addition to a charming and hugely inventive *Candide* for the Goodman (2010, which toured to the Shakespeare Theatre in Washington D.C. and Huntington Theatre Company in Boston thereafter), Zimmerman has now directed three productions for the Metropolitan Opera: Donizetti's *Lucia di Lammermour* (2007), Bellini's *La Sonnambula* (2009) and Rossini's *Armida* (2010).

Contemporary playwrights figure rarely in her work, if at all—which is not unusual for an auteur whose productions have historically been devised with an ensemble. She is much more interested in her own visions of the classics she reads, which provide so much fodder for her fertile, visual imagination.

Born in Lincoln, Nebraska in 1960, Zimmerman is, ultimately, a theater phenomenologist. Phenomenology is that strain of postmodern theory that attempts to understand how theater works on its audience: what is the experience of watching a play? Zimmerman analyzes her work from this point of view, as opposed to, say, a textual one, or even a symbolic one, despite the ample symbolism in her style.

Which is to say, Zimmerman is primarily interested in the transaction between performer and actor; she strives to repay the audience for the sacrifice of attention it makes, and she aims to provide spectators with "maximum delight." As she has become famous, having won the Tony Award and seen her work performed all over the world, Zimmerman still believes in an aesthetic of simplicity, because the surprise of watching a simple transformation—a length of blue fabric turning into a river, or a mechanical bird winging across the stage—is the theatrical phenomenon that interests her most.

Zimmerman believes the theater's job is to mirror the world back to the audience. And she has found great success in that endeavor, especially in Chicago, where she is revered for her fantastic creations. The Manilow Resident Director at Goodman Theatre, and an ensemble member of Lookingglass Theatre Company (as well as a professor at Northwestern University), Zimmerman has more than enough artistic homes to experiment in any way she likes. Through her teaching at Northwestern, she has inculcated a generation of artists who routinely create work that fuses the imagistic with the narrative. In a post-9/11 world, when audiences want their intellectual content filtered through layers of fantasy and escape, Zimmerman is providing just what the audience craves.

MARCH 2007, ZIMMERMAN'S APARTMENT, CHICAGO

You were born in Lincoln, Nebraska. Is that where you fell in love with theater?

Both my parents were professors at the University of Nebraska. When I was five and six, my dad had an opportunity to work in Cambridge and London, so we lived in England, and that's where my primal scene of theater occurred.

It happened on the outskirts of London. We lived in a place called Hampstead Garden Suburb, and our house backed onto the Little Woods—which is so English, don't you think? I played in there every day by myself. Unbeknownst to me, there was an annual production in the summer there of *A Midsummer Night's Dream*, and one day, I came across a rehearsal in a clearing of the woods.

They were rehearsing that scene early in the play: "Ill met by moonlight, proud Titania." They played the argument about the changeling boy, Oberon and Titania separated, and Oberon started to run around in a circle on the stage (which was just a grassy area). There was even music on a little record player plugged into a generator or something. He ran a few times, followed by his fairy retinue, and then he suddenly interrupted himself and said, "How many times do I go around?" And everyone started laughing and laughing, and even falling on the ground. That was so startling and profound to me.

A literal "fairy tale." Can you identify what in the experience was so profound?

The point of the story isn't that for a moment I thought they were fairies, or anything like that—I understood that they were playing. But that's what was so extraordinary: they were playing pretend, and really having fun, and laughing...and they were *adults*. I'd never experienced that before.

The woods themselves had been my own scene of invention and make-believe. I had a whole world going on there; I had names for a lot of the trees. I went back about eight years ago as an adult for the first time, and it was shockingly familiar. Everything was smaller, but certain trees were very much still there. I was sort of overwhelmed with the feeling of it.

My mom took me to a lot of plays in England, too. We went and saw the famous Christmas Pantomime, with Cinderella's ugly sisters played by men. I vividly remember that one of the ugly sisters had a big ball gown with little Christmas lights in it, and I've used that in shows, Christmas lights sewn into a dress.

So those two years in England were perhaps more formative than sixteen years in Nebraska, in terms of your career?

England is where I learned to read and write, which I think is important. I also had a teacher there who read aloud to us every afternoon, and she read us *The Odyssey*. *The Odyssey* has been really important to me, all my life. I think I had an identification with it: being in a strange land, separated from home, on an island. She also read us stories of King Arthur and the Knights of the Round Table. I remember the pictures she would show us.

You've spoken of images sticking with you from childhood—in particular, those pen-and-ink drawings from Edith Hamilton's *Mythology*.

Yes, those line drawings were very gripping to me as a child, even though they're quite simple.

It's no surprise to learn that images were so meaningful to you as a child, given the director you've become. Fairy tales, pictures, images, dreams . . .

I did fantasize as a child that there was a machine I could buy or invent that I could plug into at night to record my dreams, so I could watch them the next day. And I've since thought that the theater is that machine, where you can see, externalized, these elaborate, somewhat unconsciously informed images.

Did you try acting in your childhood, or did you go straight into directing?

I'm a *late* director, in my opinion. These days people are aware of the *job* of directing much earlier. All of my students know what directing is, and they want to be directors.

I acted in plays as a child, in community theater and in school. But when I came to Northwestern, I came as a comparative literature major because I thought I wasn't pretty enough to be an actress. In fact, I'd been told that, both explicitly and implicitly. It was in the way people looked at me when I said I wanted to be an actress: "Well, that's *really* hard, that's *really* competitive."

So I came in as a comp lit major, but that only lasted about two weeks, and then I transferred into the theater department.

If you didn't think you were going to become a professional actor, why the change?

I couldn't *not*. I *one hundred percent* believed I was throwing away my parents' money, but I was just going to do it for four more years. I had no thought that I would ever have a career in it. I had no concept of a life in the theater that wasn't the visible presence on stage. That was true through my undergraduate work, until I got back into graduate school in the performance studies department.

It was there I took a performance art class, and we were asked to stage things ourselves, *on* ourselves. We performed these pieces that were image-based, or based on fairy tales, or this or that, using no language. I was so interested and so moved by it that I started doing more and more elaborate pieces. Eventually it was just easier to *not* be in them, to just arrange them and make them. That non-narrative, visual, performance art thrust—combined with the fact that I'm an obsessive reader: all my life I've been absorbed in books—is probably what led me to what I do today.

In fact, the other half of the performance studies department was engaged in the study of adaptation. There was an actual *focus* on adaptation of literature. So I ended up combining this really strongly narrative impulse with its opposite: a non-narrative, visual, metaphoric, abstracted way of creating feeling, and images, and so forth.

All of my work figure-eights between those two impulses. Almost every show I do contains a section in which no one's speaking, but things are being understood through visual and musical means. On the other hand, almost all my shows contain narrative, where someone's actually talking to the audience and saying, "The next thing that happened was . . ."

From the Little Woods to Northwestern University: that's the story of your theatrical maturation.

Northwestern is a mammoth influence in my life. I went when I was eighteen and I haven't left. I got all my degrees there. I was officially out for two years between undergraduate and graduate school. There were some lean years when I was a graduate student, not really writing my dissertation, teaching an occasional class, teaching other places, that sort of adjunct life that one has. After three years, a position opened up there and I got it, and it became permanent.

Those formative years, the 1980s and early 1990s, were also a time of great visual experimentation in the theater generally, with artists figuring out how to combine the narrative and the visual. I'm thinking of Mabou Mines, Ping Chong . . .

Although I would never use the verb "figure out." Your work when you're working is immediate; the only thing you're figuring out is the problem that's six feet in front of you. You're not thinking theoretically.

But surely, the theoretical background you attained from Northwestern must influence how you tackle those problems six feet in front of you.

Sure, my theoretical background, my ability to describe things in a certain way that's informed by theory, has helped me in my profession immeasurably.

I was once trying to decide between two actors at the Public Theater for Shakespeare in the Park. And I said to the casting people, "I'm going to say something pretentious and incomprehensible: I believe that the *semiotic* choice is Actor A, and the *phenomenological* choice is Actor B. And if we were indoors I would go with the phenomenological, but we're outdoors, so I have to go with the semiotic one."

And they understood me entirely. One actor *was* the character; the other was capable of *signifying* it. The theory clarified this decision in an unbelievable way. So really, seriously, all my Derrida, Foucault, Bakhtin, all that way of talking about performance and representation, the mimetic versus the presentational and the representational and on and on . . . all of that really does help me articulate to myself, "What is wrong with this picture? What would fix this?"

But at the same time, you're working very up close. It's later that you look back and see the theoretical. This occurred to me just a couple of months ago: "You know, I guess I'm postmodern." All these qualities that you describe as postmodern: collage, parody, quotation . . . I am of my era. And that had never, ever, occurred to me.

You studied all those figures you mentioned, and became fascinated by questions of representation, how experience is mediated and formed on stage. That's exactly how your plays function. It is on one level an explicit, theatrical act of storytelling, and on the other a very thoughtful considera-tion of how stories are told, and have been told, through the centuries.

Yes: how am I going to make this clear? I want the audience to acquire a vocabulary early on in the evening that is going to pay off, enormously. So as the evening goes on, you can say less and less, and they read more and more. Because you've taught them early on: every time you hear this sound, it means it's the next day; or every time someone drops a red handkerchief it means someone died (I've never done that in my life, but you know what I mean). You teach a vocabulary, and the audience becomes fluent in it.

When that's being accomplished without words, it creates an enor-mous sense of intimacy between audience members and people on stage, because—like lovers or members of the family—they have gained an unspoken understanding and agreement, and they know how to read the metaphor in exactly the same way. It's as though they have an entire history with each other, even though that history has only been created in the past couple of hours. It draws on an entire cultural history, of course, but all that's been intensified and refined in just a couple of hours.

Your work has been compared to that of Pina Bausch, and you share a similarity in creating vocabularies, exactly as you say. I'm thinking of your production of *Silk* at the Goodman in 2005: every time the Narrator, played by Chris Donahue, swung his cane it meant another journey had begun. The accretion of that image became breathtaking by the end of the play.

I like that you spot Pina Bausch in me. I saw her work at the Brooklyn Academy of Music when I was in my early twenties, and it was a pro-found experience. It's exactly what you're saying: there's an emotional vocabulary. She's the first artist in which I recognized that extremely deep feelings can come outside of a story, outside of narrative, which can be really surprising in our tradition—that you can touch wells of feeling and meaning through images that aren't being explained, that aren't necessarily unrolling with the shape and pace of narrative.

At the same time, *Silk* has a huge amount of language. In fact, I think it's my most explicitly narrative piece, almost too much so.

Is that why you once said that *Silk* was the riskiest work you've ever done?

It was really risky. It's such an intimate, tiny little story that I was absolutely obsessed with. It's just an almost perfect work of art as a novel [by Italian writer Alessandro Baricco]. I left the narrative of that book ninety percent intact. The opposite would be *The Secret in the Wings,* which is based on fairy tales, and almost ninety percent written by me. *Metamorphoses* is maybe seventy percent my language, thirty percent the translations I used. They're usually more like fifty-fifty.

But *Silk* was like an illustration of the novel. I do think there were things to be gained by staging it and seeing it—and, for myself, by seeing my way through my obsession with that novel, and bringing it to completion.

What was successful about it for you?

I think it was beautiful; and for those who fell into it, it was shattering. It depended a great deal on Chris Donahue, who I often say is my most important artistic collaborator. We've done fifteen or so different shows together. I wouldn't have done *Silk* had he not been available to play the Narrator; there's no one who can narrate like he does. He's transparent, subtle. He lands on the text as lightly as a dragonfly. He's played Odysseus for me [in *The Odyssey,* which premiered at the Goodman in 1999], and narrated *Silk,* and in *The Arabian Nights* [Lookingglass, 1992], he was the king.

What about other influential artists you've seen, beyond Pina Bausch?

I saw Laurie Anderson in concert when I was younger. I remember describing every moment to people after seeing it.

Peter Brook?

I almost never mention him because the influence is so overwhelmingly obvious. I saw *The Mahabharata* in Paris when I was young, at the Bouffes du Nord. But it's clearly a big epic adaptation of a mythic text, and the cast was hyper-international, from everywhere in the world. I remember being drawn to that diversity, the ensemble quality of it, the live music.

You directed *The Baltimore Waltz* by Paula Vogel at the Goodman in 1993. It was your last contemporary script. Why?

My first and last, other than a small play by David Greenspan [*Jack,* 1990]. I had just joined the Goodman [as a resident director], and I was

Kyle Hall in Eleven Rooms of Proust *by Mary Zimmerman. About Face Theatre and Lookingglass Theatre Company, in association with Goodman Theatre, 2000. Credit: Rich Hein.*

sort of suggested, or offered, or "assigned" *The Baltimore Waltz*. I would never have done it had I not liked it, but they said, "We think you'd be good at it." I think it was my first thing in the Studio. Chris Donahue was in it. I thought our production was really good, but it was sort of misunderstood, critically. Richard Christiansen felt the play made fun of AIDS and he lambasted it.

Was it a conscious choice to leave contemporary playwrights behind?

No. After that play at the Goodman, they were casting about for projects for me to do next. And I remember [then associate artistic director] Michael Maggio said to me, "Why don't you just do that *Michelangelo* thing?" And he meant *Da Vinci*, which he'd seen. [laughs]

I'd produced *The Notebooks of Leonardo da Vinci* myself; it was my very first off-campus production. I borrowed $800 and I produced the first version of it. It's also how I met Lookingglass Theatre Company. They had a space I rented. And I did everything myself: took the publicity photos, ran the sound, got all the costumes, everything, everything,

everything. I was a graduate student at the time, and I used undergraduates and a lot of people who were in Lookingglass. I think we had three performances, there was virtually no set, and I'd always wanted to revisit it. I so loved Leonardo's writing; the quality of it was astonishing to me.

How did you first come to do that show, which was clearly so instrumental in you finding your voice?

I was doing a piece in school called *The Mystery of the Fourth Wall,* and I wanted a little "performance break" in the middle of it. I was looking for a scientific text that had to do with seeing and the eye, and I remembered watching Kenneth Clark's *Civilisation* series on TV as a child and seeing da Vinci's drawings of the eye, with lines radiating from it. So I went to the library to find that text, and to my utter shock, there were volumes and volumes of his writings. The last thing he's famous for is his writing, and yet there is so much of it and it is so varied and rich.

Immediately, the text felt like it had metaphoric resonance. When da Vinci speaks about something artistic or scientific, the writing has a quality that is infinitely rich and open. He will write, say, twenty-three chapters of anatomical description of the heart; and then, as he's justifying why anatomical drawing is superior to description, he says, "With what words can you describe this heart without filling a whole book?" The resonance of that is so clear.

Or when he's talking about painting, he has a section called "How white bodies should be represented," and he argues that there *is* no such color as white. If you see a woman walking in a field, dressed in white, "notice how her clothes are tinged with the yellow of the field nearby, and the other side by the sky. For white has no color in itself, but is tinged and transformed by the colors and the objects opposite."

That feels to me, believe it or not, like a statement about identity, even race, and how we are contingent on everything that is around us, shaped and influenced by everything around us; we are not discrete objects. Even though it's just a discussion of how you shouldn't use pure white when you paint white figures.

To this day, *Leonardo* is a piece that's really deep within me. Without being narrative, we told a life's story. It begins with an image, or memory from his childhood, a memory of being touched by a falcon on his mouth as he lay in his crib, which to me is an image of annunciation, or the moment of the passing on of divine wisdom. It ends with his speculations on death and ultimate transformation, how everything becomes everything else. There's an apotheosis at the end where he becomes a bird. So the piece had, I think, a very strong arc, even though at no moment did anyone ever play any character in a scene of dialogue, or come out and say, "When are you going to finish the painting?" [laughs]

You and Leonardo are a perfect pair—you both perceive the world visually.

He was so in love with the world, and his curiosity until the day he died was unabated.

When we're children, we ask, "Why's the sky blue? Why does the water look blue in the lake when it's clear in the faucet?" But as adults we become inured, we get habituated, we stop asking those questions. He never ever, *ever* did. He was so desperate to represent the world that he approached it from both sides, artistically or metaphorically representing the world, and then also through scientific description—which I suppose is another form of metaphor. He understood the value of both of these approaches, and also the *failure* of both, how the world exceeds any representation, any description, any lifelong pursuit.

That in the end is a huge acknowledgement. It's a huge praise of the world, of its abundance and richness, and its ultimate unknowability. The theater itself is on the same mission of representation. Of replication, of mirroring the world back to the audience. There's a line in *Da Vinci:* after a long description of painting, he asks, "Who would believe that such a small space could contain all the images of the universe?" That's true of the proscenium stage as well.

Not long after *Da Vinci* came *Journey to the West* [Goodman Theatre, 1995], which was the first production of yours that traveled to major theaters.

I love to travel. And I love remounting shows. I prefer to do them with a majority of the original cast. For one thing, they deepen with time. If you start over with a lot of new people, you're in a different place on the first day of rehearsal than the new cast is. You feel at times that you're *teaching* the show instead of making the show. Particularly the way I work, because there's no script when I start, the first experience is always this incredibly intense adventure. The second time it's a million times easier, but it doesn't have that first breath of inspiration and creativity surging through it. On the other hand, often the productions are improved.

What besides *Journey to the West* has been a major turning point in your career?

I suppose *Metamorphoses* has been the most important production of my life. I went a huge distance with that show—I was with it for six years. It started at school with students, then a year later I did it with Lookingglass (using three of those students), where it was meant to run six weeks, and we ran it eight months. And then it went on tour to three regional theaters, and then it went to Second Stage in New York, and then it went to Broadway . . . and I still had those three students in it. Three marriages came out of that show.

By now, because your work is so well known, do you feel it's easier to teach an audience that visual vocabulary you talk about?

Maybe, but here in Chicago, because of Frank Galati [who also taught at Northwestern] and his influence in this community, audiences are very aware of the whole narrative adaptation thing. It's not news to them. There are companies virtually devoted to adaptation. Frank, by the way, is my artistic father. We all came out of Frank's overcoat here in Chicago. But generally I don't have any sense that I've influenced anything. Some people have told me it's apparent in things they've seen, but we're all part of the same river.

One of the first shows I saw in Chicago was Eric Rosen's production of Whitman at About Face Theatre.

About Face came out of Northwestern; Eric was my student.

I was struck by how clearly it had been influenced by your work. It was episodic, and it told each story visually. We were in a field, so he brought on standing grass in a planter; a pond in the next episode was suggested by blue fabric.

I don't think Eric would deny this; I think *Whitman* is influenced by my work. I'm proud of that.

Any other shows that stick with you?

Eleven Rooms of Proust. It is an unreplicable experience. It has something in common with *Da Vinci*: both shows are episodic, they're non-narrative (even though the individual passages tell stories, maybe), they're fragmentary and they accrue meaning by putting things next to each other.

The "Proust House" (that's what we called the warehouse where we performed it) was unique in the world. The only reason we closed was because by July in Chicago it became unbearable; there was no air. And it was unsustainable. It had a cast of thirty, and only audiences of thirty could move through it each night, six audiences starting every half hour. It just couldn't sustain itself, even though there was a line to the end of the street to get tickets—to see Proust in a warehouse.

Where do the ideas for your plays come from?

For decades I've been harvesting the passions of my childhood. *Argonautika* [premiere at Lookingglass, 2006], *The Odyssey*, *The Arabian Nights*, and fairy tales and myths are all from my childhood. I loved them before I ever thought of staging them.

What do those texts have in common?

First, they were oral tales before they were codified in one or another particular version. And since they were oral tales, they have *embedded performance* in them. They are meant to live in the air, and in the moment, and in the transaction between the live audience and the teller. I don't consciously seek that out, but those texts all have an unreleased theatricality in them.

On the other hand, the people who were telling them or making them up were not trying to accommodate a twenty-first-century stage. So they're filled with impossible things to stage—and I love that. Sea monsters and flying carpets and camels and turning into a bird and drowning . . . All those things can't be represented on stage in a mimetic way, unless you have a zillion dollars, and want to do it that way.

You can do it with film.

They're absolutely made for film. They're film before there *was* film. But the stage has a heavy, gross materiality to it, so you have to find ways to represent those things metaphorically. You have to use all those tropes: that the part represents the whole, this stands for that, this looks *like* that but isn't that. That's the field of play that attracts me; that's what playing *is,* it's pretending and making up. It's not called a "play" for nothing. Theater's always the site of metaphor. In order to bring a whole world into that one little space, you have to use tricks and devices and imagination, which is the largest trick of them all.

So the texts you like demand transformation.

They demand transformation. You have to figure out how to represent them.

Has that task become easier in your career?

I feel I'm gaining confidence in finding narrative story where there isn't any. When you read *The Argonautika,* you *want* it to be this band of brothers on a trip in which there's lots of vivid characters, but seriously, there's so many men on that boat, too many men. They seldom appear twice: someone will come forward and speak a paragraph, and then he doesn't exist anymore, and next time there's a similar argument but it's a different character who steps forward and then never appears again. When I began the project, I set a goal for myself to pick out narrative threads to make all of the people on the boat have their own stories.

Since that isn't prioritized in the original text, I had to really massage it in a way, different from the work I've done previously. In my long-ago training at Northwestern we were very literal: "Don't change a word of that text. Stick to that text. Use the narrative. Text, text, text." That's why I found it liberating and rewarding to think, "You know, I'm combining these two characters, giving them different names than they have in the book, because the names they have in the book are too hard to understand . . ." I was faster and looser with it. These are oral texts that undergo transformation every time they're told, anyway; that's what they are supposed to do. But at one time in my life I would have felt very inadequate in relation to the text—too small to think of changing a word.

You've said that you don't begin with a script—but you can't tell me that you find all of your shows through rehearsals.

Sure, I have ideas before the show, and I make a lot of notes, but my process is misunderstood a lot. Even you saying, "Did you find that through rehearsals?" "Through" isn't quite the preposition I'd use. I'd say "during that period." The only difference between me and a regular playwright is that my period of writing is laid *on top* of the period of rehearsal. It's not that my actors are improvising, and then I'm writing down what they say. I'm writing in the hours *in between* rehearsals, and every day bringing it in, seeing if it works, going on, filling it in. My cast and designers influence the script enormously, but indirectly. For example, I write for the people in the show. I look at what they are like, and that convinces me to make certain choices. Sometimes they're reading the text, and they say, "I love that moment where such-and-such happens," and I go, "Oh really? We'll put that in."

The set, which has to be designed before we start, shapes the script—nowhere more so than for *The Notebooks of Leonardo da Vinci* and *Eleven Rooms of Proust*. In *Notebooks,* there was all this stuff built into the cabinetry that I did not quite know how I was going to use, and it kept giving me ideas; I have a hundred examples of that. I would pick selections because there was something on the set that was very useful.

It's the same with the cast. I might, for example, have thought I wasn't going to have any songs in a show, but oh, suddenly, the people I cast can really sing. We can exploit to the fullest all of their abilities.

Now sometimes people think that means we're improvising, but we're not. Definitely, I'll do physical improvisation: "How many different ways can we fly you? How are you going to get up there?" Obviously, you work that out with the actors in rehearsal. You go in with an idea, but it doesn't work, and what they come up with is a million times better. But in terms of the text, it's just like regular playwriting, except I'm doing it the morning of rehearsal.

What's the hardest part of the work in between rehearsals?

The hardest part of the process for me is the nightly casting. A lot of what I do is episodic: "He plays the old man in this scene, but wait: I think I want him to play the old man ten scenes from now . . . What am I going to do?" And later on, that other scene ends up not happening. That happens *constantly*.

Does that create insecurity in the cast? Is that difficult for them?

My process is hardest on props and costumes. Because I can say, for every person in the cast, "They're at least playing *this,* but I don't know what else they're playing." And the designers will say, "Well, how many suitors do you have in this scene?" And I'll say, "Well, *probably* four or five, but then the next scene has so many sailors . . ." Every single day it's revise, revise, revise. Which is why, when I work with Mara Blumenfeld (who does virtually all my costumes), we come up with an ensemble costume, and then add and take off pieces. There's just no way to plan for full costumes beforehand. Almost all the texts I do are much, much, much larger than the shows that I pull out of them. Most of the texts I do are thousands and thousands of pages, and I'm pulling an evening out of them.

I ask sometimes why I work this way. There are a lot of reasons, including a fear of dramaturgy. When I'm reading, the image comes to me simultaneously with the idea for the text. It's not a separate thing. Sometimes people ask, "When did you decide to do *Metamorphoses* in water?" Well, it was myths and water to begin with.

It's a freefall, and all of those clichés are true: as you fall you grow wings, and the result is very organic. It's tied to the people who are doing it, and tied to the *time* we're doing it. Many of my shows are bent by the very specific politics of not just three months ago, or that year, but *that morning,* and the events in the lives of the people I'm working with that morning. There's a strong immediacy and flexibility to the scripts and the texts. Besides, I'm always dealing with texts that *apply.* They're so archetypal, and they're so about what it is *to just be a person,* and have to experience loss. That's why they've hung around for thousands of years.

I can't imagine you have any fear of dramaturgy in the design process. That's where I read the theoretical in you most clearly. In many of your works, you identify a controlling visual gesture that informs the play as it's built by you: cabinets of wonder in *The Notebooks*, the pool of water in *Metamorphoses*, the abstract ship of *Argonautika*. These controlling gestures have to be just right, and based on intense dramaturgy, for your shows to work.

Yes, you're absolutely right. There is one controlling gesture. My sets have to be both highly defined and open fields of play. And they are *one grand gesture*.

Can you give me an example of the process?

Argonautika was a struggle, and of all my sets, it's one of my favorites. I said, "It's a ship, we need to make the whole theater a ship." We had all these ideas: the ship was really literal for a long time. So I have to credit set designer Dan Ostling. With most of my sets, I do have the idea super-strongly, and then he improves the idea a million percent, and makes it work, and makes all the volumes and the proportions eight billion times better than I ever could. But the idea, the thrust is mine.

With *Argonautika,* that abstract box was his breakthrough. We're going to go on the road with it, and put it on a proscenium stage, which means we're going to modify it. But the way that set sits in that space, at Lookingglass, for which it was conceived—

I can't imagine it without the alley staging you used, putting the audience on two sides.

Enough of my shows have been popular that theaters have wanted to get in on new ones before they've existed and to make them coproductions but I've always turned that down. Because I want the design to be perfect for the space we're in. I don't want it to be compromised before we start. So I prefer to just do a show for *that theater,* and if other theaters come and say, "We have a very similar space, and that'll fit very well," then that's great.

That must limit the ability of your shows to tour, right?

Absolutely. *Metamorphoses* can't be in a proscenium; you have to be looking at the surface of the water, or there's no point in doing the show. It has to be a thrust; you have to look down. You'd think *Argonautika* has that limitation, and I'm sure there will be stuff lost in the proscenium, but there will also be stuff gained.

For example, I have this idea that maybe we have the gods walking across the top of that box on stage, and poking their heads down through the holes. There's a dimension to be gained by using the top of the box. Also, we'll back it with a sky, or something that maybe has openings in it, so the gods are up in the sky. There are things to be gained.

I'm eager to take *Argonautika* on the road because, though Lookingglass is fantastic, we don't have any money. Our budgets are pathetic! I once said—and they understood me when I said this—that they don't produce me best, but I produce my best work there. I'm looking forward to not having people on stage wearing something that cost two dollars in a thrift store!

I wanted to ask how money has changed your work. Because your aesthetic has always been based on simplicity, and the magic of transformation with the simplest ingredients.

Yes, it was derived from having to make do, and it still is. I have a hard time spending money. I still don't like motorized things. I've never pulled a big wagon onto a stage. I'm like a little goldfish that's been in a little bowl so long that even when I'm in the big tank, I'm still swimming in a small circle! My aesthetic is based on playing in the backyard in the first place, and I think it always will be.

Where I like to spend money is in quality of fabric—that is great. Quality of shoes, quality of props, quality of wigs. As opposed to just using a glue gun and some cardboard. But I'm very guilty about spending anyone's money. Even at the Met [for *Lucia di Lammermoor*, 2007], Mara and I will be deciding between two fabrics, and I'll be asking how much they cost. I don't like to spend a lot of money on something that's on stage for a brief amount of time. It's decadent, it's wasteful and decadent, and it's a failure of imagination in some way.

Surprise is a big part of how you fire the audience's imagination. Money and technology aren't that surprising anymore.

Well, you can use money extremely imaginatively; I'm just not sure I'm very good at it. I'm very jealous sometimes when I see a big Broadway extravaganza, and I think, "I never would have thought of that." Although at the Met I'm starting to have some big ideas. It's a requirement to fill up that space. But I just contain a poor-person mentality. It almost killed me when I had to take a cab to Heathrow the other night instead of public transportation, because my bag was too heavy!

I don't mean to put myself down. I take great joy in making people *think* they saw something that wasn't there. They think they saw this

Erika LaVonn in Metamorphoses *by Mary Zimmerman. Hartford Stage, 2004. Credit: T. Charles Erickson.*

incredibly rich, fabulous thing, but it was really small and inexpensive, actually, just suggestive, and in the end kind of easy.

And there's magic in that transformation.

I love the fact that the water to fill the *Metamorphoses* pool on Broadway cost four dollars and twelve cents.

There was an effect in *The Odyssey* which is one of my all-time favorites: when the suitors get killed. Little bags of sand are hanging above their heads, and Athena pokes the bag of sand with a twelve-foot spear, and a little stream of sand comes down individually on each of their heads. There's a kind of optical illusion where it looks as though the sand is rising from their bodies rather than falling. It has so much metaphorical resonance: sands of time, and dust to dust, and being buried and time running out, and all of that. And it's the cheapest trick in the world.

Since the sand from all the different bags over the suitors never ran out at the same time, I had to solve a problem: how do I stop the image? We came up with this *dropping* of bags. The suitors stand up—they're already dead, but they take a step back, and the bags drop, and then they carry them off, these little half-empty bags of sand that are like their own ashes, their own organs, their little thing they're carrying to the underworld.

Death on stage seems to beg for metaphor.

And sex. Sex and death are two things about which I feel that the more realistically you do them on stage, the more false they seem. Sex doesn't *look like* how it *feels*. The subjective experience of it is very, very different from the objective viewing of it. Those are fun things to constantly refigure how you're going to show, and make them felt and understood in a poetic way that also feels real.

Do you have a favorite myth in *Metamorphoses* where you really aced that transformation?

Possibly "Eros and Psyche" (which is not actually in Ovid). I couldn't figure out how to do it at first because it's full of incident. If we'd represented each of those incidents, it would have been very highly plotted and taken twenty minutes. And that was one of the first times I hit on a new way, for me, of representing action: why don't I have two people having a conversation about the incidents? One of them asking the other one, "What happened next?" At the same time, I illustrated the one sequence that comes directly from Edith Hamilton. In one of those drawings, Psyche pulls the curtain aside to look down on Eros. So the only image that's shown during the whole telling of this myth (which involves Psyche having to do many tasks) is a sustained slow image of her sneaking into his room at night. We have nude, winged Eros floating in the water on a red raft, and she's looking at him, and the wax drips on him, waking him up. And that moment of *startle*. Then, a kind of slow separation of the two, and a very slow coming together. That's essentially all that happens. The blocking is slow and has literally three movements in it. And it's very delicately poised against this little conversation between these two people whispering on either side of the water.

Psyche means "the soul," and the story seems to be saying that the soul cannot look directly on love. That's a kind of unfathomable dictate. I don't know to this day what it means, and why it feels so urgent, and so profound. That's why I don't ever get tired of seeing that image. I've seen ninety performances of that play, probably, and I would never grow tired of that image, because it remains at the core of a mystery.

It goes without saying, you think imagistically as you write.

Yes. The novel *Journey to the West* has a hundred chapters. A huge criterion that determines which of those get into the play is whether I know how to stage it. Can I stage it in a way that adds something, that expresses it really well, that's imaginative and interesting? If I can't figure out a way to stage it, I might press against it (like with "Eros and Psyche") for a long time, but if an image doesn't come to me, I can't put it up there.

What are the other criteria?

A balance. All these story collections—*The Arabian Nights,* Ovid, *Journey to the West*—have a great variety of tones: funny, sad, adventurous, magic. And you try to find the very best of those. You're looking for a balance or length, you're looking for a rhythm of the evening that's emotional but has to do with the expansion and compression of time. Another criterion is: "Do I have a story yet for Actor X?"

So how do you cast if you don't know who's going to play what, or what you'll end up needing?

People come in and read sides that I've made up, some of which make it into the show. Then I call them back and I do a group audition. They come in groups of eight to twelve, and I spend forty-five minutes with them. We do a series of exercises—a lot of which I stole, some of which I made up—but to tell the truth, I'm really just spending forty-five minutes with them.

What are you looking for in those forty-five minutes?

They couldn't really *fail* at an exercise and therefore not get into the play. But they could fail to participate, and fail to be game, and fail to be supportive of the other people in the room. There are a few exercises that are incredibly telling in terms of people's ability to understand composition, to not upstage, to be part of a group, to be more interested in the big picture than in getting people to look at them.

But ultimately, it's a way of spending time with them. They get a little worn out physically, their nervousness and their pretenses get weaned away, and you get a better feeling of who they are.

Without a script, how do you determine the number of actors for a piece?

That's based on economics, for the most part. *Argonautika* is way understaffed. They were running around like madmen backstage. The most Argonauts I ever had on stage at one time was eight, and I should be able to have twelve for such a big story.

On occasion it's determined by other things. The way it works in *Mirror of the Invisible World* [the Goodman, 1997 and 2007]—this is its big trick—is there's a king and he has seven brides, and each bride tells a story one night a week for seven stories, so there are many, many characters. But our show has a cast of eight, and so all the parts in those stories are played by the other women. So women are playing men throughout the evening, and children, and kissing each other. The king only listens, until he actually enters as a character in the final story, which is startling for the audience. In that instance, I would not want to have more people, because the women doing everything is beautiful and unusual and really sexy. But, truthfully, that choice came about through economics; it was originally produced in the Studio at the Goodman, which is a very small space.

It sounds like the parameters of the cast determines the text to an enormous degree. How long do you have in rehearsal to put it together?

Exactly as long as anyone typically has for an already written show—no more. And I don't do workshops; I don't believe in them. I just have to step off the cliff, and that's all there is to it.

Very early on I was forced to write a script in advance, and to this day, it was my least successful: an adaptation of Nabokov's novel *Laughter in the Dark*. I'd love to take another crack at it, but I was very young, and it was a relatively big theater gig for me, and they were insistent, and I think it restricted my imagination a lot.

I'm slightly lying: I usually have four weeks of rehearsal as opposed to three. I insist on four. But most people think I'm in the room for six months—no, four weeks.

Of course, I've been obsessively reading the text, and it's not like I'm starting from nothing. I'm adapting; there's a source text there. It's not a leap into nothing. The people and place make what's going to happen inevitable: personalities are going to come through, and it's going to happen in certain ways.

That's why when I'm doing something new it's important to have some people who have worked with me before—about a third of the cast, at least. They're like those quarter horses that live with racehorses and walk with them to calm them down. The new actors are like, "Am

I going to have a part? Is it going to be any good? Is there going to be a play?" And the veterans say, "Yes, there's going to be a play, and she'll give you something to do, and you'll be fine."

How's your approach different when you're working with Shakespeare, or staging, rather than adapting, other classics? Are you still looking for visual cues?

Obviously it's a much more conventional process. When I do the auditions, we don't do the physical thing, especially not with Shakespeare; that's just not the priority. The priority is intellectual clarity. Obviously I'm thinking visually in the design process. But I'm trying to serve this text, which has its own demands, and those demands are pretty clear: the shape of it, the length of it.

Some people refer to *Pericles* [the Goodman, 2006] as my adaptation of *Pericles*. I made some cuts, and everyone played Gower instead of me casting just one Gower, and I reversed the order of something at the very beginning, but that's it. I don't mess with a text that's been written as a play; the stage already accommodates it.

Pericles is right up my alley. It's considered a difficult text, it has a narrator, it's episodic, it's more obscure. But nonetheless, I think I'm a pretty conventional Shakespeare director. I don't seek to set them in the Carter Administration, or whenever. I accept plays because they work, not because I want to change them into something else. I have the same kind of near-religious regard for them that I do for my favorite books, and they're written for the stage, so what do I need to do except follow them?

And when I'm directing a play that's already been written, I can go out to dinner, and see a movie! Because I'm not writing the play at the same moment; all I'm doing is staging it, figuring it out with the actors. They're in the same place with me in relation to the text. When I'm doing an adaptation, much as I try to keep them up to date on what I'm thinking, there's a lot going on in my head that's not being shared. Not because I'm trying to withhold. I just don't want to say to them, "Oh, I'm definitely doing that episode," because I might change my mind that night.

Why do you love Shakespeare? I would have assumed a more "open field of play," like the Greeks, would attract you more.

It's the epic scope of him: his plays have scale and scope and depth. I love poetry, I teach it at school, and with any Shakespeare play I do, my goal is to understand every word we're saying. Giving yourself over to that study of text is exhausting yet really rewarding; and I hope I'm absorbing something about dramatic structure and variety and surprise. His skills are just limitless: the story's good, the characters have depth and they speak to us today. The language isn't just ornamental: it's active, it functions. There's just so much to learn there.

What would your collaborators say about you?

I think they must like working with me or they wouldn't keep doing it—it's not like the pay's that great. You develop a history with your designers and your actors, and that makes everything so easy. At Lookingglass it's not the first day of rehearsal; it's the first day of the twentieth year of rehearsal. That's a tremendously efficient, rich way to work.

My relationship with my designers is so close that preproduction is almost my favorite phase. I adore conceiving design, picking out fabric . . . I just love laying the ground for maximum delight and maximum pleasure for the audience.

I'm not interested in lecturing or haranguing the audience. There are lecture halls and churches for that. I don't think they should have a shallow experience, but first and foremost they should be engaged and rewarded for the sacrifice they've made by diminishing their own presence—sitting in uniform rows in the dark . . . not being allowed to speak . . . quieting themselves bodily . . . not being allowed to eat or drink or answer their cellphones—*for removing themselves from the world and giving me their attention*. You need to appreciate that attention and respond to it because it is a sacrifice, it's a very big thing that they're doing.

I think that's what accounts for what we sometimes experience as the nearly crazy rage of the critic who's been disappointed. They have made this sacrifice and it's been thwarted, ignored, dismissed by people being boring or sloppy or clichéd or empty or pretentious or arrogant or insulting to their intelligence.

That's why I always use act curtains when I can—because who would want to receive a present that's unwrapped? There's that moment when you get to see what the set looks like! You want the evening to keep unfolding, to keep *blossoming*.

Obviously, brilliant things can happen in naturalistic theater, when it works. I have huge admiration for it, and all delight in it. My own impulses have taken me in a different direction. Although I will say I'm sad that I don't get offered *play* plays, sometimes, because I'm good with text. I think I understand pacing and how to do psychological reality. I wish someone would offer me a *play* play, but no one thinks of it.

What are the biggest challenges you face as a director?

I'm impatient sometimes. When I'm making up my own work, my actors have to be really self-sufficient, because I don't have time to have long discussions about what is needed in a scene. Typically, in the texts I'm dealing with, the characters don't even have names; they're boy, girl, master, slave, sailor, suitor . . . they're archetypal. And I need actors who are content to embrace that, and not be too full of the modern discourse of acting. I don't have the luxury of time for that.

When I'm doing Shakespeare, it's different. We have endless discussions. But that's also because I didn't author it, so I can't answer those questions right away. We have to figure it out. When I author it, I know the answers, and I'm less interested in all those intricacies.

Back to the power of myth to transform. It's frequently been said that people needed the kind of image-based, transformative power of *Metamorphoses* in the wake of 9/11. So what do people need now?

I'm not sure I know enough to address that, but I can say that the theater has proven remarkably fleet-footed in its response to 9/11, quicker than other media. Plays both documentary and fictional sprang up almost immediately. One thinks of the theater as being a bit slow to respond, but when there's a will, you can get a play up in a couple of months.

To me, the theater gives the world back to us—whatever that image is. The theater is a place of reflection, as well as a very active place. So whatever effort you make to respond to the world should play to your own strengths. The baker should make the best bread he can, and I should make a good play if I can, because that's where my skill and inclination lies.

For example, I was supposed to remount *Leonardo* at Goodman Theatre when the war in Iraq was about to start. Very late in the day I said to the producers, "Let's not do *Leonardo*, I want to do *Trojan Women*; I want to do something about the war." And the Goodman, this huge steamship of an institution, to its great credit, altered its course and took *Leonardo* off the calendar and put *Trojan Women* on. We had our first preview about three days into the invasion.

It's funny, because people don't commonly think of you as a political artist.

All my life I've been drawn to texts from far away that felt very close to me in terms of what they have to say about the world, about life, about being a person. *Mirror of the Invisible World,* for example, is a Persian text, written in a place that's now part of Iran. It's important to be reminded that these places are not sites of the grotesque and inhuman Other, but the home of our brothers and sisters. I remember a particular general gloating that we were going to "bomb Baghdad back to the stone age." He was saying this about a civilization that is so much older than our own, one that was entirely sophisticated and cosmopolitan at a time when most of Europe, let alone North America, was truly in a dark age.

My original mounting of *The Arabian Nights* was prompted by the run-up to the first Gulf War, when I saw a news report about how many children Muslim women tended to have in Iraq, and how they expected to lose a lot of them to disease and violence. The clear implication was that Iraqi women don't attach themselves to their children in the same way we do. I was young, but I could clearly see what was going on: they were diminishing the humanity of the Other so that dropping bombs on them would feel acceptable. And my work, across the board, swims against that stream, and constantly asks you to see yourself in something that you think is thousands of years away, and thousands of miles away, and thousands of gods and demons away, but is actually a mirror of yourself, with your own hopes and fears for the future, and attachments to the past.

This is no put-down, but the simplicity and naivete of your work is something people desperately want to have in a complicated world.

Yeah: "What's so funny about peace, love and understanding?" I want what I do to be absolutely clear. When I was talking about *Metamorphoses* to someone who hadn't seen it but wants to produce it in London, he asked, "What kind of education do we need to do?" And I said: "Absolutely none." It should be accessible to a child.

Nonetheless, as you said earlier, there's complexity beneath. A lot of these epics can be experienced by children on a certain level, and they can be experienced by adults on another level. There's something Nietzsche said that I like a lot: that the deep thinker wants the surface of the pond to be clear so you can see to the very bottom, and the shallow thinker wants the surface of the pond to be muddy and obscure so you don't see how shallow his thoughts are.

Given your very strong aesthetic bias, I'd like to hear more of your thoughts about naturalism's power.

I remember seeing [Steppenwolf Theatre Company's 1988 production of] *Grapes of Wrath*. Terry Kinney and Gary Sinise were squatting down, some distance from each other, having a conversation, and I realized they'd known each other almost since high school. And as they spoke to each other, there was such a profound reality. Two realities at once. You know you're looking at actors, and yet it is so persuasive and convincing to me as life.

Whereas my plays can't really be mistaken for life. They have this theatrical edge to them. They're moving in a way that depends more on the coming together of all kinds of elements: light, sound, music, movement, language, visual metaphor, composition, story. Still, to see people being hyper-real is very thrilling.

I'm for all forms of theater. One does not eliminate the other. True sophistication is to be able to respond to a broad range; to hate everything but one thing is the masquerade of sophistication. Frank Galati can find the beauty and skill in anything. I've always found that indicative of a profound understanding of the whole enterprise of representation and structure.

One of my philosophies is this: there's a thousand ways for a thing to be perfect, not just one. Just look to the natural world, in which there are thousands of perfect landscapes: angles on a certain mountain, times of day, blades of grass, flowers, skies . . . You can't say one is better than the other. So whenever I'm uptight in rehearsal, wondering if I've made the right choice, or wondering if this is exactly the way I should phrase this, I remember that perfection is a multiplicity. You *make* your choice the right one. You choose it; you love it; and it becomes perfect.

 **JASON LOEWITH** has been a producer, director, playwright and dramaturg in Los Angeles, New York, Chicago and now Washington, D.C., where he serves as Executive Director of the National New Play Network, the country's alliance of theaters that champions the development, production and continued life of new plays. As a playwright, his work includes *Adding Machine: A Musical* (Lucille Lortel, Outer Critics Circle and Jeff awards, cowritten with composer Joshua Schmidt) and *War with the Newts* (cowritten with Justin D. M. Palmer), both of which premiered at Evanston's Next Theatre Company, where he served as Artistic Director from 2002–2008. Jason directed a dozen regional and world premieres there, along with new plays for Atlanta's Alliance Theatre, D.C.'s Studio Theatre and Baltimore's CENTERSTAGE, where he also served as Associate Producer for Special Programs. Prior to his work at Next, Jason served for two years as Artistic Administrator for Chicago's Court Theatre, five years as General Manager (and frequent dramaturg) at off Broadway's Classic Stage Company, worked in the literary departments of the Mark Taper Forum and the Public Theater, and mounted fifty productions in three years as Production Manager at the Odyssey Theatre in L.A. His work has been supported multiple times with NEA grants for Artistic Excellence, as well as the Rockefeller/MAP Fund and MacArthur's International Connections Fund. Jason was a TCG New Generations mentorship grantee in the first year of the program, received his MA from the University of California at Santa Barbara and his AB from Brown University.